History Repeating Itself

History Repeating Itself

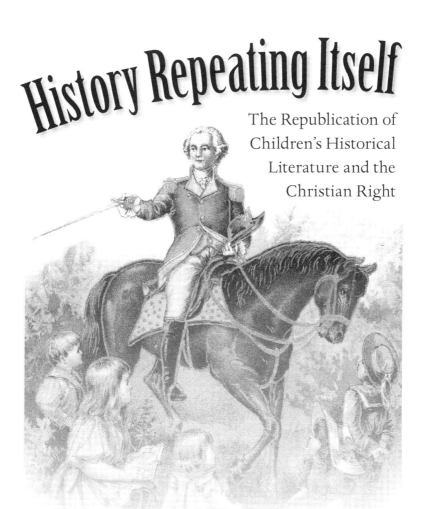

The Republication of
Children's Historical
Literature and the
Christian Right

Gregory M. Pfitzer

University of Massachusetts Press
Amherst & Boston

Designed by Jack Harrison
Set in Monotype Dante
Printed and bound by The Maple-Vail Book Manufacturing Group
Library of Congress Cataloging-in-Publication Data

Pfitzer, Gregory M.
History repeating itself : the republication of children's historical literature and the Christian right /
Gregory M. Pfitzer.
    pages cm. — (Studies in print culture and the history of the book)
  Includes bibliographical references and index.
  ISBN 978-1-62534-124-2 (pbk. : alk. paper) — ISBN 978-1-62534-123-5 (hardcover : alk. paper)
1. United States—History—Textbooks. 2. History publishing—United States—History.
3. United States—Historiography. 4. Historiography—Religious aspects.   I. Title.
E175.85.P48 2014
973—dc23
                         2014019800

British Library Cataloguing-in-Publication Data
A catalogue record for this book is available from the British Library.

For Gary, Gordon, and Margaret

CONTENTS

Acknowledgments ix

INTRODUCTION. "The Past We Choose to Remember" 1

1. Narrative History: Samuel Goodrich and
Truth in Children's History 15

2. Pedagogical History: The Abbott Brothers and Progressive
Approaches to the Past 57

3. Gendered History: Josephine Pollard and Monosyllabic Histories 96

4. Providential History: Charles Carleton Coffin
and the Home Study Movement 137

5. Biographical History: Elbridge S. Brooks and the
Childhood Lives of Great Men 177

6. Doctrinal History: Charles Morris and the Search
for "Lost History" 217

CONCLUSION. The Recycled Past 251

Notes 261

Index 299

ACKNOWLEDGMENTS

I'm reasonably sure this book will never be republished. That seems ironic given that its subject is the republication of works of history, but republication as it is practiced today is a phenomenon associated primarily with volumes written prior to the twentieth century that appeal to the Christian Right. My book does not qualify on either ground. Then again, most of the nineteenth-century authors whose histories are being reissued in the twenty-first century probably did not anticipate the resurrection of their works more than 150 years after they were written. Greater miracles have occurred, I suppose.

Even if I never experience the "rapture" of republication, I want to thank those who have helped me with this limited edition. I am especially obligated to archivists and librarians whose staffs I have kept busy in searches for obscure volumes of children's historical literature, particularly at the de Grummond Collection at the University of Southern Mississippi, the San Francisco Public Library, and the American Antiquarian Society in Worcester, Massachusetts. I have been all over the country collecting primary source materials related to the authors, publishers, and illustrators of these popular histories as well, including the Huntington Library in San Marino, California; the Lilly Library at Indiana University in Bloomington; the Rutherford B. Hayes Presidential Library in Fremont, Ohio; the Amherst College Archives in Amherst, Massachusetts; the Smith College Archives in Northampton, Massachusetts; the Somerville Historical Society in Boston; the Bowdoin College Library in Brunswick, Maine; the Colby College Archives in Waterville, Maine; the Duke University Archives in Durham, North Carolina; the Knox College Library in Galesburg, Illinois; the Newberry Library in Chicago; the New York Public Library; the Congregational Library of Boston; the Houghton Library at Harvard University; and the New England Historic and Genealogical Society in Boston.

As the extensive footnotes to this project attest, I have obligations to many scholars who have preceded me in the field of American children's literature. I want to acknowledge here my special dependence on the work of three experts—Steven Mintz, Bruce VanSledright, and Gillian Avery—each of whom has advanced my understanding of what children read in the nineteenth century, how they did so, and what implications literacy trends had for children's understandings of the past. I also wish to thank Leslie Howsam for her contributions to the fields of print culture and the history of the book. I have relied extensively on her insights throughout this work as well.

I owe a great debt to respective Deans of the Faculty Muriel Poston, Paty Rubio, and Beau Breslin as well as to members of the Faculty Development Committee of Skidmore College for financial support at various phases of this project. I am also indebted to my colleagues in the Department of American Studies at Skidmore, with whom I have exchanged ideas about history and pedagogy over the past decade, including Joanna Zangrando, Mary Lynn, Dan Nathan, Beck Krefting, Joshua Woodfork, Winston Grady-Willis, andré carrington, Janet Casey, and Megan Williams. I relied on Sue Matrazzo and Sue Blair for technical support throughout this project as well. I would like to thank the students in my American Studies 374: Senior Seminar at Skidmore—Liz Artz, Emily Bresnick, Rachel Cohen, Krista Glencross, Jordan Klein, Andrew La Sane, Elena Milius, Keke Mullins, Emma Newcombe, Claire Solomon, and Gemma Striker—who critiqued portions of my manuscript in a series of colloquium sessions from which I benefited greatly.

To Max, the former manager at Panera's Bread Shop in Wilton, New York, who asked nearly every day whether this book was done, thanks for being patient and so gracious in allowing me to use the restaurant as a second office in exchange for my meager purchases of coffee and pastries.

I wish to acknowledge the tireless efforts of my editor at the University of Massachusetts Press, Brian Halley, and his coworkers, including Bruce Wilcox, Clark Dougan, Carol Betsch, Mary Bellino, Jack Harrison, Sally Nichols, Lawrence Kenney, Yvonne Crevier, and Karen Fisk, all of whom helped shape my manuscript into a book. I am grateful as well to the editorial advisory board of the series Studies in Print Culture and the History of the Book—Greg Barnhisel, Robert Gross, Joan Shelley Rubin, and Michael Winship—of which this volume is a part.

I am most thankful to my wife, Mia, my late father-in-law, Charles, and my children, Michael and Sally, for accommodating themselves so generously to a project that required them to rearrange (literally and figuratively) the furniture of their lives. Over the years they have had to make room for stacks of popular history books that appeared first as a modest assortment in the dining room, grew into a collection in the family room, and eventually swelled to a library in the basement. I should apologize to these housemates for my habit of purchasing popular histories when, as one of them pointed out astutely, I had not finished reading the ones I owned already.

Finally, I dedicate this work to my siblings, Gary, Gordon, and Margaret, who as youngsters shared my curiosity about and love for the small collection of popular children's works housed in our two-bedroom rental home in Pittsburgh. Surely they remember the delight we felt when one of those books was selected for bedtime reading. Children have been experiencing that thrill for centuries, of course. In 1846 the children's author and popular historian Samuel Goodrich, whose pen name was Peter Parley, received a letter from a friend testifying to the remarkable reaction of children to the release of his latest work. As soon as announcements of the publication appeared in the shop windows of booksellers, the acquaintance noted, children acted "as though they had been touched by an electric spark which filled their hearts with joy. They would jump and frisk about, clap their hands, dance and stamp in front of these big handbills, and sing out in the perfect fullness of delight, begging their mothers and nurses . . . to get them the 'new Peter Parley.'" Anticipating such reactions, parents used the occasion of such a release to encourage desired behaviors in their children. Goodrich's friend remarked, "Sometimes I have heard [a child] thus answered, 'Oh, no, you cannot have Peter Parley, because you have been a bad child, and none but good children are allowed to read Peter Parley.'" The contrite and tearful youth inevitably replied, "Oh, indeed, indeed, ma, if you will only get me Peter Parley this time, I will never be bad again." "I concluded," the friend informed Goodrich, "that all children . . . were taught to feel it was a privilege and luxury to read Peter Parley."

In having such works read to us at bedtime, my siblings and I were each, like Goodrich's juvenile readers, frequently "touched by an electric spark which filled [our] hearts with joy." We may not have promised our parents "never to be bad again" (and if we did we certainly did not keep such pledges), but we were always grateful to them for the "privilege and luxury" of having wonderful children's books to listen to as we settled down for the night. Sadly, they are gone now—our parents and our books—and it remains for the four of us to keep the memory of childhood alive. *History Repeating Itself,* dedicated to you, is my effort to do just that.

History Repeating Itself

"The Past We Choose to Remember"

Those who cannot remember the past are condemned to repeat it.
George Santayana, *The Life of Reason* (1905)

Like many scholarly projects, this one began as a matter of happenstance. For the better part of a decade I had been working on a manuscript about nineteenth-century popular histories written for young readers, and, as part of my research for that project, I purchased on eBay as many of these anti-quarian volumes as I could afford. One day several years ago I ordered what I thought was a copy of Josephine Pollard's *The History of the United States Told in One Syllable Words,* published in 1884 by McLoughlin Brothers of New York. I was excited when the package arrived a few weeks later, but my enthusiasm ebbed when I discovered I had purchased not a first edition of the book but a reissue printed in 1998 by a company in Texas known as Mantle Ministries.[1] My mistake was perhaps natural, as the cover art was nearly the same in both editions, but I was irritated that I had not paid closer attention to the details of the eBay ad, which specified that the book was a republication (fig. 1). I was annoyed as well because I had paid $29.95, a fair price for the original, for a book that retails on the Mantle Ministries website for $17.95 and has sold on eBay in its recycled edition for as little as $5.95 (with free shipping!). As a book collector with great ambitions and limited resources, I learned a painful lesson about the republication phenomenon that day.

I discovered after further investigation that there is an active cottage indus-try devoted to the practice of recycling old books, and, for reasons I consider in detail throughout this book, parents who homeschool their children have been especially interested in these nineteenth-century children's histories. A website called "Resources for Homeschoolers," for instance, indicates that PrestonSpeed Publications is reprinting volumes from the series Makers of

FIGURE 1. Josephine Pollard, *The History of the United States Told in One Syllable Words* (New York: McLoughlin Brothers, 1884); Josephine Pollard, *A Child's History of America Told in One-Syllable Words* (Bulverde, Tex.: Mantle Ministries, 1998).

History by Jacob and John S. C. Abbott, published originally by Harper and Brothers between 1848 and 1856.[2] Books by Elbridge Streeter Brooks in the series Children's Lives of Great Men, first produced in the 1890s, have circulated widely as valuable homeschool offerings in digital formats designed by Kessinger Publishing.[3] In fact, dozens of such companies, some with interesting retro names like Nothing New Press, Dodo Press, and Resurrection Press, are reproducing nineteenth-century juvenile books. Many of the publishers of these recycled works are affiliated with religious organizations that cater to homeschooling parents on the Christian Right who are looking for history books that have a traditional spiritual perspective on the past. They advocate the republication of texts that promote a "recall of heritage-based heroes and events." Works like Pollard's *The History of the United States Told in One Syllable Words* fit the bill nicely.[4]

After I got over my disappointment at not receiving the volume I thought I had purchased on eBay, I became intrigued by two related questions: Why would publishers reissue nineteenth-century works such as Pollard's *The History of the United States* for twenty-first-century readers? And why would anyone today take the time to read them? Finding answers to these questions turned out to be more engaging and complicated than I imagined, so I decided to expand my project to address them.

One explanation—not a surprising one—for this republication phenomenon, I learned, was financial. Historical books published before 1923 are not protected by copyright and are therefore in the public domain, fair game for any publishing house that might want to reissue them under its brand. Given the substantial costs required to research, write, and produce a new history text, it makes economic sense for firms like Mantle Ministries to choose to republish established works rather than create new ones. It is estimated, for instance, that an original textbook in history takes five years to develop and costs between two hundred thousand and five hundred thousand dollars to produce and market. Publishers of new works hope to recoup these costs from consumers (in 2008 the average price of a new book on the history of the United States was seventy-five dollars), whereas Pollard's *The History of the United States* sells in reissued form for less than twenty dollars.[5] From a homeschooling parent's point of view, then, lower costs of production translate into affordable volumes. Since the homeschool textbook industry is a one-billion-dollar-a-year undertaking, recycling also pays sizable dividends to publishers.[6]

A second, more substantial reason for the emergence of this practice is that many homeschooling parents are attracted to republished works for pedagogical and ideological reasons. Often they have chosen to educate their children at home because they do not approve of the ways in which subjects such as history are taught in public schools, and they wish to have greater control over curriculum and reading lists. The numbers of homeschooled children are not insignificant. In the early 1990s just over 100,000 students were schooled at home; by the late 1990s the number had jumped to nearly 850,000 and by 2003 to over 1 million.[7]

Why have such dramatic increases in homeschooling occurred in the past several decades? Part of the answer lies in the intense debate that took place in the mid-1990s over the development of national standards in education, particularly historical education. In 1987 Diane Ravitch and Chester E. Finn Jr. published *What Do Our 17-Year-Olds Know?*, the first systematic assessment of the proficiencies of public high school juniors with respect to history and literature. The book reported the startling news that most American high school students were woefully ignorant about the basic facts of the American past. Three-quarters of seventeen-year-olds could not identify within twenty years the period in which Abraham Lincoln was president, barely half knew about the internment of Japanese Americans during the Second World War, and almost a quarter could not identify Richard Nixon as the president who was forced to resign because of Watergate. Ravitch and Finn's report also called into question the capacity of American youth trained in public schools to "think historically," that is, to understand the laws of historical explanation as well as concepts of chronology, cause and effect, and continuity and change.[8] These findings were corroborated in 1989 by the Bradley Commission in *Building a History Curriculum: Guidelines for Teaching History in the Schools*, a report produced by sixteen prominent members of the history profession. The writers argued that deficiencies in student knowledge had impacted profoundly the teaching of core historical values in American public schools and had jeopardized the ability of such institutions to produce better citizens.[9]

These revelations set the history community on its head and prompted a massive reconsideration of the national school curriculum for history. Charlotte Crabtree, Gary Nash, and others affiliated with the National Center for History in the Schools (NCHS), an organization based at the University of California, Los Angeles, received a $1.5-million grant from the National Endowment for the Humanities (NEH) to establish national standards in American and world history.[10] Over the next few years public school educators worked closely with university professors, school superintendents, public interest groups, and parent–teacher organizations in a collaborative effort to create guidelines for the teaching of history at all levels of public education. In 1994 the NCHS team produced the National Standards, a series of voluntary guidelines and accompanying teaching modules for redirecting the study of history in American schools.[11]

The National Standards were controversial from the start. Some admired their nontraditional approach to historical literacy. Operating under the assumption that the record of the past is variable and subject to multiple interpretations, the creators of the standards acknowledged the relevance of a contested past and challenged students to abandon old consensus models of history for ones centered on conflicts among races, classes, genders, and ethnicities. Hence, the NCHS consultants developed teaching exercises for the standards that highlighted the contentious relationships between Native Americans and European expansionists, African Americans and white slave-holders, and Japanese Americans and the U.S. government. The report also introduced discussions of gender politics, especially in the matter of female representation at the polls and restrictions on participatory democracy. Finally, the standards shuffled the conventional roster of American heroes to make room for some little-known figures of the American past, such as Ebenezer McIntosh, whose career as a poor Boston shoemaker-turned-activist underscored the class issues at the heart of the Revolution. Not surprisingly, perhaps, given the space limitations of books, the standards gave correspond-ingly less attention to such established heroes as George Washington.[12]

Traditionalists reacted negatively to this prioritizing and the breakdown of consensus implicit in it. They claimed that in advancing a contested past the NCHS group had threatened the stability of history and undercut the faith of American youth in standard symbols of national pride. Lynne Cheney, the former director of the NEH, which sponsored the assessment project, wrote a scathing review of the standards in the *Wall Street Journal* even before they were released. Provocatively titled "The End of History," Cheney's piece, along with other articles written by her that followed on its heels, asserted that the "revisionists" who directed the standards project had "hijacked" his-tory by infusing it with "multicultural excess." In emphasizing the contested past, she added, these revisionists had introduced an inappropriate, insidious divisiveness into the master narrative of American history, in the process irresponsibly debunking American heroes. The fact that Harriet Tubman was mentioned six times in the standards while Washington "makes only a fleet-ing appearance and Thomas Edison gets ignored altogether" caused Cheney to question further the priorities of the report's creators, especially with respect to dead white males.[13] Woody West of the conservative *Washington Times* echoed these claims, charging that Nash and others had "crammed U.S. culture into the Cuisinart" and "whirled and chopped, mashed and sliced [it], into an unrecognizable and unpalatable mass." In their "frantic effort to make sure no racial or ethnic group is left out, the true believers are fragmenting the consensus that bonds the whole," West concluded.[14] Leery of the supposed politically correct version of the American past that the guidelines offered and disgusted by the victimization model employed by its revisionist authors, traditionalists derided the standards as an "un-American" contribution to "oppression studies."[15]

Part of what angered conservatives was their belief that the National Standards directed public school children toward unstable models of historical understanding that were counterproductive to proper learning about the past.[16] These critics desired instead what the historian Michael Kammen has described as "stabilized history," that is, "history as the repository of 'true' heritage" that children should learn and memorize.[17] Supporters of this "consensus view" of the past believe that history is "a collection of putative facts" and that the primary function of historical education is to teach students to learn such facts in the context of agreed-upon narratives.[18] Advocates of stabilized history argued for assessment tools that measured "recall of heritage-based heroes and events" rather than those that questioned established traditions.[19] The concept of historical truth was at the center of this conservative challenge, with its accompanying belief in what the education historian Bruce VanSledright calls "history's inert but applicable moral role." According to this thinking, "students understand history as a fixed tale, a body of inert facts, holding within it a series of important moral lessons that must be learned, stored in memory, and acted upon at the proper time."[20] For many conservatives, homeschooling was the only viable alternative for protecting their children from the instability of a history curriculum that challenged such a master narrative.

Nash and others mounted a vocal defense of the National Standards, acknowledging, along with conservatives, that "the American past . . . embodies many of the most fundamental messages we, as a nation, wish to send to young citizens" but disagreeing on which lessons to emphasize. "The past we choose to remember," Nash noted, "defines in large measure our national character, transmits the values and self-images we hold dear, and preserves the events, glorious and shameful, extraordinary and mundane, that constitute our legacy from the past and inspire our hope for the future."[21] Stressing the mastery of concepts over facts, Nash and others lobbied for an inquiry-based approach to the past that challenged the "referential illusion" of traditionalists that "historians' interpretations literally *mirror* a past reality."[22] The result was a more diverse and nuanced history, one that embraced multiple perspectives on numerous and competing pasts, but such complexity was accomplished at the loss of a certain moral absolutism.[23]

A crucial issue in the debate over the National Standards was the question of what children were capable of learning about the past and when they should learn it.[24] Traditionalists drew on the logic of the child psychologist Bruno Bettelheim, who, in *The Uses of Enchantment* (1975), contended that myths, legends, and biographies should be the foundation of the K–4 curriculum, since young children "had a psychological need to confront life's basic human predicaments through fairy tales and fiction."[25] While "history proper is largely beyond the comprehension of children, they are able at an early age to understand and enjoy anecdotes of people, especially those of civilization," wrote one advocate of this philosophy, "as well as the lessons of perseverance, courage, patriotism, and virtue that are taught by the noble lives described."[26] Young children might not understand either the philosophical implications of the passage of time or the rectilinear structure of chronology, the argument went, but they could learn stories if they were presented in digestible narrative form. On this point, revisionists agreed. "Parents, children's librarians, and teachers of the young have long known the power of superbly written biographies, myths, legends, folktales, and historical narratives to capture children's imagination and to hold their interest," Crabtree wrote of this outlook. She added, "Incorporating enduring themes of conflict and personal choice; of sacrifice and responsibility; of power and oppression; of struggle, failure, and achievement, sometimes against overwhelming odds, these stories connect in powerful ways with these same impulses and conflicts in children's own lives. . . . They engage children vicariously in the experiences and perspectives of others, expand their ability to see the world through others' eyes, and enlarge their vision of lives well lived and of their own human potential."[27]

While traditionalists and revisionists alike agreed that the narrative tradition in history is a powerful inducement to an appreciation of the past by young people, they disagreed on the types of narratives best suited for young readers. Traditionalists preferred a simple, single-minded, "nationalist narrative" that emphasized "all things American." Revisionists, by contrast, argued that children are capable intellectually of understanding ambiguity and that they are prepared from a young age to handle multiple perspectives on the past. Acknowledging that "history can be a controversial subject precisely because the serious investigation of it has the power to undermine cherished 'common culture' heritage mythologies," VanSledright recognizes that more diverse approaches to the past invite students in "deeply enough to create powerful responses that often run contrary to cherished beliefs and assumptions about who Americans are supposed to be."[28] The accompanying risk of iconoclasm is justified in his estimation, since "encounters with primary sources drawn from conflicting perspectives on an event help to offset the adoption of a singular, one-sided perspective and teach novices to read all manner of historical texts more critically."[29] Calling for a "shift in how American history courses are configured and taught," revisionists like VanSledright have espoused a new epistemology with respect to historical knowledge and the education of children.[30] It was precisely this modifying ambition that frightened conservatives, who worried that a conflict-based approach to the past would erode the faith of young Americans in their nation and its founders.

By the late 1990s suspicions about assessment efforts like the National Standards spilled over into a general cynicism about the effectiveness of public educators in teaching children, encouraging the emergence of a so-called family values agenda and a related homeschooling movement. Leaders of conservative political advocacy groups, including Ralph Reed of the Christian Coalition, Gary Bauer of the Family Research Council, and James Dobson of Focus on the Family, lobbied for congressional legislation that would "strengthen the rights of parents in their children's education," especially their rights "to protect their children against education programs that undermine the values taught in the home."[31] Many homeschooling parents alleged a conspiracy on the part of educators such as Nash and Crabtree to erode the values that made the United States an exceptional culture. They acted out of fear that a destabilizing history curriculum like that of the proposed standards would compromise their children's patriotism.[32] Citing the important role of homeschooling as a protection against the subversive nature of compulsory public education, the editorialist Kim Weissman rejected the standards as "nothing more than a cynical ploy to indoctrinate children with their own hatred of America; to steal the American birthright from the children of our country; [and] to teach our children to feel guilt over their own heritage."[33]

These factors help explain why a republished version of *The History of the United States Told in One Syllable Words* might have currency in today's popular book market. To promote their own specific version of the past—one that would protect children from the threatening debunking spirit of public school history readers—homeschoolers have created shared reading lists in history with traditional titles that they trade actively on Internet websites. Perhaps more than any other element of the conservative backlash against the National Standards, these lists are responsible for establishing a new (or rather renewed) curriculum for homeschoolers centered on old texts and still older philosophies of education. What's so revealing about these homeschool catalogues in history is the degree to which they are dominated by republished nineteenth-century texts like Pollard's.

Advocates of homeschooling span the ideological spectrum, but many of those involved in republication efforts are political conservatives who embrace the American exceptionalism implicit in these antiquated texts. Dissatisfaction with the divisiveness of the National Standards caused some homeschoolers to long for works of history that were unquestioning of national motives and "free of political correctness."[34] Ravitch wrote that her early enthusiasm for the National Standards project was dampened by the "negotiating and log-rolling" of revisionists who "had forced historical 'truth' to be sacrificed at the altar of political correctness."[35] Cheney agreed, arguing in an article titled "Kill My Old Agency, Please," that the NEH had been hijacked by special interest groups on the political Left and needed to be disbanded by congressional fiat.[36] Congress did not go that far, but the persuasiveness of the conservative argument in the ensuing culture wars was evident several months later, when the U.S. Senate, at the urging of Rep. Newt Gingrich, passed by a vote of 99 to 1 a nonbinding resolution condemning the standards.[37]

Those on the political Right who appreciated Gingrich's censorship efforts offered popular nineteenth-century narrative histories as alternatives to the National Standards, implying that these older volumes provided truer guidelines for historical competency than the NCHS benchmarks. One blogger, filled with contempt for the revisionist public school standards, suggested that children should read Guerber's Historical Series, originally published in 1869 and republished by Nothing New Press in 2008. "I really like [Guerber's] books," she wrote, "because they are reprints from an earlier time so I trust them to be more accurate than most of today's revised history books."[38] Nineteenth-century authors had great respect for American heroes, she added, as opposed to those professional historians with political agendas who sought to subvert the established educational conventions for teaching children about the past. "Our heroes are precious few," one critic of such revisionism concluded. "Don't make us learn history all over again."[39]

A final impulse for the reissuing of these works, perhaps the most substantial one, has been the desire of many homeschoolers to center history curricula on a conspicuously Christian platform. Some 33 percent of all parents who homeschool cite religion as the primary factor in their choosing to keep their children out of public schools (in the United States most of these parents are Christian), while another 9 percent list morality as a related incentive.[40] Many works from the nineteenth century that appear on homeschooling republication lists appeal to the Religious Right because they challenge the allegedly anti-Christian, child-centered teaching methods of public school administrators and educators, including, as the curriculum analyst Linda

Symcox notes, "cooperative learning groups, peer tutoring, discovery or inquiry learning, multicultural curricula, and performance-based assessments."[41] As a result, the Christian Coalition, which has criticized reading lists produced for public schools by the Department of Education, endorsed efforts by Christian publishers to redirect public funds toward Christian-based homeschooling alternatives.[42] For instance, the coalition applauded Richard Wheeler of Mantle Ministries for reprinting the works of the nineteenth-century popular historian Charles Carleton Coffin because Coffin was committed to the "values of Christian living." Like Pollard's works, Coffin's were proclaimed to be "Christ-honoring books which have been recommended for Christian school, church, and family heritage libraries, as well as Christian home education curricula."[43] Cathy Duffy, a reviewer of homeschooling texts, concluded that Christian books such as Coffin's offer the "religious perspective" that must be the centerpiece of any history curriculum for children.[44]

What practical effect have these republication efforts had? Among other things, they have given new life to the nineteenth-century storylines featured in many of these works as well as to the principles of continuity and consensus that distinguish them. Reissued historical series such as Samuel Goodrich's Peter Parley's Tales from the 1820s and the Abbott brothers' Makers of History biographies of the 1840s have not only reinvigorated the master narrative of American history established so rigidly in the late nineteenth century but also contributed to the illusion that the interpretive orthodoxies of the early national period have never been challenged in any meaningful way in American historiography. As the journalist Frances FitzGerald observed, such works give rise to the idea that the history of historical writing in America throughout the nineteenth century and most of the twentieth has been "implacable" and "seamless"—that if one were to line up the most popular histories of those years end to end, one would discover a continuous narrative in which "the country never changed in any important way: its values and its political institutions remained constant from the time of the American Revolution."[45] The worth of reissued popular texts thus resides in their ability to repeat and reaffirm canonical beliefs implicit in the originals. In short, the concept of history repeating itself was both an abstract philosophy and a practical strategy for promoters of popular histories in the nineteenth century as well as for the homeschoolers who recycle them in the twenty-first century. Repetition, even redundancy, implies something meaningful about how the past functions to stabilize and sustain a culture over time.

The belief in the importance of repetition in history calls to mind the oft-quoted warning of George Santayana that informs the title of this book: "Those who cannot remember the past are condemned to repeat it." Santayana's habitually misunderstood dictum is frequently used by traditionalists to imply that since history is an endless cycle of repeated events, the future can be read from the past. Those who have not learned history's lessons are doomed to repeat its mistakes when such events inevitably reoccur, the argument goes. Their failures are largely those of misperception, of not seeing that which is inevitably coming. Sadly, the pervasiveness of this condition leads many to be blindsided by the past. Implicit in this argument is the theoretical assumption that those who have learned their history according to the master narrative can anticipate the recurring patterns of the past and are better equipped both to deal with the present and to predict the future. According to this logic, the science of history, if perfected, could reveal the explicit trajectories of events in the future based on those of the past.[46]

A closer reading of Santayana suggests, however, that he intended something very different from what is supposed conventionally in the oft-quoted passage from a volume in the series The Life of Reason in which Santayana was attempting to establish the practical uses of knowledge. Santayana sought to distinguish between history as the sum total of events that have occurred in the past and history as the record of those events. His book on reason implied that one can never know this first kind of history in any objective way because historians are restricted to the use of explanatory theories that shape facts, and these ordering schemes are always subjective.[47] As the great historian and intellectual Henry Adams discovered after years of searching for calculable phases of history, there is no objective or meaningful way to anticipate or predict the phases of the future as read backward in the past.[48]

Santayana was far more concerned, however, with the second definition of history (the narrative record of events) and with the psychological implications of studying history in order to arrive at explanations of life in the present and the future. Analyzed in context, the passages on history in The Life of Reason imply that by "remembering the past" Santayana is really referencing the practical value of trying to make sense of events that have come before as a way of fixing and holding experience steady amidst the flux and inconsistency of present human experience. To Santayana, history was unquestionably an "imaginative reconstruction," "assisted and recorded memory" that helps people shape experience in highly personal ways. Accordingly, history "might almost be said to be no science at all, if memory and faith in memory were not what science necessarily rests on," he wrote. "It is relative and useful and must be rewritten constantly to suit the purposes of its practitioners." In fact, according to Santayana, history as the constant act of reconstruction of past events is the only consistent protection against the inconsistency of history as the sum total of all events that have occurred in the past. Hence,

Santayana argued that we are doomed to repeat the mistakes of the past not because bad things inhere in the past that will reoccur in the future unless we anticipate their cycles, but because order and meaning cannot be brought to the inchoate mass of past events unless we remember them in ways that help us order and contextualize present and perhaps future experiences. Put more simply, there is a natural human propensity (evident especially among children) to seek "consecutiveness and persistence" in historical accounts.[49]

If this reading is accurate, then we have to invert the typical understanding of Santayana's famous maxim to recognize its true significance for the consensus-minded traditionalists who employ it on behalf of their republication schemes. Conservatives are attentive to the master narrative of history not because they are *condemned* to repeat it, we must acknowledge, but because they *want* to repeat it.[50]

Given this insistence on consensus as a bastion of homeschooling philosophies, one is compelled to ask certain additional questions of its usage: How and why did this cult of consistency develop over time? what consequences has it had in children's historical education in the United States? This book tries to answer these questions by charting the gradual emergence of this consensus paradigm within the genre of popular historical literature for American children from the nineteenth and early twentieth centuries. My thesis is that the remarkable consistency evidenced in this literary market for over a century and a half and the related revival of popular juvenile histories in the homeschooling republication market reveal two related tendencies: a conscious desire for self-renewal as suggested by the passing of formulaic children's books from one generation to the next, and a psychological aversion to change as evidenced by resistance to the idea of a contested past.[51] I illustrate these points by studying in detail the lives of the men and women who wrote popular histories for children, especially Samuel Goodrich, Jacob and John S. C. Abbott, Josephine Pollard, Charles Carleton Coffin, Elbridge S. Brooks, and Charles Morris, as well as the production histories of the juvenile works they marketed and their reception in the literary marketplace. In pursuit of these goals I have consulted the archives of the popular writers, publishers, and readers involved in the circulation of these texts. I have investigated the absence of alternative stories and counternarratives in this marketplace as a way of noting the persistent hold of the master narrative on American readers. Since the issue of what and when children are capable of learning about history informed most of the exchanges among writers, publishers, and readers, I have considered as well the various and changing philosophies of education associated with the original production and subsequent reissuing of these works.

The juvenile texts featured here, both original and republished, are not identical in every aspect. To be sure, there are distinctions among them. Sometimes quirky iterations developed from misappropriations of original narratives, such as the perversions that resulted from the misuse of Washington Irving's popular biography of Columbus by Goodrich and others. As in the case of the children's game of telephone, in which participants seated in a circle pass a message along to their neighbors, each to the next with some loss of accuracy, these texts reveal humorous inconsistencies in their borrowings. Many of these distortions, however, were not purposeful; they were not intended as radical critiques of the dominant paradigm. They emerged instead as the unintended consequences of attempts to play variations on the same old themes. While nineteenth-century popular publications displayed some of what the literary historian John Bryant calls "textual fluidity" in the republication process, including sampling, reappropriation, and repackaging, adaptations were offered in such apologetic terms as to betray a lack of commitment on the part of their authors to revisionism as a policy.[52]

Finally, I aim to evaluate in this book the practical effects of these republished works on the homeschoolers who read them. Given the pervasiveness of such texts among a growing portion of the population, especially young readers, it seems advisable to consider in detail what volumes like Pollard's *The History of the United States Told in One Syllable Words* were like in their original iterations and to investigate thoroughly the historical methodologies that informed them. I also contemplate the implications of centering a homeschooling history curriculum on such republished editions. Thus I explore the production histories of reissued books and consider why and how they are being reprinted in such large numbers today. I recreate the educational context in which these volumes were written and investigate the prevailing conceptions of childhood that underlay them. I also consider why changes are made to original texts in the republication process, and how such alterations affect their interpretive meaning. Above all, I ask what intellectual risks do those who use these recycled books to educate America's young today incur?

There's no point in obscuring my intentions here. I do not think a policy by which twenty-first-century children learn their history from nineteenth-century texts is a wise one. There's room to disagree on this matter, but I hope my book will convince readers that there is more than just politics at stake in the debate: the historical literacy of future generations of Americans also hangs in the balance. In order to address my concerns in this area, I have begun and concluded each chapter of this book with commentary on the efforts of a particular publisher on the Christian Right to recycle nineteenth-century popular histories for homeschool use. Serving as framing devices for analyses of the volumes themselves, these discussions are intended to alert readers to the distorting qualities of such republishing efforts, which, while undertaken for acceptable spiritual reasons, are often compromised by the financial, political, and ideological motivations that accompany them. Insofar as my book is a contribution to the history of the book and print culture in the United States, then, it is a cautionary tale about the dangerous things that can happen when centuries-old texts are used out of context and in anachronistic ways to train students of history or when original thought is transferred from one source to another without paying proper attention to the methods and consequences of transposition.

Ralph Waldo Emerson spoke prophetically, if ambiguously, two centuries ago about recycling impulses when he noted in his essay "Self-Reliance" that "a foolish consistency is the hobgoblin of little minds."[53] If we take "little" here to mean young minds, then Emerson's quote helps explain why juvenile readers might be drawn to popular histories that appeal to their need for comforting repetitions. If we understand "little" to mean "small-minded," however, then the popular texts I analyze here may well be among the hobgoblins against which Emerson warned, since they repeat and perpetuate conceptualizations of the past that are perhaps foolishly consistent. With respect to these juvenile histories, then, the question is whether we should heed the philosophical implications of Emerson's admonition against silly redundancy, or whether we should dare to ask, as some have through the ages, if there can be such a thing as a "wise consistency."[54]

CHAPTER ONE

Narrative History

Samuel Goodrich and Truth
in Children's History

There are two quite distinct purposes of history; the superior purpose, which
is its use for children, and the secondary, or inferior purpose, which is its use
for historians. The highest and noblest thing that history can be is a good story.

G. K. CHESTERTON, "The Duty of the Historian"

"God Knows the Best Way to Teach History": A True and Sacred Past

In 2002 Hearthstone Publishing of Oklahoma City reprinted an edition of
Parley's History of the World from 1858 (fig. 2). Written originally by the popular historian Samuel Goodrich under the pseudonym Peter Parley, the book
evokes, according to its Christian republisher, the important moral "lessons
of history" that were once the basis of education for children in the United
States. Nineteenth-century readers understood that the value of history
resided in its storytelling qualities, Hearthstone's publishers assert, whereas
twenty-first-century histories are committed primarily to the dissemination
of random facts disassociated from any synthesizing narrative. These points
are expanded on in the introduction to the Hearthstone edition by Noah
W. Hutchings, a syndicated evangelical radio broadcaster who specializes in
biblical prophecy. "Anyone watching the multitude of TV quiz shows would
surely note that the questions usually missed by the contestants under forty
are questions about history or geography," Hutchings observes. Challenging
readers to scrutinize their own educations, he asks, "Do you really remember
anything about the history you were taught?" "Do you remember anything
but a few isolated events floating out there in history somewhere, unrelated
to each other?" Most would answer no to these questions, he claims, because

FIGURE 2.
Samuel G. Goodrich,
Parley's History of the World
(Oklahoma City: Hearthstone
Publishing, [2002]).

children are taught history as a series of "unrelated isolated events" and as disembodied facts without connection to a centralized story.[1]

Goodrich's history is different, Hutchings insists, because it is narrative in structure and employs traditional nineteenth-century storytelling devices to facilitate the easy retention of moral facts. In this case *traditional* means biblical, since the storyline in *Parley's History of the World* is hermeneutical, adopting a structural approach inspired by the books of the Old Testament that "tell the story about [God's] people from Genesis to revelation, from the beginning to the end." This scriptural methodology is the only acceptable one for getting at the moral truths of history, Hearthstone's promoters insist, because only "God Knows the Best Way to Teach History." History "MUST Be Learned in Chronological Order in the Context in Which It Happened," they argue, since the scriptures employ a temporally sequential pattern.

"Why wouldn't we want to follow the example of the best and most important history text ever written?" the publishers ask. They suggest that because the Bible represents the unimpeachable word of God as offered in narrative form, it should be the standard by which all written history is measured. "If you want your children to remember history, they must learn it in it's [*sic*] chronological context, as one big interesting story," Hearthstone's advertisers assert. "If there was a better way to teach history, God would have used it in His Word."[2]

Because Goodrich's work references the Bible "as a credible record of both the world and humankind's past," the republishers promote *Parley's History of the World* as a theological aid to learning. History that is studied as one flowing Christian narrative "is much easier to remember," Hearthstone's circular notes, adding that the convenient learning aids scattered throughout Goodrich's book allow young twenty-first-century readers to "commit to memory the whole volume during a winter's schooling." Improving the power of memory in the instruction of history for children is crucial, according to this logic, in that "each generation bases its future or fall upon the [record of the] previous generation." Whether the American Republic "rises to the next generation or falls upon the present one," Hutchings argues, depends on the ability of young citizens to recall with absolute clarity the vital moral lessons of the past preserved in such historical narratives.[3] Predicting that the "great tribulation" is coming soon, the radio pastor warns that the impious children of the "anti-God United States" who fail to absorb their nation's history as told by Christians like Goodrich will discover only after it is too late that "they are living in the most perilous times since the flood in Noah's day." Cautioning that twenty-first-century children may be members of "the last generation of this age," Hutchings advises young readers to take up *Parley's History of the World* with an urgency that reveals their awareness that the Antichrist is upon them—in the form of computers, government data banks, and, most of all, revisionist historians.[4]

In asserting the need—in fact, the moral imperative—to reissue *Parley's History of the World,* Hearthstone presumes that Goodrich had gotten history right in the middle of the nineteenth century and that revisionists following in his wake had somehow gotten it wrong. Like many presses reprinting works primarily for the homeschool market, Hearthstone believes that the pedagogical strategies developed in private homes in the nineteenth century were more successful than those used in public schools in the twenty-first, primarily because the former were grounded in the steadfast moral lessons and narrative structure of the Bible while the latter are based on the vague, irreligious tenets of postmodern relativism.[5] In this view, revisionist history is sacrilegious and synonymous with the biblical fall from grace. The value of *Parley's History of the World* "is that it predates the revisionists who change history to accomodate [*sic*] current social and world political goals," publicity circulars for the Hearthstone edition explain, the original scriptures representing "true history," that is, sacred, unadulterated history, handed down from generation to generation in the consecrated form of canonical religious texts.[6]

For Hutchings and others, history is not conditional or negotiated, then, it is fixed and sacrosanct. It is received, as Moses received the tablets from Mount Sinai, rather than constructed, like the golden calf. The very first line of Goodrich's work—"In this book I am going to tell my readers the history of this world on which we live: how God created it, and placed human beings upon it"—bears out this ecclesiastical point, as it acknowledges the biblical creation story as the only genuinely acceptable narrative approach to the past. Revisionists "who rule over the publications of present day textbooks," Hutchings notes, seek to "get rid of the Creator" by insisting that "man appeared first in the form of a single cell amoeba in a slime pit and developing and evolving over billions and billions of years." In doing so, they blaspheme the authority of God as revealed in the original creation story.[7] The same pertains to the efforts of revisionists to downplay the hallowed nature of foundational events in American history, a perspective that has been lost to historians working in the relativistic climate of the twentieth and twenty-first centuries. Not surprisingly, then, the republication of Parley's work, its resurrection, if you will, is advertised by Hearthstone as a redemptive exercise directed at saving a discipline marred by impure impulses and practices. For Hutchings and others, Peter Parley's return, his "rising again," represents a deliverance from the twin sins of revisionism and twentieth-century iconoclasm.

Certainly in his own day Goodrich's histories had a devout following among Christian parents, who believed he provided their children with a pure, godly strategy for understanding the past. Estimated sales figures of fifty thousand volumes annually for Goodrich's publications indicate how extensively his works were read.[8] Yet despite these successes, no one would have been more uncomfortable with the republication efforts of a firm such as Hearthstone, particularly with the casting of Peter Parley as a redemptive Christ figure, than Samuel Goodrich. At the end of his life, in fact, Goodrich was inclined to think his literary contributions were not very valuable or enduring in the least, and he expected (even hoped) they would die off. He had written nothing, he claimed, that would or should last. "In looking at the long list of my publications, in reflecting upon the large numbers that have been sold, I feel far more of humiliation than of triumph," he wrote in his memoirs. "If I have sometimes taken to heart the soothing flatteries of the public, it has ever been speedily succeeded by the conviction that my life has been, on the whole, a series of mistakes, and especially in that portion of it which has been devoted to authorship." Goodrich recognized that he had written too much, too quickly and that he had done "nothing really well." Obscurity was what he deserved and desired. "You need not whisper it to the public, at least until I am gone," he confided, "but I know, better than any one can tell me, that there is nothing in this long catalogue [of publications] that will give me a permanent place in literature. A few things may struggle upon the surface for a time, but—like the last leaves of a tree in autumn, forced at last to quit their hold, and cast into the stream—even these will disappear, and my name and all I have done will be forgotten."[9]

The gloomy substance and tone of these late-in-life reflections by Goodrich beg answers to obvious questions: Why did he feel so worthless given that he had achieved national and international recognition as a writer of children's books and significant literary success in his day? And if his insights into the "series of mistakes" he had made as an author are sincere and accurate, then what do we make of the fact that the books he had set adrift on the metaphoric stream 150 years ago have resurfaced recently in reprints by Hearthstone Publishing and others?[10] Is it appropriate or even ethical to reissue books for use in the twenty-first century that their nineteenth-century authors admitted were inadequate? To answer these questions with special reference to Goodrich's popular histories for children, one must first understand the nineteenth-century cultural and literary worlds he inhabited, including the shifting historical sensibilities and changing conceptions of childhood that defined them.

Childhood as a Time Set Apart

Hearthstone's interest in republishing *Parley's History of the World* is predicated in part on the recognition that Goodrich valued stability in an age of rapidly changing historical conditions. While a remarkable consistency of subject matter has existed in the master storyline of history as articulated in national histories from the nineteenth through the twenty-first centuries, conceptions of childhood have varied markedly over that same period, impacting the way book publishers have packaged history and the manner in which young readers have received it.[11] The historian of children's literature Gillian Avery and others have pointed out, for instance, that prior to the nineteenth century childhood in America was viewed as a highly dangerous period in which vulnerable young people, especially the "unconverted," were thought to be susceptible to the corruptions of the Devil.[12] Children in colonial America were treated as little adults, and the goal in educating them was to accelerate the process of maturation as quickly as possible as a protection against corruption.[13] "What strikes us now," Avery notes from the perspective of several centuries, "is the absence of all concessions to childhood as some later generations came to see it," that is, as "a time of innocence and make-believe, when children ought to be sheltered from harsh realities."[14] Instead, parents and teachers in the eighteenth century "regarded childhood as a time of deficiency" and "focused on childish mischief-making and youthful vice, especially blasphemy, idleness, disobedience, and Sabbath-breaking" as sinful behaviors to be controlled.[15]

The effect of these beliefs was to truncate unnaturally childhood in the United States by forcing literacy on children often before they were ready to assume its responsibilities. The publisher Samuel Osgood observed with concern that "reading begins very early with us, and the universal hurry of the American mind crowds children forward and tempts them in pleasure, as in study and work, to rebel at the usual limitations of years, and push infancy prematurely into childhood, childhood into youth, and youth into maturity." He added reproachfully, "Our heads are apt to be much older than our shoulders, and English critics of our juvenile literature say that much of it seems written for the market and counting-room rather than for the nursery and playground."[16] A British traveler to the United States confirmed that impression when he wrote, "I have never discovered that there were any American *children*. Diminutive men and women in process of growing up into big ones I have met with, but the child, in the full sense attached to that word in England, a child with its rosy cheeks and bright joyous laugh, its docile obedience and simplicity, its healthful play and its disciplined work, is a being almost unknown in America."[17]

If there were few true children in the United States, there were even fewer genuine children's books. The Bible was introduced early to youngsters in the many American families that valued religious education, but reading the holy word required mastering complex sentence structures and pronunciations. Many children struggled to understand portentous biblical narratives crammed full of heavy thematic and symbolic content. The exegesis of texts so central to biblical interpretation was beyond the grasp of most children as well, a condition that may explain why they found church sermons grounded in textual analysis so stultifying. Viewed as a necessary and often painful precondition for gaining salvation through scripture, biblical literacy was pursued aggressively and became a tedious burden to many parents who felt obliged to commence this aspect of their children's spiritual training "at the earliest possible moment," sometimes before the age of five.[18] Versions of the Bible that made special concessions to children in the form of simplified storylines and lavish pictorial aids were not yet popular in the United States, in part because such works were thought to violate the sanctity of the holy text by denaturing it.

A small number of children's books did circulate in late eighteenth-century America, primarily fairy tales imported from Europe and sold by itinerant peddlers in the form of chapbooks. John Newbery's *Mother Goose Tales,* with rhymes grounded in lullaby tradition, was appreciated for its lyrical qualities, while the folk stories of the Brothers Grimm, including *Snow White* and *Hansel and Gretel,* became part of the libraries of some young American readers by the late eighteenth century.[19] Editions of Charles Perrault's works, including *Sleeping Beauty, Little Red Riding Hood, Blue Beard, Puss in Boots,* and *Cinderella,* were translated from French to English and eventually made their way to America as well. The impact of such works in the United States was not substantial, however, at least not at first. The attractions of these "little, irreverent chapbooks," Daniel Roselle has noted of the American book market, "could not erase the solemn background of religious and moral orthodoxy that had prevailed for many centuries." In fact, they "furnished additional impetus to the growth of the didactic spirit in America."[20] Works with a strong moral message, like *Little Goody Two Shoes* (1787), were more acceptable than fairy stories and folktales, which were viewed with deep skepticism by those in the United States who proclaimed them the idle indulgences of puerile fantasizers.

For similar reasons history books for children were virtually unknown in the early national period. Before the publication of the first of Goodrich's popular volumes in the 1820s, only Mason Weems's *Life of Washington* had had much circulation among the young, and, although Weems's work focused on the moral residue of Washington's boyhood adventures, including the apocryphal cherry tree tale, it was primarily targeted at adult audiences.[21] Historical fiction was beginning to appear as well, but the genre was condemned as too "picturesque and lurid" for young readers.[22] Otherwise, there were few literary options for children interested in the past. "Just imagine a nation of children who had nothing to read [about the past], and you can picture the joy with which [Goodrich's work] was welcomed," the literary critic William Stevens has written.[23]

Some of this lack of juvenile histories can be attributed as well to the long-held belief that young readers were not capable of comprehending the foundational principles of history, especially periodization and causation. Many educators anticipated Bruno Bettelheim by recommending that children not be introduced to the discipline of history before the third or fourth grade, at which age, and only slowly, they could be exposed to the past through such biographical stories and myths as King Arthur, Roland, and Hiawatha. These would "arous[e] interest . . . when ideas of time and place relations are only imperfectly developed."[24] Even such stimulating alternatives were judged inadequate by those who were concerned that such accounts might feed a child's objectionable tendencies toward excitability and excess. Historians should stick to facts organized in narrative form and hope that children would eventually grasp their relevance, teachers insisted. As the children's historian Anne MacLeod observes, writers of "historical tales" favored "literary restraint in writing for children. They were not given to vivid descriptions, whether of landscape or characters. Even less were they likely to describe or depict strong emotion since they believed that 'passions,' as they called them, should be governed, not indulged."[25]

By the 1820s changing conceptions of childhood and child-rearing practices began to impact perceptively the juvenile book culture in the United States, especially with respect to historical literature. As Avery notes, the Enlightenment era witnessed a reduction of fear in the vulnerability of children to the Devil and a greater appreciation of youth as a distinct, valued time of life.[26] The eighteenth-century belief in a "prepared" childhood, in which children were taught as quickly as possible "the skills and rules necessary to function in the adult world," gave way in the nineteenth century to the concept of a protected and protracted childhood, one in which parents sought to "shield children from adult realities."[27] The expansion of life expectancy rates in the mid-nineteenth century also afforded opportunities for greater indulgence in nostalgia for lost youth among book-buying mothers and fathers. These trends allowed childhood to be reimagined as a "time set apart," an age of innocence to be protected and cultivated rather than accelerated and impugned. MacLeod has written of the emergence of a Victorian sensibility that "cherished children as children and gave childhood a value in and by itself, rather than as a preparatory school for adult life."[28] Increasingly "the figure of the child lent itself to idealization," concurs the literary scholar Julia Briggs, "since it appeared to possess vitality and spiritual insight as yet uncontaminated by adult desires."[29]

Educators attentive to these changing conceptions of childhood insisted that the young should not be in an impetuous rush to learn; instead, they should be trained slowly with an eye to building self-esteem and a lifelong love of knowledge. This logic was adopted eventually by the publishing field as reading was reconceived by bookmakers to be not merely an educational but also a leisure activity for the young.[30] Publishers initiated new genres of children's books to accommodate these changing cultural conditions, including works of history that were didactic but also age appropriate. The fresh conception of childhood reversed the previous literary calculus by encouraging authors to produce simple texts expressly for juvenile readers rather than requiring young readers to expand their phonetic proficiency in the unrealistic expectation that they could master adult texts. The genre of popular history came to occupy a central role in this altered landscape of juvenile literature since its status as nonfiction made it more palatable to reluctant parents who still feared the effects of fictional works on their children. Even in a changing juvenile book industry, a work's veracity remained its most salient and sellable feature. "Is it a true book, John?" asks the grandmother in one nineteenth-century publication. "Because if it isn't true, it is the worst thing that a boy can read."[31]

Books about the past for children were introduced initially into the home market, partly because compulsory education laws had not gone into effect in most states until midcentury, and many children were educated at home rather than in public schools. Additionally, even those states that mandated schooling did not recognize history as an independent discipline and therefore did not encourage the purchase of history books for school use. Instead, the study of many subjects was overseen by parents, especially history, since it was presumed to have important religious associations. As Goodrich wrote in a homeschooling manual from the 1830s, *Fireside Education,* "It is to be remarked, as a part of the same great scheme of Providence, that the controlling lessons of life, those which last the longest, those which result in fixed habits and permanent tastes, and usually determine the character for good or ill, are given . . . at the fireside seminary; and that here the parent, as well by the ordinance of God as the institutions of society, is the teacher." Insisting that the lessons of history were the bedrock of moral education, Goodrich urged parents to use the past to encourage the kinds of behaviors they wished their children to exhibit in their daily lives in the present. Since the fireside is "the great institution furnished by providence for the education of man," the family hearth should be used to reveal the ways in which history exerts "a decisive influence on character." The "sagacity and benevolence" displayed in historical narratives, he concluded, "afford a striking manifestation of that wisdom and goodness which we behold in all the works of God."[32]

These trends eventually influenced the place of history in the curriculum of primary schools throughout the United States as well. The historiographer George Callcott has remarked that in selected areas of the country in the late eighteenth century the "study of the past first entered the elementary school curriculum as a part of the reading exercises" for children. Benjamin Franklin led this charge on behalf of children by advocating that history be made "a constant Part of their Reading" in schools, while leading educators like Benjamin Rush and Samuel Harrison Smith "maintained that primary readers should include history 'above all,' and that the quantity of history in readers should be 'greatly increased.'"[33] Initially such works tended to be unwieldy distillations of adult volumes, books reduced in scope and language for the benefit of children but committed to adult themes of citizenship, statehood, and virtue. They were marketed as a literature "above fiction" that, if approached properly, could serve as inducements to learning for children. As in the case of Goodrich's fireside children's literature, the test of the worth of such works of history was whether their moral values could be readily absorbed by young readers.[34] In one such representative nineteenth-century work, for instance, the hero checks out Charles Rollins's *Universal History* from the library in an effort to learn history's valuable lessons while simultaneously avoiding the dangerous distractions of those cheap books of fiction that interest his friends. "I like stories very much," the protagonist proclaims, "but I have only a little time to read, and I must learn something."[35]

With these changing cultural conditions as inducements, some forward-looking publishers imagined a market for children's history that reached beyond the compass of moral guidebooks. As attitudes toward childhood and play altered in favor of leisure activity, so did the motivations for writing history books expressly for children interested in pleasure reading. In response, a new cottage industry of children's works emerged at midcentury in the United States, including volumes that were not only useful but also interesting. As Callcott comments, the Victorian era brought a new concept "of what history was supposed to be" for children: not merely a tale of "moral and pious reflection" but "a pleasant and exciting subject of stirring narrative and intellectual adventure."[36] The key for publishers in this new field was to move slowly in these transitions because many adults remained dubious about the literary benefits of popular history for children. For such skeptics, the works of Samuel Goodrich were an acceptable option, as he remained committed to moral truth as a thematic standard even as he experimented with literary style. Eschewing the fabrications and distortions implicit in fairy tales and mythologies, Goodrich argued that history was of inestimable value to children because by studying it they would learn the value of truth. "After possessing a knowledge of religion, and the duties we owe to God and our neighbor, history is the most important of all studies," he claimed. "It relates to us what has been done by mankind, and thus teaches us what they may do. It acquaints us with the true character of our race, and enables us to know ourselves better. It apprizes us of the existence of evil and the way to shun it; it acquaints us with the existence of good and shows us how to attain it."[37]

This reasoning, evidenced in the advertisements for popular histories such as *Parley's History of the World,* convinced many parents that Goodrich was appropriately mindful of the moral implications of the changing literary appetites of their children to warrant the purchasing of his books. Some of these guardians also shared his outlook on how and when it was appropriate to teach children to read history as well as what sources and techniques were most helpful in accomplishing these tasks. Goodrich's background as an early childhood educator and his deep desire to keep the wrong materials out of the hands of vulnerable children were ample evidence to parents of his commitment as a popular historian to the didactic narrative tradition, and they help explain why Goodrich is favored among republishers and homeschoolers today.

A Field for Improvement: Narrative History as Moral Education

In order to understand the importance of these transitions, one must ask, What kind of popular children's historian was Samuel Goodrich (fig. 3)? Born in 1793, one of ten children, Sammy grew up in Ridgefield, Connecticut, in a family of preachers and farmers who were deeply spiritual but "never gloomy."[38] Owing to financial constraints, he had little formalized education, doing only short stints at the West Lane School and at Master Stebbins's Seminary, but he was a precocious fireside learner who undertook a rigorous program of home education. "Finding that his memory was bad for dates," writes his biographer Roselle, "he made a chronological list of events and riveted them in his mind by constant repetition."[39] Goodrich's historical sensibilities were honed further in conversations with his relatives, some of whom had been involved personally in historical events central to the founding of the nation. His maternal grandfather, Colonel John Ely, had had "a large and painful share in [the] vicissitudes" of the Revolution, and he was not closemouthed about his experiences. The colonel recited for Sammy and his siblings rousing stories about the British attacks on Ridgefield, about the cannonball still embedded in the corner post of the local tavern, and about "men who had seen service and won laurels in the tented field."[40] Many tales told and retold around the hearths in American homes were commonly embellished. Given that history was viewed as a device for teaching children vital family lessons, stirring filial emotions was deemed more important to the colonel than demonstrating fidelity to facts. From Ely, Goodrich developed a strong sense of self-importance, historical relevance, and validation. He also learned the value of allowing history to be told in personalized ways in order to make it useful to children living in "post-heroic" ages such as his own.[41]

FIGURE 3. Portrait of Samuel G. Goodrich. Print Collection, Miriam and Ira D. Wallach Division of Art, Prints and Photographs, The New York Public Library, Astor, Lenox and Tilden Foundations.

The oral tales told by Colonel Ely were rivaled only by those of Ridgefield's most "profound and erudite village oracle," Lieutenant Ebenezer Smith, who also had fought in the Revolution and who held forth regularly near the stoop of Keeler's Tavern, reciting historical stories to the children of the village. Smith "was a man of extensive reading, and large information," Goodrich remembered, one whose powers of "observation and experience" made him the town's most valued citizen. Sammy recalled listening in stunned rapture as this venerable figure narrated tales about "the Purchase of Louisiana; the Expedition of Lewis and Clark; the death of Hamilton in the duel with Aaron Burr; the attack of the *Leopard* on the *Chesapeake;* Fulton's attempt at steam navigation, and the other agitating topics of those times, as they came one after another." Sometimes the stories were military, such as General Edward Braddock's defeat at the outset of the French and Indian War, "embellished with romantic episodes of Indian massacres and captivities." At other times the accounts were political, such as when the lieutenant expressed disdain for the atheism of Thomas Jefferson and the "republican rabble" for whom the

third president worked.[42] In either case, Goodrich was enthralled with the historical acumen of this "Yankee Pickwick," a member of that "useful race of fussy philosophers to be found in most country villages" who were full of knowledge and yearned "to make everybody share in [their] learning."[43]

As attracted as Goodrich was to the military and political opinions of Lieutenant Smith, it was the orator's delivery as much as his subject matter that intrigued the youngster the most. "I have the impression that Lieut. Smith after all, was not very profound; but to me he was a miracle of learning," wrote Goodrich. "I listened to his discussions with very little interest, but his narrative engaged my whole attention." Smith's oratorical style inspired a lifelong interest in the techniques of storytelling and oral history that served Goodrich well as a popular historian and have since recommended his works to those at Hearthstone Publishing and elsewhere who value their narrative thrust. Privileging firsthand testimony over accumulated legend, Goodrich appreciated the "living presence of history" in the elderly gentleman's discourses and admired his habit of not resorting often to inventions or historical untruths. Smith's testimonials, though overdrawn, "were always descriptive of actual events," Goodrich remembered, "for he would have disdained fiction." From the lieutenant's narratives, he added, "I derived a satisfaction that I never found in fables."[44]

Fables were a sore spot for Goodrich, especially with regard to the theme of verisimilitude, since he believed most children were incapable of distinguishing meaningfully between fact and fiction. "There is little difference, as to moral effect upon children, between things real and things imaginary," he lectured. "All that is strongly conceived by the young, is reality to them." Betraying a lingering eighteenth-century concern for the vulnerability of children, Goodrich agonized over the pernicious effects of nursery rhymes on the youngest readers. As a boy, he had been sent a copy of Mother Goose by an uncle in London, which he read "with no relish." He was frightened by Little Red Riding Hood, Jack and the Beanstalk, and especially by the story of Blue Beard, which "made a stronger and still more painful impression" on him. "Though I knew it to be fiction, it was still in some sort a reality to me," he remembered, adding that Blue Beard's castle, "with its hideous chamber hung with ghastly corpses of his murdered wives, was more a living truth in my imagination, than any fact in history or geography." In spite of his best efforts to cast it out, the impression "remained with all its horrors—a dreadful burden upon [his] mind." Its "supper of horrors" familiarized him "with violence" and "defaced that moral sense, which is common in children—leading them to prefer the good, the true, and the beautiful if it be duly cherished." Such corrupting stories teach "meanness, deception, and crime," Goodrich concluded; they bring "evil communications" to the soul. "Had it not been for the constant teaching of rectitude, by precept and example, in the conduct of my parents, I might, to say the least, have been seriously injured," he intoned. "I am convinced that much of the vice and crime in the world are to be imputed to these atrocious books put down, with more or less efficiency, to their own debased moral standard." That they should be "put into the hands of children, and by Christian parents, and that too in an age of light and refinement" excited in him "the utmost wonder."[45]

Goodrich was so disturbed by the harmful influence of fairy tales on his and his generation's development that he waged a lifelong crusade in the United States and Europe to keep such works out of children's hands.[46] Fables and folktales, he argued in a series of discursive letters and public lectures, were counterproductive to the attainment of moral truth and should be banned from circulation among young readers. As was true of many other such censorship campaigns, Goodrich's message was not well received in Europe, especially among those who accused him of coddling young readers by suppressing too severely their literary appetites. In England, where a more indulgent Victorian sensibility about childhood had emerged, Goodrich's critics urged children's authors to continue to write "nursery rhymes" produced for a "race of real children not too wise, too learned, or too good."[47] Sir Walter Scott, who was "a strong advocate of fairy tales and their ability to stir childhood imagination," stated his preference for the genre "over the moralizing 'good-boy stories' that dominated the American juvenile fiction of his time." Scott wrote, "Truth is, I would not give one tear shed over *Little Red Riding Hood* for all the benefit to be derived from a hundred histories of Tommy Goodchild."[48] The literary arbiter Henry Cole agreed, attacking Goodrich in the guise of a "quaint, quiet, scholarly old gentleman" named Felix Summerly, who became a spokesperson in *Puck's* magazine for an "Anti-Peter-Parleyism" campaign. Summerly's self-proclaimed mission was "to preside over the enterprise, to rap the knuckles of Peter Parley, and to woo back the erring generation of children to the good old orthodox rhymes and jingles of England."[49] From Summerly's point of view, it was the "fancy, imagination, sympathies [and] affections" of this literature that had been purged unnecessarily by unimaginative American writers like Goodrich.[50]

England's most prized authors joined in the assault on Goodrich. William Makepeace Thackeray, writing under the pseudonym Michael Angelo Titmarsh, attacked Goodrich's "anti–Mother Goose and anti–fairy tale position," noting facetiously that "ogres have been a good deal maligned. They eat children it is true, but only occasionally."[51] Charles Dickens was even more waggish in his commentaries on the suitability of traditional fairy tales for children. Dickens's close friend, the illustrator George Cruikshank, had tried to improve on such tales by rewriting them to serve certain moral ends, among them "warnings against the evils of alcohol."[52] Dickens rejected Cruikshank's revisions as "Frauds on the Fairies" and "burlesqued them by turning Cinderella into a member of the Juvenile Bands of Hope, dressing her in sky-blue satin pantaloons, and sending her to the ball in 'a virtually democratic vegetable.'" Dickens claimed that fairy tales should be left alone, as they were "'harmless little books,' inculcating gentleness and mercy," and he urged parents not to deny their children the pleasure of reading about giants and wolves, despite what naysayers like Goodrich might conclude about the ill effects of such tales.[53]

This controversy paralleled later debates over whether fanciful and mythological writing should appear in history books for the very young as a way of easing children into the study of the past. Annie Cole Cady's *The American Continent and Its Inhabitants Before Its Discovery,* published under the pseudonym Robin Goodfellow, Fairy Historian, introduced juvenile readers to the lessons of the past through the literary device of a fictional narrator.[54] As nineteenth-century readers knew, Robin Goodfellow was the disguised name of the ubiquitous Puck character in British literature, a mischievous hobgoblin who led people astray through tricks and distortions.[55] Puck's appearance as the narrator in Cady's history introduced a spirited, playful element into the storyline of history and drew young readers more irresistibly to the past. Goodrich believed, however, that impish, fairy-tale narrators such as Cady's were counterproductive to juvenile learning and should be accompanied by the disclaimer that their use was "calculated to familiarize the mind with, things shocking and monstrous; to cultivate a taste for tales of bloodshed and violence; to teach the young to use coarse language, and cherish vulgar ideas . . . ; to turn the youthful mind from the gentle pleasures of home, of love and friendship at the fireside, at the school, in the playground, and to stretch it upon the rack of horrible dreams of giants, grinding the bones of children between their teeth, and satisfying their horrible thirst upon the blood of innocent men and women and infants."[56] Needless to say, there was no place for such puckish elements in Goodrich's popular histories for children.

A similar mischievous narrative element was evident in Dickens's own foray into the discipline of history, *A Child's History of England,* which was serialized between 1851 and 1853 in *Household Words* and later produced in a separate three-volume publication for young readers (fig. 4). Dickens dedicated the history to his "own dear children," whom, he hoped, "it may help, bye and bye, to read with interest larger and better books on the same subject." Certainly Dickens's work was a much more irreverent look at British history than Goodrich would have tolerated. The British author referred to King James I as "His Sowship," for instance, and poked fun at the corpulence and incompetency of other British monarchs, such as Henry VIII, who was described as "a blot of blood and grease upon the History of England."[57] Dickens's history was also more graphic than Goodrich would have preferred. As one advertisement noted, A Child's History of England "offers an engaging reminder of the English history we ought to know: who was Hereward the Wake, how was it that Thomas à Becket was murdered in Canterbury Cathedral, and was Canute really trying to stop the tide?" "Interesting, informative and accessible," Dickens's work was characterized as a history "full of sensational plots, gallant heroes and brutal villains, high adventure and terrible tragedy," appealing "to anyone who enjoys a good story and some horrible [that is, dramatic] history!"[58] By contrast, Goodrich's Pictorial History of England (1845) focused on the history of Great Britain as "a source of useful and interesting knowledge" for the "instructive" benefit of the general reader.[59]

Goodrich's distrust of fables and puckish works like those by Cady and Dickens conditioned his alternative approaches to popular histories for children.[60] Children were capable of grasping the truth of history, he reasoned, provided the past was approached in serious, high-minded ways. Goodrich's belief in the vulnerability of children coupled with his recognition of the increasing literary opportunities available to them encouraged him to write children's history books "of a purer and more exalted tone." In pursuit of this dream he traveled to England, where he consulted with Hannah More, the author of Cheap Repository Tracts, who affirmed that verisimilitude was the key to literary influence among children. It was not necessary to over-stimulate children with fiction, she reasoned, when history, natural history, geography, and biography could "become the elements of juvenile works, in place of fairies and giants, and mere monsters of the imagination." The idea as Goodrich came to understand it "was to make nursery books reasonable and truthful, and thus to feed the young mind upon things wholesome and pure, instead of things monstrous, false, and pestilent." He determined not to administer "cruelty and violence, terror and impurity" to children; as alternatives he offered "beauty instead of deformity, goodness instead of wickedness, decency instead of vulgarity."[61]

When Goodrich returned from his trip to Europe, he took up offices in Boston on the floor above the Ticknor and Fields Old Corner Bookstore, the epicenter of activity for book culture in early nineteenth-century New England. For the next thirty years, from the late 1820s to the late 1850s, he wrote and published dozens of children's textbooks designed to implement this new philosophy of education—books on popular history, geography, natu-

FIGURE 4.
Charles Dickens,
*A Child's History of
England* (London:
Estes and Lauriat,
1886).

ral history, arithmetic, and art. His advertised goal in producing these works was "to enlarge the circle of knowledge, to invigorate the understanding, to strengthen the moral nerve, [and] to purify and exalt the imagination" of children. The teaching of "morals and manners, particularly in their more familiar application to our daily duties," was his first priority. Goodrich hoped to lighten the weight of his heavy moral program by communicating simply and directly with his young charges. Narrative voice was especially important to him. He noted of his technique, "I imagined myself on the floor with a group of boys and girls, and I wrote to them as I would have spoken to them."[62]

To facilitate these goals, Goodrich knew he would have to start at the very beginning of a child's educative process, instilling an early love for reading and learning among the preliterate. He determined "to supply helps for the acquisition of the mechanical art of reading" by writing and publishing a series of five readers, each part of a developmental strategy grounded in experiential learning. The *First Reader* established the foundations for literacy by focusing on rules for posture, breathing, and pronouncing words when read aloud. The *Second Reader* encouraged children to read by using words and images as a way of making sense of the world around them. Children learned through their senses, Goodrich reasoned, and because children's "first ideas are simple and single, and formed of images of things palpable to the senses," he chose for his texts subjects "capable of sensible representation."[63] Sound was a filter for knowledge that he had learned to appreciate as a young boy listening to Lieutenant Smith. Sight was even more important—"the master organ of the body as well as the soul"—so Goodrich larded his texts with substantial visual embellishments that highlighted the eye as the central instrument of insight.[64] Subsequent volumes introduced various mnemonic devices for mastering the letters of the alphabet and then listed simple words in verse and prose, almost always with a strong moral, even biblical, message. As one student recalled, "There was no escape for his readers from the continual barrage of advice, suggestion, and demand" in such works. "Even the tiniest babe could find no sanctuary or pardon for breaking the rigid rules," as evidenced by the following aphorism found in *Goodrich's Second Reader*: "Then when about to do amiss; Though pleasant it may seem to be, I will always try to think of this, I am *not too young* for God to see!"[65]

No one was more indispensable to the practical application of these philosophies than Goodrich's friend the Reverend Thomas H. Gallaudet. As director of the American Asylum at Hartford in the 1830s, Gallaudet had developed a "sight-word method" to aid the deaf in reading by encouraging young readers to "memorize the appearance of words" through "slide[s] or cards with a picture next to a word, teaching children to associate the whole word with its meaning."[66] The sight/word technique emphasized the correspondence between image and fact, and it relied on rote memory as the primary tool for learning. This approach, reminiscent of the visual strategies used in eighteenth-century hornbooks, was popular among many schoolteachers, who issued to their youngest students manuals for refining memorization skills and who oversaw regular weekly classroom recitation exercises testing a student's capacities for retaining facts as revealed through visual channels.[67] The pedagogical goal was to stockpile specific information linked to pictorial cues until a sizable vocabulary of facts had been mastered. Only then might a student be encouraged to consider the more complex and integrative processes of learning. In the 1830s this system was adopted as uniform policy for the state of Massachusetts by Horace Mann, the secretary

of the Board of Education, and its word lists and core vocabulary charts circulated widely throughout the country, even into the late nineteenth century
and early twentieth.[68]

Goodrich applied Gallaudet's sight/word method to the discipline of history, arguing that students should develop the capacity to memorize factual
material central to the story of the past. "There are a few things I wish you
never to forget," he wrote young readers in a series of history manuals for
use in schools, and "I will therefore put them down, and you may study them
over till you have learned them all by heart." Facts were an essential part of
the overall program of achieving historical literacy, he suggested, because
they grounded education in lived experience, serving as a check on the tendency among teachers to encourage their students "to live in the world of the
imagination."[69] His second and third books of history, for instance, warned
against the excesses of ancient historians, whose works were more poetic
than factual and were "so mingled with fiction as to render the real occurrences which they relate, nearly unintelligible." Goodrich offered instead a
catalogue of facts that might equip students with the rudiments of the past
so that they could understand what distinguished "fabulous histories" from
truthful ones.[70] Even the youngest readers of *The First Book of History* were
asked to "commit to memory" forty-six dates for each unit, including some
very obscure ones, for example, the date of the incorporation of the Massachusetts Agricultural Institute (1848).[71]

Critics of these techniques voiced their discontent over the constrained,
self-righteous character of the literary and historical standards established by
Goodrich. In a review of Dickens's *A Child's History of England,* the British
critic G. K. Chesterton claimed the British novelist's approach to the past was
less high-minded than that of a popular historian such as Goodrich, whose
works personified the "mystical perversity of a man of genius writing only
out of his own temperament" and advancing a moral agenda. But in Chesterton's view virtuosity of the kind practiced by Goodrich was overrated among
historians. "If a man has a new theory of ethics there is one thing he must
not be allowed to do," the critic quipped. "Let him give laws on Sinai, let him
dictate a Bible, let him fill the world with cathedrals if he can. But he must not
be allowed to write a history of England; or a history of any country." The
danger in Goodrich's strategy was that young readers would not learn how
to distinguish between "ordinary morality" and this "extraordinary morality"
and would try to act in unrealistic ways by striving for the latter rather than
the former.[72]

Chesterton had a point, at least with respect to the literary habits of the
most zealous of Goodrich's followers. Many juvenile readers of Goodrich

accepted his moral pronouncements as articles of faith and considered him an indisputable voice on all matters of historical question. H. A. Chambers remembered how, as an impressionable boy, he "read and re-read" *Peter Parley's Common School History* "until it was torn to pieces." "I can recall the wood cuts in it of Knight's Errant, of the Kings of England, Cromwell, Charlemagne, and the other French monarchs, and of Napoleon," he noted, adding, "It was the unquestioned historical authority which was used in the great debates which occurred sometimes at the neighborhood schoolhouses on winter nights."[73] For Chambers and his friends, *Parley's History* had a power comparable to that of the Bible to adjudicate disputes. If Goodrich declared something to be true, then it was true, they believed. Chesterton worried aloud about the long-term effects of such slavish devotion to an author who wrote texts from which there was no acceptable deviation. "Historically speaking, it is better to be Dickens than to be this," Chesterton concluded; "better to be ignorant, provincial, slap-dash, seeing only the passing moment, but in that moment, to be true to eternal things."[74]

Supporters of Goodrich over Dickens, however, admired the commitment and loyalty of children to Goodrich's moral program. Even his detractors concurred that by the late 1830s Goodrich had established himself as a preeminent authority on childhood historical literacy in America, and, in the eyes of publishers like Hearthstone, he remains so today. He recycled the moral lessons of an earlier age but in new forms more easily digested by young children. His fame spread quickly as a result. "He has made the discovery, and established a conviction of the fact throughout the world, that truth may be made as attractive to youth as fiction," a reviewer for the *Southern Literary Messenger* wrote. "He has shown that truth, upon which nature and philosophy alike teach us that the young intellect should be fed and fostered, may be rendered as palatable as matters of mere fancy." In so doing he had opened a rich field for others, redeeming "the writing of children's books from the contempt in which it was once held." Some of his works "have acquired a popularity altogether unparalleled," the journal pointed out, adding that one of his textbooks, "now published in several languages, and disseminated throughout the five divisions of the globe, is more widely circulated than any other book produced within the present or the last century."[75]

Twenty-first-century republishers of Goodrich's works on the Christian Right have greatly appreciated this truth-seeking penchant as well. Goodrich's moral philosophy of history as expressed through his sight/word methodology and his insistence on the recitation of canonical historical facts implied that he was a traditionalist when it came to presenting a reliable record of the past. In Goodrich's estimation, certain historical facts were unassailable and must be included in any narrative that purported to be a true history of the human race. In addition, he rarely missed an occasion to draw strong ethical lessons from these essentials, and he made "no apology" for having availed himself "of occasional opportunities to inculcate lessons of morality and religion upon the youthful heart."[76] For those at Hearthstone Publishing who believe that one can know the past definitively and with precise reference to God's intentions for his people, Goodrich's texts hold out the intriguing promise of direct access to divine moral truths. He convinced readers, even young readers, of the ethical benefits of an intense, catechistic study of the historical record and the value of having an appreciation for the accuracy attained by working from original texts that revealed an unimpeachable past.

The "voice of truth," with which Goodrich came to be associated, was revered by youth—so much so, in fact, that he "was mobbed by excited children when he made a tour of the South in 1846."[77] Parents extolled his virtues as well. M. M. Cohen of New Orleans appreciated the high character Goodrich displayed on his visit to the Crescent City, which was marked by expressions of the value of accuracy and honesty that seemed to rub off on southern children. "For, sir," Cohen wrote the popular historian, "who knows into how many thousand habitations in the United States Peter Parley's works have found their way, and made the hearts of the inmates glad, and kept them pure? Who can tell how oft, in the humble cottage of the poor, sorrow has been soothed and labor lightened, as the fond mother read to her listening child Peter Parley's Tales, while tears of pity started in their glistening eyes, or pleasure shook their infant frames?"[78] Roselle notes that Goodrich was popular and trusted enough by the 1840s to be nominated for president of the United States on the "children's ticket" by the children's magazine editor Haley Thorne.[79] This quaint tribute had real-life consequences for Goodrich's career, as it turned out, for it attracted the attention of the future president Millard Fillmore. In a letter dated 31 August 1850, Fillmore offered Goodrich a diplomatic post in Paris on the grounds that he had proven himself a trustworthy, valuable public figure. "I think you have done more to diffuse useful knowledge among the rising generation, than any other modern writer, either English or American," he wrote, referencing one of Goodrich's "supervised-histories" as "admirably well calculated to give to the youthful mind a knowledge of history."[80] Goodrich's daughter agreed. She was fond of repeating the great statesman Charles Sumner's story about finding in the depths of a Cornish coal mine a copy of Parley's *Tales of the Sea* "side by side with one other book—the Bible." "In telling my father this," she added, Sumner remarked, " 'Goodrich, this is fame.' "[81]

"Fiction Lay at the Foundation of My Scheme": The Parley Persona

Despite Goodrich's reputation for fidelity, both in his own day and now, one is obliged to ask whether it is rightfully earned. Is it true, that is, that Goodrich's works embody the kind of trustworthiness and reliability that Hutchings and those at Hearthstone Publishing assume? Closer inspection reveals that Goodrich resorted frequently to fictional devices that distorted the historical record in significant ways. Still worse, he knew that in embellishing the past as he sometimes did, he was being unfaithful to the very literary principles that had motivated him to write history in the first place. The sad irony of this condition did not manifest itself immediately, to be sure, but by the end of his literary career Goodrich came to think of himself as more similar than dissimilar to Colonel Ely, Lieutenant Smith, and the Brothers Grimm as purveyors of historical truth.

Consider, for instance, the assumption that Goodrich was committed to facts over fiction and did everything he could to avoid the excesses of contrived approaches to the past. Goodrich did indeed eschew the influence of fairy tales on children's minds and worried about the pernicious effects fictive devices might have on a child's historical imagination. But he was not a mere compiler of historical facts who ignored the literary elements of his craft. Indeed, as the Hearthstone marketers have specified approvingly, he was also a storyteller who was interested in the power of the mind to shape historical narratives. It was not enough to require children to memorize the historical facts of a sensate world, Goodrich realized. "Repetition, drilling, line upon line, and precept upon precept, with here and there a little of the birch" was only the starting point for children to learn, he argued.[82] One must also encourage children to move beyond the outward senses—the "external organs"—to the internal organ of the mind, where ideas are formulated. Reading should not be "a mere act of running over the sound of letters and syllables, without a corresponding effort of the mind to grasp the ideas which the words convey," Goodrich averred. If a child learns "to read only with his lips and not with his understanding," he runs the risk of developing "some of the worst and most obstinate bad habits."[83]

The solution, Goodrich contended, was to require students to reflect on what they have seen and heard while studying and reciting a lesson and then to teach them how to extrapolate from the physical to the ideational. At the end of each section of his readers, therefore, Goodrich asked age-appropriate questions designed "to make the pupils think of, and reflect upon, what they have read." As might be expected, these tutorials were almost always overtly moral. For instance, the first lesson in the *Third Reader,* called "The Bible," was a short story about a little boy who discovered that his local soap maker was wrapping her product in the detached leaves of a worn-out Bible. The boy expresses his worry over this irreverent practice and tries to procure enough money to buy the remaining pages of the Holy Book. In such lessons, students are not only asked to evaluate how to spell and define certain words and warned about potential faults of pronunciation while reading the narrative, but also encouraged to consider why they "should read every word distinctly," presumably because (as with the Bible violated in the story) each word is sacred in terms of its relevance to the overall moral lesson of the exercise.[84]

Goodrich's primary pedagogical goal here and elsewhere was to find reading materials suitable for the teaching of the moral lessons while encouraging the young to approach the subject matter of history with joy as well as reverence.[85] He understood, however, that children represented challenges for historians, since chroniclers of the past often lacked "a language at the same time copious enough to express a great variety of ideas, and simple enough for the limited comprehension of children."[86] Such barriers had convinced most educators to abandon the effort, and, as a result, history was not regularly taught in American schools in the mid-nineteenth century. The deficiency arose not from a lack of history to narrate, in Goodrich's estimation, but "from the want of historical books written in a style which shall render them both interesting and profitable" and exhibiting suitable illustrations and narrative coherence. Most history textbooks were "but little more than extended chronological tables, and offer nothing to the reader but a tedious mass of dates and general observations," he claimed.[87] Such catechistic approaches had the same dulling effect that requiring children to memorize the endless genealogical record of the Bible (the who begat whom of the Old Testament) had on religious education. The key, he reasoned, was to move beyond the litany of essential facts to a discovery of the pervasive moral spirit informing them, since historical meaning inhered less in facts than in universal laws derived from facts.

In order to attract children to these weighty lessons of history, Goodrich sensed, the story of the past had to be told in inspirational ways. He was mindful, however, that in doing so historians must not be so imaginative as to invite undesirable comparisons to distorting fairy tales. He set out to develop a series of readable juvenile history books that young readers could enjoy outside of school during their leisure hours. Goodrich was not afraid to write "flesh-and-blood" history, and he employed romantic tropes and conventions to convey how the past could be used to impact the moral imaginations of the young. Of all types of reading material, Goodrich noted, "there is none that so readily attracts the attention, and lays hold of the sympathy of children and youth, as lively narratives of the enterprises, adventures, dangers, trials, successes and failures of mankind, and these it is the business of history to display."[88] The idea was to balance narrative exuberance with factual restraints. Put differently, Goodrich sought to deploy the kind of powerful oratorical devices of his townsman Lieutenant Smith—those "descriptive of actual events"—without resorting to Smith's blatant ornamentation.

Redeeming the children's book "from the contempt in which it was held" was a mission to which Goodrich remained committed throughout his career, although his more specialized goal was to make his mark in the field of juvenile popular history. He was not all that successful at first. He began by abridging several works of history that he and his brother, Charles Augustus Goodrich, had written for adult audiences.[89] He then collaborated with a friend, Samuel Kettell, on a series of pictorial works on the history of England, France, Greece, and Rome.[90] Some of these volumes were hurried into press, and the entire run betrayed signs of sloppy bookmaking. "Many of the engravings were quite poor," Roselle has noted of the *Pictorial History of France,* adding that the "ten small representations of the heads of European monarchs" were bad enough that they "presented a convincing argument in favor of royal decapitation."[91] The *London and Westminster Review* agreed, characterizing Goodrich as "a bad dealer in slip-slop on many subjects" who, although voluminous and amusing, violates readers' fundamental "right to insist" that an author "shall know what he is talking about!"[92] The *American Annals of Education and Instruction* added to the chorus, sharply criticizing Goodrich for "unnecessary violations of the truth."[93]

Goodrich's most famous and most controversial collaboration during this period was with Nathaniel Hawthorne, who was paid one hundred dollars to help Goodrich write a book titled *Universal History* for children.[94] Goodrich was not thrilled with Hawthorne's manuscript when it was first submitted. "Your letter and the two folios of 'Universal History' were received some days ago. I like the History pretty well," Goodrich wrote without much enthusiasm. "I shall make it do." For his part, Hawthorne felt underappreciated and underpaid for his work, noting that for a pittance he had been asked to become "an historian of the universe." Hawthorne admitted he possessed "rather a kindly feeling" toward Goodrich," whom he regarded as a not "unkindly man," but he condemned the publisher's "propensity to feed and fatten himself on better brains than his own." Hawthorne uncharitably concluded, "He was born to do what he did, as maggots to feed on rich cheese."[95] Goodrich remained solicitous of Hawthorne throughout his career, although he abandoned the *Universal History* in favor of a slightly revised *Common*

School History issued under his name. It is this work that has been re-released by Hearthstone Publishing.

These early failures in the children's book market motivated Goodrich to strike out on his own as a popular historian. Stating that "it is impossible for one man to do everything; or to do many different kinds of things well almost simultaneously," the *American Monthly Review* urged Goodrich to rely less extensively on the authority of others and to develop an original literary voice.[96] In response, Goodrich created an innovative narrative persona for his juvenile histories known as Peter Parley, an "old silver haired gentleman with a gouty foot and a wooden cane" who told stories (parleyed) about the past (fig. 5). The edition of 1828 of the *Tales About America* begins, "Here I am! My name is Peter Parley! I am an old man. I am very gray and lame. But I have seen a great many things, and had a great many adventures, and I love to talk about them."[97] Goodrich tinkered with the Parley narrator over the next three decades, varying his age, his background, and even which foot was gouty to suit his immediate needs but always retaining his commitment to honest storytelling through a narrator who was not real but believable. No "Robin Goodfellow, fairy historian," Parley exuded an air of truthfulness and reliability in everything he said and did. "The character of Peter Parley is drawn with a verisimilitude, quite equal to that of Robinson Crusoe," noted the *Southern Literary Messenger* appreciatively. "The cheerfulness, benevolence, condescension and piety of the good old man, have given him grace in the eyes of all; and many an eye has glistened, many a lip quivered in believing sympathy with his pains and pleasures." Fittingly, the hobbled Parley appears on the frontispiece of many of Goodrich's histories, usually surrounded by the children to whom he is telling a story and thus a welcoming channel into the books for young readers.[98]

The Parley narrator influenced how the past was absorbed by Goodrich's young readers in several ways. He allowed Goodrich to personalize the past by convincing children they were learning history from one who had experienced it directly. As the literary historian Allan Luke has noted, "Narrational presence or absence can underline the didactic element of the story, invoking the narrator's reality as distinct from that of the characters, reinforcing or undercutting the particular rules and parameters of a specific . . . reality."[99] In Parley's case, the narrator is a first-person voice that lent authenticity to Goodrich's accounts and reaffirmed his political and moral ideologies. Ingratiating himself to young readers by appealing to their curiosity about the past, Parley recounted many things he claimed to have seen and heard firsthand. Speaking of the two-hundredth anniversary of the settlement of Boston, which took place with a great deal of pomp and circumstance in 1830, Parley

FIGURE 5. "Peter Parley Telling Tales," from *Peter Parley's Winter Evening Tales,* rev. ed. (Philadelphia: Charles DeSilver, 1855), frontispiece.

reminded readers with moral intent, "I was there myself, and I was delighted at the long rows of good little boys and girls."[100] Goodrich's narrator in *Tales of Peter Parley About America* noted that he had been at the Battle of Bunker Hill as well and that he had clear memories of its heroic episodes. "I was there myself, and recollect the scene perfectly well," Parley noted. "The soldiers lay upon the ground with their guns loaded and ready. The British came up in front of us, all dressed in bright red coats." American soldiers "did not complain. . . . Everywhere, the Americans fought like good fellows," he added.[101] Goodrich's you-are-there approach to history gave his readers a participatory sense of the past and made them feel as if history was a real, even mildly dangerous, presence in their lives.

In other instances Parley was a time traveler of sorts, bouncing back and forth across time periods to give readers personal insights into the details of varied historical epochs. For those events that Parley admitted he had not experienced firsthand and for which "no man could be found old enough to tell you their story from his own observation," Goodrich expanded Parley's temporal reach. History, he noted metaphorically, "may be compared to an old man who has lived for thousands of years, and who has seen cities built and fall into decay; who has seen nations rise, flourish, and disappear; and who, with a memory full of wonderful things, sits down to tell you of all that has happened during so many years." In the introduction to *Parley's Universal History,* the narrator employed the following strategy: "I shall therefore sometimes assume to be the old graybeard of history, who has lived for thousands of years, and tell you of what has come to pass."[102] There was a temporal looseness to this narrative strategy, as even Goodrich was aware, but it allowed him to make use of a "consistent present" as an organizing device for moral and practical purposes by bridging the gap between the biblical creation story and the lives of the young readers who were so far removed from such events. "The world has existed for almost 6000 years, and in every age, some great events have happened. Now, it is the story of these events that I am going to tell you," Goodrich wrote in *Parley's Methods of Telling About History.* Whether studying "Jesus Christ, who lived at Jerusalem about 1800 years ago, and was often seen by the inhabitants of that city walking about the streets" or "Solomon and his temple; of King David, who wrote the Psalms; of Moses who led the children of Israel out of Egypt; and of Adam and Eve who dwelt in the Garden of Eden," Goodrich claimed, one finds the same "lessons of wisdom, truth, and morality" in each event.[103]

This idea of a consistent present constituted a pattern that was especially appealing to children, who had little concept of the passage of time. It catered to their desire for what David Lowenthal has called a "timeless past," that is, a history "characterized by little change" and focused on "timeless human nature."[104] By proclaiming the importance of a present which represents all time in distillation, Goodrich's scheme reduced the scope of his histories in ways that benefited young readers, who had little sense of temporal distance. Comforting as this technique was, however, Goodrich did not intend to coddle children by overusing it. "I aimed at making education easy," he wrote, but he had no intentions of "bringing up the child in habits of receiving knowledge only as made into pap" or of "putting it out of his power to relish and digest the stronger meat, even when his constitution demanded it."[105] To Goodrich, narration, even lively narration, was compatible with authenticity and rigor, and he was not averse to recounting in his histories some of the "tales of battle, bloodshed, injustice, and crime" and other "horrid scenes" over which some might be inclined to throw a veil. "These things have really happened," and it is "the duty of a faithful story-teller to hide nothing which is necessary to give a true picture of what he undertakes to exhibit."[106] What Goodrich objected to was gratuitous violence and warmongering in histories for the very young—histories like Dickens's *A Child's History of England* that were calculated "to erase from the young heart tender and gentle feelings, and substitute for them fierce and bloody thoughts and sentiments."[107]

Not everyone was convinced that Goodrich had maintained a proper balance between literary expression and accuracy of detail in his popular histories, however, especially those who found Peter Parley's "truthful fictions" inherently contradictory. Professing a profound respect for the sanctity of the past, Goodrich nonetheless took liberties sometimes with the historical record for the sake of literary effect and in the process falsified its elements. According to his naysayers, Goodrich sacrificed the dispassionate facts of history for the emotional pull of romance and in so doing gave children false impressions about the past and its relevance as a tool for understanding the present. His treatment of Native Americans was a case in point, for he described them as displaying savagery of a shocking variety and frequency. Indians "would often come at night, when the inhabitants were all asleep," Goodrich wrote in *The First Book of History,* and they "would first set the houses on fire, and as the defenceless people came forth in terror, they would shoot, and cut them down. Grey haired and tottering old men were not spared, women were slain, and innocent little children were often killed by the savages, as if in sport."[108] Such graphic depictions seemed to violate Goodrich's prohibition against fairy tale embellishments and Dickensian exaggerations, but he rationalized the inclusion of these graphic depictions of death by reminding young readers that these things really happened to settlers, whereas Blue Beard's horrors were fictional. It was the higher moral purposes to which his descriptions were put that justified their presence in children's literature, according to Goodrich.

Children were not always able to distinguish between the righteous and the audacious while reading Goodrich's stories, however, and their failure to do so worried some teachers. "Solemn educators became alarmed over the eagerness with which children took to his school-books, and they wrote heavy articles condemning him because he was making education too easy and attractive," one reviewer of Goodrich's career wrote.[109] Failing to provide "the sober narration that an age of self-restraint demanded of its historians," Goodrich was accused of violating the sanctity of history by employing the conventions of fiction and thereby subjectivizing the past in ways that distorted the truth.[110]

In this sense, Goodrich was impacted by a tension intrinsic to all historical narrative, namely, that the objective reality historians seek to describe in their works is influenced inherently by the subjective storytelling devices they use in their literary descriptions. As Hayden White has written, "The dream of a historical discourse that could consist of nothing but factually accurate statements about a realm of events which were (or had been) observable in principle, the arrangement of which in the order of their original occurrence would permit them to figure forth their meaning or significance," was just that: a dream. Goodrich was a popularizer first and foremost, and he was heedful that his histories, like those of all historians, were primarily what White has called a "literary (even fiction-making) operation." Indeed, at the end of his life he came to regard himself as nothing better than a falsifier of history, one who had relied too heavily on the "fictive or merely imaginable" to convey adequate messages about the fidelity of the past to vulnerable young readers.[111]

That Goodrich was sensitive to the implication that he had falsified the past is evident in the lengths to which he went to obscure his identity as the creator of Peter Parley. He maintained that he was motivated in this obfuscating behavior by the fact that when he began his writing career, in the early 1830s, "nursery literature had not then acquired the respect in the eyes of the world it now enjoys."[112] Yet this excuse does not explain why Goodrich continued to obscure his identity even as the genre increased in popularity. Deeper motivations for this concealment seem at work. He refused to reveal his authorship, for instance, even when his recently deceased friend and publishing associate Kettell was identified incorrectly in the *Boston Daily Courier* as being Peter Parley.[113] Still more problematic was his reaction to various imposters who claimed to be the real Peter Parley, including a man named Greene, "who deliberately dressed himself in the black coat and tight knee breeches" of the narrator and gave "public performances" as Parley that embarrassed Goodrich. Without the slightest sense of self-consciousness or discomfort about representing himself as the embodiment of a fictional character, Greene "toured the northern parts of New Hampshire and Vermont, attended religious meetings, affectionately patted little children on the head, and in many respects became old Parley incarnate." When another imposter was introduced to children in one of the New York public schools as "the veritable author of Peter Parley's Tales," Goodrich finally came to regret his ruse, complaining, "Perhaps I shall ere long be obliged to defend myself against a claim that he is I, and that I am not myself!"[114]

When Goodrich's identity as the creator of Peter Parley was revealed at last by Sarah J. Hale, the editor of *Ladies' Magazine,* he felt instantly the pangs of conscience that result from perpetrating a deception. "I was indebted to Hale for many kind offices in my literary career," Goodrich said of his revealer, "yet I could have wished she had not done me this questionable favor. Though the authorship of the Parley books has been to me a source

of some gratification," he noted, "it has also subjected me to endless vexations."[115] Among other things, being discovered exposed him to the ridicule
of those in the "Anti-Peter Parley" school, whose members discerned that
Goodrich, who had assumed a holier-than-thou attitude during his fables and
folktales campaign, was now engaged in an imaginative and sometimes misleading enterprise of his own. Indeed, the question of Parley's truthfulness
spoke directly to the integrity of the emerging discipline of history, since the
narrator of Goodrich's works was offered to gullible children as a contrived
character who masqueraded as a genuine person in a series of books that
professed a strong commitment to fidelity on behalf of a discipline that honored truth. "The real existence of such a person," opined the *Southern Literary
Messenger*, "has fastened itself upon the readers of the books issued under his
name, with a firmness of conviction that can hardly be shaken off."[116]

The deception confused his young admirers, who, on meeting him, often
expressed their disappointment and even anger that the man before them was
not the same gouty Parley described in the literature they had read. In his
memoirs Goodrich recorded the following exchange that captured perfectly
these disjunctures:

> "Did you really write that book about Africa?" said a black-eyed, dark-haired girl
> of some eight years old, at Mobile. I replied in the affirmative.
> "And did you really get into prison, there?"
> "No, I was never in Africa."
> "Never in Africa?"
> "Never."
> "Well, then, why did you say you had been there?"

On another occasion, in Savannah, a gentleman called on Goodrich, eager to
introduce his two grandchildren to Peter Parley. "The girl rushed up to me,
and gave me a ringing kiss at once. We were immediately the best friends in
the world," Goodrich wrote. "The boy, on the contrary, held himself aloof,
and ran his eye over me, up and down, from top to toe. He then walked
around, surveying me with the most scrutinizing gaze. After this, he sat
down, and during the interview, took no further notice of me. At parting,
he gave me a keen look, but said not a word." Goodrich's friend explained
the following day that his grandson, as they were on their way home, said
to him, "Grandfather, I wouldn't have any thing to do with that man: he
ain't Peter Parley." "How do we know that?" said the grandfather. "Because,"
said the boy, "he hasn't got his foot bound up, and he doesn't walk with a
crutch!"[117]

Goodrich conceded the painful irony and potential contradiction of his use of a fictional narrator in his works of history given his professed commitment to the fidelity of facts. "I, who had undertaken to teach truth, was forced to confess that fiction lay at the foundation of my scheme!" he wrote years later with some embarrassment. "My innocent young readers, however, did not suspect me: they had taken all I had said as positively true, and I was of course Peter Parley himself."[118]

The betrayal some children felt on discovering that Parley was only a literary contrivance was profound. A studio photograph of Goodrich reproduced in one of his magazines, for instance, outraged one young reader named Fanny with its nearly scandalous revelation of duplicity. "You have come to us every month, in the form of a venerable old man, requiring the support of his cane, surrounded by a troop of children, talking of old age and rheumatism," she wrote with a sense of outrage, "and when by such false pretences you have enticed us into an affectional correspondence, you spring a mine upon us, and come forth such a good-looking, smart, middle-aged gentleman that we blush to think how familiar we have been."[119] Another reader recorded his upset at discovering Goodrich's true identity. Of Parley he wrote, "What a rare old gentleman he was to be sure! And with what a grandfatherly, homely, fireside way, he told us youngsters—with pricked ears and most eager—about the Turks and the Greeks, and about London Bridge and the terrible Bastille. It was a great breakdown of our young cherished image to learn in after-life that the cocked hat, and staff, and big pockets were only purest, untruthful fancies, and that this master of boy-literature was a dapper man with an active, nervous step, who held consular office and stamped passports for the 'regulation' fees!"[120] The "shock was severe" indeed.[121]

Adult reviewers of Goodrich's career were less shocked than dismayed by Goodrich's artifices. The *Southern Literary Messenger* attempted to defend Goodrich, rationalizing the Parley ruse by noting that truth could be attained through many channels. "We have said," the reviewer noted, "that Mr. Goodrich had taught the lesson that truth may be made attractive to you; yet it is to be remarked, that he has by no means discarded the use of imagination as an instrument for teaching and training the understanding." Goodrich worked at the edges of truth, the magazine implied, using "the power of imagination" to evoke universal truths. "The character of Parley is a fiction, yet the inculcation of truth is the object and result of the whole. The power of rendering fiction subservient to truth—of using the fancy in such a manner as to make it the servant, and not the master, of the understanding—is Mr. Goodrich's highest qualification."[122]

Despite these defenses, Goodrich remained sensitive throughout his life to the insinuation that he was a mere "children's author" who had made his living by deceiving his young readers.[123] In trying to present the truthfulness of history in an entertaining manner, Goodrich sometimes failed to strike an adequate balance between a fidelity to facts and a commitment to storytelling. This imbalance reflects a fundamental tension in attitudes toward child development in the mid-nineteenth century, especially with respect to how and when children could and should be expected to achieve historical literacy. Those at Hearthstone Publishing and elsewhere who would republish Peter Parley's volumes in the twenty-first century on the grounds that they constitute a truthful record of the human past have failed to recognize not only the liberties Goodrich took with historical facts in order to advance the narrative elements of his histories but also the sense of contrition he felt at the end of his career for the choices he had made in this regard.

Killing Peter Parley and the Return of the Literary Undead

Homeschool republishers warrant that Goodrich's works are more reliable because they are original texts that preserve in unadulterated form a pure record of the past. Much depends here on what one means by the word *original.* At Hearthstone Publishing, *original* implies temporal proximity to the historical events under consideration. In the introductory essay to the Hearthstone reprint of *Parley's History of the World,* for instance, Hutchings notes that prior to 1854 the political landscape described by Goodrich was clearer and more in keeping with national goals than descriptions of the mid-nineteenth century by revisionist historians today. In 1854, Hutchings argues, "only seventy years after the end of the Revolutionary War of Independence, the citizenry understood that this nation was a republic and the Constitution was the unchanging law of the land." Revisionists, however, have "change[d] history to accommodate current social and world political goals," the radio evangelist insists, the present system of public education serving as a form of "political indoctrination" of children. The founders have been especially profound victims of this programming. "Slowly but surely after the turn of the twentieth century the social and political change agents began to exert influence upon the nation's textbooks and public schools," Hutchings writes. "Instead of our founding fathers being brave and stalwart Christians whose faith and fortitude founded a great nation, the revisionists remade them into philandering, self-serving, hypocritical deists." If the "textbooks of 1854, and before, were so bad," he adds, "how did we become such a great nation?"[124]

The debate over whether America was or still is a "great nation" is beyond the scope of this book. But Hutchings's curious, unhistorical statement about political life in 1854 must be addressed, as it ignores the fact that in less than a decade after the publication of the 1854 edition of *Parley's History of the World* the United States was shattered by a bloody fratricidal war in which the meaning of the Constitution was contested with tragic consequences and the Republic was nearly lost. Goodrich can be forgiven perhaps for failing to anticipate the emerging Civil War, but history educators teaching children today about the decade of the 1850s cannot ignore its presence, knowing what they know now about the war's results. Hutchings makes further unsubstantiated claims about the purity and consensus of Goodrich's age: "Since 1854, the moral and ethical standards of the American people have changed drastically" and for the worse, Hutchings writes. "In 1854 there were very few divorces; very few abortions, if any; very few illegitimate children; and even if there were exceptions, they were judged to be sinful and immoral by public standard." These misleading historical assertions (see Laurel Ulrich on illegitimate births and abortions in the pre–Civil War era, for instance) are a reminder that Hearthstone's most salient impulse for "resurrecting" Parley is not historical but religious.[125]

Those on the Christian Right, in short, see in Goodrich a missionary in the cause of using history to advance their ecclesiastical work. Hutchings, for instance, recommends Goodrich's volumes as a protection against anti-Christian ideas associated with the evolutionary theories that postdate such works as *Parley's History of the World*. He prompts readers that Goodrich begins his history with a discussion of Adam and Eve and the story of the Creation as told in the one true source of all history, the Bible. While avowing that readers must historicize some of Goodrich's statements with respect to their nineteenth-century contexts if they are to discern their true meanings, Hutchings intimates that Goodrich's books are as unimpeachable in their truth claims about Creation as those of the Old Testament on which they are based. He then attacks the counternarratives emanating from alternative historical sources, especially those grounded in Darwinian thought, to which it is anachronistic to assume Goodrich was reacting. "Contemporary science cannot accept the proposition that God created the world," Hutchings insists. "In fact, contemporary science cannot accept the reality of God, because God cannot be analyzed in a test tube." Here again it is the revisionists that Hearthstone holds responsible for such scientific heresies. Threatened by the sanctity of the biblical creation story, "revisionists must get rid of all these 'mythological' references to God who made the world and things therein," Hutchings pronounces with disdain.[126]

Yet Hutchings's criticism of revisionists seems hypocritical given that the Hearthstone edition of *Parley's History of the World* is itself a revisionist work. While Hearthstone advertises Goodrich's volume as providing a pre-

Darwinian perspective on the world before 1854, for example, it is not actually a reproduction of Goodrich's original work; rather, *Parley's History of the World* is a reissue of an 1881 edition of an 1858 reprint. This bibliographical fact is relevant because, as an editorial note in the Hearthstone reprint makes clear, the 1881 edition of *Parley's History of the World* had been "carefully revised" several times since its original publication by someone other than the primary author, who had died in 1860.[127] Indeed, the correct full title of the 1858 edition of the work Hearthstone reissued is *Parley's Common School History Revised*.[128] In other words, readers of the Hearthstone edition of the history who might think they are receiving the past in unadulterated form from the pre-Darwinian pen of Goodrich are deceived in two ways: first, in imagining that the edition they are reading is the 1854 edition that Goodrich alone prepared, when, in fact, it is a revised version; and, second, in assuming that the original work was written by Goodrich himself, when in fact it was adapted from multiple sources and updated as late as 1881. Understanding the production history of a work such as *Parley's History of the World,* in short, is crucial in terms of establishing the context of history and its acceptable uses.

Embarrassments over the lack of authenticity and stability in Goodrich's writings partially account for some of the negative outlook he expressed in his memoirs when he spoke of the humiliation of his career and his expectation, even hope, that his collective works would disappear or be forgotten forever. Sadly, however, even this sobering wish for obscurity went unfulfilled because of the large number of copycat editions of his works that appeared on bookstore shelves. There was no international copyright agreement in the mid-nineteenth century and therefore no protection for authors from literary pirates who crossed the oceans stealing intellectual property with impunity. Typically a novel published in London was republished in the United States within months of its release, with no royalties going to the author or to the original publisher. Less frequently, British publishers reproduced without compensation the works of rising American writers, such as Washington Irving and James Fenimore Cooper. To avoid such thievery, in fact, many American authors published their books first in London and only secondarily in the United States. But even this tactic did not protect them from more subtle misappropriations of their writings. England passed a Copyright Act in 1842 that safeguarded the work of living British writers for forty-two years, but for only seven years after they died.[129] This inadequate law prompted Augustine Birrell to say of the British book market, "You may buy twenty books of dead men at the price of one work by a living man." Evidently Birrell's dead men "neither asked for fees nor quibbled about sales."[130]

British republishers not only pirated Goodrich's texts but also altered and even rewrote them in ways to suit British audiences. Thomas Tegg paid Goodrich four hundred pounds for the privilege of republishing a single Parley volume, an unusually fair-minded act of compensation, but he then proceeded, without the author's permission or further recompense, to appropriate the Parley name for use in dozens of additional reprintings of Goodrich's works. Less scrupulous was John Darton, a British publisher who issued volumes containing tales written by a group of hired ghost writers trained to mimic Goodrich's narrative style. One day in 1854, while traveling in London, Goodrich entered Darton's office and noticed that a copy of *Peter Parley's Annual* was on display, a volume he had not written or approved. He complained directly to the publisher: "Many of these counterfeit Parley books are to me nauseous in style, matter, and purpose. . . . According to my taste, they are full of vulgarisms, degrading phrases, and coarse ideas. In some cases they advocate principles which are not mine, and manners and customs I disapprove." He added with disdain, "This very volume of yours, for 1854, in spite of its gold edges, colored engravings, and embossed binding, is mainly written in a low, bald, and vulgar style; and withal is ridiculous from its affected Parley-isms. Rich outside, it is within smitten with poverty." Declaring the Parley surrogates filled "with passages incompatible with good manners and good morals," Goodrich asked the publisher to cease and desist from counterfeiting his works and to compensate him for his losses.[131]

Goodrich seems to have had a case in that many of the Darton editions altered the original texts in inappropriate ways. Careful readers of Parley volumes can spot a Tegg or Darton version by the exclusion of the antimonarchical statements that appeared profusely in the original texts. Goodrich had written in *Tales of Peter Parley About America,* for instance, that monarchs were not to be trusted. "You will not read much about kings, before you will learn that they care little whether what they do is right or wrong," he wrote. "They are generally governed by selfishness, and do what they please, without regard to justice or humanity," and, by means of "oppression and subjugation of the weak and defenceless, kings have been accustomed to increase their wealth and power, and call it glory."[132] In Darton's version of *Peter Parley's Tales of America* these lines were deleted. Furthermore, in his 1828 version, published in Boston, Goodrich filled many pages on the American Revolution with detailed descriptions of battle scenes, and he placed blame for the conflict on British shoulders, especially those of the aggressive king who sent troops to harass his own colonial subjects. In describing how the British, unprovoked, fired on colonial militias gathered at Lexington, Goodrich conveyed his anti-Anglo sentiments to young readers in a highly personalized (perhaps inappropriate) appeal: "Would it not make you angry, if soldiers should come from England, and shoot your dear father or your brother?" he implored. "Certainly it would; and so the Americans were excited to resistance by this act of the English soldiers, and they determined to resent and revenge it."[133] Yet the American Revolution was dismissed in just a few sentences in Darton's edition, and the provocation by King George III went unnoted. "I need not enter on the events of the war," Darton's Parley asserts. "It ended in the triumph of the American settlers, and in the declaration of American independence and the formation of the United States."[134]

More insidious still was the tendency of British editors of Parley to recast Goodrich's narrator in the guise of a fawning Anglophile. As Roselle writes, "Indeed, the Yankee characteristics of old Peter Parley were so distorted that he began to appear as a genial British 'tar,' with a wooden leg and a patriotic devotion to England." The English *Peter Parley's Annual* included the following pro-British sentiments, anathema to Goodrich: "Peter Parley loves our good Queen, and delights to follow her in her various progress," and "He loves the sea-breeze and he would sing with his poor old voice, like a shattered clarionet, 'Rule Britannia,' and thank God that he lived to see the day when England exhibits to the world that she is still able to 'rule the waves.'" Goodrich was angered also to discover that Charles Till of Fleet Street in London "wrote and published in 1838 *Peter Parley's Visit to London during the Coronation of Queen Victoria,* a work lavishly praising the royal family." Goodrich had not attended the coronation—he was in Connecticut at the time—but even if he had been in England he likely would have skipped the event as he was a well-known scoffer at the "maudlin pageantry of English nobility." As the popular historian later noted derisively, "I have great respect for the Queen of England . . . but it [is] not pleasant to find these things in a book, issued in the name of Peter Parley."[135]

Darton's defense of these misappropriations was the largely untenable one that in making changes to Goodrich's original texts he was hoping to further secure Parley's reputation among young readers. Goodrich admitted that Darton had helped circulate the Parley name, but he stressed that the British publisher had besmirched it in the process. "My reputation has been attacked, my literary rank degraded, by being made responsible for works I never wrote," he protested. Goodrich noted later in his memoirs, *"The Westminster Review,* some years ago, criticised the Parley Books, as sullied by coarse phrases and vulgar Americanisms. Extracts were made to verify this criticism, and yet every extract was from a false book, or a false passage foisted into a true one. Not one line of the damnatory examples did I ever write. Precisely this process of degradation must have been going on against me, for the last dozen years, in the public mind of England, through the influence of your counterfeits."[136] Goodrich discovered after much complaining that he had little recourse in these matters, although he did try, unsuccessfully, to sue Darton to recover royalties from pirated books.

Goodrich took a slightly different tack with the London publisher George Mogridge, "a sanctimonious fraud" who, according to Goodrich's daughter, Emily, "was writing unwholesome books for children under [Parley's] name, making thousands of illegal dollars thereby to the detriment of father's purse."[137] In the 1840s and 1850s Mogridge issued a series of Parley histories, none of which had been written by Goodrich and for which he received no compensation. Goodrich's strategy in this case was to go on the offensive. As a preemptive strike against the exportation of such fake works to the United States, Goodrich bought up as many Mogridge copies of Parley's works as he could find in London, rewrote them to his satisfaction, and then reissued them in the United States under the Parley label. Unlike Mogridge, Goodrich made full disclosure of the authorship of these American versions. "Among the several books lately published in London and falsely attributed to me, is one giving an account of the manner in which the Christmas holidays are celebrated in England, with sketches of ancient Christmas customs," Goodrich wrote in the introduction to *Peter Parley's Christmas Tales for 1839*: "The work is cleverly done—much better, no doubt, than I could have done it,—but there are many thing[s] in it not fit for young readers, and of very little profit to old ones. Thinking it likely that the book would be republished here, I have thought it well to revise it and give it to the public, with the proper story of its origins."[138]

The appearance of such books being issued as revisions of revised originals that had themselves been pirated internationally indicates how volatile and unprotected nineteenth-century works were in the expanding children's book market and how difficult it is in this or any other age to reissue them with any confidence that they approximate the intentions of their presumed authors. So confused was the landscape of Parley literature, in fact, that Goodrich felt compelled to add an appendix in his autobiography detailing "Spurious Peter Parleys." This was accompanied by what Pat Pflieger calls a "rant about those who had published books using Parley's name."[139] Goodrich condemned book manufacturers like Darton and Tegg, who displayed an "utter disregard of truth, honor, and decency, on the part of respectable British authors and publishers, in this wholesome system of imposition and injustice." Can it be that a man might be sent to Newgate Prison for passing a counterfeit five-pound note, Goodrich asked, "while another may issue thousands of counterfeit volumes, and not destroy his reputation?" The conduct of all these "parties places them, morally, on a footing with other counterfeiters and forgers," he grumbled.[140] Aggrieved by these matters and the amount of energy he had to devote to them, Goodrich concluded that disreputable British publishers "cut Peter to the heart" and "served greatly to shorten his life."[141]

The comment about a shortened life was in reference to the momentous decision Goodrich made in 1840 to kill off his embattled narrator. In *Peter Parley's Farewell* as well as in a subsequent magazine article in *Robert Merry's Museum*, Goodrich announced that Parley was "no more," having been laid to rest by his creator as an unfortunate casualty of those who were "palming off trumpery works of their own as Peter Parley's."[142] But Parley's death didn't take. Within months of the announcement of his demise, Parley resurfaced in various unauthorized book and magazine publications in the United States and England, publications whose plagiarizing authors were unaware of or unconcerned with the fact that Goodrich had terminated his narrator. Darton continued throughout the 1840s to issue Parley annuals as well as unsavory counterfeit works such as *Parley's Peeps at Paris,* while Tegg introduced a new line of sensationalized adventure books commencing only months after Parley's supposed death, including *Peter Parley's Shipwrecks.* There was no clearer confirmation that Goodrich had lost control of his own narrative voice than this unauthorized resurrection of Parley. Rising from the dead, Lazarus-like, Parley took on a posthumous life of his own, and even his original creator was powerless against the "gross and shameful imposition" of the narrator's disinterment. Just as he attempted to do by burning his personal papers one despondent day toward the end of his life, Goodrich hoped to eviscerate the past with the erasure of Parley, but "alas, how fallacious my calculation!" he moaned. No matter how "we may seek to cover our lives with forgetfulness," he added, "their records still exist, and those may come up against us when we have no vouchers to meet the charges which are presented."[143]

It is suggestive as well that Goodrich's memoirs, *Recollections of a Lifetime,* were reissued after his death in a truncated form for children with the revealing title *Peter Parley's Own Story.*[144] Even in death the Goodrich and Parley personae could not be disentangled. That death came in May 1860 in New York City, and Goodrich was mourned by thousands.[145] His funeral was an elaborate affair of state, and his pallbearers included the publishers Appleton, Derby, and Goupil. Many tributes to the man known around the world as "the Children's Teacher and Friend" were issued, including some that evaluated his contributions as a writer.[146] The eulogizers were generally more optimistic and insightful about Goodrich's longevity than the author himself was. Although little known today, Goodrich's works remained popular throughout the remainder of the nineteenth century. "As late as 1902 *The United States Catalogue of Books in Print* showed twenty-eight Peter Parleys in print, and in 1912 there were still five coming off the press," Roselle has written. "The total sale of Peter Parley was probably near twelve million."[147] Goodrich's daughter captured her father's staying power best when, in 1898, she remarked on a Parley revival that was in evidence nearly forty years after her father's death. "Every generation or two there is a return wave, which bears upon its crest the name of some prominent character in the past, *quiescent,* though not forgotten," she wrote. "Writers and publishers are quite aware of the fact, and are keenly on the watch for the first sign of a returning wave. Within the last three or four years, the name of the children's friend, Peter Parley, has been made in educational articles in the newspapers, and the magazines have brought him back to mind again."[148] It was a revival, she might have added, that her father would have found unjustified and that surely would have embarrassed him.

These trends reveal the extent to which popular historical literature for children was still in its infancy during Goodrich's life. The success Goodrich enjoyed in the popular book market indicated that an interest in juvenile histories existed in American homes and schools, but the abovementioned "vexations" hinted that there was no general agreement about whether history could be both meaningful *and* entertaining to children. Some, like Goodrich, wished for children's historical literature to retain a strong moral focus, evidencing its didactic potential and modeling in its heroes the desired behaviors of young people. Others demanded that such literature expose children to the harsher realities of human existence and prepare them for less sentimental approaches to life. The debates over Goodrich's legacy impacted perceptibly the kind of juvenile literature that emerged in the history field in the late nineteenth century and the popular histories that are being recycled today by presses like Hearthstone. In the years after Goodrich's death, the genre of juvenile historical literature expanded dramatically, moving in various, more diversified directions and with an unharnessed energy that pointed to both the richness and confusion of the industry.

The pattern of Goodrich's career as an author of juvenile texts shows that evidentiary standards for popular history books had not established themselves fully at midcentury. Certainly such works did not and should not be expected to meet the scholarly norms of later eras; they barely met the less rigorous ones of earlier years. Their faults and limitations were conceded by Goodrich himself once his identity as a children's historian had been revealed. He had no special training in history and had relied extensively on the researches and writings of others. He violated consistently his own prescriptions for appropriate children's books by trying to reduce adult literature for use by youth. His histories were reissued in multiple editions and by numerous presses in versions that reflected inconsistent alterations and problems of transmission. Different authors moved in and out of the editors' chairs for these works, and different audiences with distinct needs patronized them (parents, schools, recreational readers). In some cases, adult texts were abridged for children, while in others books written first for children were expanded to meet the needs of adults, creating an accordion-like inconsistency in such works. And there were many pirated and counterfeited copies of Goodrich's works, editions bowdlerized by London publishers who wished to transform Peter Parley into a Brit. These texts were at times reclaimed by their author and rewritten in an effort to recapture some of the intellectual ideas they contained. In short, Goodrich's volumes are so jumbled in their production histories as to evoke little or no confidence in their reliability as historical sources. Even the author, who felt he had no control over these runaway texts, failed in his attempts to commit intellectual infanticide by symbolically killing off his literary offspring.

Unfortunately, the details of these complex production histories are often lost on twenty-first-century homeschooling purchasers of such volumes. Their comments betray a troubling lack of awareness of these complicated origins. A recent blogger for "Yes Lord Ministries," for instance, offered *Parley's History of the World* to readers as a truthful alternative to revisionist histories that deliberately distort the past. In a blog titled "Daily Interesting Things," a correspondent noted that recent histories of the United States remove from the Mayflower Compact key words testifying to the godliness of the enterprise, specifically, the phrases *"In the name of God, Amen"* and *"for the Glory of God and advancement of the Christian Faith and Honour of our King and Country."* This legitimate complaint is then followed by the pronouncement that while "not many words were left" of the Mayflower Compact, "they were very significant words" since "students who read this abbreviated, edited, revised version of history will have no clue or understanding why the USA was founded and the underlying principles." So, "what to do" with such obvious revisionism? "Well, for one thing, read history books that have not revised history," the blogger writes, adding, "If you are wanting to know about the history of the world, without any revisionist bias, then, do I have the book for you. It is *Parley's History of the World* and is now my all time favorite history book." The presumption is that Goodrich would never modify his history recklessly the way revisionists do; why would he, after all, as it represents "what reallllly happened in the past instead of the 'revisionist' stuff that is being foisted upon us today"? The blogger fails to note, however, that Goodrich's volume was constantly under revision, both authorized and unauthorized, from the moment of its inception and throughout its nearly 140-year reproduction history.[149]

What is the purpose of obscuring the revisionism at the heart of Goodrich's work as a popular children's historian? To some, the ends justify the means. Since *revisionism* is an evil word to those who believe in history as singular truth, it must not be associated with any title in the homeschooling curriculum. As recent debates over the National Standards suggest, those on the Christian Right fear the prospect of a contested past—a history of conflicting interpretations rather than those characterized by single explanatory devices—which they see as the "utmost corruption" introduced by revisionists. They embrace a brand of "historical fundamentalism" that Jill Lepore describes as a "belief that a particular and quite narrowly defined past . . . is ageless and sacred and to be worshipped; that certain historical texts . . . are to be read in the same spirit with which religious fundamentalists read, for instance, the Ten Commandments"; and "that the academic study of history (whose standards of evidence and methods of analysis are based on skepticism) is a conspiracy and, furthermore, blasphemy."[150] Insinuating that historical literature since Goodrich's day has served to erode the confidence of children by complicating the master narrative with multiple non-Christian perspectives, Hutchings warns that American historiography might come to emulate the unproductive cacophony of Middle Eastern history, spurred on by Jewish and Palestinian historians who fail to agree on even the most simple facts of the history of the region they share. Evoking Santayana (again, without fully understanding the philosopher's meaning), Hutchings asks, "Are we going to make the same mistakes again or will we do it right this time?"[151]

The philosophical question concerns what *right* means in the context of historical interpretation and reinterpretation. For some, especially those who will admit of only one sacred version of the past, right is synonymous with Truth. Multiple interpretations of history and diverse perspectives on the pedagogy of childhood literacy are liberal conceits, they claim, that diminish the "One Truth." Parley's histories recommend themselves, Hutchings believes, because they were "written before the revisionists re-wrote history to suit their own social, political and religionist viewpoints." Hutchings's personal social, political, and religious viewpoints, however, do not seem to invite much corresponding scrutiny. "Sure, we might question the historicity of some of the traditional accounts in this book just as we would question some of the politically and anti-Christian revisions in modern textbooks," he concludes of *Parley's History of the World*. "But on a whole, I have found it to be far superior, and infinitely more interesting and reliable, more honest and accurate in presentation, than any in our public schools today."[152]

That is an assertion that even Samuel Goodrich, the creator of the well-meaning but fictionalizing and falsifying narrator Peter Parley, would have condemned as "wholly imaginary" and completely inappropriate in regard to the historical education of impressionable young children.

CHAPTER TWO

Pedagogical History

The Abbott Brothers and Progressive
Approaches to the Past

That which has been is that which will be, and that which has been done is that which will be done. So, there is nothing new under the sun.

Ecclesiastes 1:9

Heritage and History

Despite his justifiable concerns about the lasting value of his works, Samuel Goodrich reckoned correctly that the market for juvenile books in the last half of the nineteenth century was robust. There was no question that a new mass industry of books for children had established itself. "Let any one who wishes to comprehend the matter," Goodrich wrote in 1856, "go to such a juvenile bookstore as that of C. S. Francis, in Broadway, New York, and behold the teeming shelves—comprising almost every topic within the range of human knowledge, treated in a manner to please the young mind, by the use of every attraction of style and every art of embellishment—and let him remember that nineteen[-]twentieths of these works have come into existence within the last thirty years. . . . He will then see how differently this age estimates the importance of juvenile instruction, from any other that has gone before it."[1] As the popular historian understood, these books had a special capacity to command the attention of children, and their packaging, pictorial embellishments, and strong narrative elements were captivating enough to allow Goodrich and others to sustain lengthy careers.

Goodrich did not anticipate, however, that such works would have a life that lasted into the twenty-first century. Yet they have, largely through the preservationist and reclamation efforts of presses that cater to homeschooling educators. A case in point is Nothing New Press, a publishing firm in

Sarasota, Florida, established in the late 1990s when a group of homeschooling mothers began reprinting and trading nineteenth-century popular histories in the homeschool market. According to its website, Nothing New Press has a Christian, traditional orientation and emphasizes the "ancient paths" of education, "beginning with the first historical act of import, God's creation of the universe out of nothing."[2] It endorses a curricular initiative known as History Through Literature that attempts to restore time-honored, Christian pedagogies through a guide series called All Through the Ages. Spearheaded by Christine Miller, a homeschooling mother, the series seeks to revive "the wonderful curriculum that was commonly used in schools in centuries past, when academic standards were more rigorous and the acquiring of a Biblical worldview was considered just as important as the acquiring of reading, writing, and arithmetic skills." In the promotional literature for All Through the Ages, Miller urges homeschooling parents to pursue Christian education as a way of reversing the insidious effects of "modern educational methods" that "continue to produce high school graduates who are not only functionally illiterate and lacking in critical thinking skills, but morally bankrupt as well."[3]

The Nothing New Press website notes that because the women who direct its enterprises are "wives and mothers, homemakers and homeschool teachers" and because these roles are the first priority in their lives, "the new curricula are completed without regard to deadlines" and are not marketed at homeschool curriculum fairs.[4] Many retailers do supply materials from Nothing New Press, however, including Heritage History, a web-based e-book distribution center in Newman Lake, Washington, run by two proprietors who identify themselves only as Adam and Alice. "Imagine the lead comic strip character, 'Adam', from Adam@home, married to the 'Alice' character from Dilbert, and head of a homeschooling family with five children," the website advises, and you will have an adequate depiction of the pair. Under the banner "Old-fashioned history straight from your great-grandparents' bookshelf," Heritage History has solicited volunteers to scan hundreds of nineteenth-century history books for the enjoyment and edification of young people and the general public. The firm reproduces between fifty and sixty history books a year in seeking to attract young readers to a study of the past by reviving works that showcase "the lost art of telling historical tales."[5]

Like the proprietors of Nothing New Press, Adam and Alice subscribe to Miller's strategy of encouraging young readers of history to study texts that highlight universal characteristics of the human condition. "The Heritage Classical Curriculum is a study program based on classical juvenile history books," the website notes, and "it was founded on the belief that well-written, age-appropriate history books could be of such natural interest that with sufficient guidance, many students can actually 'teach themselves' history." The real facilitators of the curriculum, they add, are the "wonderful authors and learned scholars who produced the outstanding collection of histories that we drew upon to create the Heritage History libraries." These writers are "the 'permanent faculty,' so to speak" of a pedagogical initiative "whose works are simple and cost-effective." Like the publishers of Goodrich's volumes at Hearthstone Publishing, this couple emphasizes the grounded narrativity of the works it reproduces. "To keep a student's interest in history flourishing you need only refrain from smothering it," Adam and Alice note. "History is a natural outlet for a student's interest in the world around him, and as long as his natural curiosity is not overwhelmed by the hype, chaos, commercialism, and exploitation of modern culture, he is likely to enjoy the subject," they remark. "Assuming a young person is protected enough from the distractions of the modern world so that he can focus his energies on reading," the couple adds, "well-written history books, such as those found on Heritage History, are usually not a hard sell."[6]

It is easy to see why such a self-taught approach would be attractive to homeschooling parents. The idea of children teaching themselves has a certain practical appeal, to be sure, but Adam and Alice of Heritage History note that the e-books they reproduce are valuable not simply as learning tools for self-motivated students but also as meaningful alternatives to inadequate public school texts. Something has gone horribly wrong with the twenty-first-century textbooks written by professionals and used in public schools, they argue, noting that such volumes are bland and uninviting because they are purged of material deemed offensive by progressive educators oversensitive to identity politics. Echoing the complaints of Lynne Cheney about the political correctness of the National Standards, the couple asks, "How can modern books possibly avoid being vapid when they are bound by a thousand constraints imposed by an army of well-meaning meddlers? They must be comprehensible to every dullard, and unoffending to every thin-skinned partisan. How can human interest possibly flourish in such shackles?" The Heritage History website contrasts these substandard modern textbooks with traditional nineteenth-century volumes of history produced by teachers and writers described as "actual *authors*" with passionate opinions "who were generally trying to entertain and inform, rather than to steer clear of political pitfalls, or avoid upsetting the hyper-sensitive."[7] Producers of modern textbooks are not actual authors, the couple implies, but mere automatons doing the bidding of those special interests that facilitate publications but require subservience to their stultifying restrictions as compensation.

The promoters at Heritage History and Nothing New Press have three basic objections to the textbooks being used currently in public schools, all of which relate to the lingering influence of the turn-of-the-twentieth-century movement they identify as the most insidious force impacting historical literacy among children today: social studies. First, they reject the pragmatism of social studies, with its "new-found pressure to focus on usefulness and tangible results" while transforming "the field of history within the Universities from the centerpiece of the humanities to a laboratory of the social sciences." Disgusted by progressive educators such as John Dewey, who asserted that "history might become a useful vehicle of scientific inquiry," Adam and Alice reject the idea that history should be used "to serve the noble purpose of 'improving society'" rather than merely amusing its readers in the tradition of the humanities. Progressive pedagogy was "the ruination of traditional history," the Heritage History website claims, as "social science theories and related hokum" destroyed the traditional values associated with a classical curriculum. Twentieth-century educators chose to teach from works of history "most conducive to promoting current social theories, and combined them with selected geographical facts, civics lessons, economic theories, a bit of psychology, and a considerable amount of moral exhortation," Adam and Alice write, "[foisting] this mishmash on young people in lieu of actual history." The result has been disastrous for history education. By the 1960s and 1970s, they calculate, "college-educated, social-science enamored, intelligentsia began to expand far beyond its traditional bounds," and "juvenile history was entirely subsumed into the newly created discipline of *social studies*."[8] Rejecting these trends, the couple asserts that "historical knowledge has very few *practical* applications." They prefer to have students study history not for what it teaches, in short, but *"because it is Fascinating!"*[9]

Second, Adam and Alice reject the large, synthetic or comprehensive treatments of the past implicit in the structural modeling of the social studies movement. According to the website, the "great benefit of the Heritage Classical Curriculum" is that its books "do not attempt to explain the 'underlying forces,' that influence history, or critique ancient notions of human rights, or focus on contrasts between cultures" the way texts by progressive educators do. By their own admission, Adam and Alice choose books that never "put the cart before the horse, by putting their conclusions front and center, and using stories only to buttress the grand analysis"; instead, their goal is always to keep history "from becoming a chore by deemphasizing its fact-collecting elements and its bells and whistles and to focus on compelling narrative." For those at Heritage History, therefore, metahistorical considerations should always be subordinate to story. "We believe that young people should be allowed to absorb history without being required to analyze it," Adam and

Alice note. "Pointing out ironies, competing values, and historical disputes is a fine thing, but asking students to write position papers on complicated issues with a sophomoric background is usually a waste of time and paper."[10]

Third, Adam, Alice, Miller, and other homeschoolers question the place of the "contemporary" in social studies practices with regard to the past, especially the obsession of public school history teachers with current events. According to the Heritage History website, "It is an open question whether the study of contemporary politics and current events is even appropriate for young people who are not yet grounded with a solid understanding of history," since "contemporary history is not actually history at all" because "there is no way to objectively present the relative importance of events that are still working themselves out." Such pedagogies encourage an unhealthy presentism in historical works based on the "self-absorbed belief that everything relevant to a student must be something that he or she is immediately and materially effected [*sic*] by," Adam and Alice note. They shift inappropriately "a student's focus from the timeless panorama of history to the petty political squabbles of the hour." The unfortunate consequence of this transition is that "one of the great benefits of the study of history—the ability of a student to be engaged and interested in persons and events outside of himself—is again completely undermined." Rather than being "challenged to seek wisdom outside themselves, in the experience of others," the couple adds, "students are flattered that their personal feelings about current events, no matter how ignorant, are relevant and worthy of consideration." The curriculum promoters at Heritage History and Nothing New Press believe that reading the works of traditional historians "completely obviates the problem" because these older texts were written by authors who "all died a hundred years ago, and never have a thing to say about current events, unless perchance, a lesson from yester-year still echoes its relevance through the ages."[11]

All three of these objections to social studies methodologies—their pragmatism, their preference for analytic over narrative forms of literary expression, and their contemporary, ideological perspectives—are components of a distinctly antimodernist philosophy of education characteristic of many republishers on the Christian Right. The proprietors at Heritage History and Nothing New Press believe that children of the rising generation, trained mindlessly by social studies strategists with progressive agendas, view the past in inappropriate, even dangerous, ways. "Be suspicious of anything written after 1970," Adam and Alice warn their prospective customers, whom they pity for having been so "bombarded" throughout their lives "with the music, values, advertisements, fads, neuroses, politics, and universal media over-saturation" that they are incapable of imagining a time when things were simple and traditional. "It's not just that these children have never lived through such times," the couple states; it's that these "narcissistic" representatives of an "ever-present and nauseatingly self-important generation" lack the capacity to think historically about eras prior to the contemporary moment. Advertising the works of Heritage History as "an enjoyable and fascinating *escape* from the overwhelming and often tiresome modern world," the couple exhorts parents and their young readers to "try it, and you may find, as we do, that the study of the timeless stories of the past can serve as a much needed antidote to the bombast, commercialism, and relentless hype of the present."[12]

The most promising alternative to the repugnant utilitarianism of the progressive social studies movement, homeschoolers argue, is the narrative, storytelling qualities of pre-twentieth-century historical texts for children. Nothing New Press and Heritage History promote books that are "based simply on stories that have been retold for dozens of generations regarding individual characters, important conflicts, and events of special interest" without the falderal of meta-analysis. Consider, for instance, that Heritage History reproduces the histories of two brothers from Maine, Jacob and John S. C. Abbott, who wrote over three hundred volumes of popular literature between the early 1830s and the late 1870s. Their most widely read works for children were thirty-two short biographical volumes (Jacob authored twenty-two and John ten) in the series Makers of History, published by Harper and Brothers from the late 1840s through the early 1870s. Produced in burgundy bindings for school-aged readers, these "little red histories" introduced children to such historical figures as Alexander the Great, Cleopatra, Genghis Khan, and Elizabeth I. They were priced reasonably at $1.20 per volume, and the entire set sold for $38.40, placing it within the reach of many families. For those without sufficient resources to purchase all thirty-two volumes, Makers of History was repackaged into smaller topical subgroups, including the English Series, works on Queen Elizabeth, Charles I, Charles II, etc.; the Ancient Series: Cyrus the Great, Cleopatra, Alexander the Great; and the General Series: Josephine, Genghis Khan, King Philip.[13]

According to a nineteenth-century review by R. H. Fleming in the *New York Tribune*, these Abbott subseries were "very popular with the young," and "had an extensive circulation" in their day.[14] She averred that the "mere mention of Mr. Abbott's name" recalled "the sunny days of childhood, when in some sunny corner or under a wide spreading tree" she and her playmates "mingled study and pleasure gathering in the facts of his historical biographies."[15] The volumes also had a profound impact on the novelist and historian Edward

Eggleston, who considered himself fortunate to have been exposed as a child to the "red-backed histories of the Abbotts."[16] Their influence was felt even among those who impacted public policy. "I want to thank you and your brother for Abbott's series of Histories," Abraham Lincoln reportedly wrote to Jacob and John S. C. while he was president. "I have not education enough to appreciate the profound works of voluminous historians, and if I had, I have no time to read them," he noted, but "your series of Histories gave me, in brief compass, just that knowledge of past men and events which I need. I have read them with the greatest interest. To them I am indebted for about all the historical knowledge I have."[17] If the Abbott biographies were good enough for Lincoln, homeschooling advocates suggest, then they should be suitable for children in this day as well.

The major republishers of the series Makers of History have been less preoccupied with the potential influence of such works on public policy, however, than with their prospects for improving the unpretentious minds of children with their "simple narrative threads" that are "completely shorn of complicated analysis."[18] The Abbott brothers' works are promoted by Nothing New Press as being "full of excitement, adventure, and heart-wrenching drama," "living books" that "bring the 'story' back into 'history'" by making "historical figures come alive, giving them depth and character and thoughts and feelings and struggles and joys in ways that textbooks cannot possibly do." Such books reaffirm what Miller contends histories for children should be, that is, texts that highlight "historical figures as real people we can relate to, facing many of the same kinds of situations we have to face." Consequently, the works Miller endorses are advertised by Nothing New Press as "made up principally of stories about persons; for, while history proper is largely beyond the comprehension of children, they are able at an early age to understand and enjoy anecdotes of people, especially those in the childhood of civilization." Biographical texts such as those of the Abbott brothers "also aim," according to Miller, "to enforce the lessons of perserverance [*sic*], courage, patriotism, and virtue that are taught by the noble lives described."[19]

Equal sentiments are echoed by two other homeschool presses: Dodo Press, a British firm that has republished dozens of the Abbott brothers' texts, and Canon Press, the publishing arm of Christ Church in Moscow, Idaho. The little red volumes are worthy of republication, according to both of these Christian republishers, in part because they were produced in the nineteenth century, making them preferable to anything written in the twentieth century or the twenty-first. The assumption is that any text written before 1900 escaped the corruptions of the progressive educational strategies, especially the ill-advised attempts of Dewey and others "to lead impressionable

minds through some prescribed exercises in 'critical thinking.'" Part of such
antimodernism is predicated on the idea that nineteenth-century historians
shared a pervasive consensus about the meaning of American life and the
priorities of the nation-state. That consensus, the proprietors at Heritage History believe, is now gone. "The modern mindset loves innovation and novelty," Adam and Alice write, and readers "often think of the modern world
as progressing in a positive fashion and always value the latest research and
newest ideas. . . . But when relating ancient stories that have been passed on
for dozens of generations, innovation is not a plus." Regretting the tendency
of twenty-first-century historians "to tell old stories from an oppositional,
modern perspective" that distorts their messages, the couple attests that "one
of the greatest benefits of studying [traditional] history is to learn the stories
just as they have been told for generations," helping students "to distinguish
between permanent values, and those that are mere fashion. Re-interpreting
all of history according to modern ideas destroys the very breadth of perspective that the study of history is capable of giving."[20]

In considering the value of the republication of works by authors like the
Abbott brothers and by such presses and distributors as Nothing New Press,
Heritage History, Dodo Press, and Canon Press, then, one must once ask
whether it makes sense to center a twentieth-first-century history curriculum
on texts written in the nineteenth century. Decision makers at these presses
believe the discipline of history in the twenty-first century is too dominated
by politically correct, social studies practitioners and methodologies, too dis-
figured by recklessly overgeneralized metanarratives, and too compromised
by disturbing ideologies and presentist elements. They favor the reintroduc-
tion of traditional narrative approaches to the past grounded in biography
and written in pre-ideological contexts. But were the Abbott brothers' little
red volumes really traditional works? and, if so, is it sound educationally to
build a curriculum in history around them today? To make this judgment, I
want to discuss first the historical context in which these nineteenth-century
works emerged and isolate the motivations of their authors. Do these republished works have a legitimate and vital role to play in educating children
today? or are they truly nothing new, obsolete works that should be allowed
to go the way of the dodo?

The Abbotts as Progressive Educators

Consider the first contention of the republication presses: the Abbott brothers' little red histories offer an essential safeguard against the corruptions of
social studies approaches to the past. This assumption is predicated on a very

limited and skeptical assessment of the influence school educators such as the Abbotts had in the mid-nineteenth-century development of progressive educational strategies.

At the end of the eighteenth century, when public schools still played only a small part in the educations of most young people and when children were conceived of as vulnerable little adults who needed to be educated quickly lest they succumb to life's depredations, teachers had fewer opportunities to affect the historical learning of their students. As conceptions of childhood changed among the general populace, however, vulnerable children were granted more time to absorb these lessons and given more space to work out their implications. By the mid-nineteenth century, middle-class parents felt special pressures to provide what Steven Mintz has called a "sheltered childhood," a state in which children were viewed "as symbols of purity, spontaneity, and emotional expressiveness, who were free from adult inhibitions and thus required parents who would ensure that their innocence was not corrupted." Guardians sought to prolong the pre-adult worlds of their offspring by seeking the assistance of public institutions in educating and protecting them. In the process, teachers took on a greater role in nurturing historical perspectives among their students. According to Mintz, the "shifting power relationships between parents and children, especially parents' increasing psychological investment in their children," altered fundamentally the way schools went about educating the young. "The new stress on children's fragility, malleability, and corruptibility resulted in the establishment and construction of an array of institutions for children, from Sunday schools and public schools to orphanages, houses of refuge, reform schools, and children's hospitals," Mintz writes. The rise of mandatory school attendance laws and child labor restrictions was predicated on the idea that "children were fragile, innocent, and vulnerable creatures who needed adults' paternalistic protection." During this period, "childhood dependency was prolonged, child-drearing became a more intensive and self-conscious activity, and schooling was extended."[21]

An illustration of these changes can be found in the lives and careers of the Abbott brothers, who were among America's first and most prolific pedagogical theorists. The Abbotts were members of an extraordinary Maine family of teachers and writers who belonged to "the strictest class of Christian" educators.[22] The most prominent of the seven children in the family was the second, Jacob, who was born in 1803 and became the collaborator on the series Makers of History with the fourth child, John Stevens Cabot, born two years later (fig. 6). The two brothers were cut from the same cloth. Both went to Hallowell Academy and then to Bowdoin College, and both eventually attended Andover Academy to study theology in preparation for becoming ministers and eventually teachers and authors. Three other brothers, Gorham, Charles, and Samuel, followed in this exact path from Bowdoin to Andover to pastorates and classrooms. All became gifted teachers and ministers and were beloved by their young students and parishioners. Jacob Abbott's granddaughter remembered her grandfather as representative of the collective virtues of all his brothers: "a gentleman somewhat above middle height, with a peculiarly benignant and kindly bearing, an unvarying courtesy in word and ways, a genial smile, a cordial outstretched hand, and a quick apprehension of a child's pleasure, trouble and wants." In common with his siblings, Jacob had a Peter Parley–like ability to capture children's imaginations. School-age boys and girls were "his constant companions," she recalled, and they "were always drawn to him by his simplicity and affection."[23]

Jacob Abbott occupied a pastorate for several years, but, finding that he did not enjoy delivering sermons as much as writing them, he left the pulpit for the classroom, followed shortly thereafter by his brothers John and Gorham.[24] Between the late 1820s and the 1860s they operated a series of private schools dedicated to implementing elements of their moral reform program for children, beginning with the Mount Vernon School in 1829, a first-of-its-kind private high school for girls in Boston.[25] At Mount Vernon the Abbotts adopted some novel approaches to teaching and learning. They embraced wholeheartedly, for instance, the new commitment of American educators to the concept of a prolonged childhood; they had no interest in returning to a puritanical practice of rushing children toward adulthood. They differed from their contemporaries, however, in arguing that many schools dedicated to sustaining and extending the experiences of youth smothered children in the process. They believed that parents could be too protective of their children, and they worried about the prospects of generations growing up coddled and shielded unnaturally from the rigors of life by an approach to education that was too scripted and programmatic to be useful. The idealization of youth had encouraged providers to make too many concessions to children, the brothers argued, and the result was an educational system that was overnurturing and therefore counterproductive to the developing child.[26]

The ruling pedagogical assumption of the Mount Vernon School was that children should be given more responsibility for their own learning and behavior.[27] This strategy was adapted from the pedagogical philosophy of the eighteenth-century Swiss educator Johann Heinrich Pestalozzi, who had advocated that children should be encouraged to learn on their own through direct experience and hands-on activities.[28] In *How Gertrude Teaches Her Children,* Pestalozzi argued that "observation was the basis of all knowledge." The

FIGURE 6. (*top*) Portrait of
Jacob Abbott. Print Collection,
Miriam and Ira D. Wallach Division
of Art, Prints and Photographs,
The New York Public Library, Astor,
Lenox and Tilden Foundations.
(*bottom*) Portrait of John S. C. Abbott.
Photography Collection, Miriam and
Ira D. Wallach Division of Art, Prints
and Photographs, The New York
Public Library, Astor, Lenox and
Tilden Foundations.

first principle of education "was to lead a child to observe with accuracy," he wrote, while the second "was to teach a child to express correctly the results of his observations."[29] As the historian John Manning has remarked, the Pestalozzi experiment involved "put[ting] theory into practice, attempting to proceed from the known to the unknown, from the concrete to the abstract, from perception to expression," through the presentation in the classroom of concrete objects such as pieces of coal or chalk. Teachers were expected to elicit from the class the name, spelling, uses, and qualities possessed by the objects in question. Hence the name 'object lesson' came into current and common usage, and potential teachers were trained in its application."[30]

As the headmaster at Mount Vernon, Jacob Abbott implemented these fresh pedagogies by advising parents that "the students are as much as possible to be led to instruct and govern themselves."[31] Employing techniques that today would be labeled educational constructivism, the Abbotts favored instructors who took the role of facilitators rather than teachers.[32] At Mount Vernon, therefore, students policed their own classrooms by holding each other accountable for their actions. "He threw responsibility upon them, great responsibility," Lyman Abbott remembered of his father, Jacob, "and they realized it."[33] Self-progress charts were used to record work accomplished, and the standards were often quite high. When questions were raised by parents about the feasibility and desirability of this self-policing system, Abbott "objected to the idea of making things too easy and simple for the child." He wrote that "while it is important that the child be happy, it is more important to lay a firm and permanent foundation."[34] He admitted, in fact, that often the schoolrooms at Mount Vernon were without a teacher or monitor and apparently "did not suffer from the absence." "I place very great confidence in the scholars in regard to their moral conduct and deportment," Abbott wrote, "and they fully deserve it."[35]

The Abbotts urged that school curricula should become more free and unstructured; that children should be encouraged to make mistakes and to discover for themselves through self-exploration, self-reliance, and independence even if this invited occasional failure or introduced momentary self-doubt. In the promotional literature associated with the school, Jacob Abbott made it a point to clarify that no more than half the designated hour for the study of geography, history, natural and intellectual philosophy at Mount Vernon was given over to recitations; the remainder was for self-guided exploration and object lessons.[36] In keeping with these investigatory ambitions, the Abbotts kept a "Cabinet of Nature for the Year" that featured "curious particulars characteristic of each month"—including minerals, shells, and models—as a way to "direct young people to the innocent and agreeable

employment of observing nature."[37] The goal was to exercise the imagination of students through contact with tangible realities. "I remember well,"
recalled one acquaintance fondly, "how much Mr. Abbott used to strive to
interest children in sensible things for amusements, rather than nonsense
games. He used to collect them about him . . . and by propounding questions,
or suggesting games, insensibly lead them into some new and useful plan of
amusement or instructive conversation, accomplishing his purpose without
in the least arousing their suspicions that he was teaching them. He simply
guided them to think for themselves the things he wished them to think."[38]
The educator and reformer Lydia Child applauded the Abbott method for
what it could teach students about themselves in relation to the items they
studied. "The habit . . . of directing the attention of very little children to
surrounding objects, lays an excellent foundation for obtaining clear and
accurate ideas of what is read," she wrote. "The same habit of observation,
that leads them to remark whether a thing is round or square, likewise leads
them to attend to the sense of what they find in books."[39]

The policy of restricting recitations at Mount Vernon in favor of lessons
centered on direct observation was in reaction to the tendency of public
school teachers to rely too heavily on rote memorization in the learning process. The Abbott brothers were worried that as school attendance became
mandatory across the nation and as the number of hours per day the average
child spent in school increased, the curriculum would become too structured
and regimented. Unable to keep up with demands posed by exploding enroll-
ments, teachers had imposed mindless exercises and harsh disciplinary measures—even physical punishment, which the Abbotts detested—as strategies
for maintaining order in schools. The sight/word memorization techniques
of Goodrich, Gallaudet, and Mann had led to daily recitation periods, in
which, as one commentator explained, "the children are obliged to stand in
the line, perfectly motionless, their bodies erect, their knees and feet together,
the tips of their shoes touching the edge of the board in the floor."[40] Dickens poked fun at this fact-based approach to children's learning through the
character of Thomas Gradgrind in *Hard Times*. "Teach these boys and girls
nothing but facts. Facts alone are wanted in life," Gradgrind insisted. "Nothing else will ever be of any service to them. . . . This is the principle on which I
bring up these children. Stick to facts, Sir!"[41]

Hoping to avoid the Gradgrindian conceits of memorization and recitation, the Abbotts rejected sight/word methodologies in favor of phonetic
approaches to learning based on the orthographic rules of written language
and the alphabetic principles that accompanied them. In the 1830s Jacob
Abbott wrote a series of children's books, the Rollo and Lucy stories, whose

main characters modeled the kind of phonetic learning he wished to encourage in his young readers.[42] In the lesson "How to Read Right," the narrator endeavors to teach children the orthographic rules of reading, including "the comma, and the period, and the interrogation mark, and all the stops." Abbott tells the story of a man who climbs up a mountain for some obscure purpose, interrupting the narrative continually to call the readers' attention to large and small fonts, paragraphing, italics, and capitalization. By the end of the tale it is clear that the real purpose of the story is not to determine why the man is climbing the mountain but to acquaint children with the rules of punctuation. In this way Abbott tried to impress young readers with the "difficulties of language" and alert them to the importance of the "conquest of them." In *Rollo Learning to Read* he elaborated that in his works "the more difficult words and phrases, in common use, are not *avoided,* for the very object of such a reading book should be to teach the use of them. They are freely introduced, and rendered intelligible by being placed in striking connections" and made familiar by "being frequently repeated." By a "wonderful provision in the structure of the mind, children thirst for repetition," Abbott wrote, redundancy being "the very thing essential to give security and permanence to the knowledge they acquire."[43]

This phonetic approach, in which children are taught to read first by learning the letters of the alphabet as the building blocks for comprehending words in their constituent parts, emphasized the construction of language by connecting sounds and letter patterns for the mastery of unknown words through various alphabetic correspondences. Such a method of having children learn their "letters" had been in use in the United States since the circulation of Noah Webster's Blue-Backed Spellers in the early nineteenth century. In fact, it was to Webster's "systematic phonics," with its "numerous tables of words illustrating an easy standard of pronunciation," to which Boston schoolmasters wished to return when they complained to Superintendent Mann in 1844 that the sight/word system was not working. Their criticism was that children using that method were capable of recognizing words but had no appreciation for "grammar, spelling, capitalization and punctuation" and could not master the orthographic rules by which words are strung together in meaningful sentences.[44] Even students who gained a "rudimentary ability to decode written text," the sociologist Allan Luke notes, did "not develop the capacity to get meaning from text, much less to analyse critically and act upon it." They were capable of learning word recognition but not the construction "of meaningful sentences."[45]

Critics contended that the sight/word reading method reduced English "to an ideographic language, using symbols to stand for whole words and

negating the advantages offered by alphabetization." As in most pedagogical matters, the Abbotts encouraged language proficiency in their students
through trial and error rather than rote memorization. They complained that
students trained under Goodrich's system were competent at word recognition but were unable to construct meaningful sentences. "We have decided
to forget that we write with letters and learn to read English as if it were
Chinese," a critic of the Goodrich technique noted.[46] The popular historian
Charles Carleton Coffin corroborated the point, noting his reaction as a small
boy to first hearing the line "The cat doth play, / And after slay" in a rhyme
about an unfortunate mouse. "Having heard of and seen the sleigh before
learning the synonym for 'kill,'" Coffin noted, "[I] was as much bothered as a
Chinese child who first hears one sound which has many meanings, and only
gradually clears up the mystery as the ideographs are mastered."[47] Experts on
both sides of the debate agreed that whole-word memorization "enables children to get off to a fast start" as they rather easily memorize a select number
of words by using abstract visual symbols; but critics noted that any "initial
success is deceptive because it does not provide the foundation for learning
thousands of additional [more complex] words."[48] The phonetic approach is
based on the assumption that unless students are exposed to phonics in addition to their whole word training, "they cannot learn more than about 2,000
words by sight alone." The "word burden," as it is called, is simply too great.[49]

Phonetic approaches to learning revolutionized the study of many subjects
at Mount Vernon, but perhaps none more so than the discipline of history.[50]
Certainly the Abbotts' process-oriented techniques challenged the prevailing
mid-nineteenth-century view that history was a fact-based subject that young
children could not master except by memorizing lists of names and dates.
According to Bruce VanSledright, many educators of the day believed that
children "are first concrete thinkers, who need things spelled out in systematic steps tied to objects they can touch and manipulate." The Abbotts would
have accepted this assertion. They would have disagreed, however, with the
corollary contentions that "young children cannot effectively do much more
with history than commit dates, events, and actors to memory" and that they
would not "acquire the capacity to deal with abstract concepts such as revolution, capitalism, democracy, and the like" until much later in life. Instead, the
Abbotts held that school-age children could be taught to think historically at
a very young age. They anticipated twentieth-century social studies educators who encouraged in their students "a deep understanding of the processes
involved in investigating the past," including, as VanSledright describes,
"knowing where to obtain the sources of evidence, knowing what to do with
that evidence, understanding how to read difficult texts and analyze sometimes

mysterious artifacts, and honing the ability to get into the hearts and minds of people whose worlds were different from our own without unfairly imposing our contemporary assumptions on them." The phonetic approach to literacy employed by the Abbotts facilitated this pedagogy because it emphasized process over content, and it encouraged students to "draw their own conclusions supported by evidence drawn from primary sources." A sight/word method of historical study was, in the estimation of the Abbotts, a less personal, noncreative mode of inquiry. "Without the capacity to do history" and to "investigate the past oneself," VanSledright has written of such thinking, "learning about history" is inappropriately "reduced largely to rote memorization of dates, events, and people, or, in other words, the consumption of other people's facts."[51]

The value of history to the Abbotts is best evidenced in the curricula employed at two additional schools founded by the brothers in the mid-nineteenth century. The first was Abbotts' School for Young Ladies (later known as the Spingler Institute), located in the Union Square neighborhood of New York City and overseen by Jacob, Charles, and Gorham.[52] The school attracted young women from all over the country and even from abroad and was dedicated, as the *First Report, with Catalogue* notes, to the goal of providing women with a liberal education.[53] Its prevailing philosophy was that the "American woman" was an undervalued educational commodity in the United States and that "she had a right to be something more and higher than either cook or housekeeper, a right to be a woman, with every part of her nature developed by study and enriched by culture; a right as a daughter of God, to share with her brother in the fruits of the tree of knowledge which God has made free to all his children; was neither claimed by herself nor allowed her by others."[54] The second school was Upper Spingler, an affiliated collegiate institute in which the Abbott brothers served as instructors and administrators.[55] As at the Mount Vernon School, the foundations of the learning experiences at Upper Spingler rested on self-government. "The scholars were encouraged to make their own selection of studies, under the guidance of their parents or guardians, and much of the discipline of the school was left to their discretion," remembered one former student.[56]

The Abbotts believed that students should be encouraged to think creatively and independently about history, and they did not try to impose a singular interpretive tradition on their students. Each fall, for instance, Jacob Abbott lectured to pupils at Spingler from his little red volume on Mary Queen of Scots, and rather than asking them to regurgitate the facts of the narrative as he had relayed them in class, he requested that students write him individualized notes about what of significance they thought they would retain about

Mary's life. Why was Mary important to them and why should they remember her, he asked? It's clear from the responses to this exercise (preserved in a letter book at Bowdoin College) that the students were encouraged to be open, honest, and highly personal in their evaluations of their teacher's work. One felt comfortable enough to admit the following, for instance: "Dear Teacher: I do not think I shall be able to remember much of Mary Queen of Scots."[57] Such facile responses discouraged less patient instructors, such as Child, who decried the fact that one of her young charges cared only about "whether Queen Mary had sandy hair, or dark hair." The girl "was naturally bright and intelligent; but she had not been accustomed to attend to anything, except what related to dress and personal appearance," Child wrote. "The descriptions of Scottish scenery, the workings of religious prejudice, the intrigues of political faction, the faithful pictures of life and manners, were all lost upon her. She did not observe them because she had never formed the habit of observing. She read through [several], so full of historical interest, without feeling interested in anything but the color of Queen Mary's hair."[58] Abbott, however, believed that sufficient habits of observation could be cultivated in the young, and he commented with pride that some of his pupils became lifelong students of the queen and the lessons her life imparted. Harriet A. Smith, for instance, a student at Spingler, wrote to Abbott to thank him for her newfound fascination with the Queen of Scots: "I am very much interested in her history and I go home and tell my friends all about it."[59]

Historical study at Spingler was a mixture of classical subjects and contemporary approaches to learning. On the one hand, the faculty was quite academic in its background and methodologies, including professors from various local colleges and universities hired to teach courses on Greek, Roman, and British history, as well as special lecturers such as John S. C. Abbott, who gave weekly presentations on his favorite topic, French history.[60] A set of class notes kept during the 1856–57 school year by Adaline T. Allen includes the abstract of a high-minded lecture titled "Philosophy of History" given by Henry Boynton Smith, a Presbyterian minister and historian who also taught at the Union Theological Seminary.[61]

On the other hand, part of the history curriculum at Spingler was given over to more casual conversations about pertinent present topics, and, as they had been at Mount Vernon, students were expected to teach themselves about the major events of the day through newspaper study and discussion. Comments from students in the Abbot Memorial volume imply that one of Headmaster Gorham's favorite "quarters of an hour" came at the close of the six o'clock dinner, when he quizzed them on local, state, national, and international news. "We can hear, at this moment, the rap, rap, rap, that came at the close of the meal, from his place at the head of the table, where Mrs. Abbot sat always at his right hand," reminisced one student. "At once, every one sat up, conversation ceased and quiet reigned." Interested in what would later come to be known as current events, the Abbotts made conscious efforts to link the contemporary moments to their historical antecedents. "This would lead to geographical or historical questions, and these would be given to one and another for the next evening," the student continued. "Sometimes, he would call, suddenly, for a thought from the lessons of the day. . . . It was surprising how soon the new students adjusted themselves to these conditions, and how rapidly they improved in self-possession and in power of expression. These table exercises gave the girls conversational power and were invaluable. I have known of no other school that has pursued this plan."[62]

Why is this educational background relevant to my consideration of the efforts of publishers such as Heritage History to recirculate the histories of the Abbotts? Because these pedagogical strategies anticipated by many decades the inquiry-based learning techniques that came into prominence in the Progressive Era. They reveal that quite apart from being a corrective to the constructivist approaches of the twentieth century, as some homeschooling parents imagine, the writings and pedagogies of the Abbott brothers actually anticipated the development of process learning that culminated in the emergence of social studies in American schools. As much as any of the founders of the progressive education movement, including Pestalozzi, the Abbotts embraced the concept that children could and should be taught history by other than mere content-driven pedagogies and "in contrast to memorizing details in a textbook." They offered strong evidence of what modern research in cognitive learning has confirmed: "Children do have the intellectual capacity to judge the validity, reliability, and perspective of . . . documents and images."[63] And the Abbotts believed these aptitudes pertained to girls and women as well as to boys and men. The Abbott brothers were also conspicuously interdisciplinary in their teaching in ways that presaged the efforts of progressive educators to make connections among disciplines. As the historian Abigail Hamblen writes, "Long before the all-embracing term 'social studies' had been coined, the Abbotts, born pedagogues, incorporated geography, sociology, and psychology into their historical accounts."[64]

Accordingly, to advocate the republishing of the works of the Abbott brothers today as correctives to the so-called misguided progressive history texts of the twentieth century points to a gross misunderstanding of what the Abbotts aimed to accomplish in their pedagogy and writing. Indeed, as the historian Mary Stimpson has written, the Abbotts were the forerunners of "several progressive educational movements" in the United States, including the social studies initiative, and they were more closely aligned with progressive pedagogical initiatives than most other teachers in their day.[65] Certainly they would have had little sympathy with the idea that history should "steer clear of political pitfalls" or that it should be taught primarily for its entertainment value. The goal of history for the Abbotts as educators was to make the past usable for students and to employ its insights and judgments for the improvement of society through the cultivation of critical thinking skills. Jacob and John Abbott would have agreed in theory with the contention of the proprietors of Heritage History that students are capable of "teaching themselves history," but the brothers would never have acceded to the abandonment of those "modern educational methods" that Adam and Alice reject so resoundingly. Indeed, the Abbott brothers had done more than most educators to create and implement those progressive techniques in the first place.

"Mere Republication": Biography and the Usable Past

The second affirmation of the Nothing New Press and Heritage History—that the works of the Abbott brothers should be republished and used in homeschool settings because they represent entertaining prose narratives rather than analytical investigations—is equally dubious. The assumption that the Abbott brothers were interested only in storytelling and did not seek to make large, comprehensive statements about a usable past is not supportable. The best way to document this incorrect presupposition is to examine how the Abbotts approached the study of historical biography, the genre they believed was most appropriate for educating young children in the lessons of the past.

To begin with, the prolific careers of Jacob and John Abbott as writers were an extension of their work as educators. They never published books without contemplating their educational effects on readers, especially young readers. In writing the little red volumes of their Makers of History, for instance, the brothers alerted educators to the fact that they had pitched the narratives to the needs of multiple audiences, each with different literary expectations (fig. 7). "Persons sometimes wonder why we should have so many different accounts of the same thing," Jacob Abbott wrote in the introduction to the volume on Mary Queen of Scots in the series. "The reason is, that each one of these accounts is intended for a different set of readers, who read with ideas and purposes widely dissimilar from each other." With respect to very young audiences, for instance, "a mere republication of existing accounts is not what they require. The story must be told expressly for them," the brothers remarked. "The things that are to be explained, the points that are to be brought out, the comparative degree of prominence to be given to the various particulars, will all be different, on account of the difference in the situation, the ideas, and the objects of these new readers, compared with those of the various other classes of readers which former authors have had in view."[66]

The Abbotts had no objections to lively narratives. As Adam and Alice of Heritage History correctly point out, the brothers valued the power of prose as an inducement to reading among learners, especially those at slightly more advanced reading levels. Throughout Makers of History, Jacob and John S. C. Abbott included picturesque accounts of battles, floods, political intrigues, and diseases, focusing often on the human dramas emanating from natural and unnatural catastrophes. In their zeal to write compelling history that would appeal to older children, they occasionally resorted to sensationalized descriptions that were as gratuitous as they were spellbinding. In depicting the maritime travails of William the Conqueror, for example, Jacob Abbott noted in ghoulish detail the human losses associated with the sinking of William's vessels at sea. "The fragments of them, with the bodies of the drowned mariners, were driven to the shore," he wrote. "The ghastly spectacles presented by these dead bodies, swollen and mangled, and half buried in the sand, as if the sea had been endeavoring to hide the mischief it had done, shocked and terrified the spectators who saw them."[67] In narrating the cruelty of the Saxon invasion of the Danes, Jacob described how Ethelred authorized the killing of women by burying them up to their waists before setting dogs on them "to tear their naked flesh until they died in agony." The brothers conceded that "it would be best, in narrating history, to suppress such horrid details as these," but they claimed a civic responsibility to educate vulnerable readers to the realities of life in a politically contentious age, noting that "in a land like this . . . it is very important that we should all know what civil war is, and to what horrible atrocities it inevitably leads."[68]

Critics reacted to these literary excesses at times. A reviewer wondered how the undiscriminating public could be protected from such authors as the Abbotts, "who cared more for picturesque narrative than for sober interpretation."[69] Such criticisms, though justified, obscure the more restrained strategies the Abbotts employed in their efforts to encourage the very youngest readers to take an interest in history. The brothers wrote lively narratives, to be sure, but they also guarded against being too animated in their prose for fear that young students would miss the larger moral points of their writings. "Every parent knows there is a great danger that children will run over the pages of a book where narrative and dialogue are introduced to illustrate religious truth," Jacob Abbott wrote, and "that they will, with peculiar dexterity, find out and read all that has the interest of a story, and skip the rest."[70]

FIGURE 7. John S. C. Abbott,
*The History of Henry IV: King
of France,* Makers of History
Series (New York: Harper
and Brothers, 1856).

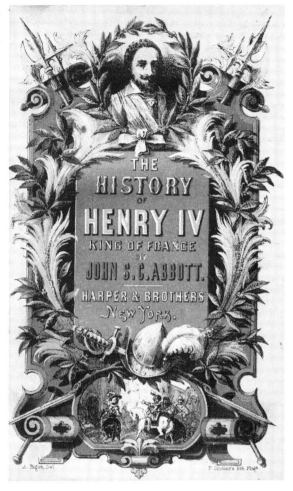

Authors such as the Abbotts, therefore, searched diligently for material that
would, according to Avery, "engage children's interests without telling them
lies, while trying to counteract the prevailing thirst for fiction."[71] The brothers
erred often on the side of temperance. Decades after reading one of Jacob's little red volumes, Fleming remembered and appreciated its less melodramatic
approach: "Few hairbreadth escapes and no romantic, wonderful deliverances
does Mr. Abbott record" in his efforts to reach young readers, she wrote. "We
may not care much for the simple stories now, but some of us have reason to
be thankful, in looking over the many sensational, frothy books for juvenile
perusal with which the press teems to-day, that to our youthful intellect was
given a healthier nourishment and such as we desire for our own little ones."[72]

A late nineteenth-century reviewer for the *Lutheran Observer* agreed, asserting, "What a public blessing it would be, if the popular taste would incline to the sweet, pure and instructive literature of Jacob Abbott," instead of the "pernicious and sensational trash which is now devoured by millions of our young people, all over the land."[73]

The Abbotts were very serious about the academic rigor of their works. Rejecting the use of fictionalized narrators like Goodrich's Peter Parley, the Abbotts insisted on a straightforward authorial voice that would offer "useful, and not merely entertaining, knowledge."[74] In his introduction to the Harper volume on Louis Philippe, for instance, John S. C. Abbott alerted young readers to the factual authority of his work. "Every event here narrated is sustained by documentary evidence beyond the possibility of a doubt," he assured readers.[75] Jacob made similar claims for his volume on Richard I. "The author of this series has made it his special object to confine himself very strictly, even in the most minute details which he records, to historic truth," he wrote in the introduction to the volume, adding, "The narratives are not tales founded upon history, but history itself, without any embellishment, or any deviations from the strict truth so far as it can be discovered by an attentive examination of the annals written at the time when the events themselves occurred. . . . Nothing is stated, not even the most minute and apparently imaginary details, without what was deemed good historical authority."[76] Even on those rare occasions when a lack of verifiable sources encouraged the brothers to rely on ancient myths and legends (the works on Cyrus, Darius, Xerxes, Romulus, and Pyrrhus, for instance), they warned readers against the seductiveness of such "fabulous and mythical" sources. "In writing this series of histories, therefore, it has been the aim of the author not to *correct* the ancient story," Jacob wrote, "but to repeat it as it stands, cautioning the reader, however, whenever occasion requires, not to suppose that the marvelous narratives are historically true."[77]

Consistent with their educational philosophies, the Abbotts underscored these characteristics of scholarly rigor in their works not so that young readers would feel obliged to memorize facts or dates but so that they would come to appreciate how valuable truthful narratives can be as inducements to proper behavior. Realizing that small children lacked the maturity of mind and capacity to understand how rote learning can be made practical, the brothers rejected textbook approaches that devolved into "a mere mechanical committing to memory of names, and dates, and phrases" and "which awaken no interest, communicate no ideas, and impart no useful knowledge to the mind."[78] They believed that applied learning could be achieved best in young students through exposure to short, spirited biographies that documented accurately the lives of exemplary historical figures, volumes that allowed young readers to exercise "their reflecting and reasoning powers" by making connections to their own lives. In studying the "history of individual monarchies or the narratives of single events," Jacob wrote in the *History of Cyrus the Great,* children "take notice of the motives of conduct, of the gradual development of character, the good or ill desert of actions, and of the connection of causes and consequences, both in respect to the influence of wisdom and virtue on the one hand, and, on the other, of folly and crime." In a word, "they reason, they sympathize, they pity, they approve, and they condemn. They enjoy the real and true pleasure which constitutes the charm of historical study for minds that are mature; and they acquire a taste for truth instead of fiction, which will tend to direct their reading into proper channels in all future years."[79]

If the Abbotts had relied solely on these biographical techniques for narrating the past, perhaps Adam and Alice of Heritage History might be justified in arguing that the brothers were not analytic or comprehensive thinkers. The Abbotts believed, however, that young children were capable of appreciating the larger synthetic elements of history if these were presented in age-appropriate ways. In the Harper series, for instance, the Abbotts employed the concept of collective biography to encourage youth to acquire a comprehensive chronological knowledge of the past by tracing the connections among the life stories of major historical figures across volumes. Advertisements for Abbott's Juvenile Histories stressed that each narrative in the series was not only succinct but also comprehensive with respect to the whole enterprise.[80] Seen from the perspective of the entire collection, in fact, the little red volumes composed a metanarrative that connected one age to the next in meaningful chronological progression. "The successive volumes of the series, though they contain the life of a single individual, and constitute thus a distinct and independent work, follow each other in the main, in regular historical order," the Abbotts averred in the introduction to the volume *History of King Philip,* each book continuing "the general narrative of history down to the period at which the general history from the present age back to the remotest times."[81] Readers of all volumes in the Makers of History could expect to gain a comprehensive, analytical perspective on the past, therefore, since, as the historian of British print culture Leslie Howsam has observed of such "sustained literary ventures," the "sum of the collected books was greater than their individual parts."[82]

The marketing and production histories of the Abbott brothers' little red histories bear out this interest in a comprehensive history characterized by metahistorical perspectives. What Howsam says about the historical series format in England holds true for the United States as well; that is, it "had particular advantages for the publishers of history books, in that the development of a set of connected works on a single theme, with one volume succeeding the next in both chronological and thematic sequence, allowed them to conceptualize projects on a grand scale."[83] Series publishing was also an astute promotional strategy on the part of Harper in that, as another student of the business of literacy has written, the "'piggybacking' of products by publishers under a similar brand name [led] to the development of mass 'product loyalty.'"[84] The series approach of the Abbotts certainly appealed to middle- and upper-class parents who encouraged their children to collect handsome volumes with long runs, uniformly bound and consistently priced.[85] As Luke has pointed out, the repetitions among volumes in series such as Makers of History created in readers "a sense of dependency on the continuance of its conventions, codes, and messages." Any boredom one might expect from redundancies that might emerge in the process was obviated by the mass product loyalty of the purchasers of books like these, as readers developed what Umberto Eco calls "a hunger for repetition." While commitment to formulaic history created its own dependencies, then, the "design of a redundant, recognizable and predictable text was intentional."[86] Additionally, surmising that children might become collectors of books, assembling small libraries of coveted works, Harper and Brothers remained committed to the Abbott series for decades.[87]

These tendencies indicate that the Abbotts aspired to a comprehensiveness in their works that republishers such as Adam and Alice have underestimated. Their biographies did much to reaffirm the master narrative of world history, for instance, by emphasizing the commonalities of human behavior across time and highlighting the basic moral lessons endemic to all human history. In his volume on William the Conqueror, for instance, Jacob Abbott reminded readers that "the same qualities of courage, energy, and fearless love of adventure and of danger" characteristic of eleventh-century Norman discoverers could be found in "their descendants at the present day." The energy and willingness to endure "privations and hardships" that one discovers "on nineteenth-century whaling voyages in the Pacific Ocean or in mining expeditions in California," Jacob added, derived from the exploits of the descendants of William, who braved "every hardship and every imaginable danger, to find new regions to dwell in, more genial, and fertile, and rich than their own native northern climes." The times and circumstances have changed, "but the race and spirit are the same."[88]

An identical impulse toward consistency held for races whose records the Abbotts viewed as less stellar, such as the Mongols. In his volume on Genghis

Khan, for instance, Jacob Abbott truncated his narrative of the succession of Mongolian leaders, noting that to chart their histories "would be a repetition of the same tale of rapine, plunder, murder, and devastation." Genghis Khan's excesses presaged the failure of all his descendants, in Abbott's estimation: "The fate of the grand empire which Genghis Khan established was the same with that of all others that have arisen in the world, from time to time, by the extension of the power of great military commanders over widely separated and heterogeneous nations." Abbott continued, "The sons and successors to whom the vast possessions descended soon quarreled among themselves, and the immense fabric fell to pieces in less time than it had taken to construct it."[89]

Such pronouncements about the imperfections of inherited racial traits reveal the degree to which the Abbott brothers were products of their time. Many of the volumes in the Harper series make racial assumptions that are inappropriate when viewed from a twenty-first-century perspective, calling into question the value of their republication in the current literary marketplace. As Hamblen has written, "*Alfred the Great* contains several pages which fashionable modern educators would certainly deplore," including references to the preeminence of the Anglo-Saxon races. "[Abbott] implies that their superior qualities adhere to their descendants (among whom he and the reader, too, of course, are proud to number themselves)," Hamblen adds. "Here is a writer unabashedly striving to make young readers proud of their heritage."[90] Conversely, Jacob Abbott is quite derogatory about Asian peoples, whose physiognomy he does not admire. In describing the Mongols, for instance, Jacob wrote, "To obtain a clear conception of a single Mongol family, you must imagine, first, a rather small, short, thick-set man, with long black hair, a flat face, and a dark olive complexion. His wife, if her face were not so flat and her nose so broad, would be quite a brilliant little beauty, her eyes were so black and sparkling."[91]

Apart from its inherent racism, this statement reveals a good deal about a disturbing sexism typical of the misogynistic age in which the Abbotts wrote. We know from their work as educators that the brothers were more enlightened than most nineteenth-century teachers on the subject of the educability of women, yet they could not escape completely the limitations of a Victorian outlook on femininity. Hamblen says that a casual perusal of the little red volumes reveals a persistent antifemale bias. "The modern advocate of 'Women's Lib' would smile grimly at the opinion, given over and over again, that a woman must be 'womanly,' must rule by her 'gentle personality,'" she maintains with reference to the Harper volumes.[92] In his biography of the French Girondist Madame Roland, for instance, John S. C. Abbott writes that "her case is one of the most extraordinary the history of the world has presented, in which the very highest degree of heroism is combined with the most resistless charms of feminine loveliness." He then moralizes as follows: "An unfeminine woman can never be *loved* by men. She may be respected for her talents, she may be honored for her philanthropy, but she cannot win the warmer emotions of the heart."[93]

Republishers of the Abbott brothers' books often ignore these expressions of overt racism and sexism. Indeed, Adam and Alice of Heritage History market the little red volumes as works sympathetic to the cause of women. Selling reprints of nineteenth-century books at a recent homeschooling conference, for instance, Adam was confronted by a female customer who expressed concern that "older history books were well known to 'exclude women.'" He failed in several attempts to persuade her that women were important to many nineteenth-century narratives. Not wishing to concede the point regarding how "'enlightened' the old authors really were," Adam called her attention to "the works of Jacob Abbott in the *Maker's* [sic] *of History* collection, 'a full quarter [of which] are about women heroines, and there are interesting secondary female characters in almost all of them.'" Unconvinced, the skeptical woman "disappeared into the crowd." Adam inferred that this would-be female customer could not be converted to the Abbott texts because she refused to look at the evidence that was squarely before her with respect to the brothers' appreciation of the role of women in history. "It seems the best way to determine whether or not women are actually 'neglected' in old history books, is to read old history books" themselves, Adam argued, and to "see for oneself, rather than to except hearsay from modern historians, who need to make a case for studying history from a modern, rather than a traditional viewpoint." This woman, who professed "concern about the supposed neglect of women in older history books," was obviously "not concerned enough about the truth of the assertion to actually investigate the claim," Adam concluded.[94] He, in turn, seems to have missed her point: that by the "neglect of women in older history books" she meant perhaps not the exclusion of women necessarily but their inclusion under unsatisfactory terms.

Those like Adam and Alice of Heritage History who reprint the Abbott brothers' histories because they believe them to be lively narratives unencumbered by analytical and metanarrative intentions fail to identify the degree to which the Abbotts wrote with the instructional needs of their young readers in mind. As educators, they were committed to making the past serve pedagogical purposes, and they produced volumes in Makers of History that were distinguished by large, synthetic understandings of human history, by conscious employment of a usable past, and by acute awareness of the relevance of the contemporary moment. Just as fictionalizing tropes were intrinsic to the narrative form practiced by Goodrich, so meta-analysis was central to the accounts of the past produced by the Abbotts in series format. Interested more in process learning than in literary effect, the Abbotts never wrote for mere entertainment value, as Adam and Alice would have it. They were self-consciously methodological in everything they produced, and this analytical outlook was emblematic of many works in the genre of pedagogical history to which they were committed explicitly.

The Abbotts as Ideologues: *The History of Napoleon Bonaparte*

The third assertion by republishers of Abbott brothers' histories—that their works were pre-ideological or even nonideological—is the least defensible of all their claims, primarily because it is the most inaccurate historically. In making such an argument, Adam and Alice assert that the Abbotts managed to avoid the two major pitfalls of twenty-first-century historical writing, partiality and political correctness, by writing at a time when chroniclers of the past and their readers agreed on a consensus-based master narrative. What the couple fails to divulge, however, is that the Abbotts were not operating in an ideological vacuum in the mid-nineteenth century, when they published Makers of History; they were in fact active in debates over dogma and interpretation as well as in petty squabbles over historiographic perspective. The decades of the mid-nineteenth century were contentious ones for the nation as a whole, and the various personal, regional, and philosophical preferences of the Abbotts vis-à-vis the events of those years insinuated themselves consistently into their texts just as they do in all works of history.

The best evidence of such ideological involvement is the controversy surrounding John S. C. Abbott's little red volumes on French history. Abbott was fascinated by the Bonapartes, and he wrote biographies for the series Makers of History on Josephine Bonaparte and on Hortense Bonaparte, Josephine's daughter and the mother of Napoleon III. In 1851 he began to write a volume on Napoleon I, but, finding himself too restricted by the page limitations of the series, he published it in installments in *Harper's Magazine* instead. In 1855 these articles were issued as a two-volume biography, *The History of Napoleon Bonaparte*. This work was pitched primarily to an adult audience, but, because it was initiated as one of the little red volumes, Abbott expected many children to find it accessible as well. He was not disappointed. "His histories have found an especial popularity among young people and in the general reading classes of all parts of the country," one reviewer noted, adding, "Few school-boys have not read his *History of Napoleon I.*"[95] Another reviewer, writing for the *Christian Leader,* recalled his own youthful first encounter with the biography: "We shall never forget the fascination which the . . . work had for us in our boyhood," he noted. "We used to read and reread it, until we could almost repeat some of its passages from memory. Even now the old spell has some power, and to imagine how we felt when a boy, we have only to take down the well-thumbed 'Napoleon,' and turn over its familiar pages."[96]

These young readers likely did not understand the complicated ideological factors that induced Abbott to write about the Bonapartes for Harper and Brothers, but they were present nonetheless. Among other things, John S. C. Abbott took pride in being an iconoclast who confounded historical authorities with his interpretations. The very moment of inspiration for working on Napoleon was, in fact, an act of historiographic rebellion, he remembered. "I was trained to believe Napoleon a monster," as "Scott's life was the only one I had ever read," Abbott admitted of his early, limited exposure to Napoleonic studies. One day, while sitting in the study of a friend, Abbott alluded to "that scourge of the human race, Napoleon Bonaparte," at which point his acquaintance went to the shelves, took down a volume of the *Encyclopedia Americana,* and read an extract recounting Napoleon's inspired directions to his minister of the interior. "When he had finished, he returned the book to its place, without saying a word," Abbott wrote. "I was then and there led to feel that there was another side to Napoleon's character." A friend recalled how this encounter motivated Abbott "to pursue the matter further and the result was his conviction that a true history of Napoleon had not been written, and [he] felt that it was a work which he should undertake."[97] He determined to write a popular history of the man "in the interest of the people, and in an entirely different vein from the general histories of the Revolution, which have been written either in the interest of English Tories or restored Bourbons."[98]

Abbott's distrust of the British Tories and his eagerness to condemn Anglo scholarship on Napoleon revealed how politically motivated he was in writing about the Bonaparte family. In distinction to debunking British historians, he defended Napoleon, confessing boldly that he was "one who reveres and loves the Emperor." He professed unabashedly that he admired Napoleon because the French leader "abhorred war, and did everything in his power to avert that dire calamity; because he merited the sovereignty to which the suffrages of a grateful nation elevated him; because he consecrated the most extraordinary energies ever conferred upon a mortal to promote the prosperity of his country; because he was regardless of luxury, and cheerfully endured all toil and all hardships that he might elevate and bless the masses of mankind; because he had a high sense of honor, revered religion, respected the rights of conscience, and nobly advocated equality of privileges and the universal brotherhood of man."[99] In his biography of Josephine Bonaparte for Makers of History, Abbott took issue with British historians who had condemned Napoleon for the despicable divorce of his wife. Acknowledging the "great wrong" and tremendous pain Napoleon inflicted "upon the noble Josephine," Abbott nonetheless called attention to the selfless quality of the French emperor's actions. Again, England was a useful point of reference. Compared to the "brutal butcheries of Henry VIII," whose wife "was compelled to place her head upon the block, merely to afford room for the indulgence" of the king's "vagrant passions," Abbott wrote, Napoleon's parting with his wife, motivated by the needs of the state, was almost humane.[100]

Abbott was driven to write positively about Napoleon in part because he sympathized strongly with the ideological bent of so many of the French leader's personal and political priorities. For obvious reasons, given his educational philosophies, for instance, Abbott was impressed by the fact that as soon as Napoleon assumed command of the French government "he immediately and energetically established schools for female education, remarking that France needed nothing so much to promote its regeneration as good mothers." He also applauded Napoleon's insistence on strict moral comportment by members of France's notoriously debauched court. Additionally, Abbott, a committed pacifist, regarded Napoleon as a lover of peace who was compelled to fight against his will to safeguard democracy against the crumbling but still formidable bastions of European monarchical rule. England, the nation Abbott identified as "the unrelenting inciter of these wars," was culpable in this matter because its leaders convinced other countries to attack France, thereby sealing Napoleon's fate and derailing France's democratic initiatives. Abbott warned Mother England that "the hour of her punishment" and "the day of retribution is at hand." She "now groans beneath the burden of four thousand million dollars of debt" brought on by the Napoleonic Wars, he wrote, and this "weighs upon her children with a crushing pressure which is daily becoming more insupportable."[101]

Perhaps Abbott's strongest impetus for reassessing the life and career of Napoleon was his personal relationship with Bonaparte's nephew, Louis-Napoleon Bonaparte (Napoleon III), who was in power during the Second French Republic while Abbott was working on his biography of Napoleon I. Abbott had corresponded with a number of high-ranking members of the French government about his project, including Louis-Napoleon, who invited him to Paris for a personal interview. After this encounter Abbott became an unrepentant supporter of the Second Republic, and he openly avowed his allegiance to the French republican system. In his little red book about

Napoleon III's mother, Hortense, for instance, Abbott wrote that if "from spirit-land" she could "look down upon her son, her heart must be cheered in view of the honors which his native land, with such unprecedented unanimity, has conferred upon him. . . . Every well-informed man will admit that the kingdom of France has never, since its foundations were laid, enjoyed so many years of tranquility, and of mental and material advancement at home, and also of respect and influence abroad, as during the reign of the son of Hortense."[102] Abbott conversed with Louis-Napoleon about the "principles of the government" that Bonaparte "was then so successfully administering for France," and he made a special study of the ways in which Napoleon I's policies had left a mark on his nephew's practices. Abbott eventually presented his completed two-volume biography of Napoleon I as a gift to the French leader, and Louis-Napoleon in turn gave the historian a gold medal as a sign of his gratitude.[103]

Abbott's outspoken admiration of the French in general and of Napoleon I and Napoleon III embroiled him in disputes with historians who did not share his ideological positions or his overly generous disposition. By the late 1850s, in fact, Abbott had become the whipping boy of a whole community of nascent professional scholars who were attempting to formulate acceptable codes of operation for members of the rising historical profession. These professional critics questioned consistently the research techniques used by the Abbott brothers in their little red volumes. A reviewer of Makers of History for the *Christian Leader* speculated that the "histories were evidently compiled from the sources nearest at hand, with a direct view to immediate and popular effect" and could not be "the result of long research and careful investigation."[104] John's nephew Lyman acknowledged the validity of this charge, explaining that his uncle prepared for each volume by "read[ing] up on the topic till he was thoroughly familiar with it"; then, "closing his eyes, he would by a rare power of historic imagination transport himself into the scene which he was about to describe and paint with his pen what he had seen in a mental vision. The elements of this vision were made up out of the previous studies," Lyman added, "but I think after the studies were completed he rarely consulted authorities while he wrote."[105] Abbott's nephew and the editor of the *Literary World*, Edward Abbott, admitted as well that the "pressure under which he toiled operated unfavorably as respects carefulness and exactness."[106] Abbott's daughter confessed the same, although she had fewer problems with the technique. "I know for a fact that he always went alone into his study and there sought divine guidance that he might write only the truth as he could best discover it, without fear or favor." Under the circumstances, she added, "how could father be wrong?"[107]

Others, above all, people who were not members of the Abbott family, were less convinced of John S. C. Abbott's infallibility. Edwin Godkin complained in a lengthy review article in the *New York Evening Post* about Abbott's "persistent, laborious, untiring efforts at panegyric," which struck the reviewer as distinctly unprofessional. "The author daubs, plasters and overwhelms his hero with superlatives, until all other heroes of all time are literally 'nowhere,'" Godkin added, "if actual merit is to be estimated by the quantity of praise bestowed upon it." Godkin took further issue with the nature of the proof Abbott offered for his contentions about the Bonapartes as feminists, moralists, pacifists, and burgeoning democrats. An admitted autodidact with no formal training in history, Abbott did not have an adequate understanding, in Godkin's estimation, of what historians meant by factual information or what was acceptable regarding the proper use of sources in making these arguments. Despite assurances by Abbott that *"his* life of Napoleon can be relied on for 'facts,' and that the American people 'constitute the only impartial tribunal which can now be found on earth to pronounce judgment on Napoleon,'" Godkin warned readers not to be gulled into accepting the author's undemanding assessment that all they must do "is to 'find the facts' as Mr. Abbott finds them, and to 'pronounce judgment' in conformity. When the rest of the civilized world hears what the verdict is they will doubtless know what to do about it."[108] A reviewer for the *Universalist* agreed, noting of the Napoleon biography that Abbott had written a pandering life from which "hosts of young readers . . . will find they have much to unlearn."[109]

Other professional critics warranted that Abbott's distorting embellishments and his misappropriations of facts were enough to disqualify him altogether as a historian. In *Little Journeys to the Homes of Eminent Artists,* Elbert Hubbard classified the Napoleon biography as a piece of historical fiction, and a bad one at that. "Next to Weems in point of literary atrocity," he wrote disdainfully, "comes John S. C. Abbott, whose life of Napoleon is a splendid concealment of the man."[110] A writer for the literary magazine the *Jewell* echoed this sentiment: "Abbott has done more than all men to make us doubt whether all history is not fiction." In reading Abbott's works, this critic added, one receives the impression that "Bonaparte was a charitable old gentleman in a drab overcoat who went about promoting Sunday schools and other benevolent objects, and was never to blame for the awful accidents which happened all around him. His main characteristic was that he was always begging for peace, but unfortunately there were so many bad men in his day he could rarely obtain it. They kept this benevolent old gentleman fighting nearly all his life sorely against his will." Admitting he had never read nearly five dozen of Abbott's works, the reviewer nonetheless proclaimed himself a "victim of an overdose" of Abbott's misleading prose. "Having taken in his 'Life of Bonaparte' while a freshman in college," he wrote in the first person plural, "[we] were enthusiastic admirers of Bony and Abbott for a time, and we suppose the whole sixty would have been swallowed then if they had come in our way." The critic elaborated: "After more reading we began to conceive that the character of Bonaparte was overdrawn by Abbott, then we concluded it was not drawn at all, and finally we came into such a skeptical state of mind with regard to the 'Life' that we always resort to the Arabian Nights for unalloyed fiction in preference to it."[111]

Critics of Abbott contended furthermore that distortions in his works were not just a matter of sloppy technique but were ideologically motivated as well. Of primary import in relation to twenty-first-century homeschoolers' evaluation of the Abbotts' works, this line of argument appeared in a strong attack on John S. C. Abbott's treatment of the Bonapartes in Horace Greeley's *New-York Daily Tribune.* In a ten-column review of *The History of Napoleon,* conspicuous for its length and vitriolic tone, Greeley's associate William Henry Fry accused Abbott of betraying the sanctity of the ecclesiastical robes he once wore: "There is a man called John S. C. Abbott who prefixes to his name the title Reverend, which belongs to the elect disciples of One whose teachings were all of purity and peace; of One who exhorted his followers to do justice, love mercy and walk humbly before God—to love, likewise, their neighbors as themselves; of One who said, Blessed are the peacemakers." Abbott was not worthy of the title reverend, Fry implied, and neither was the publication that first serialized his biography, *Harper's Magazine,* which the *Tribune* referred to as a "motley" periodical "made up partly of original contributions and partly of matter taken without credit from the English journals." Fry fumed that Abbott had misrepresented Napoleon knowingly in portraying him as "a model of genius, talents, patriotism and all the virtues—to hold . . . up for the admiration and imitation of American youth." Trumpeting the career of a man such as Napoleon, who was "a scourge to the world" and a "monster" who had "lost his 'moral character,'" amounted to an unforgivable "attempt to debauch . . . [the] youthful mind[s]" of those vulnerable children who, unfortunately, had been encouraged to read it. Appalled by the publication, Greeley and Fry dismissed Abbott as a mere amateur historian, too incompetent to be entrusted with the biography of a figure as important and complex as Napoleon I.[112]

The *Tribune* was especially outraged by the fact that Abbott had made a gift of the biography to Napoleon III and in exchange had received a gold medal. This was "a humiliating spectacle," the paper declared, "of an American clergyman, a technical republican . . . bedaubing and begilding the memory of [an] Imperial criminal" for the sake of pecuniary reward. In the *Tribune's* estimation, Abbott's acceptance of the monetary gift, which in Fry's estimation might as well have been thirty pieces of silver, made him little better than a "court toady, crawling in slime up to the imperial footstool." More untrustworthy even than most court historians, Abbott had written a thinly veiled political biography whose ultimate goal was to use a distorted past in the service of an abusive present. Fry elaborated on this nefarious behavior:

> When we find an American, and a clergyman too, like this Abbott, seeking a private interview with this matchless criminal and deeming it an honor; presenting to him a work which is a disgrace to American authorship; accompanying the presentation with sanctimonious protestations of its truthfulness and with a foul slander on the memory of Washington; receiving a gold medal in return; and when we consider that as the historian of *Harper's* magazine—perhaps the cheapest picture-book ever published and one of vast circulation—he has had the opportunity to poison the minds of American youth with such a history of his Napoleon I., and may, through the same channel, send out an equally pernicious history of Napoleon III.; when we take all this into account, we believe we have not absolutely wasted our labor placing these facts before the million readers of *The Tribune.*"[113]

From the point of view of the *Tribune,* at least, John S. C. Abbott had no business trying to educate children or adults in the proper modes of historiography.

To many readers, even Abbott's detractors, Greeley's *Tribune* review appeared overly aggressive in its condemnation of a reverend and teacher-turned-historian. Allowing that Abbott's *The History of Napoleon* failed "to observe a calm, unimpassioned spirit of justice in the narration of none but the best authenticated facts," a reviewer from the *Criterion* nonetheless criticized the *Tribune* for working too hard to find fault with a popularizer, Greeley having exhausted his "copious vocabulary of abuse" to condemn Abbott unfairly. The effect was so intense that the *Criterion* believed an apology was due Abbott, who must "consider himself utterly annihilated."[114] Edward Abbott, referred to Fry's review as the "atrocious" disgorgements of a "fierce assailant" who "wrote quite as much under passion of one kind as Mr. Abbott, in the work itself, wrote under passion of another."[115] Forty years after *The History of Napoleon* was first reviewed, Edward was still angry about the personalized nature of Greeley's attack, and he reminded readers that his uncle had been vindicated to an extent by the revival of Napoleon's reputation in late nineteenth-century Europe.[116]

Critics notwithstanding, John S. C. Abbott's volumes were popular and sold well. As Abbott pointed out proudly in a later interview, "Old Mr. Harper once said to me: 'You are making us rich; we are getting quantities of letters every day from people who write to subscribe for the magazine, and who wish their subscription to begin with the first number of the 'Life of Napoleon.'"[117] Nathaniel Hawthorne, too, conceded this success, albeit grudgingly, when he quipped about the stronghold the Abbotts had on children's works in the mid-nineteenth century: "If I saw a probability of deriving a reasonable profit from juvenile literature, I would willingly devote myself to it for a time, as being easier and more agreeable (by way of variety) than literature for grown people. . . . But my experience hitherto has not made me very sanguine on this point. In fact, the business has long been overdone. Mr Abbot [sic] and other writers have reaped the harvest; and the gleanings seem to be scarcely worth picking up."[118] The "voluminous information" contained in the Abbott brothers' books may have "made [for] convenient burlesque in later generations," a scholar of those "pre-homeopathic days" noted, but they were set apart by "conspicuous common sense" and their "sugar-coated pills were extraordinarily popular."[119]

Far from being merely "lively narrators," then, the biographies of the Abbott brothers were also progressive, analytical, and ideological in their approaches to the past, tendencies encouraged by the philosophies of education and history they preached in their schools. These proclivities would seem to disqualify the Abbotts' histories from suitability for republication, at least as judged by the nonideological standards of Adam and Alice of Heritage History, but they have not done so. The question remains: Does it make sense for some on the Christian Right to reproduce works by Jacob and John S. C. Abbott today when, even in their own day, they were thought by many critics, professionals among them, to be motivated ideologically and to be questionable historically?

The Abbott Legacy: "Redundancies Possibly Occur"

Perhaps the truest measure of the worthiness of the Abbott brothers' publications for twenty-first-century readers is how they have fared since the deaths of their authors. Of the two, Jacob's works have done better than those of John. Jacob seems to have realized earlier than his sibling that it was time to put down his pen. Having written hundreds of quickly produced histories and textbooks, he spent his last years living restfully at his home, Few Acres, in Farmington, Maine, where, according to his son Lyman, he was daily "honoured by his fellow-citizens" and "adored by his children."[120] After a short illness, he died in 1879 and was buried at Mount Auburn in Cambridge, Massachusetts. At the time of his death, many of his books, some written

fifty years earlier, were still in print. In the early twentieth century a successful campaign was waged to preserve Abbott's home as a monument to "the
author of the Rollo Books" by placing it on the National Register of Historic
Places.[121] A bronze tablet was affixed to a granite boulder on the lawn in front
of his former study. It reads, "Preacher of the Gospel of Christ; Teacher of
the Laws of Nature and Literature; Pioneer in the education of Youth; Friend
and Guide of Children; Master in the Art of Gentle Measures; Minister in
the Higher Life of Man."[122] The literary critic Fletcher Osgood believed
these accomplishments secured Jacob's place in the pantheon of important
American writers. His demonstrated abilities to show us how to "restrain our
literary straining, to give repose (not pose) to what we write, to make our
writing genuine to the core and very limpid, to aid our characterizations to
be strong and true—and yet not super-microscopic," implied, according to
Osgood, that "we need to-day—we sorely need, I think—a Jacob Abbott literary cult."[123]

John S. C. Abbott's legacy was less secure. Even his death, which was lingering, in the best Victorian sense of the word, did not protect him from
his critics.[124] When he died on 17 June 1877, just a few days after the British
historian John Lothrop Motley, their nearly simultaneous departures invited
numerous comparisons. The *New York Tribune* was somewhat generous in its
assessment of Abbott, the obituary columnist noting that "while the writings of Mr. Abbott have not been accorded the preeminent position, as contributions to historical literature, which Mr. Motley's hold by the common
consent of the most learned men, some of them have been widely read, and
the name of the writer is probably as universally known."[125] A commentator for the *Methodist* was less munificent, however, holding that the primary
difference between the two historians "is that Mr. Abbott will not be read at
all ten years from now, while Motley will be read more widely than during
his lifetime for several decades to come." Abbott "served his generation,"
while Motley's services "were rendered to the human race," he concluded.[126]
Even his devoted nephew recognized that John must suffer by comparison. It
would "not be a correct estimate to call Mr. Abbott an historian in the sense
in which Mr. Motley was an historian," Edward averred. "Mr. Motley was
an historical *scholar*. Mr. Abbott was an historical *writer*. It is the function of
Mr. Motley to bring out to the surface from their long and profound concealment, and to display in scientific and orderly manner, the materials of
history; it was Mr. Abbott's sole employment to adapt those materials to the
popular taste." He was an educator, not an original investigator in the field
of history. "His mind was not constructed for work of that kind," Edward
summed up. "His mission was to popularize knowledge. He never professed

to write for scholars, but for the people; his sympathies were profoundly with them; and his object steadily was to bring the facts of history to their apprehension."[127]

Such criticisms at the time of John S. C. Abbott's death remind one of just how controversial he was in his day. One would think this kind of reputation should give pause to twentieth-century republishers of Abbott's works, but it has not. I have discussed why the primary justifications of Adam and Alice of Heritage History for reissuing the Abbott brothers' little red volumes—their value as counterpoints to modern textbooks marred by social studies orientations, by metahistorical perspectives, and by ideological predispositions—are insufficient since the Abbotts embraced all of these qualities in their historical narratives. In addition to these discrepancies, one must consider whether the little red histories were *ever* viewed as adequate, even by the standards of their own age. Writers for some of the most influential newspapers in the land, including the *New York Herald,* the *Evening-Post,* and the *Tribune,* found the Abbotts wanting when it came to the practice of writing history. Adam and Alice argue that "the latest is not the greatest" in the business of publishing history books, and they insist that "older books, written by traditional authors" like the Abbotts are better able "to engage, entertain, and actually teach history" than modern books, which are "so often dull, uncompelling, and riddled with propaganda." But is this true? Are older books always more reliable? Heritage History alleges that the greatest value of the Abbott brothers' works is that they were (and still are) fun and entertaining to read.[128] Fiction is fun to read as well, yet most people do not (or at least should not) use it to anchor the study of history.[129]

Equally troubling is that many of the presses that have chosen to republish the works of the Abbott brothers on the grounds that they are valuable educational tools for homeschoolers have not produced very reliable copies of the originals. Dodo Press, for instance, has reprinted a copy of John S. C. Abbott's *Napoleon Bonaparte* from scanned images of the original *Harper's Magazine* articles from the early 1850s. Unfortunately, the scanning was not completed with much skill or attention to detail, and several important pages were omitted in the process. In one instance, paragraphs from a piece that flanked the original segment of June 1852 of Abbott's serialized biography are included in the Dodo Press volume as if they were part of Abbott's narrative. In another case, whoever scanned the material from the article of August 1852 on Napoleon's campaign interpolated passages from Jacob Abbott's "Memoirs of the Holy Land," which appeared next to his brother's piece in the original *Harper's* volume. This is an example of the kind of introduction of extraneous material and unacceptable transposing of historical information that occurs when works of history are repurposed without paying attention to detail and scholarly rigor.[130]

The insidious effects of these republication irregularities are multiplied when they appear in electronic formats. The Heritage History website assures readers that its "e-Books" can be "read on a variety of devices and copies can be saved on your home computer so they can never be lost or destroyed," guaranteeing their permanency.[131] That is a frightening prospect given that such duplication processes are indiscriminate in their reproductive capacities, preserving errors as readily as truths. As hard copies of nineteenth-century texts are discarded or succumb to the ravages of time, inadequately scanned electronic versions such as those put out by Dodo Press will be substituted in their place, increasing the likelihood that the original mistakes made by writers such as John S. C. Abbott will be amplified and distorted while proving less easy to correct.

Given the announced antimodern intentions of these presses, there is a considerable irony associated with the use of electronic formats by companies that recycle old books, especially those that do so inadequately. Nothing New Press suggests that e-readers are the best means to access their recycled inventory, despite the fact that they associate "classical education" with the physical, tactile experience of holding and reading a classical text. As a writer for Open Source Living comments, "The book as an object of knowledge has a firm historical and cultural standing. . . . I love the experience of book design, the smell of paper, the possibility of manual annotations, the sense of partaking in an age-old tradition and all the other idiosyncrasies that make up the relationships between humans and paper books." Yet that same writer admits that e-readers are much more than "simple book emulation devices"; they are also "interfaces with a vast distributed network of online content from blogs to newspapers and beyond," and they widen the scope of texts, classical and otherwise, that readers have available to them.[132]

If so, then works such as those of the Abbott brothers, which are oftentimes flawed in their originals, are subject to all manner of manipulation and distortion in reprintings, leaving potential readers confused as to their content and intent. There are now even publishing concerns, such as ReadHowYouWant, that allow purchasers to customize books like John S. C. Abbott's *Napoleon Bonaparte* by using "PC, Mac and modern smartphones and tablets," thereby increasing the chances of the wide circulation of texts that have been tampered with (fig. 8). Having developed conversion technology that "reformats existing books into high quality, alternative formats quickly, easily, and at price points comparable to standard format books," ReadHowYouWant offers readers the narcissistic opportunity to turn books

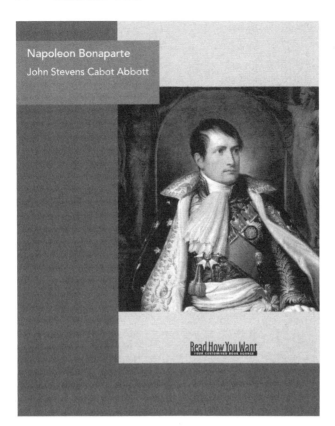

Napoleon Bonaparte
John Stevens Cabot Abbott

Read How You Want
YOUR CUSTOMIZED BOOK SOURCE

FIGURE 8.
John S. C. Abbott,
Napoleon Bonaparte
(ReadHowYouWant:
Your Customized
Book Source).

like Abbott's biography into formats they "can design for themselves."[133] Such practices borrow dangerously from the "altered book" movement in which artists challenge the authority of books as material objects by cutting, tearing, and folding pages to create new sculptural forms. While this brings us closer to Carl Becker's utopian vision of "everyman his own historian," it also pushes us more quickly toward the dystopian corollary of an unfettered relativism in which the integrity of historical documents is compromised by the publication of revisions masquerading as originals.[134]

Even if history books such as those written by the Abbott brothers can be transposed from one format to another in authoritative, accurate ways, they cannot escape the context of their creation. They are still nineteenth-century works, particular to their age and the conditions of their times, being recycled by homeschoolers in misappropriated forms for use in twenty-first-century educational contexts. That fact suggests that some republishers on the Christian Right may be asking too much of these older texts—volumes that were themselves flawed, written by popular historians who were untrained, who were not original thinkers, and who were inattentive to proper historical technique. It also implies that the mechanical recycling of their works may be superfluous and harmful. This is a case where the blind repetition of history is not a satisfactory pedagogical strategy. Certainly the Abbotts, who advocated a process-oriented pedagogical style in keeping with the changing pedagogies of their day, a style in which students extrapolated from the objects of history to their inner meanings and practical uses, would not have been pleased with such perfunctory duplications. To them, rote learning was never as conducive to the acquisition of knowledge as independent thinking.

And familiarity in this case does breed contempt. To cite one of the nineteenth-century commentators who cautioned against overuse of the Abbott brothers' original writings in the education of children: "This is not ideal literature. Redundancies possibly occur."[135]

CHAPTER THREE

Gendered History

Josephine Pollard and Monosyllabic Histories

Not to know what happened before one was born is always to be a child.

MARCUS TULLIUS CICERO

Reeducating Youth: The Republication of Monosyllabic Histories

The works of Samuel Goodrich and the Abbott brothers reveal that changing conceptions of childhood and childhood literacy conditioned the kinds of popular histories published in the mid-nineteenth century. While there was great consistency in the themes and structure of the volumes of these writers, there were also marked distinctions among them in terms of narrative strategies and historical methodologies. These differences influenced crucially the manner in which young readers were introduced to juvenile historical literature and the lessons they took away from it. Because nineteenth-century works were rooted firmly in the intellectual and educational contexts of the eras in which they were published, they are distinctive temporally and do not translate well into all learning environments. The danger of using such volumes in twenty-first-century homeschooling settings is that they are presumed by republishers to contain universal, omniscient messages that transcend time and place, when in fact they are grounded in the issues and needs of very specific pasts. Misappropriation of such texts and the failure to historicize them properly lead to misuses and abuses of history, especially when associated with children's literature. As the scholars Ann Curthoys and John Docker warn, the historian should never assume that "historical sources can be read and presented as if the past is speaking in the present, unassisted, unmediated in extensive and complex ways."[1] Popular juvenile histories may *speak to* historical themes that are ubiquitous, perhaps, but they should not be presumed to *speak for* them in all contexts.

A case in point is the effort of one republisher, Mantle Ministries, to revive the works of Josephine Pollard, a popular historian of the 1880s and 1890s. In 1998 this small, Texas-based publishing firm began reprinting Pollard's juvenile histories as part of a mission to protect young people from the depravities of contemporary life by exposing them to the supposedly more righteous moral culture of the nineteenth century. Operated by Richard "Little Bear" Wheeler, an actor-turned-evangelist and historian, Mantle Ministries is dedicated to "passing along the mantle of Christian heritage from one generation to another, thereby preserving a Godly legacy and Christ-honoring standard given to us by the Founding Fathers." According to the company's website, Wheeler achieves these goals through dramatic presentations, motivational workshops, and keynote speaking engagements in which he assumes the identities of historical figures, complete with "authentic costumes and props," and delivers "accurate, engrossing, and unforgettable dramatized messages" about the "Lord Jesus Christ's mighty hand" in guiding the nation's history.[2] In addition, Wheeler republishes books from the eighteenth and nineteenth centuries that "focus on our Christian heritage and biblical value" and that present "enthralling portrayals of historical events and true stories not found in public instruction nor in books published during the last 100 years." Among the bestselling of these "Christ-honoring books"—works that are "recommended for Christian school, church, and family heritage libraries, as well as Christian home education curricula,"—are those of Pollard from her series of histories "told in one syllable words." These reissued monosyllabic volumes are bought and sold with great frequency at homeschooling conventions, at Wheeler's "Living-History" reenactment camps, and, as I mentioned in the introduction, on eBay auction sites.[3]

Why is Mantle Ministries so interested in reintroducing these one-syllable books by Pollard? For four reasons, primarily. First, the moral content of Pollard's volumes reaffirms Wheeler's belief that God should be at the center of the master narrative of American history. The back cover of the Wheeler re-release of Pollard's *The History of the United States* recounts how "our nation began because a handful of utterly devoted men and women [that is, the Pilgrims] 'committed themselves to the will of God.'" Wheeler urges readers to see the miracle at Plymouth Plantation as a sign of the favor God granted the United States. "Think about that," he writes. "This remnant of the faithful was six times smaller than Gideon's army, yet we are here today because God blessed the efforts of about fifty people who vigorously purposed to submit themselves to His will."[4] Wheeler counsels that Pollard's stirring personal narrative of the Pilgrims at Plymouth should serve as an inducement for a massive reconsideration of the country's educational mission. He hopes that in reissuing works like Pollard's he can "correlate historical facts with Christian influences and traditions" and thereby reeducate youth to the spiritual foundations of the nation.[5] Many Christian readers have found this goal compelling, as evidenced by the robust Internet activity associated with Pollard's collected books. Her monosyllabic histories were offered recently as the grand prize in a reading competition for children by Homeschooling Mommies.com, an online Christian network devoted to finding "good Christian literature [that] can challenge and inspire readers of all ages."[6]

Second, the Pollard volumes serve as ammunition in Wheeler's prolonged campaign against the separation of church and state. The Mantle Ministries website alleges a conspiracy on the part of public educators to keep Christian themes out of schoolbooks and schools.[7] In fact, Wheeler has written a book, *Warning! Public Schools Aren't for Christians!,* about the "life-destroying pitfalls of public education." In this work he claims that a handful of powerful but misguided educational theorists have conspired to control school curricula, school boards, and textbook requisitions in an effort to deny basic religious information to young people in public schools.[8] Wheeler's solution for offsetting the negative effects of this pedagogical plot of the irreverent is to eschew public education in favor of homeschooling, a strategy that encourages parents to make their own decisions about the suitability of religious texts like Pollard's for curricular use. Creating an alternative domestic environment for learning outside the many-tentacled reach of public schools is not always easy, Wheeler acknowledges, but it is necessary and can be heroic. To buttress this argument, Mantle Ministries promotes on its website Christopher Klicka's *Home School Heroes: The Struggle and Triumph of Home Schooling in America,* a history of those who "blazed the trail of freedom for homeschoolers today" by recounting "the stories of the brave fathers and mother who faced intense and difficult legal opposition while choosing to obey God's biblical commission to teach their children." *Home School Heroes* not only "document[s] the stories of God's miraculous deliverance of these homeschooling parents in the courts and in the legislatures" but also advises homeschool parents what to do "when faced with social workers, police, and truant officers at [the] door."[9] Pollard's histories serve these heroic homeschool educators well, Wheeler asserts, because she tells "the true story of America's birth," a story that "has been removed from the history texts which populate the libraries and classrooms of the modern governmental school."[10]

Third, *The History of the United States* employs a literacy strategy that is consistent with Wheeler's pedagogical outlook. Pollard and other popular historians of the late nineteenth century used a monosyllabic technique to narrate the American past on the assumption that children learn to read better when exposed to easy whole words they can pronounce and understand rather than polysyllabic words that can be complex and disorienting. This approach, which had its roots in Goodrich's sight/word mode, is uncomplicated, direct, and in keeping with the simple Christian message authors conveyed in original nineteenth-century texts that encouraged "the young student to develop reading skills while thrilling at examples of faith, fortitude and freedom."[11] The justification for this methodology is religious and historical, Wheeler notes, grounded firmly as it is in the Protestant tradition of affording unrestricted access to the Holy Word. "When [Martin] Luther was at work on the word of God he took great pains to find short and strong words, so that all might read it and learn the way of life," the monosyllable historian Helen Walls Pierson explained in the 1880s. "He did not wish to write it in terms that the poor man did not know. So it was his way to go out in the streets where there were throngs of poor, to go to the house of birth and death, or where feasts were held for those who wed, that he might hear the mode in which the poor spoke on such themes." Luther declared, "'I can not use words of the rich and those heard in courts, I must give pure and clear Ger-man.' And he said he and Me-lanc-thon would oft seek three or four days for one short and strong word."[12] Luther, Pierson, Pollard, and Wheeler believe complex words obscure meanings and distract readers from the simple moral messages implicit in the past. Why gloss the lily, they ask implicitly, when in its least encumbered form, the Bible, God's word is at its most pure. Read it, learn it, recite it, implement it, and one cannot go wrong.

The fourth reason Mantle Ministries desires to reproduce Pollard's volumes is that they speak to gendered approaches to the past that are compatible with Wheeler's outlook on the varied ways in which boys and girls learn history. In the nineteenth century many educators believed that the genders were substantially different in terms of cognitive makeup and intellectual potential. Males were thought to be predisposed to mathematical and scientific analysis and to be adept at "acquiring and using power" while less naturally "inclined toward caring for others." Females were presumed to be better at verbal communication and to be more empathetic, while less proficient in analytic fields.[13] Pollard considered military history the private domain of boys, for instance, since, as she wrote, "man has to fight his way through the world, from the time he comes into it till he goes out of it; not all the while with guns and firearms, but in ways that tend to make the nerves strong, and the heart brave and true."[14] Girls, however, need not trouble themselves with such things, she reasoned. Pollard warned would-be female readers of her juvenile biography of the war hero Ulysses S. Grant that "it is not a book for girls at all. They will not like it."[15] Some teachers, including the Abbotts, preached the intellectual equality of the sexes, but most followed Lydia Child's advice to train children to appreciate the fact that "time and perfect companionship

... gives both man and woman complete freedom *in* their places, without a restless desire to go out of them."[16]

Education in the United States was profoundly affected by these gender-specific assumptions. "Although boys and girls increasingly attended the same schools, the cultures of boyhood and girlhood were defined in opposition to each other," Mintz has written. "Boys and girls were assumed to differ in their constitution, stature, temperament, and behavior. Femininity was defined in terms of self-sacrifice and service; masculinity, in terms of aggressiveness and daring."[17] This gendered thinking fell out of favor in the twentieth century, but it has been revived recently by the educational psychologist Leonard Sax, who avers in *Why Gender Matters* that "girls and boys behave differently because their brains are wired differently."[18] Drawing on the work of Sax and Michael Gurian, among others, some on the Christian Right accept the premise that "boys have brains naturally wired for understanding systems, due to high testosterone, low serotonin, low oxytocin, and a smaller 'corpus callosum,' a bundle of nerve fibers that aids language by connecting the brain's two hemispheres"; girls' brains, on the other hand, are equipped with "verbal parts" that "are larger than men's and they are hard-wired for empathy, but they lack a natural ability to reach the top levels of math and science." According to this logic, boys and girls are attracted to diverse kinds of learning and with differing intensities because of their distinctive neurological and physiological makeups. On the basis of such thinking, some educators have proposed separate curricula for boys and girls in public schools. In such states as South Carolina, school districts have even begun to make sex-segregated classrooms available for all children.[19]

In the view of Mantle Ministries, the value of monosyllabic books like those written by Pollard is that they supply rationalizations for gendered approaches, not only for historical study but also for learning and life. For instance, at his Little Bear Adventure Camp at the Horn Creek Conference Grounds near Westcliffe, Colorado, Wheeler offers homeschooling families, including "dads, moms, sons, and daughters, and even grandparents," the opportunity to experience the pioneer past through living history demonstrations. According to the Mantle Ministries publicity packet, fathers and sons learn "wilderness survival skills, like hunting and skinning wild game, fishing, and building traps and shelters," while mothers and daughters are offered the services of a "special women's ministry team" whose leaders offer "breakaway sessions" devoted to developing "family skills."[20] The gender-segregated character of these history conferences is justified in addresses Wheeler organizes in tandem with his fellow evangelist Mark Holden. Delivering talks with titles such as "Letting Go: The Difference Between Sons and Daughters," Holden instructs listeners that "God's defined role for men is different than that for women" and that such dissimilarities should impact the approaches "taken in releasing a son as compared to releasing a daughter." Wheeler agrees, adding that after a woman completes secondary school her life should be devoted primarily to "supporting her husband by being a helpmeet and raising Godly children." He concludes that it is a waste of money for women to attend college. "A better investment," Wheeler argues, is to apply the money that might have been used for college "toward a house and baby furniture, leaving the support of the family to the bread winner—the husband—to toil by the 'sweat of his brow.' " As for "me and my house," Wheeler notes, "we have chosen to keep our daughters home—protected, sheltered in love, and trained to become Godly, submissive wives someday."[21]

Not everyone on the Christian Right shares Wheeler's limited perspective on women's education. Indeed, there are many who doubtless find it misogynistic and antithetical to the Christian mission. Even if one regards the value of books like Pollard's solely from the point of view of reading proficiency and spiritual recovery, however, one must still ask whether these texts are the best choices for the teaching of history to homeschooled children today. At the very least they raise some vital and perplexing questions about how children retain information about the past.[22] If reading is the primary conduit for learning about history among school-age children, for instance, then what does a monosyllabic approach imply for historical literacy among children? As the Abbott brothers wondered, if children are encouraged to absorb history through recall-based, sight-method systems, can they be taught to think historically and to develop the critical skills of historical investigation valued by historians in all ages?[23] And what is one to make of the gender implications of the Wheeler approach? Do the monosyllabic works of Pollard and others justify sex segregation in public school classrooms and gender distinctions in homeschool environments? or, conversely, as the American Civil Liberties Union (ACLU) argues, are such works being promoted in a misguided effort to encourage teachers "to treat girls and boys differently" on the basis of "imprecise" and "inaccurate" "overgeneralizations" and "old stereotypes" about "how boys and girls learn?"[24]

"May I Have a Small Word with You?": Monosyllabic Histories and Literacy

Some of the answers to these questions about the sustainability of monosyllabic histories in the twenty-first century can be found in the changing conceptions of childhood that motivated their authors to write them in the first place. In the last third of the nineteenth century, perceptions about how children developed shifted in response to several factors affecting social conditions in the culture at large. Prior to the Civil War, the concept of a protected childhood was relevant primarily to those upper- and middle-class families whose breadwinners could afford the luxury of sheltering their children "from the stresses and demands of the adult world." However, as Mintz has written, the "grim realities" of postwar industrialization, including "child poverty, juvenile delinquency, and child abuse," called wider attention to low-class families whose offspring had been forced to experience a "useful childhood" before their time. The nature–nurture debate raged also, as those traditionalists who argued that poverty, even in children, was a moral failing lost ground to reformers, who held that living conditions among the young were the dominant factor determining their social standing as adults.[25]

By the mid- to late nineteenth century, an emerging generation of progressive educators influenced by social Darwinism began to study populations of children, especially those at risk, to see what could be done to improve their lives by altering their environments. The resulting "cult of the child" led to the promotion of exposé as a historical genre. Works in this vein included Jacob Riis's *How the Other Half Lives* and George C. Needham's *Street Arabs and Gutter Snipes* as well as paintings of street urchins by J. G. Brown, all of which described in maudlin images and sentimental texts the wretched conditions under which impoverished juveniles lived and struggled.[26] Dickensian depictions of "destitute and delinquent" youths motivated reformers to try to "protect children from the dangers of urban society" by establishing reform schools devoted to rescuing "vulnerable victims of exploitation" and redeeming "misguided souls." Children's relief associations developed educational programs designed, according to Mintz, to "solve social problems and reshape human character by removing children from corrupting outside influence and instilling self-control through moral education, work, rigorous discipline, and an orderly environment."[27]

Childhood was reconceived by these educators—collectively known as child-savers—as a crucial stage of life associated with the earliest years of cognition, during which time pedagogical mistakes were presumed to have lifelong consequences. Young children, they argued, needed stronger instructional guidance than that prescribed by the permissive Pestalozzi method employed by the Abbotts. For older children who had been exposed to educational deprivations at the youngest ages, the effects of a carefully constructed reading program were thought to be especially ameliorative. When the minister Charles Loring Brace witnessed the sight of "thousands of New York children supporting themselves as beggars, flower sellers, and prostitutes," Mintz notes, he attempted to "protect destitute children from [such] pernicious environment[s]" by establishing reading rooms through-out the city. Assuming that children are often indiscriminate consumers of literature, Brace worried that if left to their own devices, as educators like the Abbott brothers had encouraged, young readers would choose sensational-ized works, such as cheap dime novels, rather than more instructive, but also more expensive, literary offerings. Much of Brace's fundraising, therefore, was directed at purchasing morally upright books for use by children who could not afford to discriminate among the literary works they consumed.[28]

Brace may have underestimated the extent to which children of greater means were at least as vulnerable as their underprivileged peers to cheap lit-erature insofar as they had financial access to publications of a frighteningly unrestrained variety. Catherine Beecher warned that "there is a tide of wealth and prosperity setting in to our country unparalleled in extent and power," a tide with the potential to draw the Christian sons and daughters of the nouveau riche "into a current of worldliness and self-indulgence from which they now would shrink with dismay."[29] Disposable income meant that some of these children would undoubtedly make poor decisions with respect to what to read. "Whereas Victorian domesticity had valued the family reading hour, during which a parent read aloud from Charles Dickens, Louisa May Alcott, James Fenimore Cooper, or other approved classic authors," the chil-dren's historian Gail Murray has written of this period, "now children were choosing their own books, which were targeted specifically to adolescents, not families. As a consequence, critics felt an obligation to monitor these juve-nile texts more closely."[30] According to the curators of the Baldwin Library Children's Collection, the sheer number of children's books in the mid-nine-teenth century "belie[s] the way in which societal views about children and the social construction of childhood were becoming more complex during these decades." Indeed, "during the period from 1850 to 1869, it was increas-ingly more difficult for readers, critics and authors to speak of 'childhood,' 'children's literature' and even 'children' as monolithic categories. Through-out these years, these terms were fracturing and splintering in ways that were both delightful and devilish."[31]

The most vigilant of the new custodians of juvenile culture was Anthony Comstock, whose *Traps for the Young* warned of the dangers of indiscrimi-nate reading by children. A special agent of the Post Office Department and a founder of the New York Society for the Suppression of Vice, Comstock con-ducted a decades-long campaign against what he called the menace of "evil reading." He particularly disdained dime novel elements in children's books, which he claimed emptied the youthful mind "of lofty aims and ambitions" and "shrivel[ed]" the soul with their "perverting taste and fancy." Like Goodrich, Comstock condemned such works as "devil-traps" and warned against their "silly, insipid" plots and their "coarse, slang" stories in the "dialect of the barroom, the blood-and-thunder romance of the border life, and the exaggerated details of crimes, real and imaginary." He regretted that "these stories are allowed to become associates for the child's mind and to shape and direct the[ir] thoughts," since such "products of corrupt minds are the eggs from which all kinds of villainies are hatched."[32] Rejecting the unstructured philosophy of the Pestalozzi method of literacy, which left too much up to the unpracticed reader, Comstock advocated more traditional back-to-basics approaches to literacy. At least the works of writers like Goodrich, he reasoned, were characterized by clear, unmistakable moral lessons.[33]

These changing definitions of childhood and the heightened awareness of the power of books to influence young minds that accompanied them had striking effects on the production of popular monosyllabic history books for children. Complaining of historians who presented the past to children "in a style beyond their comprehension," Lydia Sigourney preferred an approach to juvenile writing in which "the memory may be exercised without weariness, and the understanding strengthened, without being disgusted at its nourishment."[34] Given the grand expectations for the genre, it is not surprising that there is little subtlety in histories told in words of one syllable. Their messages are overtly didactic and designed to leave few doubts in the minds of young readers about the right and wrong of history. The religious foundations of the monosyllabic approach to historical learning also encouraged its practitioners to ascribe unusual redemptive qualities to their works. That is, these volumes not only advanced literacy among children for the sake of gaining access to the sacred word of God but also offered extraordinary potential for saving the moral lives of vulnerable young readers. To a publisher like Wheeler, who has reissued monosyllabic works in the name of spiritual revitalization, the moral values implicit in their simple plots and characters are presumed to be eternal. "We present *Stories of American History and Home Life* not as a mere relic, but rather as a vital tool for parents during family devotions," wrote Wheeler of one of his republishing efforts. He argued, "Herein lies the wit and charm of bygone days, when biblical values were standard in an overriding majority of American homes. By exposing your children to the following stories, as parents you have the privilege of elevating your young listeners' vocabulary and instructing them to be God's fearing patriotic citizens who will help to steer the future of the country. Without such training, America has little hope for the future."[35]

This morally grounded monosyllabic technique, reinvigorated by Wheeler in the late twentieth century, had been in limited use as early as the first part of the nineteenth century, when the British author Lucy Aikin, under the pseudonym Lady Mary Godolphin, translated works of great literature, among them *Pilgrim's Progress, Swiss Family Robinson,* and *Robinson Crusoe,* into words of one syllable for children.[36] Her primary goal was to make complex words and sentences simpler for juvenile readers to understand. "By this method the labor of dividing and accentuating words is avoided: a difficulty which pupils who have only attained to the knowledge of monosyllables cannot conquer by independent effort," Godolphin wrote in her preface to *Pilgrim's Progress.*[37] As Amy Weinstein has observed, Godolphin called attention to "the novelty of her approach in bringing one-syllable construction out of the bland spelling book and into the realm of the adventure novel," thereby encouraging children drawn to action tales to master her condensed editions on their way to tackling more complex works. "As soon as you can read yourself," Godolphin advised in the case of her most popular abridgment, "you should read the complete life of Robinson Crusoe."[38] She strove to reduce complicated adult literature into simple monosyllabic texts in keeping with Goodrich's practice rather than requiring simpleminded children to expand unrealistically their phonetic proficiency by trying to master more complex texts, as the Abbotts had recommended. A secondary goal was to help adult beginners who struggled with reading literacy. As Godolphin wrote in her preface to *Pilgrim's Progress,* "There is a large class of persons who do not begin to acquire the art of reading till somewhat late in life, and it is for such that I think a book of this Character is peculiarly applicable."[39]

Although a number of publishing houses experimented with variations on Godolphin's monosyllabic mode throughout the nineteenth century, the British bookseller George Routledge was the first to produce a successful series of popular history books in that format. In the 1880s Routledge's firm printed histories of countries "Told in Words of One Syllable," including heavily pictorialized volumes on the histories of the United States, Ireland, France, Germany, England, Russia, and Japan by such writers as Helen Wall Pierson, Helen Ainslie Smith, and Agnes Sadlier. Although no copybooks of general correspondence or letters from the authors of these works exist in the voluminous archives of George Routledge and Company, extensive contract records suggest that the firm remained committed in its publication of monosyllabic histories to its "original policy and vision, a vision which ran entirely contrary to the high prices and protectionist methods of conservative contemporary publishers."[40] That policy was implemented as early as the summer of 1848, when Routledge marketed volumes of his "Railway Library" to a bookstall in London's Euston Station, "and other outlets soon sprouted in stations throughout the country." The literary historians James and Patience Barnes note that as "demand for titles in the series grew, [a vendor] placed a standing order for one thousand copies of each new volume, ushering in the era of mass marketing."[41]

Routledge, the nineteenth-century publisher who was most responsible for initiating the genre that resulted eventually in twenty-first-century republications of works such as Pollard's *The History of the United States,* was also one of the industry's first republishers. According to the company's archivist, the Routledge firm "started in a somewhat raffish manner in the middle years of the century by pirating works of fiction and then producing them cheaply for the new and enormously influential railway bookstalls."[42] As the historian Aileen Fyfe acknowledges, "It was an uncertain business in which Routledge did not always have the law on his side."[43] Although he compensated financially a few authors who sought legal redress from such thievery, most were not reimbursed. Routledge continued to thrive throughout the mid-nineteenth century by reprinting at reduced costs the works of authors, primarily British and American ones, whose books were not protected by copyright.[44]

In the field of history Routledge was especially forward-looking, defying the conventional wisdom of Goodrich and others that young readers should have access primarily to scaled-down versions of adult works written without concessions to juvenile audiences. Routledge recognized that children constituted a growing new market in England and elsewhere, and he designed books with their specific needs in mind. He perceived that new conceptions of childhood in Victorian Britain, with their attendant interests in childhood play and leisure, meant the prospect of more and better-educated young readers of history. Routledge enjoyed original success with versions of Dickens's *A Child's History of England,* which the publisher reproduced in multiple design layouts in response to the "transformation of the market for children's books from a limited upper-middle-class market to a mass market."[45] As Fyfe notes, Routledge "often published the same titles in formats varying in sixpenny increments from 1s ("Every Boy's Library") to 3s6d ("Reward Books"), depending on the quality of the paper, the number of illustrations and the style of the binding."[46] As the "stratification of readership intensified," the publisher circulated internationally a *Catalogue of a Thousand Juvenile Books* that included listings for works in "Routledge's Historical Course," for example, *Home Lessons; or Learning Made Pleasant by Means of Pictures and Stories.*[47]

By the 1880s, however, it was the monosyllabic histories that really established Routledge's place in the popular history book market.[48] Everything about these works was highly formulaic. The Routledge recipe was as simple and as clear as the monosyllabic methodologies employed by the firm's authors: don't overwhelm children with convoluted narratives that require complex laws of historical explanation or that introduce confusing new perspectives on the role of causality in history. Instead, Routledge promoted standardized works that catalogued monarchical reigns and presidential administrations and provided the foundations necessary for the stockpiling of factual information about the past. Helen A. Smith, who produced the volume on the history of Russia, found the formulaic regimentation of the Routledge outlook a bit limiting. "In bulk I have written more than ½ the ms. of my Routledge book," she wrote to a friend, "but thru some misunderstanding part of it will have to be laid out, as giving too much on one subject. I'm 'in heaps' with it, with new matter & proofs just now, but that will all be straightened out by the end of the week."[49] Smith also balked at the seeming disinterest of the editors at Routledge in the subtle peculiarities of Russian history, which she felt warranted more copy space. Presentation, she concluded, was often valued over substance in such formulaic works: "After all the *subject is* little to talk about; it's the *treatment*—the conception of it & the language that makes the book."[50]

Routledge's histories relied heavily on the rote learning principles implicit in the sight/word approaches to literacy instruction introduced decades before by Goodrich, Gallaudet, Mann, and others. Children who read "Histories Told in One Syllable Words" were encouraged to memorize a lexicon of discrete historical episodes that corresponded to the simple word lists used in monosyllabic readers (fig. 9). Specific peoples, places, and dates were the morphemes of this language of historical discourse, and they collectively defined the master narrative of the past for young readers. This routine was popular among schoolteachers, who issued their students handbooks for refining memorization skills and who oversaw regular weekly classroom recitation exercises that tested a student's capacity for the retention of facts.[51] Readers were asked to commit to memory answers to questions sprinkled throughout Routledge's texts, such as, "Do you know the name of the ship [the Pilgrims] came in? It is a sweet name, and you must keep it in your mind—the *Mayflower?*"[52] The pedagogical goal was to stockpile specific information until a sizable vocabulary of exact historical facts had been mastered. Only then might a student be encouraged to ponder the more complex, integrative processes related to causality and historical explanation. The key was for young readers to be able to discriminate between bona fide facts and unsubstantiated opinions. To these ends, Smith warned consumers of her *History of Japan in Words of One Syllable* that much of the early history of that country "is naught but tales; and though these form a part of the story of the growth of the realm, all folks on our side of the globe at least, know that they must not be read for truth." They show readers "more of the strange forms of the Japanese faith than of real facts in their history."[53]

Purchasers of Routledge's histories believed the monosyllabic volumes had a salutary effect on the historical sensibilities of children. A reviewer for the *Critic* in 1887 appreciated the concessions made to young readers by these popular historians: "It was a capital idea of Miss Helen Ainslie [Smith]'s to tell the story and dramatic history of two such nations as Japan and Russia 'in words of one syllable,'" the commentator wrote. "Such difficulties for the young readers as 'military,' 'necessary,' and the uncondensable proper names are removed by skilful dissection and the separate parts skewered together with hyphens." Special praise was directed at Smith's attention to factual detail: "We are glad that these books, though intended for beginners in reading, have been written by a competent author, who has followed the best authorities, so that the young minds will not be perverted by false statements." The reviewer added, "Occasionally we find a word misprinted, but altogether the performance is commendable." Timed smartly by Routledge's business department for a Christmas release, Smith's books "will doubtless bulge out of many a Christmas stocking in the year of grace, 1887," the *Critic* predicted, and must have a positive reconciling impact on the young disciples "of Mikado, Tsar, and President . . . respectively. Long may the double-eagle, eagle and dragon keep peace!"[54]

Routledge's monosyllabic texts were so successful in England that the firm began marketing them in the United States at an office in New York City set up for that purpose. The volumes were quickly—and ironically, given Routledge's own history of pirating—copied by other American publishers eager to capitalize on their format. Lax copyright laws being what they were, it was common in the United States to find a single work issued by multiple publishing houses simultaneously, each trying to edge out its competitors by capturing the lion's share of a variegated market. As noted earlier, one of the first authors to be victimized by this practice was Goodrich, but he was by no means the last. Works with titles like *Histories Told in Words of One Syllable* were published by the thousands during the late nineteenth century, not necessarily by Routledge alone even though he had commissioned most of the originals.[55] For instance, A. L. Burt Publishers of New York advertised *One-Syllable Histories* in clothbound sets at prices ranging from twenty-five cents to a dollar a volume. These books were similar to the Routledge edition in almost every detail save for their slightly inferior cover art, a cost-cutting measure that allowed Burt to underprice Routledge and thereby outsell him.[56] Routledge's monosyllabic texts were altered more noticeably by some American publishers, who hired their own authors to produce knockoffs of

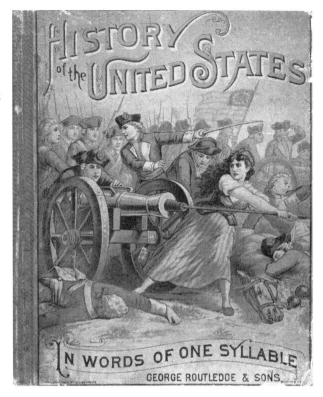

the originals. In light of these editorial practices, it is fascinating, in the view of the curators of the Baldwin Library of Historical Children's Literature, "how different versions [of these works] were typeset, bound, and marketed in different historical eras and the impact that these changes had on critical interpretation as well as popular reception."[57] While the process was consistent, the complex production histories of works in the one-syllable genre during this era of appropriation and adaptation reveal that no portion of a manuscript was immune to revision, no passage was sacrosanct.

An American firm, McLoughlin Brothers, led the way in this redactive behavior, using inventive means to control the market for books "not chock full of great big words."[58] Founded in the 1830s by a former coachman's apprentice, the New York City publishing house manufactured games, toys, puzzles, and paper dolls and reprinted mainly illustrated children's works.[59] McLoughlin beat Routledge at his own game, not only outperforming the piratical British publisher in establishing a mass market for recycled juvenile works among American children, but also plundering Routledge's treasure trove of works to accomplish the feat. Cutting costs by abridging and altering

Routledge's texts and reducing the number of pages, McLoughlin Brothers sold its histories for seventy-five cents each, while Routledge's *One-Syllable Histories* cost one dollar apiece.[60] The firm also introduced middle-class children to a genre of history books designed expressly with American needs in mind.[61] Hence, the McLoughlin Brothers' file at the San Francisco Public Library includes British books that have been annotated by the McLoughlin editorial staff to accommodate the American market. For instance, the library owns a British edition of *Mrs. Dove's Party* with marginalia that include an editor's proposal to "change Rule Britannia to Hail Columbia." Suggestions for name changes—Harry to Hank, Jackdaw to Bluejay, Kine to Kitten, and Queen to Quince—are sprinkled throughout the annotated works as well, and even McLoughlin's artists were asked frequently to redraw images, such as when an art editor requested that a colorist make the gate in one vignette of the *Blue Bells on the Lea* "look American."[62]

McLoughlin's writers stayed truthful to the general storylines created by Routledge's authors, to be sure, and they did not alter purposefully the historical record to accommodate their marketing needs, but they were not above doctoring texts tonally to account for the ideological demands of American readers. Hence, when Routledge's Helen W. Pierson wrote of the faults of Native Americans in her *History of the United States* (1883), she did so by intimating to British readers that American settlers in the New World had failed these tribes. "They made their wars in a strange and fierce style, and wore at their belts locks of hair, cut from the heads of those slain by their hands. These locks, cut from the head with part of the skin, they call a scalp," Pierson wrote. "It was the pride of an Indian to have scalps hung at his belt. No one taught him that this was wrong, and he did not have the Word of God to show him the right way."[63] A year later, in 1884, Pollard described the same traits in McLoughlin's *History of the United States,* drawing directly on Pierson's text but altering it slightly to shift the blame away from white Americans, whom she depicted as intent on promoting "the Word of God," and to make use of it to reform an unresponsive native people (fig. 10). In describing Native Americans, she wrote, "When they killed a man, they would cut off his scalp, which was the skin of his head with the hair on, and these scalps were tied to their belts and worn with much pride." But Pollard then came to the defense of American colonists: "These were not nice men to meet with in a strange land, and as you read on you will learn how the white men had to fight these foes, and in what ways they tried to make friends with the red men."[64]

McLoughlin Brothers experimented with literary voice and narrative presentation as well. Critics had complained that Godolphin's system, by her own admission, "involves the use of words which, though short, are difficult to

FIGURE 10.
Josephine Pollard, *The History of the United States Told in One Syllable Words* (New York: McLoughlin Brothers, 1884).

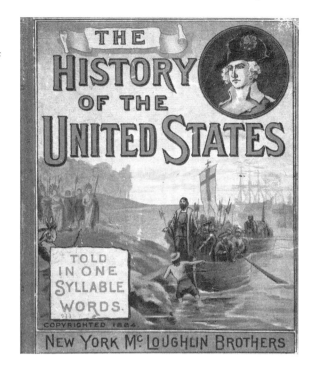

understand and might be made more intelligible in polysyllabic language."[65] Jacob Abbott, who rejected this practice, argued that the "difficulty with most books intended for children just learning to read, is, that the writers make so much effort to confine themselves to *words of one syllable,* that the style is quaint and uninteresting, and often far more unintelligible than the usual language would be."[66] To address this challenge, McLoughlin hired so-called fanciful writers such as Annie Cole Cady, who wrote whimsical volumes under the aforementioned pseudonym Robin Goodfellow, Fairy Historian.[67] Harry Thurston, a literary critic, editor, and scholar, applauded this and others of McLoughlin's imaginative strategies in *Bookman:* "Had we the revenues of a multi-millionaire we should send each Christmas Day our personal cheque for ten thousand dollars to the Messrs. McLoughlin of this city. [They] still put forth those good old classics whose pages show the very subtlest literary gifts and which have long ago secured a glorious immortality."[68] As Avery points out, Thurston "deplored the theories of 'educationalists' who, he said, had thrown out nursery rhymes and fairy tales, and he praised the McLoughlin brothers for keeping 'the sacred flame alight.' "[69]

Whether produced by Routledge, Burt, or McLoughlin, these monosyllabic works were approved generally by parents and educators, who appreciated the allowances they made to young readers. "There is no book in the market filling its place," noted one reviewer of Routledge's *History of the United States in Words of One Syllable* in the *New York School Journal*. "Mrs. Pierson has done her work well, and this is great praise, for it is a most difficult task to write history so as to be interesting to young people and yet keep out all but history. This work is here done, and for this we heartily commend the book."[70] The *New England Journal of Education* praised Helen Ainslie Smith's *One Hundred Famous Americans* for its presentation and commitment to facts, remarking, "Happy the boy into whose life *this admirable array of great men and women,* with all the illustrations, portraits, and designs, enters." The reviewer added, "The selection of characters, and the characteristics of each, are as noticeable as the attractive way in which the facts are put."[71] A teacher, M. Louise Comstock, concurred, adding with respect to Pierson's work, "The one syllable 'History of the United States' has been used in my school with great success, and I regard it as a *most valuable book,* just filling a want I have long felt—an interesting account of our own country simple enough for beginners."[72]

Most important of all, children responded well to these monosyllabic volumes. Sales figures are hard to determine with precision for mass-marketed popular histories, but the sheer number of volumes issued in the category of books written "in words of one syllable" implies that sales were brisk. As Smith boasted to a friend, "From a mercantile point of view, [*One Hundred Famous Americans*] is 'doing wonders,' I hear from the publishers & dealers in the trade. I believe the publishers are already making arrangements for another edition."[73] Much of this success no doubt can be attributed to the concessions made to young readers by authors like Pollard and Smith, who worked with children's needs expressly in mind. As the McLoughlin catalogue testified, such volumes "were written in charming style" and with a "clearness and simplicity" that children appreciated.[74] "Verily there is a new era in this country in the literature for children," an essayist in *Putnam's Magazine* wrote in 1868 with reference to the booming children's book trade. "It is not very long since all the juvenile books seemed conducted on the principle of the definition of duty 'doing what you don't want to,'" the reviewer added, since all "the books that were interesting were not considered good, and the 'good' ones were certainly not interesting." Now, however, "we have a different order of things, and books for children are about as varied in their scope as those for grown people."[75] That variety was more derivative, perhaps, than the reviewer wished to acknowledge, but there was no doubt that by the late 1880s monosyllabic histories had established themselves as a distinct and substantial genre in the field of American children's literature.

But does it make sense to republish and market such monosyllabic works today, given the conditions under which they were produced originally? Are the literary and financial decisions made by Routledge, McLoughlin, and Burt as they published their nineteenth-century works relevant to republishers in the twenty-first century? Historicizing these texts and understanding the original circumstances of their publication are useful exercises for evaluating the suitability of adapting them for present-day usage.

"The Busy Daughters of Clio": Women Historians and Children's Literature

The child-savers who circulated monosyllabic histories averred that such works were most effective when introduced into controlled learning environments by facilitators with special interest in their proper receptivity among children. Tellingly, Routledge and McLoughlin employed primarily women to write the books that flooded the juvenile literary marketplace in the last third of the nineteenth century.[76] This business decision was influenced by many factors, but among the most central was the presumption that women had special insight into the historical sensibilities of children. "Convinced that the stability of the new republic depended on a virtuous citizenry, the post-revolutionary generation called for more intensive styles of child-rearing and more prolonged and systematic forms of education," Mintz has written, insisting that the "primary responsibility for instilling republican virtues in children rested with mothers, who required better education to meet this high responsibility."[77] A commentator from the *American Annals of Education* supported such initiatives, noting that books such as Routledge's monosyllabic histories were offered not merely as amusement for periods of dalliance but were to be "companions of serious hours" and "made more intelligible and impressive by the practiced voice of the mother, and, in fact, almost form the moral atmosphere in which the child moves."[78]

In the Victorian era, in which monosyllabic histories reached the height of their popularity, women were associated closely with the "domestic education" of children, which, in terms of history, meant educating their offspring to the ancient virtues of hearth and home. As Nina Baym has noted, reading histories by the fireplace was a way of strengthening familial bonds between mothers and children in a homeschooling environment. Likewise, Sigourney stressed the potential benefits of the practice in the introduction to one of her popular histories: "This book was commenced as an assistant to parents, in domestic education. Its highest ambition is to be in the hand of the mother, who seeks to aid in that most delightful of all departments, the instruction of her little ones." The "homelike institutional space" in which the mother narrates history "makes teaching seem like women's natural work," Baym added; the home, "when used for the mother's teaching, becomes a classroom." History books written by women enhanced the meaningfulness of these exchanges, since the models of learning featured in them centered on female expertise. For instance, the authors of these popular works often adopted a dialogic or conversational format in which "the provider of history" was depicted often as "a mother teaching her children of assorted ages (and both sexes) at home." The goal was to make children "feel at home with history by funneling it through the maternal voice," a channel characterized by "its frequent endearments, its endorsement of affective reactions to information, its attunement to student response, and its receptiveness to audience questions." Collectively, these works participated in what Baym has called "the project of redefining motherhood as an intellectual and civic function." By "assigning historical and doctrinal expertise to the mother," such works "confirm[ed] her domestic mission while greatly extending her intellectual reach."[79]

Women writers adopted quaint narrative devices in their monosyllabic works that affirmed the maternal links between the author and her young readers. More credible even than Goodrich's grandfatherly Peter Parley, whose veracity, as we have seen, some children came to doubt, these maternal narrators reduced the barriers between home study and school. Ella Stratton, for instance, wrote a series of juvenile histories in which children under the tutelage of Mamma Nelson took field trips to places of historical import. Not a teacher but an involved parent, Nelson impresses upon her young charges the value of integrating history into their everyday lives. In Stratton's *Child's History of Our Great Country from the Earliest Discoveries to the Present Time* (1902), a young boy named Bennie seeks out Mamma Nelson for help in learning about the "Story of Our Nation." His class at school is competing for a prize (revealingly, a library of popular histories for children) that will be awarded to those students who can prove "they understand the history of the United States the best." In pursuit of this reward, Bennie and his classmates decide to spend Friday and Saturday nights studying at the home of their matriarch. Calling themselves the Old White House Club, these students compete for the bobbles and affection that the idealized figure of Mamma Nelson dispenses after each successful foray into the past. They are transformed by Nelson's motherly methods. "I always hated history," the character Phinney admits to his matronly mentor, "but [now] I shall read every book in the historical library,—when we get it."[80]

These mothering narrative devices had a discernible effect on the perception of "women as conveyors of historical information."[81] Maternal narrators were presumed to have a long cognitive reach, extending back to the earliest stages of child development. Leslie Howsam has noticed that in England, for instance, Charlotte Yonge proposed "a new 'baby history'" for preliterate youth on the grounds that "one finds children must—or mamma thinks they must—learn names and ideas about English kings before they can read." Howsam argues that the "language used by Victorian authors and publishers about histories for children is telling," since "nursery histories" and "baby histor[ies]" point to how vital a study of the past was to the process of nurturing and developing the very youngest children's minds, the unique province of women.[82] They were also beneficial to those raising such young learners. In *Stories of Bible History for Little Ones,* Yonge adopted the persona of Aunt Charlotte to inform children of nursery school age about the value of historical narratives. Yonge said of Charlotte that for years she had trans-lated the Bible to "little scholars and friends" who were too young to read it themselves, although even "the older people used to come to the Infant Class room to hear her explain it."[83] Across the ocean, Lucy Lombardi Barber, act-ing under a similar maternal impulse on behalf of the preliterate, published *A Nursery History of the United States.*[84]

Women, it was assumed, had special insight into the gender distinctions that educators believed existed between boys and girls. For many in the nine-teenth century as well as for some republishers today, this meant that boys valued military conflicts, technology, and politics, while girls appreciated social drama and character development. "If there is fighting, action, adven-ture, rampaging elephants, blood-thirsty pirates, cannibals, sword fights, exploding cannons, despicable villains, harrowing sea-battles, horrific trench warfare, fantastic escapes, and general danger then you can be pretty sure that you've got boy stuff," Adam and Alice of Heritage History have apprised customers with regard to the gender preferences among readers of historical literature. Conversely, girls preferred "personal drama" and were attracted to the "heroine who *seduces a few Roman emperors, or assassinates the leader of the French Revolution,* or connives and manipulates her way to the throne before getting her *head cut off.*"[85] Around the beginning of the twentieth century the popular historian Kate Dickinson Sweetser published separate volumes of history for each gender, *Ten Girls from History* and *Ten Boys from History,* which were designed to underscore the unique, distinctive "deeds of patriotism and courage" evidenced by boys and by girls during times of national crisis.[86] Similarly, special McLoughlin editions of literary portraits of male and female children in Dickens's novels were released under the twin titles *The Boys of Dickens Retold* and *The Girls of Dickens Retold.* This format connoted not only the gender particularities perpetuated by nineteenth-century publishers but also the degree to which canonical works of literature were revised to serve the specific needs of niche markets, in this case gendered ones.[87]

Given the presumed sensitivity of women to gender and moral distinctions, publishers often hired them to tone down the provocative, sensationalizing works of their male counterparts. In England, for instance, Mrs. Markham's (Elizabeth Penrose) *History of England* (1823) and Lady Maria Callcott's *Little Arthur's History of England* (1835) offered their juvenile histories as "dilations" of David Hume's *History of England*. Both "were written in the voice of a middle-class woman instructing children in a domestic setting," Howsam notes. Indeed, "'Mrs. Markham' begins with an adolescent Markham grumbling about his difficulties with reading Hume, and his mother's offer to 'entertain and instruct' Richard, along with his younger brother and sister, by telling a succession of stories from the past."[88] Several decades later Mary Howitt updated Hume for mid-nineteenth-century readers, adopting Mrs. Markham's literary conventions in the process. "I have, for the sake of consistency, maintained the little fiction of Authorship by supposing the wife of one of worthy Mrs. Markham's sons, to continue the narrative to her children," Howitt confided, "and I hope in so doing I have written in the spirit of the original."[89]

The success of such reductionist works in the literary marketplace furthered the reputation of women historians for making the complex understandable. Because literacy is a way of transmitting not only knowledge but also values, female authors of monosyllabic histories demonstrated that simplicity aided in achieving reading competency in children and in addition served as a practical guide for helping boys and girls deal with the challenges they might face in life. Establishing moral rules was the key component of this process, and here again women were thought to have unusual insights into the minds and habits of children, writing feminized morality tales centered on those aspects of the "realms of human experience" in which "women were better revealed."[90] They used their powers of maternal persuasion and imposition of guilt to direct the behaviors of their young readers. Cady, for instance, urged juvenile readers of her monosyllabic books to gain a sense of their responsibilities for good behavior on the basis of their obligations to family and country. In a monosyllabic book on the State of Pennsylvania, she addressed young readers as follows: "Your fathers for over two hundred years have kept its history so pure that its very name has come to mean a just and upright people. In war and in peace its records have been the same. But a few years must pass ere you are the men and women from whose acts the history of that day will be made. So it is plain that while you thank God for giving you this grand old State for your birthright, you are in duty bound to study hard at school and make yourselves wise and good, so that when its honor rests in your hands, you may add to its luster a purer, higher light than any which has been shed upon it in the days which are past."[91]

Women historians were alleged to understand more fully than their male counterparts the subtle gradations of behavior that children demonstrated. They employed nuanced modes of analysis to instill in young readers a clear, simple sense of right and wrong, commenting on the codified rules of comportment for children (the behavioral dos and don'ts) through the good and bad actions of the protagonists in their works. Good behavior was associated with activities that advanced the causes of home and country; bad behavior, which was featured more prominently in such literature, was affiliated with the subversion of domestic and parental authority. In *Our Naval Heroes: Told in One Syllable Words,* Pollard moralized about why disobedient boys who ran away to sea often paid a high price for their wanderlust. "It used to be quite the style for boys to run off to sea when things did not please them at home," Pollard sermonized. "If they thought they could loll on deck and take their ease, play tricks and do just as they liked, they soon found out their mistake, when they got on ship-board, and oh! How some of them longed for the nice bed, the good food, and the kind of friends to whom they were so glad to say good-by!" The "deck rules" for these school-ships were quite strict, she noted, and they were directed at "bad boys" who would "sometimes get on board, and would play all sorts of pranks, if they were not held in check with strong reins." Tellingly, she added, such boys often "watched for a chance, and ran back to the homes which they had learned to prize, and proved by this act that they were not born to be heroes." Pollard was quick to advise that good boys should remain at home to be schooled until they were mature enough to adapt to the rigors of the sea and to accept the burdens of military service: "For it is a well-known fact, that when the time of need comes, the right kind of men find their way to the front, and do deeds that not only make their own names famous, but prompt all boys to be brave and true, to stand man-ful-ly at the post where duty calls and to die, if need be, for the cause they have at heart."[92]

Female authors tried to parse out transitional behaviors that fell somewhere on the spectrum between very good and very bad. Hence, Pollard was willing to point out the flaws of even so fine a good boy as George Washington in order to help young readers understand that all humans are prone to some bad behaviors, ones which were correctible under the right guidance. "But you must not think that George Washington was such a good-good boy that he could guide himself, and did not need to be kept in check," Pollard wrote with respect to maternal authority (since his father had died when he was younger). "He was too high strung, as quick as a flash, and felt that he was born to rule," she wrote, "and these traits his mother had to keep down and train so that they would not wreck the boy."[93] As awkward as specialized terms like "good-good" boy or "bad-bad" boy were, nonetheless they were important markers on a values spectrum limited in its gradations by the simplicity of the monosyllabic terms available to describe behavior. In straightforward terminology they served to remind young readers of the subtle distinctions within the broad categories of human comportment and of women's special insight into these subtleties by virtue of their abilities as mothers to understand that moral character is ever in the process of developing or declining in children. Delicate gradations could be perceived best by women historians, it was argued, because they were responsible primarily for developing and implementing the moral algorithms used in American homes to raise those special children who would someday assume their proper places in history.

For these and other reasons, publishers of monosyllabic histories such as Routledge and McLoughlin felt that women were positioned best to dispense the kind of historical wisdom from which young children could benefit most. Yet they rarely compensated women writers of history adequately for these capacities. Nineteenth-century book publishing was first and foremost a competitive business with small profit margins and high risks, and women faced serious economic discrimination in virtually every field of employment. Women writers were paid less, in some cases substantially less, than their male counterparts for writing and revising books, and any savings in the costs of production were valued. The daughters of the popular novelist Edward Eggleston, Allegra and Lillie, who had collaborated with their father on a series of biographies of famous Americans for young people, were asked by their publisher, D. Appleton, to take a pay cut so that the poor sales of the works would not reflect badly on their father's reputation. When the daughters complained of this unfair adjustment to their contract, Appleton responded defensively: "It is a very great disappointment to us that the books have not done better, and we are still afraid that quite a number of them may be returned, and we are naturally doubtful of the outlook for the present season."[94] Most such excuses were designed to camouflage the real causes of underpayment: gender discrimination of the sort that had given birth, ironically, to the genre of monosyllabic histories in the first place. That is, the very forces that had encouraged publishers to promote volumes in a gendered monosyllabic book market in which women emerged as the most powerful motive force also encouraged book manufacturers to distinguish between male and female authors in terms of financial compensation.

FIGURE 11.
Portrait of Josephine Pollard.
Marguerite Dawson Winant,
A Century of Sorosis, 1868–1968
(Uniondale, N.Y.: Printed by
Salisbury Printers, 1968), 75.

Pollard's experience is highly revealing in this regard (fig. 11).[95] The devoted daughter of a prominent architect in New York City, she had been educated at the Abbott brothers' Spingler Institute, where school records indicate that she "gave evidence of poetic talent."[96] She began her professional life as a public school teacher in the first ward school of Brooklyn, but after the premature death of her father and the departure of her only brother for the Civil War, she was forced to support her mother and sisters.[97] She took up work eventually as a nanny and tutor in Stamford, Connecticut, a job that did not challenge her intellectually. Letters Pollard wrote to her brother on the battlefield hint that she found her life in Stamford rather monotonous. "I hope to feel more ambition than I feel at present," she wrote. "It seems that the longer I remain the more stupid I get."[98] In order to stave off boredom, Pollard wrote verse, some of which she published, and eventually she supported herself, if only modestly, as a writer of "miscellaneous character," producing poetry, books, reviews, and hymns.[99] She was one of the early participants in the Chautauqua movement, a revival-style camp meeting devoted to adult education, and wrote the "call to arms" for the first Chautauqua Assembly in 1874.[100] She worked in the social gospel tradition as well, creating a series titled Gypsy Books that were popular among child-savers because they told the story of "a thorough, irrepressible child, who is wild enough and hard enough to manage, but who, under the right sort of influences, at last resolves to be 'awful good,' and means it."[101] A reviewer for the *Patchogue Advance* said the Gypsy volumes were "[as] popular as they were weird." The reviewer averred that "no writer in America ever depicted the life and romance of these wandering tribes with more consummate skill."[102]

In spite of being highly prolific, Pollard had trouble making ends meet financially throughout an independent writing career that lasted thirty years. She tried to improve her lot by associating with one of several established publishing firms, such as when she approached the publisher S. S. McClure in 1890 seeking a permanent position on the staff of one of his magazines. Presuming she was known to McClure "by reputation," Pollard judged that her freelance writing had done little to secure her financial future. "Although my work has been before the public for nearly a quarter of a century, I have led a secluded life, and am personally unknown to the literati," she wrote. "In order to avoid the uncertainties and anxieties of literary life—to some extent at least—I would like to obtain a position where my work would be acceptable, and my income assured." With reference to her preferred literary treatment in works such as her *History of the Battles of America in Words of One Syllable,* Pollard said, "I am versatile" and not wedded to any particular style "unless it is One Syllable work."[103] No offer was tendered, however, likely because McClure benefited financially from continuing to employ her as a freelance writer. Publishers held the purse strings and wielded the financial power. Perhaps Helen A. Smith summarized the financial vulnerabilities of these women best when she confided the following about her monosyllabic work on the history of Russia: "This is not a means of making money at present; . . . I suppose I must be content with that & making small moneys till I've passed though the period. One cannot always afford to make money even though one wants to."[104]

These inequities highlight the fact that the writing of history, even juvenile history, was a gendered, politicized activity in the nineteenth century, one with economic but also intellectual consequences for authors, publishers, and readers. They bespeak how power functioned in the literary marketplace and how gender conditioned the production and receptivity of popular works. Julie Des Jardins sees the effects of gender on historical practice in this period as being extensive, especially for women who wrote histories without having access to the resources available to men. In some cases these negative influences had positive effects, such as when women like Pollard, Pierson, Smith, and Sadlier demonstrated imagination and resolve in working outside established forms to tell history in personalized ways. They were among those female historians whom Des Jardins describes as "savvy marketers and disseminators of their versions of the past on the grassroots level," women who promoted their works to classrooms, popular markets, and mass consumers. A few used their positions as outsiders to challenge standardized versions of history, writing social and cultural history from the "bottom-up" by using artifacts and resources found in unconventional places.[105] In many other cases, however, women authors could not overcome the obstacles they faced in the literary marketplace, and these adverse circumstances of production made many reviewers skeptical of the value of their works. In the case of histories told in words of one syllable, such limitations did much to undercut faith in children's historical literature as a genre.

The failure to compensate women adequately was a central factor in the widespread criticism monosyllabic works received in the press, but a still more challenging obstacle was the barriers many women historians faced in gaining access to valuable archival materials needed for conducting original historical research. As Howsam has explained, the male scholars and curators who controlled historical resources often refused to allow women to use them on the grounds that "female learning had long been associated with unwomanly and even immoral conduct." These men "were condescending about women's work, and others were downright scornful," she adds, "disparag[ing] wholesale the [efforts] of 'ladies' as writers of serious history books."[106] Such attitudes and restrictions impacted unavoidably the kinds of histories popular women historians could produce as well as critics' reactions to them. For instance, as Rosemary Mitchell has pointed out, a reviewer assessing Katherine Thomson's *Life and Times of George Villiers, Duke of Buckingham* (1860) for the *Saturday Review*, "hailed her coyly as 'quite a mother in Israel among the busy daughters of Clio'" but went on to discredit her and her sister (also an author) "by ironical reflections on their limited learning, scope of subject matter, and depth and breadth of historical criticism in comparison with male historians such as Macaulay and J. A. Froude."[107]

Helen Smith experienced some condescension in her relationship with her former teacher, the Reverend Frederic A. Adams of the Young Ladies Seminary and Boarding School of Orange, New Jersey.[108] The correspondence between Smith and her mentor reveals that years after her departure from the seminary, she was still dependent on her male instructor for expressions of confidence and security. She was reluctant to submit any work for publication, for instance, until Adams had approved it. "I have a poor opinion of my judgment in fine points on literary matters," she admitted to him.¹⁰⁹ In a self-deprecating fashion not atypical of women writers of monosyllabic histories, she acknowledged her "lazy mind" and promised that it was a condition she "earnestly" hoped to be "growing out of." When she reported to Adams that she had received some encouragement from G. P. Putnam's about a monosyllabic history of Russia for children—a confidence that she said "has begun to quite rouse my enthusiasm"—Adams quickly put Smith in her place.¹¹⁰ Conveying his disapproval of the kind of juvenile literature she was writing, he scolded her as follows: "What times have we fallen upon that the children are going to read the history of Russia?"¹¹¹ On those few occasions when Smith ventured out on her own, submitting written work to a publisher without seeking preapproval from her mentor, Adams informed her that he could have saved her much embarrassment had she consulted him. His advice to her was to slow down the pace of her writing and to study her subject matter more carefully. "So *five* volumes, it seems, lie behind you, witnesses of your honest toil of eye, hand and brain," Adams wrote his charge. One might have hoped for more, he hinted, "but this is *the work* your hand has found to do, and you have done it with [all] your might. How pleasant, if you could pause now, and study!"¹¹²

Smith agreed with the criticisms of her mentor and wished for better from herself as well. "Though my aims are still the same, first class historical work in books &, a school paper for children," she wrote to Adams, "I realize that with my limitations there is even after five years of hard work, all of which has been directly serviceable, a great deal of knowledge & experience to be gained before these aims can be successfully accomplished." Smith could not "pause to study," as Adams had recommended, however, because she could not afford to do so. Badly injured in a carriage accident that resulted in a broken hip, pelvis, leg, and ankle, she was mired for years in litigation that ultimately netted her only eighteen hundred dollars in damages. Forced to write children's histories as a way to make money quickly, Smith complained frequently about the kind of disagreeable work she felt compelled to do in association with "those one syllable books" that "take up a good deal of my time."¹¹³ She confided to Adams that she wanted to "do something toward making my way before the public, i.e. articles acceptable to the best publications, to become known to the Editors of leading papers & magazines," but she despaired of her lack of education and the availability of resources. Admitting with submissive compliance to a certain laziness and "tendency to scatter," Smith identified her real problem as the superficiality associated with writing for children. "I wish I were more given to pursuing one thing a long way than taking up a great many so easily," she confessed. "I wish a beam would strike me, as it were, and make me do some one thing (& a good-paying thing, too) as well as it were possible." Adams was not very encouraging of these aspirations, advising her patronizingly, "Do not hurry, do not be—what shall I say, 'too ambitious,' or simply 'ambitious.'"[114]

What are we to make of the fact that, despite the success of one-syllable volumes in the popular book market, they were not regarded as "ambitious" even by the authors who submitted them for publication? Considering that such works for children were criticized as being superficial by those who produced them, one must ask again: Is it appropriate for the republished works of popular historians such as Pollard, Pierson, Smith, and Sadlier to be used as learning tools for educating homeschooled children in the twenty-first century?

A Problematic Past

Given all the obstructions women historians faced in the nineteenth century, it is not surprising to discover that most of their popular histories for children do not meet the minimum standards for historical acceptability as defined by the scholarly codes of professional historians in the twenty-first century. Many of these monosyllabic histories contain too many factual mistakes to be trusted, for instance. Some errors were minor, such as when Pierson wrote in her *History of the United States* that Daniel Webster and Henry Clay died on the same day, when, in fact, they died months apart in the same year. (She may have been thinking of John Adams and Thomas Jefferson, who did die on the same day, and not just any day but the fiftieth anniversary of the signing of the Declaration of Independence, 4 July 1826.)[115] Cady interpolated dates, asserting that the British major Robert Rogers attacked the French during Pontiac's Rebellion in 1670 rather than in 1760, the actual date.[116] Pollard stated that Henry Hudson traveled with John Smith on his first trip to Jamestown, Virginia, in 1607. Hudson knew Smith personally, and they corresponded after the fact about the trip, but Hudson never went on the voyage.[117] Nor did Sir Walter Raleigh travel to the New World to help found the Roanoke colony in the 1580s, as Pierson alleged. She argued incorrectly that Raleigh "took out the first folks to North America," arriving with "two ships, and found the red skins kind. They bought him gifts, and he went back to tell of all the strange things he had seen, and soon came to live on the new shores."[118] In fact, Raleigh never traveled to the American colonies, engaged as he was in political disputes in England. Cady exacerbated Pierson's misstatements by claiming that in 1603 "Sir Walter Raleigh, Captain George Popham and James Davis came once more to Virginia, and made some small forts, which the

Indians soon tore down."[119] This would have been difficult for Raleigh to do since he was in prison in the Tower of London at the time, having fallen out of favor with King James.

In addition to such misstatements of fact, monosyllabic historians were guilty of misquoting historical figures and misrepresenting historical events. In recounting the death of Edward Braddock in the French and Indian War, Pierson professed that the British general's last words were conciliatory ones to the colonial militiaman George Washington, who had tried to warn the general about the likelihood of the ambush that left Braddock mortally wounded. "Oh! If I had but done as you said, all might have been well—or at least loss would not have been so great," Pierson's Braddock laments."[120] No such self-reflexive words were ever spoken. Dozens of eyewitnesses to Braddock's death recorded the fallen general's true last words: "Who would have thought it possible?," a question that intimated that no one, not even Washington, could have anticipated the attack.[121] Furthermore, Pierson writes in the *Lives of the Presidents* that John Brown "was hung, and on his way to the place where he was to give up his life his last act was to kiss a babe in a slave's arms."[122] As the historian James C. Malin has protested, this symbolic gesture was an impossibility because the "public was excluded from any possible direct contact with the prisoner" for fear of a rescue attempt. In fact, the baby-kissing incident was introduced as a hoax in a *New York Tribune* article of 1859 and was developed into a national myth by the poet John Greenleaf Whittier, whose poem "Brown of Osawatomie" included the following words: "They led him out to die; / And lo! a poor slave-mother with her little child pressed nigh. / Then the bold, blue eye grew tender, and the old, harsh face grew mild, / As he stooped between the jeering ranks and kissed the negro's child." As Malin notes, "It is the fable rather than the truth which became a permanent part of the popular national heritage."[123]

Further difficulties with these quickly written children's books arose from their authors' overreliance on the pirated histories of others. Any given McLoughlin edition of a monosyllabic history might be a work that had been bootlegged from Routledge and then Americanized for the benefit of young audiences in the United States. In turn, Routledge's version of the text could have been a boiled-down version of a much more complex narrative that itself had been appropriated and then simplified. Such reductionism had obvious costs. One of the works on which Pierson leaned most heavily, for instance, was a two-volume *Field-Book of the Revolution,* whose author, Benson Lossing, traveled the country in the late 1840s interviewing survivors of the Revolution and collecting relics of that struggle.[124] Thirty years later, these subjects were all deceased, the last surviving veteran of the American Revolution having died in 1869.[125] But in 1884, when Pierson published her *History of the United* States, she appropriated bits of Lossing's commentary verbatim without contextualizing or even proofreading it apparently, conveying the false impression among her readers that veterans of the Revolutionary War were still living. "There are some old men who fought in that war, who are alive this day," Pierson paraphrased Lossing inappropriately, an assertion that, if she were forced to prove its accuracy, would have required her to find a veteran who was over 140 years old.[126]

Stratton, who had no formal training in history, also took to quoting lengthy passages from the texts of established historians. She relied so heavily on Henry Davenport Northrup's *History of the United States* in her monosyllabic histories, in fact, that one wonders why the children in the North End history class needed Mamma Nelson at all. When students ask their matronly club leader to settle a historical dispute, for example, she deflects their requests by calling attention to the source materials of others like Northrup. "You will find other standard histories on the table, and I would like to have you bring what you have from home," Mamma Nelson tells the children. "Truth can only be learned by comparison." Interpreted generously, this redirecting could be viewed as an application of the Abbott brothers' process-learning technique. More often, however, it appeared as an excuse for Mamma Nelson to defer to the prior authority of historians more established than she. An exchange between two children in *Child's History of Our Great Country,* one of whom, Katie, has been asked to report on maritime navigation in the Age of Discovery, brings into relief all one needs to know about the derivative quality of Stratton's work. "But tell us, Katie, how did they make boats? They had no nails," interrupted Marion. "I can answer you best by reading what Northrop says," replied Katie "taking the book from the table." Several pages of verbatim quoted material follow.[127]

These female historians were constrained not only by financial discrimination and by their lack of formal training in history but also by literary limitations associated with monosyllabic formats. The authors of monosyllabic histories faced practical challenges in presenting narratives told in words of one syllable that sometimes reflected poorly on their historical techniques. In the first place, certain texts did not lend themselves easily to reduction into monosyllabic sentences. Routledge and McLoughlin both tried to issue versions of the Old and New Testaments "told in words of one syllable," but these efforts proved controversial since the Bible as holy text was viewed as sacrosanct by many. Any attempt to alter its wording was deemed by many to be a sacrilege. In the case of the Routledge Brothers Bible, "translated" for children, Pollard was criticized for using monosyllabic words in ways that oversimplified scripture. She defended herself by arguing that there is much in the Bible that "a child cannot understand," adding that the goal of making the story "easy reading" for children should be "sufficient excuse for its presentation in words of one syllable."[128] Pierson and McLoughlin Brothers were attacked for trying the opposite strategy, that is, abandoning the monosyllabic approach in favor of a more complex lexicon closer in word choice to the actual text of the King James Bible. "It has not been thought advisable, in this story of the Bible, to adhere to words of one syllable quite as strictly as has been done in some other works," Pierson wrote apologetically. "Simple and easy words have been used which a child can read, but in order to convey exact statements these words are sometimes of two syllables. The liberties taken with other histories cannot be taken with the Bible. In places where the exact words could be used, they have been used. Where they were difficult, they have been put in a simpler form, but it is hoped that the dignity and beauty of the words of Holy Writ have not been sacrificed."[129]

With respect to more secular events and texts, the authors of monosyllabic histories faced additional technical challenges related to the translation of complex events into simple rubrics for young readers. They often found it difficult and awkward to accommodate proper nouns that had entered into the historical vernacular. Pierson converted the Reign of Terror of the French Revolution to the less satisfactory "reign of fright," for instance, while she substituted "small fat boys with wings" for "cherubs."[130] These historians discovered as well that monosyllabic words were not always ample enough in their connotations to convey complex meanings adequately. "No pen can write of such scenes of war, in words that will show them to you," Pierson warned young readers in one instance, adding in another similar case: "Then came the scenes of woe that pen cannot tell."[131] Complicated political, diplomatic, and economic issues were also difficult to portray. "It will be readily understood that many matters of statecraft—tariff, nullification and important political movements—have been excluded from this volume as beyond the limits of one syllable," Pierson wrote in *Lives of the Presidents of the United States*. "But such matters are also beyond the comprehension of the little ones who may gain from this book their first knowledge of those who have occupied the chief place in our nation." Still more troublesome, from the point of view of writing history, was the fact that it was difficult for monosyllabic historians to make use of the tense most useful for discussing bygone events—the past—since it generally required the appending of the additional syllable -ed to the end of present tense verbs. Pierson admitted in the preface to the same work that she had found this obstacle impossible to overcome: "In these *Lives of the Presidents of the United States*," she confessed, "it has been thought best to depart from the strictly one-syllable style, by using the past tense of certain verbs."[132]

The inadequacy of monosyllabic prose for conveying dramatic intent and action was pointed out by the genre's detractors. Monosyllabic authors rarely tackled complicated, controversial topics, and often they avoided contested material. Unwilling to get embroiled in the historiographic debates about Napoleon that preoccupied John S. C. Abbott and his critics, for instance, Pierson backed away from many of the most contentious elements of the French leader's career. She wrote neutrally and evasively in *Life and Battles of Napoleon Bonaparte*, "The story of the brave and fearless men who helped Napoleon in his victories, has only been touched on, as there was no space for it. But the children, who read his Life in small words, can find the famous record of these heroes when able to master the more difficult pages of larger works."[133] The failure of one-syllable language to rise to the level of a nation's most controversial historical debates meant that histories told in that way were often understated and undercharged. The effect of reading "page after page of herky-jerky one-syllable prose," a twenty-first-century reviewer of these nineteenth-century texts has complained, is like "reading a telegram" or perhaps an instant message. The texts "lack rhythm and variety," he notes, and reading these books aloud "is a choppy and robotic experience" at best. "Even beginning readers were probably bored by their general atonality," he presumed.[134]

The philosophy of literacy implicit in monosyllabic histories posed further language challenges. Those supportive of phonetic approaches to historical education, like the Abbott brothers, contended that the same limitations faced by children learning to read in the monosyllabic fashion applied to those studying history by sight/word techniques; namely, that children are capable of memorizing only limited amounts and types of information at any given time and that they quickly reach natural ceilings in terms of mental capacity in their effort to retain such knowledge. As in the case of the constraints imposed by the "word burden" of the sight/word approach to literacy, children studying history could commit to memory only a finite number of events. Such limited capacity for retention of historical knowledge on the part of the young encouraged redundancies in juvenile popular histories, a tendency that severely limited the subjects popular historians could broach and restricted unnaturally the scope of history. A case in point is Cady's apology for her inadequate portrait of the renowned astronomer and inventor David Rittenhouse in her *History of Pennsylvania:* "My dear young friends, I fear that with the short list of words you can read, I cannot say what I would like to of this great man."[135] Pierson wrote of Jean Baptiste Donatien de Vimeur, Comte de Rochambeau, who fought beside Washington in the last years of the American Revolution, as the "French General, who had a hard name, which you may learn one of these days." Elsewhere in the same text Pierson confessed that she had made concessions that violated occasionally the spirit of her educational mission to inform children of the details of the past. "There were six tribes of red men who were their friends, and I would tell you their names if they were not so long and hard," she admitted sheepishly.[136]

These limitations of language meant that most monosyllabic writers were unwilling to view their texts as occasions for taking principled stands on controversial topics, such as racism in America. Pierson noted of slaves that they were "as a class light of heart and fond of dance and song. When work was done they would meet at night and sing their wild songs, for which they made up their own words. They took small thought for the past or for what was to come. If they had their hoe cake and their bit of fat pork to eat with it, they were all right."[137] Cady spoke even less sympathetically of those "poor men who had the ill luck to be born black."[138] Rather than indict Christopher Columbus for kidnapping Native Americans during his first voyage in order to take them to Spain and there display them, Pollard justified the decision by explaining that the discoverer "took seven of them back with him to the ships that they might learn the speech of Spain and be used as guides, and prove to the king and queen that he had indeed found a new world."[139] She indicated elsewhere that Washington "had a large force of slaves" to whom he "was kind," taking "the best care of them when they were sick, but . . . quick to see that they did not shirk their work." Implying that slaves were naturally shiftless and in need of supervision, Pollard recorded in *The Life of Washington* that the nation's first president distrusted but protected his slaves: "Four of his slaves set out to hew and shape a large log. Washington kept his eye on them and thought they loafed too much. So he sat down, took out his watch, and timed them."[140]

These errors, evasions, and prejudices might have been tolerable if they had not been committed in the service of a methodology that relied so heavily on the memorization of a sanctified body of canonical facts. Implicit in the rote or recitation style of learning advocated in these monosyllabic texts, however, was a trust (shared by parents and increasingly by teachers) that their facts were unimpeachable and worth remembering. By almost anyone's standards, memorization of things unimportant or inaccurate was counterproductive to the learning process. As Sadlier noted in her *History of Ireland*, "Of course you know that a thing to be a fact must be true; it would be no fact else; so that there can be no such thing as a false fact."[141] Not surprisingly, scholars found more that was fictional than factual in many of these volumes. Such works betrayed the racial, class, and gender biases of the age in which they were written; they defied scholarly efforts to impose objectivity as the standard of worth; and they offered primarily portraits of white, middle-class, male society despite their female authorships. Like many works written in the nationalistic post–Civil War era, these juvenile histories were uncompromisingly patriotic in tone, and they admitted little dissent with respect to government policies. They reveal too often what VanSledright refers to as an "unreflective acceptance of one-sided happy talk about American virtue peddled as American history," which "can breed blind conformity to nation-state and community authority, something those in power may occasionally welcome, yet a manifest danger addressed by the Constitution."[142]

Some women writers, perhaps embarrassed by these inadequacies, tried to obscure their identities by hiding behind literary pseudonyms. Ella Stratton, who had to be convinced by her mother to send "her first brain-children out into the wide world to seek a welcome in the already crowded paths of literature," used various noms de plume to mask her connection to these projects, only to be forced to endure "hearing her work criticised, sometimes by near friends who did not suspect the authorship."[143] Pollard likewise admitted that the true degree of her success in the juvenile book market could "be ascertained [only] on inquiry at Routledge's and McLoughlin's" since so many of her works "appear without my name."[144] And Pierson signed her juvenile histories told in words of one syllable Mrs. Helen Wall Pierson (rather than merely Helen Wall Pierson, as she did her mature literary publications in *Harper's* and other national magazines), thereby linking the monosyllabic form to the educational responsibilities of married women and mothers. One clever twenty-first-century reviewer of Pierson's histories mimicked her unavoidably robotic style even as she condemned its impracticality and superficiality. Having discovered a copy of *History of England in Words of One Syllable* at a flea market, this reviewer claimed to have bought it "for its sheer dottiness." "It is by Mrs. Helen W. Pierson, and Mrs. Pierson's ghost would probably be very upset if I omitted the 'Mrs.' on subsequent references to her, so I won't," she wrote, adding, "This book must have been hell, sheer hell to write. I would not want to have to do what Mrs. Pier-son did for long at all. It would drive me mad. Just think—each word a short one but for names and places. . . . Just to write this has made me weak. I must go to bed now."[145]

As was the case with Goodrich, such obfuscation revealed much about the vulnerabilities and limitations of the authors and texts associated with the monosyllabic mode of writing. It also raises definite misgivings about the wisdom of recycling nineteenth-century works in twenty-first-century homeschool markets. What were these women historians hiding about themselves and from whom were they hiding it?

The Ironies of Recycling History

Despite rather intense criticisms of the monosyllabic as a literacy strategy, such works had their defenders, and still do today. The format persisted well into the twentieth century as a tribute to the power of simple literary expression. Perhaps the most famous implementer was Theodor Geisel (Dr. Seuss), who, on a dare from Bennett Cerf, an editor at Random House, wrote *The Cat in the Hat* using fewer than fifty one-syllable words.[146] The unadorned style was expanded in the popular "look and say" basal readers associated with the whole language movement of the 1930s, 1940s, and 1950s, especially Scott Foresman's Dick, Jane, and Sally books, which encouraged young readers to memorize words on sight.[147] The most eccentric application of monosyllabic philosophies was featured in the *Wall Street Journal* a number of years ago in a story about a group of writers so fed up with the misuse of elevated language in public discourse that its members vowed to speak to one another only in one-syllable words.[148] These practitioners of the one-syllable word strategy argue that it is still an effective way of promoting reading, especially among young learners who are at the beginning stages of the literacy cycle. More complex techniques can be introduced later in the developmental sequence, they claim, as children gain greater confidence and proficiency with words and syntax.

Many literacy experts have rejected this line of thinking, however, primarily because it ignores the fact that simplicity of presentation does not guarantee historical insight and may in fact inhibit it. Certainly the literary austerity of volumes by Pollard, Pierson, Smith, and others presents a serious problem for those who would advocate their use in home school settings today. We might forgive the authors of these monosyllabic histories for their misidentifications of historical events and their transpositions of historical figures out of context in light of the fact that the standards of historical truth were notably weaker in their day than in our own and in recognition of the condition that some of their falsifications of history were based on evidence not available to pre-twentieth-century scholars. Given that an entire century of historical scholarship has brought new material to light with respect to some of these interpretations, however, and that twenty-first-century standards of accuracy demand more rigorous attention to matters of verification and argument than in the past, it is difficult to excuse republishers who have access to improved information and techniques and yet refuse to employ them.

Richard Wheeler of Mantle Ministries and others in the homeschooling business note that professional historians who uphold academic standards have their own pedagogical and political agendas and problems as well. Some on the Christian Right argue that those who claim a professional authority to determine what did and what did not happen in the past are elitists and classists. Mocking revisionist historians who debunk America's heroes, Wheeler comments that he has reissued Pollard's works as an antidote to the kind of history that "is taught from a non-providential perspective" by scholars intent on removing "all acts of God, prayer by the Founding Fathers, and references to God directing the affairs of this nation." Deliberately ignoring the Manichean dichotomies, that is, both the good and the bad of American experience, sprinkled throughout the histories of Pollard and others, he proclaims, "We are commanded by God to teach only what is good and noble. We do not need schools that emphasize the faults of historical people and glorify those about whom we should be ashamed—a prevailing trend in today's history books. . . . We need to teach children that which is of value and that which is good in the lives of historical figures."[149] Wheeler adds that the monosyllabic histories he republishes expunged faults from the historical record, but in fact he fails to recognize that works like Pollard's are filled with indictments of historical characters as well as condemnations of those who have been glorified inappropriately.

Still worse, some of the original errors in these flawed nineteenth-century monosyllabic manuscripts are compounded by the addition of new inaccuracies introduced in the twenty-first-century republication process. For instance, on the back cover of Mantle Ministries' *A Child's History of America,* one finds the following: "From the journeys of Christopher Columbus to the doughboys of World War I, Mrs. Pollard presents the history of God's unfolding plan for our great nation."[150] This advertising blurb distorts the historical record in two important ways. First, it ignores the fact that Pollard died in 1892 and therefore had no knowledge of the First World War and never wrote about its horrors. Her volume was obviously updated by someone at McLoughlin Brothers in the two decades between her death and the end of the Great War, yet no acknowledgment of that fact is made by Mantle Ministries. This is a reminder that the republishing of nineteenth-century histories in the name of originalism requires one to have an analytical bibliographer's interest in books as evolving literary documents and a descriptive bibliographer's commitment to identifying their ideal forms as defined by the intentions of the original author. The recycled uses to which republishers such as Wheeler have put texts like Pollard's exacerbate the problems that went uncorrected in the originals published by Routledge and McLoughlin, which were themselves based on recycled and pirated texts. Wheeler's rejuvenating efforts have given new life to old texts, to be sure, but that reanimation has come at the price of accuracy, and for most historians, whether professional or amateur, that is too high a price to pay.

Second, the Mantle Ministries' excerpt alters Pollard's marital status from Miss to Mrs., a transformation to which Pierson acceded but to which Pollard would have objected vehemently. This mistake appears to be a matter of wish fulfillment on Wheeler's part rather than a simple typographic error, given the evangelist's very distinct attitudes about women and marriage. The Bible, Wheeler says, does not place any responsibilities on women other than that they support their husbands and raise God-fearing children.[151] If this altering of social title was not intentional, it is certainly ironic, to say the least, given Pollard's personal history. Unlike Pierson, Pollard never married, confiding in her brother that she had nothing but contempt for the institution. "If you are going to be married do give us at least six months' notice, if you expect anything substantial in the way of sympathy," she wrote him.[152] She deliberately signed her books Miss Josephine Pollard as a statement of her independence as an unwed woman and writer, so the error in attribution by Mantle Ministries would have been an affront to her.

In fact, Pollard makes an odd spokesperson for Mantle Ministries' causes generally given that her positions on matters of gender and marriage were completely incompatible with Wheeler's. For instance, Wheeler believes that a young woman who attends college—at large expense to her parents, he editorializes—soon finds "a well-paying job in the profession she pursued, meets *Mr. Perfect,* gets married, and within a year or two finds herself with a child, and is now faced with a dilemma. The God-given instinct is to be a stay-at-home mother, but their financial trap of relying on two incomes and a godless society pressure her to go back to work."[153] In promoting Pollard, Wheeler ignores the fact that she was a major advocate of college education for women and wrote a lengthy narrative poem, "Co-education," in which the female narrator knocks on the doors of Columbia College, asking for entry. She is rebuffed by the "Cerberus who sits on guard" and proclaims haughtily, "Madam, all the doors are barred / 'Gainst such as you. You're much too weak / To stand the exercise you seek, / And would, ere many days, succumb / 'Neath our severe curriculum. . . . / By nature you were not designed / To labor thus to train your mind." Undeterred, Pollard's protagonist at last finds "a worthy Prex / Who did not measure sex with sex, / But had the common sense to take, / A forward step for woman's sake." Behold woman now, Pollard insisted, "more emulous, / Because of all this stir and fuss, / Studying Hebrew, Latin, Greek, / And going on from week to week / In such a steady, earnest way / Her libelers have naught to say."[154]

Ironic as well is that Wheeler promotes Pollard's monosyllabic books for the home school market when Pollard herself was a former teacher and a strong advocate of public education. On page 157 of *A Child's History of the United States,* Wheeler reasserts Pollard's plea for free public schooling, even for women, over the more traditional homeschooling options. "By 1860," she wrote, "nearly all the states had free schools and since then the efforts to keep them up to a high mark has [*sic*] not grown weak." Indeed, she added with pride, "it is not out of the reach of a boy or a girl who has a real wish for it to get through college free."[155] Yet Wheeler markets Pollard's history as an alternative to the texts issued by public school educators, instructors he describes as fools who teach "godless history, sex education, and evolutionary science" through books designed "to destroy the Christian faith of children." Referring to public schools as decayed, fallen institutions "dedicated to fostering atheism and relativism," Wheeler counsels parents to "pull their children out of [such] godless, Christ-hating, socialistic, sexually perverted, unpatriotic government schools across the land." He adds for good measure that public school teachers abuse their authority in immoral ways that must be protected against. "If the teacher happens to be a homosexual," Wheeler writes, "he is transferring the power of his lifestyle to the innocent minds of children. The teacher may or may not be up-front with his lifestyle, but his world view is tainted to reflect his devious behavior, regardless, and his authority carries a power in his spoken words to alter the minds of those under his teachings."[156]

Such a statement not only betrays a disturbing homophobia but also reveals how out of touch Wheeler is with the woman whose text he promotes as a protection against such behavior. Pollard was a feminist, after all, and a charter member and officer of an organization, the Sorosis Club, that was created in 1868 by the journalist Jane Cunningham Croly in reaction to the exclusion of women writers from a dinner given by the New York Press Club honoring Dickens.[157] Protesting this snubbing, these feminists held an organizational meeting at Delmonico's restaurant in New York City, "itself a challenge to socially acceptable behavior since it was not deemed proper for women to be seen in public places without a male escort." The goals outlined in the club's constitution and bylaws included the following: "The promotion of agreeable and useful relations among women of literary, artistic, and scientific tastes; the discussion and dissemination of principles and facts which promise to exert a salutary influence on women and on society; and the establishment of an order which shall render the female sex helpful to each other, and actively benevolent in the world."[158] The women also determined to maintain their "distance from men" because they envisioned their work "in the association of women, not in integration."[159] "We were criticised and ridiculed and lampooned and cartooned until some of our members lost their courage and the husbands of some of the rest of the members—who never had any courage—made them resign," one of the founders, Charlotte Wilbour, recalled, "but we always had more applications and were able to put candidates for admission to a pretty severe test."[160] Wilbour references a cartoon that appeared in *Harper's Weekly* that satirized the Sorosis Club as consisting of women with male inclinations, implying it was "a radical effort to switch gender roles in society, with men caring for the children and women engaged in business and politics" (fig. 12).[161]

Wheeler also seems to have misjudged the intentions of Pollard and other women historians with respect to gendered approaches to the past. It is true that Pollard wrote a few of her monosyllabic books with boys in mind (as evinced by her prefatory remarks in her biography of Grant, for instance), and it is also the case that she and other monosyllabic writers accepted some of the most common nineteenth-century stereotypes about gender distinctions between boys and girls. Yet Pollard, Smith, and Sadlier believed fervently in the feminist mission of the Sorosis Club as articulated by President Croly, who wrote, "We have . . . proposed to open out new avenues of employment to women, to make them less dependent and less burdensome, to lift them out of unwomanly self-distrust, disqualifying diffidence, into womanly self-respect and self-knowledge."[162] Indeed, they modeled these behaviors in their own careers and wrote encouragements to young female readers of their texts. In *The History of the United States,* for instance, Pollard advised young women to guard carefully their inalienable rights, warning them to avoid becoming slaves to their men. Male "Indians . . . made their squaws do all the hard work," she remarked. "These poor squaws had to dig the ground, sow the corn, and weave the mats of which their huts were made; and not a smile or a kind word did they get to pay them for their hard tasks."[163] White men were no better as taskmasters, Pollard observed in describing seventeenth-century Swedish colonists in Philadelphia in *The History of the United States.* "One day it chanced that all the men Swedes went off to the woods and left their wives at home. It was soft-soap day," she wrote, "and I guess if the truth were known, that was just why the men went at the time."[164]

Finally, there is thick irony in Wheeler's choice of Pollard to be his poster child for the promotion of the Christian values he wishes to encourage in young readers. She was indeed a God-fearing woman, and she was committed to Protestantism with an enthusiasm that followers of the Mantle Ministries could appreciate. But she was also an independent writer and artist, one whose bohemian lifestyle (she was the author of several gypsy tales, after all)

FIGURE 12. Charles G. Bush, *"Sorosis, 1869," Harper's Weekly,* 15 May 1869. Courtesy of the Library of Congress.

was viewed with suspicion by some in her day. The questionable nature of her reputation was borne out in newspaper accounts of a scandalous "breach of promise" trial in 1895 of Madeline Pollard from Ohio, who claimed that Rep. William Campbell Preston Breckinridge of Kentucky was an adulterer who had reneged on a marriage proposal after she bore him three children out of wedlock.[165] In his examination of Pollard, the lead attorney for Breckinridge, a Major Butterworth, cited an article from the *Brooklyn Standard-Union* identifying her as a known "opium eater" who was on "intimate terms" with various radical writers and poets, including James Russell Lowell, with whom she was said to have walked "hand-in-hand through the streets of Cambridge" in a brazen display of unladylike behavior.[166] Madeline Pollard objected to these accusations on the grounds that Butterworth was confusing her with the writer and Brooklyn native Josephine Pollard, who had died three years earlier and to whom she was not related. The objection was sustained by the presiding judge, although Butterworth's confusion was understandable, since, in fact, Madeline Pollard had masqueraded on several occasions as

Josephine.[167] What's interesting about this moment in the trial, apart from what it suggests about Madeline Pollard's duplicity, is what it conveys about Josephine Pollard's reputation as a free spirit. Whether she was an opium addict as was alleged in the newspaper article is hard to confirm, but it is revealing that the defense attorneys for Breckinridge sought to impugn the character of Madeline by citing the behavior of Josephine, which they agreed was unbecoming of an educated woman.

Under the circumstances, then, Pollard would seem to be an unlikely selection by Mantle Ministries as the lead author in its campaign to communicate "a Christ-directed teaching to children, as well as adults, of Christian conviction and Godly standards, with a focus on eternal purpose and visionary hope."[168] The republication of her works and those of other monosyllablists raises strong suspicions about what influences their flawed texts might have on vulnerable children who read them today. Routledge and McLoughlin controlled the marketplace for popular histories so completely that they left little room for female authors to exercise independence of thought or to train themselves adequately in the proper technique of history. These conditions not only reaffirmed the master narrative of American history from which many women dissented but also undercut the ability of some women historians to make independent claims about the past.

In fact, in the present moment, when dead words can be resurrected and manipulated in print without editorial restraint and when children are more insensitive to historical context than ever before, publishers continue to wield much power in the production and maintenance of history books and the shaping of historical memory among children. Insofar as we are still influenced today by the impulse of nineteenth-century reformers known as child-savers in support of the "cult of the child," then, we must continue to question the desirability of republishing for homeschooling use popular histories by nineteenth-century women who worked under conditions quite different from our own and were employed by male publishers whose gendered perspectives on historical writing are even more inappropriate in our age than they were in theirs.

CHAPTER FOUR

Providential History

*Charles Carleton Coffin and
the Home Study Movement*

> Good children's literature appeals not only to the child in the adult, but to the
> adult in the child.
>
> ANONYMOUS

Maranatha Publications and the "History Books of Heaven"

As measured by thematic content and structural approach, the works of
monosyllablists such as Pollard, Pierson, Smith, and Sadlier were not substantially different from one another or from those of their predecessors in the
field of popular children's history, including Samuel Goodrich and the Abbott
brothers. They employed roughly the same cast of characters in the service
of comparable stories designed to reaffirm a common master narrative. The
kind and frequency of repetitions that emerged from these collective works
(both factual and fictional) gave birth to the impression that American history in the nineteenth century was a consensual enterprise practiced by like-
minded popularizers disinterested in argument or debate. Certainly those on
the Christian Right today who republish volumes from this period do so in
part because they view the consistencies among such texts as a sign of the
inherent stability of the American past. In terms of the historical learning and
literacy strategies utilized in these popular histories, however, there is a great
deal of variability among their authors about how and when to teach children
about the past. Careful examination of volumes in the genre—not just their
themes and structure, that is, but their production histories and their reception by readers—reveals that the major works of popular history for children
should be studied not as stable products of a cohesive, undifferentiated age
but as fluid texts that functioned variably in distinctive, changing cultural

contexts. Those who lump all nineteenth-century histories together as being of one undifferentiated kind miss the subtle differences among them that challenge the authenticity of a consensual past and undermine the argument for republication on the grounds of consistency and repetitive uniformity.

A good example of the misplaced expectations some republishers have for books in the genre of popular children's literature can be found in the inventory of volumes offered by Maranatha Publications, an affiliate of Maranatha Christian Ministries (MCM). In the early 1970s the evangelical ministers Bob and Rose Weiner began a small youth ministry in Paducah, Kentucky, associated with MCM, a Charismatic/Pentecostal organization dedicated to redeeming America's young from the profligacy of the contemporary world. Disciples of Maranatha sought to save the nation's most vulnerable souls, those of teenagers, by creating specialized missions in high schools and colleges that addressed adolescents' needs. Noting that "only 4% of today's Christian youth will be in church in the next decade" and that "95% of Christians get saved before they are 25 years of age," the Weiners argued that reaching American young people was crucial to the survival of Christianity in the United States. "Unless we do something now, in just a few years America will lose its Christian base and slide into complete heathenism," they warned.[1] Campus pastors, often recent graduates of the colleges in which the church had a foothold, supervised the lives of members very closely, requiring initiates to tithe to the cause and to submit to a regimen of social rules mandated by the Maranatha leadership. The movement expanded quickly in the seventies and eighties, with chapters forming at over one hundred campuses in the United States.[2] By the 1990s the Weiners had incorporated Weiner Ministries International to carry the church's mission abroad, with chapters in Canada, Argentina, Brazil, Indonesia, France, Germany, the United Kingdom, Australia, New Zealand, and the Philippines.[3]

Because Bob Weiner professes to have received direct revelations from God, he claims to be able to understand and elucidate the providential nature of history. Hoping that the nation is on the verge of a historical period of spiritual revival, the Weiners have devoted themselves to training a new generation of young religious students to help "harvest" its fruits. In particular they have sought to return the study of God to history curricula by reversing the perceived atheistic practices of secular humanists and liberal professors who "voice their philosophy on the goodness of man and his unlimited potential apart from God." In jeremiad-like strains, the Weiners have asked young people to seize history before it seizes them. "Our generation may have the greatest opportunity in all of history to experience revival, awakening and the supernatural power of God," they sermonize. "Depending on our vision, our ability to conquer our enemies and our desire to achieve our destiny, we could see a dynamic demonstration of the Holy Spirit's power in our generation." Disciples of Maranatha must not miss their opportunity to change history by sleeping through a revolution, the Weiners warn. "Let it be recorded in the *history books of Heaven,* that the young Christians of this generation responded in radical obedience and dedication to the revelation of the purposes of God for their lifetime," the couple urges. "Let us be like David who 'served the purpose of God in his generation' so that we shall discover that we came to the Kingdom 'for such a time as this.' "[4]

The curious phrase "history books of Heaven" suggests just how much the Weiners believe the patterns of history are predetermined by a higher author- ity. In the late 1980s the couple created the publishing arm of their operations, Maranatha Publications, to illuminate these providential designs through allegedly divine works marketed to the church's disciples. Many of their earli- est publishing projects were reissues of popular histories written in the nine- teenth century, an age in which, the Weiners believed, historians were purer in their intentions and more God-fearing in their views of the past. Like many on the Christian Right, the Weiners implore young readers to acquire their historical learning from such pre-twentieth-century texts rather than from those of revisionists, since nineteenth-century volumes are less tainted by the methodologies of social studies. "Yes, it's True! Our History was re-written in the early 20th Century by Progressives who wanted to erase the Christian Foundation of our nation from our history books!" the Maranatha website declares, adding with a hint of conspiratorial mystery, "Now you can read what they did not want you to know." The promotional literature states that nineteenth-century historians understood "how America became the greatest nation in the world," asserting that young people who read Maranatha works will learn "what it will take to stay the greatest." The secret to recovering lost glory, readers are told, has something to do with recognizing the "Providen- tial Hand of God in founding the American Colonies" and appreciating "the Christian idea of self-government," which has offered the world "the ideal of a written constitution based on Christian Principles that have given eagle wings to the human spirit!" While not quite "history books of Heaven," then, these older volumes by popular historians reaffirm the perspectives of the founders, who believed, according to the Weiners, that "the highest pinnacle toward which all history was moving was the day when the kingdoms of this world would become the kingdoms of our God and of His Christ."[5]

Maranatha republications have been especially popular among home- schoolers. They address many of the primary preoccupations that home- schooling parents have had about the kinds of history being taught in public

schools. "Education must return to the basic ideas of early American education, that became derailed before they were ever fully developed," the Weiners write. Among these basic ideas is the belief that children should be taught
to recognize and embrace with evangelical fervor the powerful Christian
narratives central to many historical works of an earlier age. These evan-
gelicals see the Bible as the prototype for all historical narration. The event
of "Christ's appearance on earth," with which so many of these nineteenth-
century chronicles of the past began, the historian Nina Baym has written,
"gave history its narrative structure and so in a sense invented history itself."
Consequently, children should be required to study biblical history and its
derivatives, the Weiners contend, since doing so will alert them to the "divine
narrative progressing inexorably toward a known end, the millennium that
would mark history's closure."[6] Additionally, the couple maintains that history
education must not be impartial or disinterested, as social-scientific educators
insist; rather, it should be partisan, spirited, and unequivocal in its messages.[7]
The Maranatha website proclaims in capital letters, "EDUCATION IS NOT
NEUTRAL. It will cause people either to respect God and His principles, or
to turn away from Him."[8] Embraced by the Christian homeschooling community, Maranatha history books have been described by a blogger who has
devoted an entire website to them as the perfect instrument for realizing that
elusive blend of "Christian living, family, [and] homeschooling" necessary for
the achievement of historical understanding.[9]

Among the most popular of the Maranatha republications are two works
by the nineteenth-century popular historian Charles Carleton Coffin: *The
Story of Liberty,* which covers the European background vis-à-vis the American identity, and *Sweet Land of Liberty,* treating early American colonial life.[10]
Maranatha advertises Coffin's *The Story of Liberty* as a "classic reference in
the Christian education and home schooling communities" and "a must-read
for anyone eager for a view of history unedited by secular humanists." Rose
Weiner notes in the introduction to the republished version of this work that
America was born a "Christian Republic" and must remain one by continuing
to "diligently ponder" the "divine influence behind America's history" and
"to understand the goodness of God in establishing the nation of America for
His gospel purposes." Citing Job 8:8–10—"Please inquire of past generations,
and consider the things searched out by their fathers. For we are only of yesterday and know nothing"—she claims that parents have a familial obligation
to preserve and recirculate these older Christian narratives as a protection
against the insidious impiety of newer revisionist tomes. According to the
Weiners, *The Story of Liberty* teaches children to "reach back into the records
of history to observe the hand of the Great Author of all liberty" who gives

them "direction for the days ahead" and "the keys we need to understand and interpret the future."[11]

The Maranatha republications of Coffin's works have been highly popular in homeschool history markets. His histories come strongly recommended on homeschool review sites such as Leadership Education through Discipleship (L.E.D.), where they are touted as essential alternatives to the textbooks of the twentieth and twenty-first centuries that are inspired by social science. "Charles Coffin's series was written in the latter 1800s, before revisionists were changing history to fit their agenda," the L.E.D. website notes.[12] Gregg Harris, a reviewer for the online newsletter "The Christian Home-School," agrees, adding that the historical works of so-called progressive educators were actually regressive insofar as they gave young people a false impression of what the founders intended the spiritual foundations of this country to be. "In this modern era of historical dishonesty," Harris writes, "the work of Charles Coffin stands strong. His fear of God, his love of country and his respect for historical truth all combine to give us a faithful, passionate and accurate story of our nation's fight for liberty."[13]

Other publishers have followed suit in praising and recirculating Coffin's works. Mantle Ministries also republishes volumes from Coffin's series, recommending them as antidotes to the revisionist impulses of professional scholars. "We are often asked, 'What history curriculum does evangelist/historian Richard "Little Bear" Wheeler use with his family?'" the website questions. The answer: Coffin's.[14] In the late 1990s an outfit called Exodus Books of Milwaukie, Oregon, began distributing republished versions of Coffin's works as part of a homeschooling Christian enterprise devoted to "family and faith" as well as to "education, edification and enjoyment." Rejecting the view that public schools can do a better job of educating youth than private individuals, the brochure for Exodus Books cites the Bible in warning instructors that "your children are *your* responsibility, not the State's" and in stressing that homeschooling "is an opportunity to reverse the trends of idolatry and compartmentalization" characteristic of twenty-first-century histories for children. Reading works like Coffin's in a homeschool setting "takes education out of the control of a system that hates our God and is bent on teaching your children that He does not exist," the publishers at Exodus Books contend. The discipleship Coffin preaches "is really what home education is about, having your children with you so you can use every opportunity to teach them—not just reading, writing, and arithmetic, but more importantly, how to live a Godly life in service to King Jesus." The key for parents is to find universal literature like Coffin's to which children will respond and then to teach it responsibly, the promoters suggest, adding that doing so will ensure that "your education is directed toward God's glory and that the books we carry will help you in that endeavor."[15]

Firms such as Maranatha Publications, Mantle Ministries, and Exodus Books all believe that republished nineteenth-century works can and should serve as the foundation for homeschooling efforts in the field of history. They affirm that volumes by popular historians like Coffin can alert young readers to the special destiny of the American nation, with its attendant commitment to liberty, while distracting the vulnerable young from revisionist texts whose cynical authors deny the role played by Providence in determining the American past. The further assumption held by all these presses is that Coffin's works were written at a time when parents understood that education began in the home and asserted that caregivers had ethical responsibilities to bring Christian educational sensibilities to bear on their children's domestic lives. As one impressed reader of *The Story of Liberty* avowed, "All too often, it is assumed that modern interpretations of history are somehow objective and unbiased. All historians write from their worldview, and there is nothing that says a naturalist/atheistic perspective is somehow more valid than the perspective that God directs the events of history for a purpose. The latter view is much closer to what was held by many of the people (Reformers, Pilgrims, & Catholics) that this history is about, and therefore, in my opinion, is capable of a deeper understanding of the motivation of these people to act against injustice." By teaching from such books "written by people in ages other than our own," this blogger adds, "we gain the perspective necessary to analyze our own cultures [*sic*] assumptions and beliefs."[16]

Home Study and History on the Home Front

In some ways it makes good sense for those on the Christian Right to adopt Coffin's books for homeschool use. After all, they were written before public schools had established their full authority over private homes as the central locus of educational activity. In Coffin's day, many parents believed that American public schools were not capable of keeping up with the demands of a changing world. The arrival of vast numbers of immigrants after the Civil War meant that many public schools were inundated with students, and teachers found themselves overwhelmed at times by educational mandates established by the state for instructing these new charges. According to some educators, such conditions signaled that American schools were in crisis and in dire need of reform. "The schools are handicapped by lack of time for much personal care, by lack of facilities for the best of instruction and by the multiplicity of things that must be done," opined one critic. "Under the best conditions a teacher has but a small part of a child's time and then instruction must be given usually to classes and not to individuals." Certain subjects, such as history, might thus be shortchanged in the curriculum, he noted, which could lead to sloppy intellectual and moral habits.[17]

The alternative as far as some educators were concerned was to strengthen the role of the home in educating American youth. For certain families this meant pulling their children out of school altogether in favor of having them taught by private tutors. Some theorists recommended homeschooling as the only way for parents to safeguard their children from the most pernicious elements of public school education. In making their case, these advocates revived an argument advanced nearly fifty years earlier by Lydia Sigourney in her *Letters to Mothers*. "Why expose [the child] to the influence of evil example [in schools]?" she asked. "Why yield it to the excitement of promiscuous association, when it has a parent's house, where its innocence may be shielded, and its intellect aided to expand? Does not a mother's tutoring for two or three hours a day give a child more time than a teacher at school?"[18] Parents must have the primary say in a child's education, critics of public schools insisted, and the failure to exercise that authority was an abnegation of moral responsibility. It was a sin to abandon defenseless children to a public school system in which "the parent furnishes the child at one end of the machine and receives the finished product, bound in white muslin or in broadcloth, as the case may be, on graduation day." The prevailing condition that "neither the thought nor the conscience of the parent is aroused by our present school system," the Reverend William H. Lyon remarked in a lecture titled "The Responsibility of the Parent in the Education of the Child," has come to be "a very serious fact in society."[19]

In other cases, homeschooling meant supplementing what was being taught in public school with additional reading supplied by the parents at home as resources allowed. "Outside of school for a considerable time each day the child falls under the influence of playmates who may or may not be helpful, but the greater part of every twenty-four hours belongs to the home," the educational specialist C. H. Sylvester wrote. "Parents, guardians, brothers and sisters, servants, consciously or unconsciously, wisely or unwisely, are teaching all the time. It is from this great complex of influences that every child builds his character and lays the foundation of whatever success he afterwards achieves," The home, he summed up, "is the greatest single influence and that is strongest during the early years." These conditions provided a self-explanatory justification for home study at a very young age, one that is consistent with what the Weiners of Maranatha Publications have said about the pace of teenage spiritual development today. "Before a boy is seven the elements of his character begin to form; by the time he is fourteen his future usually can be predicted, and after he is twenty, few real changes are brought about in the character of the man," Sylvester concluded. "The schools can do little more than plant the seeds of culture; in the family must the young plants be watered, nourished and trained. Then will the growth be symmetrical and beautiful."[20]

In an effort to address these conditions, a burgeoning home study movement gained momentum in the mid- to late nineteenth century. Initiated by William Rainey Harper, a wealthy entrepreneur and educational reformer who became president of the University of Chicago, home study was conceived originally as an extension school for young working-class citizens and those who labored at home who could not afford either the time or the money to attend public or private schools. Harper developed a system of correspondence courses designed to connect students with established faculty members throughout the country, who took it upon themselves (often for nominal compensation) to teach those "who are obliged to work by themselves."[21] A " 'Young Men's Society for Home Study' has been organized at Cambridge," announced a reporter for the *Harvard Daily Echo* of one such early effort; the society "aims to guide and encourage the earnest desire among many men for systematic study and reading at home."[22] In the State of Wisconsin, an Inter-State School of Correspondence was created that offered four eight-month-long courses, including one on American literature and advanced American history, to people "who are prevented from leaving home and who yet do not wish to stagnate." Students received a booklet at the beginning of each month containing an outline of a home reading program followed later in the month by a set of test questions. Responses to these queries were then mailed back to the instructors, who evaluated and returned them with corrected answers. At the end of the course, a certificate was awarded to those who had completed the work successfully.[23]

The needs of women, many of whom had not advanced in their public school educations beyond high school, were of special concern to the early promoters of the home study movement. Anna Eliot Ticknor, the daughter of the historian and Harvard University professor George Ticknor, tailored the program to women who were "confined" to the domestic sphere, establishing the Society to Encourage Studies at Home for their benefit. Ticknor created correspondence courses "to induce among ladies the habit of devoting some part of every day to study of a systematic and thorough kind."[24] Since the 1830s, girls of means had had private school options for education, including such institutions as the Abbott brothers' Mount Vernon and Spingler schools, but the parents of many young women in the nineteenth

FIGURE 13.
"Forces in Education,"
from C. H. Sylvester,
Journeys Through Bookland,
vol. 10 (Chicago:
Thompson Publishing
Company [c. 1909]).

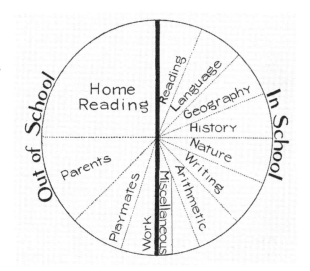

century could not afford (or did not see the necessity of budgeting for) an education for their daughters. The home study program sought to address the intellectual deficits created by these conditions, often to good effect. The educator Samuel Eliot commented that the Society to Encourage Studies at Home had generated an "increased happiness" among its female members and was "both a proof and a cause of the growth of character."[25]

In the late nineteenth century a substantial book industry developed around the home study movement, and volumes with titles such as *The Automatic Instructor: A Practical System for Home Study* became very popular.[26] Sylvester developed a literacy curriculum centered on family reading opportunities for the young titled "Journeys Through Bookland: A New and Original Plan for Reading Applied to the World's Best Literature for Children." In a brochure advertising the program he counseled that "if any mature person at home can spend each week a few hours in reading and talking with the children about what has been read he will be surprised to find how lightly the time passes and how quickly his own cares and anxieties are dissipated." Such a person would "find greater delight than he has ever known in the society of his equals; and the younger ones, whose minds glow with helpful curiosity and absorbing interest will be kept to that extent from the street and its attractions, while at the same time they are learning those things that count for most in life's great battle." Sylvester included in his promotional materials a pie chart labeled "Forces in Education" that depicted the sum total of all the influences that impact the mind and character of the growing child (fig. 13). Not surprisingly, the home was the most significant factor in Sylvester's model for determining a student's character development. "In school are the various studies taught; reading, writing, language, nature, geography, history, arithmetic," he wrote. "Other things such as morals, manners, hygiene, etc., come in for their share of force in the division 'Miscellaneous.' Out of school the child's work influences him; his playmates affect him more; the example and instruction of his parents form his habits, thought and character to a still greater extent; but more than any one, as much as the three combined, does his home reading shape his destiny."[27]

If home reading was commonly held to be the most vital force in shaping personal destiny, then it makes sense that publishing companies in the mid- to late nineteenth century began actively marketing home study readers to youngsters. Works of providential history were of special relevance in this marketplace since they offered perfect opportunities to demonstrate how national moral character had developed over time in the regulated environment of private American homes. For instance, the dime novelist Edward S. Ellis, who wrote *The History of Our Country* for the series History as Home Study published by Jones Brothers Publishers of Cincinnati, wrote that "Home Study broadens the mind, quickens the intellect, adds to and perfects the education, and is now very generally recognized as an invaluable aid to success in life." He encouraged parents to stop relying on the public schools to impart historical knowledge because they were failing children in the area of moral education; instead, parents should take up the "laudable work of home-education."[28] The writer of popular histories Benson Lossing contributed to the home study movement as well with the *Young People's Story of American Achievements, a Graphic History of the Republic and its Builders with over 300 Portraits and Biographical Outlines of Illustrious Americans,* circulated by the Home Education League of America.[29] Doubleday and McClure Company supplied an entire historical curriculum for those interested in an encyclopedic approach to home learning with the *Home Study Circle Library.*[30] "Perhaps our most important project is the Home Study Series, which will ultimately run to thirty volumes, and will be arranged and planned on new lines," Doubleday and McClure announced in its yearly inventory report for 1899.[31]

Home study history volumes were quite diverse in their approaches to education, but most shared a steadfast commitment to vivid narrative style. Young readers of Ellis and Lossing chose their works because they were fast-paced productions that were far more literary than the standard stultifying history textbooks used in public schools. Primary school students in the Boston public schools, for instance, resented having to read William Swinton's *First Lessons in Our Country's History,* which opened with an elaborate apologia from its author for the dullness of his approach. "Of histories which the child may read by the mother's knee there is no lack," Swinton wrote with reference to more popular works, "but this is not what is required for school study, which must not only convey impressions, but impart a certain amount of available knowledge."[32] Many young readers preferred lively stories that were driven less by factual content than by the personalized moral perspectives of their writers. Ellis's training as a novelist was a valued asset in this context. One reviewer of his work observed that the "juveniles of Mr. Ellis are deserving of their wonderful popularity, for not only are they stirring, interesting and instructive, but they are clean and pure, and teach boys true manliness, obedience, honesty, truthfulness and all the virtues that make a youth a true and useful citizen and a blessing to the community in which he lives."[33] Commenting on the readability and value of Ellis's *The Youth's History of the United States* (1880), the literary historian Albert Johannsen wrote, "I regret very much that I did not have a book like Ellis's *Youth History of the United States* when I was a boy, in place of a history that was simply a mass of names and dates and battles, as are, I am afraid, many of the modern school histories."[34]

Perhaps the most popular of all authors of home study histories for children was Coffin, whose works were proclaimed by such groups as the Congress of Mothers Literature as of sufficient power to "arouse the interest of any child."[35] He was the author of several children's series in the late nineteenth century, including Carleton's Juveniles (published by Estes and Lauriat and focused on Civil War studies) and Coffin's Historical Reading for the Young (produced by Harper and Brothers and addressing themes of liberty). He wrote from a conviction that school textbooks were harmful to the interests of young readers, whose parents needed to monitor more carefully than they were inclined to the historical lessons their children were learning in schools. His close friend and biographer, William Griffis, noted that Coffin "often expressed the emphatic opinion that our school histories were viciously planned and written, preserving a spirit that boded no good for the future of our country and the world." He was unhappy above all with the ways in which historians like John S. C. Abbott had disparaged American relations with potential allies abroad like England. In the nineties, Coffin "was asked by Harpers to write a history of the United States for young people," Griffis noted, and this "he hoped to do, correcting prejudices, and emphasizing the moral union between the two nations using English speech."[36] This reconciliationist impulse was just one example of how Coffin attempted to use home study techniques to correct the misimpressions children received from standardized textbooks and from their public school educations.

Coffin not only wrote for the home study market but also conducted a weekly Reading Club for Young Ladies for the educational benefit of those mothers, daughters, aunts, cousins, and grandmothers whom he called the home guard.[37] His works appealed as well to voracious young readers like the future poet Carl Sandburg, who had dropped out of school at the age of thirteen but maintained an active home reading schedule in the areas of history and literature. In one of his reading notebooks Sandburg recorded having completed joyfully Coffin's *The Boys of '76,* which made him feel as if he "could have been a boy in the days of George Washington and watched him on a horse, a good rider sitting easy and straight, at the head of a line of ragged soldier as with shotguns."[38] It is difficult to know the exact sales figures for Coffin's cumulative works, but one estimate places the total number of his readers at well over a million. Griffis reported with confidence that by the early twentieth century Coffin had become the most popular historian for children in the country and beyond: "At a particular time, as the chief librarian of a large public library told him, Carleton's books were more largely read than those of any living writer in the world." Still more revealing, perhaps, was the anecdotal evidence of Coffin's popularity that Griffis uncovered with respect to his own daughter's home reading habits. "How widely popular this volume may have been, the writer cannot say," Griffis wrote of one Coffin's works, "but he knows that one little maiden whom he sees every day has re-read the work several times."[39]

Carleton's Juveniles and "A Bright Nation of Readers"

In terms of background and literary training Coffin was well suited to represent the principles and priorities of the home study movement, although, as we shall see, he did not always do so. Carleton, as his acquaintances and readers referred to him, was born in New Hampshire in 1823 and "grew up on the family farm, attended the village school, and studied for a year at the local academy" (fig. 14). Like Goodrich, Coffin had relatives who had fought in the American Revolution and lived to tell vivid stories about its cultural meaning. "The first lore to which Carleton listened after his infant lips had learned prayer, and 'line upon line, and precept upon precept,' from the Bible, was from his soldier grandfathers," his biographer wrote. Like Goodrich's mentors Colonel Ely and Lieutenant Smith, Coffin's grandfathers sat "around the open fireplace" and "told the story of revolutionary marches, and camps, and battles." Nothing was "more real to the open-eyed little boy than the narratives related by the actors themselves, especially when he could ask questions, and get full light and explanation," Griffis noted. As a youngster he reenacted the battles of Bunker Hill and Bennington, "in which his living ancestors had fought, and of which they had told him,—using the roadside weeds as Brit-

FIGURE 14.
Portrait of Charles Carleton
Coffin. William Elliot Griffis,
Charles Carleton Coffin: War
Correspondent, Traveller, Author,
and Statesman (Boston: Estes
and Lauriat, 1898),
frontispiece.

ish soldiers, and sticks, stones, and a cornstalk knife for weapons." In later
life Coffin visited the battlefield at Saratoga, where his grandfather Eliphalet
Kilborn had fought. Griffis wrote that "Carleton picked up a bullet just uncovered by the plow, and in that bright and beautiful summer's day the whole
scene of 1777 came back before him. From the author's map in 'Burgoyne's
Defence,' giving a meagre sketch of the battle, he was able to retrace the general lines of the American breastworks. This was the first of scores of careful
study on the spot and reproduction in imagination of famous battles, which
Carleton made and enjoyed during his life."[40]

Schooling was somewhat of a hit-or-miss proposition for Coffin, as it had
been for Goodrich and other popular historians of the nineteenth century.
As a very young boy he attended the local district school, where he received
formal instruction in his letters with a heavy dose of the didacticism and recitation practices common to the age. Most of his training came from home
and church, his biographer writing that "Carleton's first and greatest teachers were his mother and father." Griffis represented his schooling as follows:
"Carleton's religious and dogmatic education began with the New England
Primer, and progressed with the hymns of that famous Congregationalist,
Doctor Watts. When five years old, at the foot of a long line of boys and girls,

he toed the mark,—a crack in the kitchen floor,—and recited verses from the Bible." Coffin matriculated at the Academy on the Plain, and he eventually spent a single term at the Blanchard Academy in Pembroke, New Hampshire, where he was exposed to the Pestalozzi method of his teacher, Charles G. M. Burnham, who was described as being "enthusiastic and magnetic, having few rules, and placing his pupils upon their honor. It was not so much what Carleton learned from books," Griffis wrote insightfully of his training, "as association with the one hundred and sixty young men and women of his own age, which here so stimulated him."[41]

When the Civil War broke out Coffin tried to enlist in the Union Army, but he was rejected because of an ankle injury he had suffered the previous decade. He became a war correspondent instead, billing himself as the only journalist to cover the conflict in its entirety.[42] Noted for his "precise but graphic reports," Coffin was regarded as "a stickler for accuracy who would venture onto the battlefield in order to obtain the facts." He wrote many of his newspaper dispatches in the first person from the fringes of the battle-fields, and he infused them with a personalized narrative voice by adopting a you-are-there style to depict the tragic events of the war. The intense presentism of his writings derived from his unique perspective as an observer of the battles he described, generally recorded from dangerous vantage points that inspired combatants as well as readers. Coffin's biographer wrote,

> An old soldier whom I was once showing through the library stopped short in front of Coffin's books and looked at them with much interest. He said that at his first battle,—I think it was Fredericksburg, but of this I am not sure,—he was scared almost to death. He was a mere boy, and when his regiment was ordered to the front and the shot was lively around him, he would have run away if he had dared. But a little distance off, he saw a man standing under the lee of a tree and writing away as coolly as if he were standing at a desk. The soldier asked who he was, and was told it was Carleton, of the *Journal*. "There he stood," said the man, "perfectly unconcerned, and I felt easier every time I looked at him. Finally he finished and went off to another place. But that was his reputation among the men all through the war,—perfectly cool, and always at the front."

Coffin may even have influenced high-ranking officers during the course of the war. Friends marveled, for instance, that he "used to ask for and give news even to the commander-in-chief," Lincoln, whom he met several times during the conflict. Staff officers were amazed "at the cheek of Carleton in suggest-ing what should be done."[43]

Coffin also offered readers firsthand, observational reports on the camp life of Union soldiers. Outspoken and ardent about his work, he anticipated the Weiners' dictum that history should not be neutral, dispassionate, or apolitical. On assignment during the war for the *Boston Journal,* for instance, Coffin devoted one of his "letters from the front" in spring 1863 to a detailed description of the training regimen of the much-discussed African American troops under Col. Thomas Wentworth Higginson of Massachusetts. Contradicting reports that they were unsuited for military regimen, Coffin watched the soldiers at drill in an oak grove on a deserted plantation and testified to the fact that they operated "with precision" as skirmishers, "advancing, retreating, rallying, deploying, loading and firing." He conceded that there was "strong prejudice in the army against employing negroes," but he insisted that the black soldiers he observed demonstrated profound "courage and patriotism" in the heat of battle. "The antipathy which at the beginning was rampant," he wrote of Higginson's troops, "quickly toned down" in light of the "deportment of the colored soldiers under insult" and of "their bravery in battle," which "compelled respect from all who had doubted their heroism or fidelity."[44]

Coffin's literary style was "flowery and somewhat melodramatic" at times, although he prided himself on avoiding the excesses of the most sensational journalists of his day.[45] He was determined to use simple words, as Pollard and others had done, a practice he followed when he lectured on the war, which he did nearly two thousand times in the years after the conflict ended.[46] Coffin gave an account of his personal literary and oratorical techniques: "I saw that what the public wanted was news in condensed form; that the day for stately editorials was passing away; that short statements and arguments, which went like an arrow straight to the mark, were what the public would be likely to read. I formed my style of writing with that in view. I avoided long sentences."[47] A few critics complained about his "aversion to conjunctions and relative pronouns" as well as about his "fondness for staccato," while others found his style "jerky" and "nervous."[48] Although one reviewer applauded Coffin's "short, sharp sentences" as an appropriate expression of the musketry that "rang in the writer's brain and moulded and winged his thought" as the battles raged, another marked the same tendency as a distinct fault and associated it with a too-deliberate effort to be lucid for his young readers by way of "popping out pellets of sentence which reminds us of Bean-shooting."[49] At times even Coffin expressed misgivings about coming too close to adopting the minimalism of the monosyllablists in his literary expression. But he stuck with it: "I thought that I went too far in the other direction and clipped my sentences too short, and did not give sufficient ornamentation, but I determined to use words of Saxon rather than of Latin or Norman origin, to use 'begin,' instead of 'commence,' as stronger and more forcible."[50]

Coffin spent the years immediately after the war reshaping his numerous newspaper articles into popular histories about the conflict, many of which were mainstays of the home study market. In 1865 he published *My Days and Nights on the Battle-Field*, which was followed by *Four Years of Fighting*, later released as *Boys of '61*.[51] Over the next fifteen years, as war literature became more popular among children, he produced a trilogy of such works for young readers in the series Carleton's Juveniles, including *My Days and Nights on the Battle-Field*, *Following the Flag*, and *Winning His Way*, all with lavish pictorial covers (fig. 15). In these "books for boys," Coffin's prose did not deviate appreciably from the texts of his war letters on which they were based.[52] He made few concessions to his young readers. He expected children to handle mature military themes, including mutilation and death, and to engage fully the historian's lively prose, which, though sometimes boyish, was written originally for adults. Coffin's juvenile books "are always enjoyable to the mature man," Griffis noted, for their author "discerns beneath the vivid picturing and simple rhetoric, so pleasing to the child, a practical knowledge and a philosophic depth which shows that the writer is a master of the art of reading men and events as well as of interpreting history."[53]

Carleton's Juveniles had widespread influence on a generation of young readers on the home front who were trying to make sense of their parents' civil feud in ways that school textbooks rarely attempted or achieved. A reviewer for the *Nation* remarked that Coffin's Civil War volumes were "well adapted to interest and instruct the young reader," while another commentator for the same journal referred to the series as "the best long history of the war yet written for young people."[54] In *The Imagined Civil War: Popular Literature of the North and South, 1861–1865*, Alice Fahs recounts the reactions of an eleven-year-old Massachusetts boy, Grenville Norcross, who kept a home reading journal in which he recorded his excitement at receiving one of Coffin's works, *My Days and Nights on the Battle-Field*, as a gift. This was one of his many war novels and war histories that "invited children to imagine *themselves* as protagonists in the war," Fahs has noted. " 'You take your place in the ranks, nervous, excited, and trembling at you know not what,' began an account of a call to arms in the middle of the night in Charles Carleton Coffin's *My Days and Nights on the Battlefield*." Such works "provided an important link to a postwar juvenile culture that stressed adventure and excitement for boys."[55] Coffin's juvenile histories were both spirited and spiritual; they were narrative and provocative; they emphasized the virtues of home and hearth; and, most of all, they did not seek to sanitize or trivialize the portentous events of the recent past.

Also popular in the home study market was Coffin's aforementioned historical series on liberty. Published originally by Harper and Brothers as part of the collection Historical Reading for the Young, works in the series included

FIGURE 15. Front and back covers of Charles Carleton Coffin, *Following the Flag* (Boston: Estes and Lauriat, 1886).

The Story of Liberty (1879), *Old Times in the Colonies* (1881), *The Boys of '76* (1881), and *Building the Nation* (1883). The first volume began with a description of the gradual emergence of freedom's light during the Dark Ages and included a discussion of the enormous price reformers paid for the acquisition of liberties in the late medieval period. The story progressed in subsequent volumes to a consideration of how the rights of individuals to think for themselves were safeguarded by political, ecclesiastical, and military battles against the forces of oppression, culminating in the creation of the American nation in the eighteenth century. This interest in liberty as a theme was a plausible intellectual transition for a man like Coffin, who believed that the Civil War had been fought to vindicate the Founding Fathers and to sustain the democratic principles that Washington, Adams, and Jefferson embraced. "If while reading this 'Story' you are roused to indignation, or pained at the recital of wrong and outrage," Coffin advised children, "remember that out of endurance and sacrifice has come all that you hold most dear; so will you comprehend what Liberty has cost, and what it is worth."[56]

In order to trace the theme of liberty in a linear fashion over time, Coffin developed a causal scheme in the series Historical Reading for the Young that linked all historical events to the revelation of God's providential plan for humanity. The idea that history had divine meaning was beyond debate in Coffin's mind. "Surely it has a meaning, else what are we living for?" he asked rhetorically in *Old Times in the Colonies*. "If there is design in the material world, there must be some meaning to history, some ultimate end to be accomplished."[57] While cynics pointed out that the history of human affairs reveals an indiscriminate pattern of oppressors getting their way, including many instances of tyrants employing ruthlessly a might-makes-right ethic, Coffin urged young readers to focus on the "other forces silently at work, which in time undermined their plans, as if a Divine hand were directing a counter-attack against them." Whoever reads *The Story of Liberty* without recognizing this providential feature "will fail of fully comprehending the meaning of history," Coffin warranted, adding, "There must be a meaning to history, or else existence is an incomprehensible enigma."[58] It is precisely this deterministic philosophy that Christian republishers like the Weiners have come to appreciate in Coffin's Juvenile Histories.

To Coffin, history was teleological, and this insight appealed to those in the home study movement, who decried the lack of moral agency in standard school textbooks. A child's understanding of the story of the past was crucial in determining God's plans for the present and the future, Coffin insisted. The narrative of the emergence of liberty "is a history not designed by man," he wrote, "for the men of one generation cannot lay a plan for the generation that succeeds it. Every person exercises his own individual will; and it is only a Divine hand that out of the greed, selfishness, avarice, ambition, and passions of the multitude out of their blunders, mistakes, and crimes—out of all the turmoils and conflicts of centuries—can mould a great Republic in which law, order, liberty, and an exalted sense of justice and right shall be supreme." Hence, in reading *The Story of Liberty* and *Old Times in the Colonies* children were instructed to look for examples of "how Tyranny and Wrong have fought against Liberty and Justice" as well as "how that banner which the barons flung to the breeze at Runnymede, inscribed with the rights of man, which Cromwell bore amidst the carnage of Marston Moor, which waved from the mast-head of the Mayflower when that lone vessel crossed the Atlantic, has never been trailed in the dust in this Western World; but Tyranny and Wrong have gone down before it." Readers were advised to know that "men die, generations come and go, but ideas live on," so that "through all the narratives of wars, massacres, and bloodshed" they might "see Right, Justice, and Liberty ever advancing." *Old Times in the Colonies* was not "an unmeaning record of events," Coffin asserted, "but the story of the rise of a great nation, the growth of individual liberty, the coming in of constitutional government in this Western World the history of the first period in the new era in human affairs. As you peruse these pages," he suggested, "the conviction, I trust, will come that, under the power of great ideas, our country is leading the human race in its march toward a state of society inexpressibly grand and glorious."[59]

In conveying these idealistic and providential ideals, Coffin was often more melodramatic than school textbooks tended to be, which was perhaps part of the attraction of his works to young home study readers. For instance, he was startlingly graphic in his treatment of Native American conflicts and their impact on the development of liberty as a guiding principle of colonial life. Depictions of Indian attacks on frontier homes were common in popular and school histories of the period, readers seeming to have an almost perverse fascination with treachery and slaughter. Yet Coffin's portrayals were more explicit than most, and he was not inclined to withhold hideous details from his young readers. His account of the kidnapping in 1697 of Hannah Dustin in *Old Times in the Colonies* is a case in point: "Mrs. Dustin rises, seizes a tomahawk, and gives one to Mary Neff, another to Samuel. Each selects a victim," Coffin wrote of the famous retaliatory incident. "A signal, and the hatchets descend, crushing through the skulls of the Indians, blow after blow in quick succession. It is the work of a minute, but in that brief time ten of the twelve have been killed." Prisoners no longer, Dustin and her compatriots "gather up the provisions, take the guns of the Indians, scuttle all the canoes but one, and take their departure down the Merrimac." But then a thought occurs to the fleeing trio: "Will their friends believe the story they will have to tell. They will have indisputable evidence. A few strokes of the paddle bring them back to the island, Mrs. Dustin runs the scalping-knife around the brows of the dead Indians, takes their scalps, and starts once more, guiding the canoe with her paddle, landing, and carrying it past dangerous rapids, reaching Haverhill, sixty miles distant, with her bloody trophies, to the astonishment of her friends, who thought her dead."[60]

One might well ask, as reviewers did, what the purpose of these graphic details was in histories intended for children. Was it justifiable as a demonstration of the power of moral retribution? or was it merely gratuitous violence? A worried mother reading the republished version of *Sweet Land of Liberty* with her son at home remarked, "We are learning a lot, but I don't know how much more of this I can take. Almost every chapter has hangings, Indian scalpings, or bodily dismemberment."[61] Part of Coffin's incentive in writing so vividly was to stay true to his tenet of not catering to the presumed sensitivities of young children. A writer for the *Atlantic Monthly* appreciated the fact that "'Carleton' ever treats his boy-readers as his intelligent equals, and considers them capable of understanding the common language of books and men."[62] Coffin's directness of approach may have left some school boards reluctant to endorse his works, but his volumes found a ready readership in the home market, and they still enjoy brisk sales today. "Probably the best thing I liked about it was how it was written," a blogger has written recently of *The Story of Liberty*. "Because [Coffin] realises that history is actually a thrilling story, full of Providential plot turns, desperate last stands, heroes and villains, the book is extremely easy to read. It's written vividly, in the present tense."[63] As another current reader of a Maranatha republication of the work notes, "It is no dry history text. It reads like a novel, bringing to life the amazing events and fascinating people who fought and sacrificed for the liberty we now enjoy. I have read it for pure pleasure myself and also used it in teaching American history to my own children at home and in the classroom. It instills a love for history and an appreciation for what we have as Americans."[64]

Strong moral convictions, opinionated prose, presentist literary conventions, and graphic, even lurid, detail assured that the volumes in Coffin's liberty series would be highly popular with children in the nineteenth century. For all of these reasons it might seem to make sense that Christian presses today would reprint Coffin's histories in support of their homeschooling cause, having as much in common as they do with the philosophies of the home study advocates who consumed his works originally. Yet the wisdom of reprinting these works in the twenty-first century is not as obvious as would first appear. Many pedagogues in the 1880s and 1890s found fault with the educational assumptions vis-à-vis child rearing and literacy implicit in the home study model, and they attacked popular historians whose works they viewed as complicit in the propagation of those erroneous beliefs. With respect to the study of the past, these critics also pointed to the limitations of providential history, which restricted the role of free will in historical narratives and took a decidedly unscientific approach to causal and temporal interpretation. Cultivating historical-mindedness in children was not a matter of convincing them of the preordained nature of human events, these critics noted, but of alerting them to the consequences of unreflective action. This, they argued, was the special role of the American public school system.

Child Study and Emergent Historical Literacy

Despite the challenges and struggles it faced from the home study movement, the public school in the United States was in the ascendancy in the mid-nineteenth century, and its trajectory conformed to the changing conceptions of childhood that influenced its growth. As we have seen, children in the eighteenth century and the early nineteenth were treated as little adults who were pushed hurriedly toward maturity as a protection against the vulnerabilities of youth. Goodrich's conception of a high-minded literature for the young, with its attendant moral edifications, was in keeping with an accelerated conception of childhood. The Pestalozzi method introduced by the Abbotts was more patient and allowed children greater time and freedom to make mistakes in the learning process, but its permissiveness worried traditionalists like Pollard, who associated literacy with building self-esteem through age-appropriate tasks. This pedagogy was consistent with a late-century Victorian appreciation for the so-called long childhood—a period extending from infancy to the age of eighteen—that identified distinct phases of sequential growth in children and contributed to a new scientific interest in the emotional, physical, and sexual development of children over time. This, in turn, led to the emergence of educational manuals written by child-rearing experts who, according to Steven Mintz, were "physicians and psychologists" rather than "ministers and moralists" and who espoused "rational rather than spiritual advice."[65]

In the 1880s the acknowledged leader of this new child study movement in the United States was the educator and psychologist G. Stanley Hall.[66] Hall's late nineteenth-century scientific work on the stages of childhood development began with minute observations of children in public schools and the compiling of detailed reports about their behaviors. These notes led to the creation of a series of questionnaires designed to identify critical transition points in the life of a child. Hall and his associates interviewed hundreds of kindergarten children in Boston, for instance, asking them extensive questions about animals, astronomy, geography, mathematics, meteorology, and plants. They arrived at some surprising findings. As Mintz summarizes, "Hall was startled by the children's ignorance. Eighty percent did not know what a beehive was. Fully 90 percent did not know where their ribs were, 65 percent couldn't identify their ankles, and 93 percent did not know that leather came from animals. Hall concluded that teachers could not assume that children came to school with a common fund of basic knowledge" in any subject area. In response, he "gathered empirical information about children's physical growth, psychological development, and sexual maturation. Through further questionnaires and close observations of thousands of children, researchers investigated language development, hearing, and eyesight; children's ethical and religious impulses; and their psychological lives, including their ideas about old age, disease, and death."[67] The results of these findings were published in various child study journals that promoted efforts to take the guesswork out of educational psychology and to bring credibility to it as a science. The forerunner of mental testing and assessment techniques, Hall's longitudinal studies deemed teaching a "scientific pedagogy," not an intuitive art.[68]

Hall's conception that "children develop through clearly differentiated cognitive, emotional, and physiological stages, marked by distinctive psychological and emotional characteristics" led to the identification of phases of early childhood development. These included an initial period that "should be devoted to free play, healthful exercise, and oral instruction, devoid of premature learning; a succeeding stage suitable for intensive instruction in reading, writing, and arithmetic; and, most of all, adolescence, a period of psychological and emotional storm and stress that began with puberty and marked a young person's social and sexual maturation."[69] Hall urged parents and teachers to "love their children intelligently enough to study them," and in sufficient depth to facilitate the creation of educational lesson plans that addressed the specific needs of each stage of a child's development.[70] At a meeting of the Committee on Child Study of the Brookline Massachusetts Education Society in November 1895, for instance, the educator E. M. Hartwell reminded listeners that childhood is not a singular condition from which one graduates instantaneously at a distinct, discernible moment, as during a religious conversion; rather, it is a series of stages through which one passes incrementally and from which one reaches adulthood slowly. Children are not "literary echoes" of adults, Hartwell argued, and therefore the "child cannot be judged by an adult standard. He is not a miniature man."[71]

The concept of sequential development revolutionized the way late nineteenth-century educators approached learning in many disciplines, especially reading. Monosyllabic historians had made some concessions to young children in terms of protecting them from polysyllabic challenges and from needing to make associations among groups of words when arranged in complex sentences. For Hall and his associates, however, even the customized literacy programs of monosyllablists were ineffective when foisted prematurely on immature students in home study settings. They held that children could not learn to read adequately until they possessed a "certain mental maturity," what specialists today call "reading readiness." Maturationists claimed that at the very youngest stages of development, reading was to be secondary to learning to live. This philosophy, which is still at the heart of Montessori instruction, was predicated on the assumption that "literacy is not a static ability that develops at one distinct point in a child's education, but rather an ongoing evolution of abilities and attitudes. The conceptualization of literacy as an emergent, or developing, skill led parents and lecturers to rethink their approach to teaching children how to read and write." At the so-called preliterate stages, students were encouraged to take part gradually in conversations, using more and more descriptive words in increasingly complex ways. Because children in this stage also like to be read to aloud, especially from short stories and poems that expose them to rhyme and alliteration, the emerging literacy model emphasizes interactive readings characterized by choral repetition, pointing, and picture associations as well as tracing letters and mock reading. The method encouraged parents to reread favorite works to their preliterate children, as repetition fosters familiarity with sounds and words. Once these skills are mastered, the theory goes, children are prepared to take on the more demanding tasks of phonetic decoding and vocabulary acquisition.[72]

In terms of historical literacy Hall took aim at the determinism of works such as Coffin's *The Story of Liberty*, which he felt were confusing to children, who had no sense of agency in the past. In 1883 Hall edited a series of volumes on educational pedagogy in which he and his associates outlined approaches to literacy based on developmental rather than providential theories of learning. He began the first volume, *Methods of Teaching History*, with editorial reflections on the poor state of history education in the late nineteenth century: "History was chosen for the subject of the first volume of this educational library because, after much observation in the schoolrooms of many of the larger cities in the eastern part of our country, the editor, without having a hobby about its relative importance or being in any sense an expert in history, is convinced that no subject so widely taught is, on the whole, taught so poorly." Hall warned against beginning history training in children too early, notably via the recitation methods used in most public and Sunday Schools, which "sometimes actually deform the pupil's historic sense, and illustrate the danger of great ideas to minds not well disciplined for them." He advised further, "The high educational value of history is too great to be left to teachers who merely hear recitations, keeping the finger on the place in the text-book, and only asking the questions conveniently printed for them in the margin or back of the book." In younger children, Hall added, the "wider altruistic and ethical interests, which it is the special function of history to develop, rarely become strong enough to control narrower and more isolated and selfish aims in life." Hence, Hall favored studying the past in discrete, calculated stages, beginning with myths and legends, which helped establish the epic drama of the past, and then moving on to biographies, which humanized history by emphasizing the human condition.[73]

At the heart of these dicta of the child study program was the assumption that school administrators, psychologists, and teachers had a right and a responsibility to monitor the physical, emotional, and even moral development of children, above all when students lacked proper information and guidance at home. As Andrew White of Cornell University explained in an additional chapter in Hall's *Methods of Teaching History,* professional historians trained in the developmental aspects of their discipline were ideally qualified to oversee curricular reforms centered on the gradual maturation of rising students.[74] The application of these progressive methodologies to the lives of schoolchildren afforded sophisticated, useful techniques for monitoring development, White noted, although it required that parents be willing to entrust their children to professional educators in public schools. The minutes from a child study committee meeting in Brookline typify the kind of relationship such educators imagined for themselves and the parents of their students. "Mr. C. C. Soule raised an inquiry in regard to the amount of help parents could properly give their children," the minutes note. Soule argued that "methods of teaching have so changed that the parent is often left behind," obligating school officials to help parents come "to know the individual characteristics of their children" and to "strengthen them upon those lines" so that they might "supplement the school work with appropriate tasks." He concluded that the home had a distinct but only supplemental role to play in the development of American children.[75] Schools had become the control centers for learning, and teachers increasingly took on the responsibility of guiding the young through the developmental stages of intellectual, social, and emotional growth.

With respect to the responsibility of teachers in the study of history, the presumption among the child study advocates was that school boards should endorse textbooks that were attuned to the precise needs of developing groups of readers at specific moments in their youthful progression. A chapter in Hall's *Methods of Teaching History* devoted to the question "Why do children dislike history?" blamed the "one-size-fits-all" approach adopted by most writers of juvenile school books for the lack of interest in things historical among secondary school children. The author of this article argued that small boys and girls had contempt for history because it was written in ways that were not age appropriate and that predisposed them against the discipline as they got older. Young children require historical texts that humanize the past, he argued, not those that focus on the complex principles of cause and effect more suitable for older readers. "The moral of it all is, that the fault is not in the child, but in us who write the books and teach the lessons," he wrote. "In truth, the whole situation, in respect to history, is described in that well-known conversation between the English clergyman and the play-actor," he added. "'Why is it,' asked the clergyman, 'that you, who represent what everybody knows to be false, obtain more attention than we who deal in the most momentous realities!' 'It is,' said the actor, 'because you represent the truth so that it seems like fiction, while we depict fiction in such a manner that it has the effect of truth.'"[76] By this logic, providential historical works such as those by Coffin qualified more as dramatic productions than as reliable liturgical tomes.

The author of this chapter on juvenile aversion to the study of the past in Hall's *Methods of Teaching History* was Thomas Wentworth Higginson, the colonel whose African American troops Coffin had followed in the spring of 1863 (fig. 16). After the war Higginson became an essayist and lecturer of some renown. On one level Higginson and Coffin had a good deal in common. They were both from the Boston area, both participants in the Civil War, and both involved in writing children's historical literature in the postwar period. They were also ardent New England reformers who had been involved in the abolitionist movement in the antebellum period, although Higginson played a more auspicious role, having been a member of the infamous Secret Six, who funded John Brown's raid on Harpers Ferry. Unlike Coffin, however, Higginson did not believe children's authors should traffic in such partisan matters as slavery and war, and he labored to produce literature that would be informative to young readers while remaining understated and even neutral with respect to the most disturbing elements of the past. As a writer, Higginson was more reductionist than Coffin, pursuing, as he noted in the introduction to one of his histories, "the lighter but not always easier

FIGURE 16. Portrait of Thomas Wentworth Higginson. Print Collection, Miriam and Ira D. Wallach Division of Art, Prints and Photographs, The New York Public Library, Astor, Lenox and Tilden Foundations.

task of the literary man to reduce accumulations into compact shape, select what is most characteristic, and make the result readable."[77]

Higginson's primary contribution to Hall's child-centric literature was his *Young Folks' History of the United States,* a mainstay of the child study history curriculum at schools across the country in the 1880s.[78] Higginson wrote this work with two literary principles in mind, both employed for the benefit of young readers: "to omit all names and dates not really needful" and "to make liberal use of the familiar traits and incidents of every day" while giving less space "to the events of war, and more to the affairs of peace." A former soldier himself, Higginson endorsed Coffin's perspective that it was "desirable, no doubt, that the reader should fully understand the way in which every important war began and ended, and that he should read enough of the details to know in what spirit it was carried on." For the youngest readers, however, Higginson contended that "the statistics of sieges and battles are of little value, and are apt to make us forget that the true glory of a nation lies, after all, in orderly progress. Times of peace, the proverb says, have few historians; but this may be more the fault of the historians than of the times."[79] If so, then Coffin was as blameworthy as anyone, and Higginson sought to rectify the error.

The publisher of Higginson's *Young Folks' History,* Lee and Shepard, promoted it as a "clear and charmingly written" volume that would be for American youth what Dickens's *Child's History of England* was for "the children of our cousins beyond the sea."[80] A circular advertising the forthcoming work promised it would be "entertaining and picturesque" and written in a style that would be more comprehensible to children than any other textbook on the market. "It is a curious fact that style seems usually the very last thing to be considered by the makers of school-books," the literary notice declared. "They respect facts, as profoundly as did Mr. Gradgrind, but they tell them as baldly as if gracefulness of expression were a crime."[81] The theory of the book "can be briefly stated," the promoters of the *Young Folks' History* continued. "It is, that American history is in itself one of the most attractive of all subjects, and can be made interesting to old and young by being presented in a simple, clear, and graphic way."[82] Advertisements accompanying specimen sheets for *Young Folks' History* promised romance as well as readability. A writer for the *Chicago Tribune* reported that one of his colleagues, whom he found "greedily devouring" the advance proofs of Higginson's book, had invoked the spirit of another brilliant writer of British prose, Sir Walter Scott, in declaring the *Young Folks' History* "as interesting as Ivanhoe!" despite the fact that it was written for children.[83]

One thing Higginson did not wish to be accused of doing in the *Young Folks' History* was overdramatizing the past in ways that Dickens, Scott, and even Coffin had. Juxtaposing passages from Higginson's *Young Folks' History* with comparable ones from Coffin's *Old Times in the Colonies* reveals the extent to which Higginson repressed such melodramatic impulses. For instance, as we've seen, Coffin went to great lengths to describe the gruesome details of the retribution sought by Hannah Dustin for her kidnapping by Indians in 1697, including mention of the fact that Dustin had taken the scalps of her victims as "bloody trophies." Higginson's treatment of the same incident is markedly different. He not only includes a raison d'être for Dustin's retaliation but also obscures some of the bloodiest details for the sake of his young readers. He wrote, "At last, when they were encamped on an island in the Merrimack River, the prisoners discovered that they were to be put to death with tortures at the end of the journey, and resolved to save themselves. At night, when their captors were asleep, the three prisoners killed with tomahawks ten of the twelve Indians, and escaped to the white settlements."[84] The discretion Higginson believed was required of children's literature prevented him, as it had not Coffin, from adding the dramatic detail that Dustin had scalped her Indian victims.

Unlike Coffin, Higginson tried to remain nonpartisan in his presentation of the past, believing that young people were capable of making up their own minds about the right and wrong of a situation if the alternatives were presented fairly. This tendency toward balance was a reflection of the child study's nondeterministic philosophy of history, in which free will was both a means and an end in the study of history. As Herbert B. Adams, a professor at Johns Hopkins University, noted in a chapter titled "Special Methods of Historical Study" included in Hall's *Methods of Teaching History*, the child study method was predicated on the concept of truth as being fluid and dynamic rather than rigid and inalterable. Calling for a proportional approach to the past, Adams made a special plea for the "application of the comparative method to the use of historical literature. Students should learn to view history," he wrote, "in different lights and from various standpoints. Instead of relying passively upon the *ipse dixit* [dictum] of the schoolmaster, or of the school-book, or of some one historian, pupils should learn to judge for themselves by comparing evidence."[85] Higginson employed this pedagogical strategy in the *Young Folks' History of the United States* (he called it persuading) with its "higher form of freedom of discussion," even with regard to religious history, "such as prevails more and more universally in all our public high schools, where Jew and Gentile, Catholic and Protestant, are encouraged to search subjects for themselves, the pupil simply looking toward the teachers as presiding officers in the debate."[86]

These reflections on the neutral treatment of religion in his popular history reveal the extent to which Higginson endorsed the balanced approaches to the past advanced first by the Abbott brothers and then refined in the child study movement. He had seen Hall's methods work in practical educational settings in which the difficult topic of religion was under discussion. In one of his autobiographical writings, Higginson recounted having observed the "classes in American history" of the educator and author Alice Wellington Rollins, who taught the Protestant Reformation to young female students by means of a debate method. Her room was "equally divided between Catholic and Protestant," Higginson noted; "the girls in succession brought out all they knew, and then, for want of ammunition, begged to have the debate adjourned until the next week, when they would come back with their cartridge-boxes replenished." In answer to Higginson's later inquiry to the teacher as to whether "either side converted the other," Rollins replied, "Probably not," but at least they now might "[hold] their own view in a larger spirit, as understanding the points at which honest minds could differ."[87] Higginson adapted this ecumenical outlook for use in his *Young Folks' History*, in which his heroes, for example, Roger Williams, consistently champion toleration. Williams was "not always moderate or judicious in his way of expressing these opinions," Higginson wrote, "but most people would now admit that his views on toleration were right and wise." Higginson admired religious leaders like John Eliot who acknowledged and respected clergy of other faiths: "There were so many quarrels between the French and the English in those early days, and between the Roman Catholics and Protestants, that it is pleasant to see any instances of harmony and toleration."[88]

A nondenominational stance toward religion was quite at odds with Coffin's providential one. In the introduction to *The Story of Liberty*, Coffin offered the pretense of impartiality when he declared, "You will also take special notice that nothing is said [in this book] against religion—nothing against the Pope because he is Pope; nothing against a Catholic because he is a Catholic; nor against a Protestant because he protests against the authority of the Church of Rome. Facts of history only are given." But in fact a strong anti-Catholic bias did run throughout Coffin's work. For instance, he described medieval England as "overrun with monks and friars" who had "taken solemn vows to have nothing to do with the world" but who actually enjoyed "bountiful tables" in a land "suffering from want." He condemned unscrupulous Catholic priests for selling indulgences and relics for personal profit. "They have relics for sale," he wrote in *The Story of Liberty*, including "shreds of clothing which they declare was worn by the Virgin Mary, pieces of the true cross; bones of saints—all very holy." There were so many vestiges in this priestly stockpile, Coffin added, that John the Baptist appeared to have "four shoulder-blades, eight arms, eleven fingers, besides twelve complete hands, thirteen skulls, and seven whole bodies—enough almost for a regiment!" The most vilified figures in Coffin's volumes were Catholic popes, who were described universally as shams and reprobates. "The Pope decrees that men must believe in religion as he believes," Coffin wrote derisively. "There is no appeal from his decree. If a man believes differently, he shall be thrown into prison, tortured till he makes confession, and then he is burned to death, and all his property confiscated." And who gave the popes this authority? "No one," Coffin proclaimed. "They took it, and, having taken it, they intend to keep it."[89]

So heavy-handed were Coffin's sentiments about Catholicism in the liberty series that he was attacked rather savagely in the press for them. The historian James K. Hosmer characterized *The Story of Liberty* as a "thoroughly misleading and harmful" book for children because of its antipapal tendencies. While Hosmer admitted that the Roman Catholic Church "can justly be called to account for many shortcomings," he insisted that "it is not the only imperfect institution which the world has seen." Protestants, too, had committed sins against liberty, Hosmer noted, and he condemned Coffin for working so deliberately to convey "a wrong impression" of the religious causes of tyranny and restricted freedoms in Europe and America. "In the hands of the young for whom [the volume] is intended," Hosmer concluded, "it is certain to be an instrument of harm."[90] Thomas K. Hanna, who grew up in a Missouri home in the 1880s in which the "Coffin classics" were readily available, professed that the books were shunned by parents and children alike because they contained "such seeds of false prejudice" as were thought to be "a potential source of harmful discord" to the "impressionable mind of a schoolboy." Responding to a reviewer in the *New York Times* who spoke "to the merit" of Coffin's works, Hanna admonished, "By all means let us avoid the Charles Carleton Coffin spirit of unfair and prejudiced partisanship at the expense of truth."[91]

Home study proponents who admired Coffin's outspokenness found themselves locked in debate with child study promoters, who refused to allow such books to become part of public school reading lists. Providential history, especially providential history of a doctrinal variety, had no place in the public schools, according to Coffin's critics. *The Story of Liberty*, for instance, precipitated "a furious religious war" in the Indiana legislature that broke out when a representative introduced a resolution condemning the anti-Catholicism of Coffin's book in the state-supported, school-endorsed Indiana Reading Circle list. Claiming *The Story of Liberty* "makes an attack on the [Catholic] Church and is aiding in keeping alive a spirit of religious intolerance which the Legislature should condemn," Representative Peter Wallrath was adamant in holding that the volume be removed from the superintendent of school's list of recommended reading because its purpose was evidently to "abuse and vilify" Catholics. After a bitter, protracted discussion about the potential impact of the book "on school children who were searching after the truth of history," the resolution passed by a vote of 75 to 12.[92]

Higginson's unbiased approaches proved more acceptable than Coffin's to school boards searching to adopt history books for young readers. Many welcomed his view that children of a certain age could be trained away from prejudices associated with doctrinal knowledge and behavior. "Children are naturally partisans; in their estimation, one side is always and altogether right, the other wholly wrong," a child study committee in Illinois warned. Consequently, the "study of the history of his own country by a person of immature years, may cause this natural tendency to develop into an intellectual habit. Guard against this result," committee members counseled, "especially if the text in use is written in a glowing style. Cultivate in your pupils a spirit of judicial fairness. Disinterestedness is one of the cardinal intellectual virtues, and this study offers exceptional opportunities to cultivate it."[93] Distinctly partisan points of view had been bleached out of Higginson's *Young*

Folks' History of the United States; personalized opinions had been obliterated. A reviewer for the *Wisconsin Journal of Education* predicted that school boards would continue to embrace the book "because the story is told in such a way as to impress the imagination and fasten itself upon the memory" in balanced and responsible ways."[94] Frederick Sheldon of the *Nation* was grateful that Higginson had shown restraint in avoiding the "rampant patriotism" and "spread-eagleism" so evident in the majority of history books written for children in the aftermath of the Civil War. "Even manifest destiny has been omitted," Sheldon marveled after reading Higginson's history, remarking how pleased he was "not to be told that America is the home of the oppressed of all nations, and the only hope of liberty and civilization."[95] "Never in my life have I been received so warmly," Higginson admitted with pride. "Everywhere I have found my books well known, one private school even using my 'Young Folks History,' and one schoolmaster in South Carolina holding my Epictetus to be next to the Bible."[96]

More rational than spiritual, more biographical than analytical, Higginson's *Young Folks' History of the United States* reaffirmed Hall's developmental theories, which were working their way gradually into American schools by the 1880s. Rapidly disappearing from school classrooms were the older pedagogical techniques associated with teleological and deterministic histories, and in their place was substituted a narrative manner that emphasized the thrill of history without its sentimentalized cant. By the early 1880s *Young Folks' History* was having a larger impact on the way children learned the lessons of history than the works of Coffin. "A taste for better reading is rapidly growing among our children," a satisfied parent avowed with respect to works like Higginson's. "It is to be hoped that the present method may obtain generally, as the results warrant us in saying history may be made delightful, and even fascinating" when introduced under the proper pedagogical restraints.[97] A parent of several young boys who were reading the volume simultaneously wrote that "Colonel Higginson has written a book that is not only valuable, but one that the boys all want to read and will fight for the chance to read." Having only one copy of *Young Folks' History* in the house, he added, "We have been compelled to take [it] away" at times "in the interests of peace."[98] According to his publisher, Higginson had "done the world great service" by inaugurating what his wife identified as "a new era in writing history for children."[99] That transition was accomplished at the expense of Coffin and other popular historians whose works failed to keep up with the latest theories of literacy and child development.

"Better No History than False History"

Coffin's growing obsolescence in the face of competition from Higginson and others in the child study movement was not a complete surprise to him or his friends. Those closest to Coffin anticipated that his writings would not withstand the test of time for three distinct reasons. First, Coffin never thought of himself as a historian but only as a journalist interested in historical themes. There's no denying he had a historian's interest in accuracy—Griffis refers to him as a "hater of lies"—and he was described accurately in his day as "a soldier of the pen and a knight of truth." Yet many of Coffin's histories consisted merely of lengthy quotations taken from his extensive travel writings as a Civil War correspondent and, later, as a foreign correspondent for several newspapers and loosely tied together in a conversational format. This literary and methodological choice limited the metanarrative sweep of what he wrote. Coffin rarely missed a journalistic deadline, his biographer noted, but he also never had much time to reflect broadly on the historical meaning of what he was writing. "Strictly speaking, in the light of the more rigid canons of historical knowledge and the research demanded in our days, and when tested by stern criticism, Mr. Coffin was not a historical scholar of the first order. Nor did he make any such pretension," Griffis argued. "No one, certainly not himself, would dream of ranging his name in the same line with those of the great masters, Prescott, Motley, Bancroft, or Parkman,—men of wealth and leisure, as well as of ability." In fact, he was obligated to these broader-thinking historians in ways he frequently conceded in his introductions. "His first purpose was to make an impression, and his second, to fix that impression inerasably on the mind," Griffis noted. "For this, he trusted largely the work of those who had lived before him, and he made diligent and liberal use of materials already accumulated." Like John S. C. Abbott, "he would paint his own picture after making the drawings and arranging his tints, perspective, lights, and shadows."[100]

Second, Coffin published more quickly than may have been judicious. He produced over forty volumes in a thirty-five-year writing career, releasing seven histories from five publishing houses in the two-year period from 1879 to 1881 alone.[101] Not surprisingly, one finds errors in many of his works, and these collectively have hampered his long-term reputation as a historian. In *The Story of Liberty,* for instance, Coffin perpetuated Pierson's mistake about Sir Walter Raleigh having traveled to the New World to found the Colony of Roanoke. Compounding this error, Coffin insisted that Raleigh made several additional trips to the region, where he traded with the Indians before returning to England "carrying with him some of the tobacco of Virginia."[102] Such inaccuracies might seem harmless in isolation, but in associating Raleigh with the marketing of tobacco as a cash crop, Coffin leapt irresponsibly to the conclusion that the intrepid adventurer promoted slavery and played a major role in encouraging the Civil War. "We shall see that a little tobacco-smoke whiffed nearly three hundred years ago [by Raleigh] has had an influence in bringing about the rebellion," Coffin wrote inaccurately and unfairly in *My Days and Nights on the Battle-Field*.[103]

Third, Coffin was never recognized by his contemporaries as a gifted writer of historical literature. His style was lively and exciting with respect to historical action, but his analyses were often ponderous, and he found it difficult to articulate the larger historical forces at work in the universe. Griffis likened him to "the father of his Country," George Washington, who was less brilliant than practical, less theoretical than strategic. A bit of a plodder intellectually, Coffin was more interested in literary impact than in metanarrative insight, especially when it came to the field of juvenile historical literature. Coffin's style "was different from anything to which [children] had been accustomed," Griffis wrote. "Peter Parley had, indeed, in his time, created a fresh style of historical narration which captivated unnumbered readers by its simple and direct method of presenting subjects known in their general outline," he added, "but not made of sufficient human or present interest." Employing the developmental language now popular in conversations about historical thinking, Griffis averred that Goodrich's works "had suited exactly the stage of culture which the majority of young people in our country had reached when the Parley books were written. It is doubtful, however, whether those same works would have achieved a like success in the last three decades of this century." Coffin's genius was more mechanical and in keeping with the utilitarian character of his age. "Education had been so much improved, schools were so much more general, the development of the press and cheap reading matter was so great, that in the enlargement of view consequent upon the successful issue of the great civil war, a higher order of historical narration was a necessity," Griffis wrote. "He who would win the new generation needed to be neither a professional scholar, a man of research, nor a genius, but he must know human nature well, and be familiar with great national movements, the causes and the channels of power."[104] Coffin demonstrated some of these traits but lacked others.

If Coffin did not think of himself primarily as a historian but as a journalist; if he acknowledged that his histories were prone to errors; and if he understood that his literary style was not noteworthy with respect to historical synthesis, then why have his texts been republished in such great numbers by companies such as Maranatha Publications and used so widely to anchor homeschool curricula in history in the twenty-first century? There are three primary answers to this question as well: first, the Christian orientation of Coffin's works has an obvious appeal to those on the Christian Right who are committed to providential history; second, the assumption that Coffin supported the home study movement and its associated pedagogies; and third, the lingering skepticism Coffin shared presumably with homeschooling advocates regarding the efficacy of child study programs as a pedagogical strategy in public schools. None of these considerations would have persuaded Coffin, however, that his books were worth republishing. Indeed, if one looks more closely at Coffin's texts, one discovers that they are not always what homeschoolers and republishers like the Weiners imagine them to be.

Consider, for instance, the first of these contentions: that Coffin's works are committed to a Christian and providential perspective. There is no question that nineteenth-century readers purchased Coffin's works because they endorsed a deterministic philosophy of history that many Christians found compatible with their own faiths. Griffis insightfully wrote, "Charles Carleton Coffin had a face that helped one to believe in God," and this divine element, when transferred to his popular histories by a process Griffis referred to as "spiritual induction," helped sell volumes. Although not trained as a minister, Coffin was a man of such "intense conviction" that one finds religious "earnestness in every tone" of his writing. The Civil War was an opportunity to sharpen "fresh axes of moral reconstruction," Griffis noted, and it furnished this "soldier of righteousness" the chance to elaborate on "things Christian and Godlike" as well as on the "phenomena of spiritual courage and enterprise."[105] Rose Weiner wrote in the introduction to Maranatha's republished version of *Old Times in the Colonies* that she was won over by Coffin's "Providential perspective of history (a perspective that is difficult to find expressed today in the closing years of the twentieth century)"[106]

Yet Weiner fails to mention that Coffin embraced a specific brand of Christianity, one whose philosophies were not mainstream in his own day and remain controversial among Christian fundamentalists even in this. Specifically, Coffin was a "free churchman," meaning he was not overly reliant on the religious credentials of those "who should preach to him or administer the sacraments," and he rejected the argument that any member of any church has "the smallest claim to any kind of authority over or among his fellow members." Instead, he believed everyone was open to the spirit of God, and he looked forward to the day when there would be a "shredding off of many things dogmatic theologians consider to be vital to Christianity." As Griffis notes, Coffin was leery especially of "evangelical churches holding the historic form of Christianity" that attempted to foist on believers an authoritarian administrative structure and to link too closely "private redemption and civil reform." Hence, Coffin was an Anabaptist who called for a strict separation of church and state, and he had a Congregationalist's sense of ecclesiastical independence. This was one of the reasons he harbored such negative feelings toward the Roman Catholic Church, whose papal authority he rejected so vehemently in his histories. While traveling in Italy shortly after the Civil War, Coffin visited Rome, where he took notice with disgust that "French bayonets were still supporting the Pope's temporal throne." He was delighted to discover, however, that within a fortnight of his arrival "the last echoes of the French drum-beat and bugle-blast had died away." Italy "was waking to a new life," he reported, and the Anabaptists "were avenged and justified."[107]

As Coffin would have understood, no policy could be more incompatible with the philosophies of the Weiners than this Anabaptist doctrine. The incongruity is especially evident when one considers the recent history of accusations against the Weiners with respect to the excessive authoritarianism of their church practices. In the mid-1980s, for instance, Bob and Rose Weiner came under harsh criticism by an ad hoc committee of United Churches whose members labeled Maranatha a cult-like institution.[108] Bob Weiner's "exotic blend of Bible-thumping, born-again Christianity and conservative politics is drawing criticism from an increasing number of angry parents," a *Wall Street Journal* article noted, recording complaints from mothers and fathers of students in the Maranatha program that it has "an authoritarian orientation with potential negative consequences for members."[109] Parents worried that their children had undergone radical personality changes while associated with the Weiners' movement: their grades fell, and they donated large sums of money to Maranatha that had been earmarked for their educations. Some refused medical and dental treatment, believing such practices demonstrated a lack of faith in God's healing power. In its report, the investigatory committee cited the Weiners for employing "faulty methods of biblical interpretation, questionable practices, and deficient theology—including an unclear view of the Trinity." The committee also "expressed skepticism about the regular revelations or 'words from the Lord' that Maranatha leaders and members" claimed to receive. "It appears to us that there is at least the potential for the final authority to rest more with the 'revelations' of MCM leaders than the Bible," the report states.[110]

Religious tyranny like this was anathema to Coffin. He went on the public lecture circuit to lobby against its insidious influences in his day. In November 1888, for instance, he gave a speech before the Congregational Club of Boston analyzing the role of the Roman Catholic Church in the education

of Boston public school children. Titled "Our Schools," the address began
with a characteristic attack on Catholic parochial schools, whose staffs, Coffin
vouched, were subjected to the "priestly command" of the pope in Rome.
Many Catholics refused to enroll their sons and daughters in the public school
system because they believed that "the state has no right or authority to control the education of the children of the church," Coffin offered. For these
parents, as for the Weiners, it made more sense initially to choose private
instruction over public education. Because Catholics recognized that the public schools were far superior to private educational institutions funded by the
Church, however, they adopted a new strategy in the 1880s to improve their
children's educations by running Catholic candidates for open seats on the
Boston school board. The idea was to gain majority control of the board and
then to influence decisions about hiring and firing, curriculum development,
and book selection. Warning listeners who might object to getting "their politics from Rome" that they must be vigilant in guarding against any efforts to
impose a similar "Roman hierarchy" on public schools, Coffin condemned
such electioneering practices as overtly biased and ideological. "I do not say
that every Catholic is an offensive partisan and sectarian," Coffin averred, "but
there are men upon the Boston School Board who are so intensely partisan &
who are so dominated by bad prejudices and who are so intensely sectarian
that they not only improve opportunity, but make opportunity for crowding
out American teachers & putting in Irish."[111]

Among other things, Catholics who managed to get elected to the Bos-
ton school board began tinkering with the required reading lists, especially
in history, gaining enough votes to remove William Swinton's *Outlines of
World History* (with its acknowledged pro-Protestant outlook) in favor of
John J. Anderson's more pro-Catholic text titled *A Complete Course in History:
New Manual of General History with Particular Attention to Ancient and Modern
Civilizations*.[112] Coffin objected to this substitution and urged his Protestant
friends to regain seats on the board and to make their first order of business
the removal of Anderson's book.[113] But, revealingly, Coffin did not call for
a return to *Outlines of World History* as a required text, since he agreed that
Swinton was prone to overstatement and "a shade of coloring" that "falsified"
history as much as, if not more than, Anderson's work. "If I am correctly
informed, the restoration of Swinton's History is to be the issue of the campaign" and that Protestant candidates for the school board "are to be required
to pledge themselves for its restoration," Coffin intoned. "Are you quite sure
that you will best advance the interest of the public schools by doing that?" he
asked. "Better no history than false history," he reasoned. Nor did he push for
the adoption of his own works as substitutes, a tack that might have satisfied

those with Protestant leanings in positions of authority within the Boston public school system. This act of self-removal was not a gesture of modesty, however; it hints instead that Coffin's anti-authoritarianism was so profound that he would have rather dispensed altogether with historical reading in schools than have a reading list imposed on students by an authority committed too stringently to "party politics or religious belief," even his own.[114]

The second assumption among republishers of Coffin's popular histories—that Coffin was a home study supporter who disapproved of public school education—is also inaccurate. It is true that many in the home study movement (in the past and in the present) have been suspicious of "compulsory and state supported" education and the so-called experts who control it. While sympathetic to these complaints, Coffin did not believe Hall's child study method conferred too much power on schools or educational psychologists. He was, instead, a strong proponent of public education. It is revealing, in fact, that Coffin chose a formal public address as his means to air grievances about the Boston school board, a clue as to how invested he was in the system itself. He propounded in a public arena that all Bostonians, Protestants *and* Catholics, should abandon parochial and home education and make public schools their highest priority.[115] In *Old Times in the Colonies,* Coffin had traced proudly the roots of public education from the colonial period to the Revolution, and he drew on this narrative to convince his listeners that their interests were tightly bound together in the success of the public school system.[116] So committed was Coffin to public education, in fact, that he served for several years as the commissioner of schools in Malden, Massachusetts, and he eventually lobbied the state legislature successfully for the issuing of free textbooks to the public school children of Boston.[117]

What kinds of books did Coffin recommend in his capacity as commissioner of schools? Not Swinton's or Anderson's histories or his own; instead, he endorsed the choices of Hall, whose *Methods of Teaching History* offered a bibliography of "Books for Collateral Reading in Connection with Class Work," which included several of Higginson's histories.[118] This support of the work of educational psychologists implies that the priorities of early homeschoolers and public school advocates were not as different as those who are republishing Coffin's works in the twenty-first century would have us believe. Indeed, in their day, popular historians like Higginson and Coffin did not necessarily see themselves as competing with each other. As a reviewer for the *Pennsylvania Monthly* said of Coffin's *The Boys of '76,* the volume is "an admirable supplement to Mr. Higginson's *Young Folks' History,* which in some respects it resembles."[119]

The third contention of republishers—that Coffin disapproved of child study and its related progressive educational reforms—is also not borne out by the facts.[120] Along with many others, he worked actively on behalf of both initiatives. If one examines the minutes of the child study committee meetings of Brookline, where Coffin resided, one finds that the professed goal of many of the professional educators who chaired such gatherings was to integrate home and school, not to separate them. The mission statement of the Brookline Society for Education, founded in 1895 celebrated the fact that "teachers and parents are coming more into conference." The school stands "midway between the family and the state," noted a keynote speaker at the inaugural session of the society, adding that "all obligations should be met by intelligent cooperation."[121] To facilitate this collaborative process, lecturers were invited to speak before the Brookline child study group on pedagogical issues. The speakers included Hall himself, who gave an address titled "Child Study: Some of Its Methods and Results" to a receptive audience that agreed when he declared that "we are now entering upon a period of more scientific development when the joint intelligence of parent and teacher is to be brought to bear in order that peculiarities of temperament, defects of body and mind, and external conditions may be taken into account in prescribing courses of treatment."[122]

Coffin was likely one of those who organized Hall's appearance, as he was a founding member of the group and had taken an active part in the implementation of its lecture series.[123] There is no record of Coffin's reactions to Hall's address, however, because the popular historian died within a few days of its delivery. He was seventy-two years old and was buried at Auburn Cemetery in Cambridge, not far from the gravesite of Jacob Abbott. At a meeting subsequent to his death, the membership of the society passed a resolution that cited the historian's interest in reform pedagogies: "*Resolved,* That in the death of Hon. Charles Carleton Coffin the town of Brookline has lost one of her most distinguished citizens, and the Education Society one of its most valued and highly esteemed members."[124] Testimonials presented at Coffin's funeral emphasized his special connection to public school children. "It is no wonder that childhood feels under special obligation to the man who has made the days of '76 and of the early sixties live again," his friend Howard A. Bridgman observed. "It reveals the hold he had on little hearts that the children in one of the Brookline schools asked to have the flag on their edifice put at half-mast on the day of his funeral, and that his picture in their schoolroom might be wreathed with laurel." He cited a note sent to Coffin's wife from a teacher at the William H. Lincoln School in Brookline confirming the sense of loss public school children felt on this occasion: "We are deeply grieved and every child feels a personal loss," the teacher wrote. "They have asked to have the flag placed at half-mast on the schoolhouse on Thursday, and a laurel wreath hung upon his picture."[125]

When one examines Coffin's philosophy of education and life in detail, then, one discovers that he was an ardent supporter of many of those things the Weiners of Maranatha Ministries and others on the Christian Right disdain. To be sure, he had a providential outlook on history, but he did not always promote home education over public school education nor did he view the two as mutually exclusive. He was not antimodern or antiprogressive, as the Weiners prefer their historians to be. And he did not reject the educational methods of the scientific pedagogues of Hall's child study movement but worked actively on behalf of that movement to improve educational opportunities for students by reconciling the needs of parents with those of teachers. In fact, Coffin had more in common with Higginson than with the Weiners. Tellingly, Higginson's *Young Folks' History of the United States* and Coffin's *Old Times in the Colonies* were both included in the "List of Books Which Have been Tested and Found To Be Helpful in the School-room" in Sarah Louise Arnold's instruction manual of 1899, *Reading: How to Teach It*. Each, in her estimation, met the requirements for "useful history" as defined by parents and teachers who were beginning to work collaboratively to meet the new standards of the discipline of history emerging in the early twentieth century.[126]

Contextualizing the popular works of Coffin reveals, then, that the "American Christian History" that the Weiners believe has been "erased from our [current] history books!" may never have existed in the first place, at least not in Coffin's works.[127] While he acknowledged the controlling hand of God in history, Coffin was not a strict determinist insofar as he was willing to work with secular humanists to arrive at suitable protocols for improving the historical literacy of children. And although he operated within the dominant historical paradigm of his age—believing that until "the millennium released individuals from history, historical memory placed them in the flow of world drama and gave their lives universal significance"—Coffin did not fall victim to the paradox at the heart of most Christian teleological thinking with respect to time, namely, that humans can never know the ultimate telos toward which history is moving or even if such a goal exists because the very narrative tropes they employ to elucidate such determinism depict them as flawed and sinful beings incapable of distinguishing between true or false reflections of the past.[128]

Given this contemporaneous perspective, it seems unlikely Coffin would have approved of the efforts of those in the twenty-first century to resurrect his texts more than one hundred years after their burial. Like Goodrich, Coffin did not believe his works had any claim to permanency because, to quote his eulogist, "Nobody knew his limitations better than himself." Indeed, Coffin anticipated Carl Becker by many decades in suggesting that every generation must write its own histories rather than recycle narratives from prior periods. "He cared very little for truths which had been shapen in symbols which had outlived their time," Griffis said at Coffin's funeral. Instead, he "hammered on the anvil of [his] age and epoch," rejecting "the truth taken out of old things" in favor of the truth emanating from the new. "He never disassociated the truth from the man who lived it." That advice might serve us well today as we consider the effects of educating homeschooled children by using history books written more than a century ago by a man "whose outward temple," Griffis noted, "lies there in the dust." Those contemplating an intellectual disinterment of the sort that Maranatha Publications has attempted with the republication of Carleton's Juveniles would be better served by leaving Coffin's coffin untouched.[129]

CHAPTER FIVE

Biographical History

Elbridge S. Brooks and the
Childhood Lives of Great Men

I knew very well that to make a real & vivid biography would require an amount and minuteness of investigation which could never be repaid in money, nor done without money.

JAMES PARTON to Charles Eliot Norton, 5 February 1867

The Child First Movement and the Need for Heroes

At the heart of the debate over whether children would benefit more from a volume such as Coffin's *The Story of Liberty* or from Higginson's *Young Folks' History of the United States* was a complicated disagreement concerning the advantages and disadvantages of home study and child study programs. Put side by side, the two histories reveal no major distinctions between them in their historical themes and episodes; the master narrative is secure in both. In terms of the pedagogical strategies, however, they could not be more different, especially with respect to audience and their authors' differing conceptions of childhood as a transitional period of development. Failure to recognize the distinctions between emergent and nonemergent approaches to the past has encouraged some to recycle nineteenth-century works indiscriminately; presses like Maranatha Publications operate as if *all* such works deserve our respect and attention for the same reason that all elderly people command our veneration—because of their advanced age. The result of this unselective publication policy has been a tendency to encourage the fallacious idea that nineteenth-century popular histories for children are essentially interchangeable. It also has fostered the misleading belief that repetition and redundancy are inevitable and desirable characteristics of the genre.

Such opinions are evident in the popular works republished by the Learning

Parent, a Christian-based company operated by Rick and Marilyn Boyer of Rustburg, Virginia. Since 1993 the Boyers have been advising homeschooling parents about the proper ways to educate their children domestically. They should know what they are talking about, as they are the parents of fourteen children, all of whom have been homeschooled. The couple has written several books and delivered numerous lectures on the virtues of the practice as well. In these publications and presentations, the Boyers advocate a distinctly Christian approach to homeschool learning.[1] "We equip and encourage parents to embrace a Scriptural pattern of home education where family life is the environment for childhood learning and discipleship," the Learning Parent website notes. "A godly character is the highest priority," and "academics and practical life skills are taught to grow children into useful Christian citizens." Home learning should be centered on the heart even more than the mind, they argue, and the ultimate purpose of education is to strengthen the parent–child relationship as a necessary first step toward producing young adults who will one day minister to themselves and their progeny. "We assist homeschoolers in raising up future generations of wise, servant-hearted children with a compelling vision for spiritual revival," the Boyers claim. They are evidently good at what they do. Marilyn is recognized on homeschooling chat pages for her "keen and warmhearted insights into parenting," while Rick, with his "humorous, folksy style," has been called "the Will Rogers of the home schooling movement."[2]

Like nearly all the Christian homeschooling advocates I have discussed in this book, including Noah Hutchings of Hearthstone Publishing, Adam and Alice of Heritage History, Richard "Little Bear" Wheeler of Mantle Ministries, and Bob and Rose Weiner of Maranatha Christian Ministries, the Boyers view public schools as counterproductive and even dangerous to the learning process. Real pedagogical authority, they argue, rests in the home with parents. In his lecture "Breaking the Shackles: Why Parents Should Trust Themselves, Not Schools," Rick Boyer asserts, "The educational system we see all around us today is bogus." Not mincing words, he calls the typical public school a "whitewashed sepulcher full of death and rottenness" and a "conditioning for passivity." The problems began, he claims, when progressive teachers and administrators of the child study movement "who thought they knew better than God" began "stealing our children so gradually that we somehow didn't see it." Alleging a financial motive behind compulsory attendance requirements in public schools, Boyer also blames the National Education Association (NEA), the largest teachers' union, for the impact of these policies on the very young. "Research shows that school kids do better if they start between the ages of 8 and 12," Rick writes accusingly. "But the NEA is not interested in the welfare of children. It is a labor union, and it knows that lower attendance ages mean more kids in schools" and "more jobs for teachers." Associating the leadership of the NEA with the "social engineers who demand ever more control over the time and therefore the lives of children," Boyer objects especially to the "snoopervision" of "government-certified elites" who scrutinize homeschooling parents and make them doubt their abilities as potential educators. "We lost our way," he criticizes, "when we began believing the lie that government institutions could, if given enough control, enough money, enough of a person's growing up time, do a better job of creating whole people than the home and the church and the community of former times."[3]

In their popular book on the subject, *Home Educating with Confidence,* Rick and Marilyn Boyer revive complaints about progressive educators like G. Stanley Hall and John Dewey, who, in their estimation, ruined public education by exposing children to the "falsehoods of psychology, sociology, and statism." The Boyers write that "professional educators have a stake in conditioning the public to believe that school people are a sort of aristocracy endued with ability and high-tech training far beyond the reach of those lower on the food chain." This has led, in turn, to a distorted sense of the value of public education. The American school is regarded as a great institution, they note, a "state-of-the-art system that has sprouted, grown, and adapted" to meet the changing conditions of the times. "That's hogwash," the Boyers carp. The public school system "is a mammoth failure," a colossal betrayal of those taxpayers naïve enough to believe in its "image as the industry standard for education . . . fostered by the billions of dollars we spend on it, the professional esteem bestowed upon its practitioners, and the massive structure we've built to maintain it." As further proof of their assertions, the Boyers cite studies that reveal that "home-educated children scor[e] consistently higher" on standardized exams than their public-school-educated peers.[4]

The Boyers contend that public schools have also de-Christianized education in ways that compromise the original principles on which the nation was founded. "To those who understand history, the hand of God is unmistakable in the story of America," Rick Boyer avows. "Our Founders built on the soil of the New World a nation organized on the principles of Scripture. The result was that early America astounded the world with its freedom, genius and productivity." When local, state, and federal government agencies began to assume responsibility for the educating of Americans in the nineteenth and twentieth centuries, however, secular concerns eclipsed spiritual ones with disastrous effects. Boyer insists that it is time for home-educating parents to oppose government interference in education by "taking back their children and raising up a generation of bright, godly, competent Americans who understand their heritage and are determined to reclaim it for the glory of God." God "designed the family, not the school, to be the primary training ground for His champions," Boyer concludes, so parents must exercise the same authority over their children as the heavenly father does over his.[5]

The Boyers are not alone in professing that profound (and they would say regrettable) changes in American public schools occurred in the first decades of the twentieth century. This revolutionary refashioning took place in part because, as Steven Mintz has noted, nearly "every act of childhood was transformed in this period." The developmental models of child growth popular at the end of the nineteenth century encouraged parents to think more deliberately about the stages of a young person's life and the crucial transitional moments between and among them. As in the child study movement, the greater attentiveness to all phases of a child's development encouraged, indeed required, parents to seek help from experts in the field of education, causing them to cede some of their traditional authority to the teachers and administrators in public schools. Children gained greater independence in the process as they were encouraged by new behavioral pedagogies to engage the world on their own terms through individual acts of self-construction. As the Abbott brothers had advised, public schools urged students to test experience through personal interactions with their learning environments and to rely on teachers to offer direction but not mandates about how to attain knowledge. The circumstances and background of the learner were emphasized. This values-based pedagogy celebrated the unique needs of individuals, and its practitioners resisted the temptation to impose a single, uniform curricular program on all students. While it is hard to discern exactly what was cause and what was effect in the matter of these exchanges, it is evident that during the "half-century between 1880 and 1930, parent–child relations underwent a profound transformation," Mintz notes, as "middle-class family life grew more democratic, affectionate, and child-centered, and the school and the peer group became more significant in young people's lives."[6]

This so-called child first movement, as it has been named both by its promoters and detractors, worried parents who recognized that greater independence on the part of children could mean less deference to elders. They were also concerned by the indulgent nature of such constructivist pedagogies, especially the creation of support systems to deal with the new "anxieties, phobias, and emotional needs" that emerged simultaneously with the growth of public schools. For skeptical parents, the child first movement meant a ratcheting up of expectations for meeting the egocentric demands of their children on someone else's terms and an intensification of the guilt experienced when expectations were not met. The consequences of inattentiveness to these matters were too great to ignore, however. According to one of Hall's students, Arnold Gesell of the Yale Child Study Center, "juvenile delinquents" were not inherently bad children but children who had been "neglected, maltreated, and subjected to intolerable brutality" by their parents and who required "psychiatric care rather than punishment." Educators "drew on psychological research to show that childish behavior that appeared to be evil, naughty, or impertinent was often symptomatic of psychological confusions or conflicts, or responses to situations and demands beyond the child's capacities." The resulting "psychologizing of childrearing" led to profound tensions between parents and children. The young sought to assert their wills, breaking free from the "tradition and outmoded authority" of their elders, while parents became increasingly "flabbergasted by their children's insolence." In 1913 the *North American Review* announced that even spiritual education had been affected by these developments. In a manner consistent with the declarations of disappointment expressed by home study educators in the late nineteenth century, the journal noted that the "time has passed when parents supervised the morals of their children."[7]

Some parents resented deeply and resisted mightily these new trends in child-rearing practice. In 1911 Cornelia A. P. Comer published "A Letter to the Rising Generation" in the *Atlantic Monthly* that railed against the impertinent younger cohort, whose members, she complained, "were selfish, discourteous, lazy, and self-indulgent." Lacking respect "for their elders or for common decency," Mintz summarizes, the young were characterized by Comer as "hedonistic, 'shallow, amusement-seeking creatures,' whose tastes had been 'formed by the colored supplements of the Sunday paper' and the 'moving picture shows.'" Values education inspired by social studies had betrayed students, she added, by failing to instill in them a means of distinguishing right from wrong.[8] Parents must reassert their authority, she noted in a manner reminiscent of Anthony Comstock, compelling submission as a way of equipping their children to make proper moral judgments.

Comer resented that the new age of permissiveness in child rearing was having a marked effect on literacy rates among American youth. She argued that the younger generation, trained by indulgent progressive educators, "couldn't spell, and its English was 'slipshod'" at best. Pedagogical experimentation in public schools had contributed to the emergence of a cohort of pampered students who, she insisted, were "'soft' intellectually" and disinterested in "proper English or outmoded standards of propriety."[9] Comer recognized that in making her case for less intellectual freedom for children she was defying current trends. Social constructivists since the time of the

Abbotts had asserted that learners must be given space and time to arrive at their own versions of the truth, and John Dewey had trained a generation of educators to be sensitive to the special needs of individual groups of learners. Books tailored to designated subgroups within the culture became more fashionable as teachers tested multiple approaches to literacy training, sometimes combining whole word and phonetic forms in the same hybrid texts. In the handbook *Reading: How to Teach It* (1899), Sarah Louise Arnold held that each child should have a literacy program of his own, "adapted to his intelligence, suited to his interest." This obligated teachers to "a study of the children as well as a study of literature," Arnold added. "We must watch them through our storytelling or our reading, and judge, by their attention, their comments, their silence, their indifference, where their interest lies," she advised. "We must begin with that which appeals to their child life" and develop educational programs directed toward "their present interest."[10]

Such efforts to accommodate individual readers on their own terms met with resistance from traditionalists in the twentieth century, and they continue to aggravate some parents in the twenty-first. Rick and Marilyn Boyer believe, for instance, that tinkering with standard approaches to reading has undercut parental authority and contributed to the undoing of society. The "sight/word systems in use in American public schools are the main reason for the decline of literacy in our country," the Boyers note, in common with Bob and Rose Weiner, adding that as a result "it took only a few generations to bring about the social, spiritual, moral and intellectual decay that permeates our society today."[11] The Boyers embrace a strict phonetic approach with a Christian twist, endorsing the products of the A Beka Book company designed to educate students in accordance with "biblical principles that address the nature of the learner and learning" and "traditional grammar and standard usage and mechanics." A Beka Book promoters contend that in such "a day of poor and lazy communication skills" as this, students must be taught "to be comfortable with correct grammar, pronunciation, and usage in conversation and other forms of speech."[12] The Boyers are also reluctant to relinquish control over what material children will and will not read. Recognizing that young readers are too strong-willed to comply with their elders' advice about such matters, the couple recommends that parents keep "plenty of good books in the house and occasionally *plant* a new one on a bed, on the coffee table, or in some other conspicuous spot," since "often it will be picked up and perused out of curiosity even though the topic or the cover may not have interested the child enough to seek out on his own."[13]

Of all the subjects taught in public schools in the twentieth century, the Boyers are most worried about the damaging effects of permissive child rearing and pedagogical practices on the study of history. The couple notes in a special blog devoted to the topic, "Why History Matters," that "young people in recent decades have displayed not only a disturbing lack of interest in history, but an outright contempt for it." This disdain derives primarily from students' "ignorance of history's importance" and an attendant inability to find any ethical value in the study of the past.[14] The blame for these deficiencies, the Boyers claim, lies with secular public educators who have dissected history and removed its spiritual and moral content. "Were it not for the fact that our public schools have robbed us of our knowledge of our own history, we would all understand why the Constitution says not one word about education," Boyer notes. "Our founding fathers knew that the upbringing of children is given by God into the hands of parents. Government should just keep its nose out of family business."[15] In *Home Educating with Confidence,* the Boyers elaborate on this "originalist" argument, averring that "when you teach the history of America without regard to the spiritual lives of the characters involved you produce a caricature of history." A more valid approach to the past, in their estimation, would acknowledge the role of God as the primary causal force in the universe and would ignore the "'vain speculations' of evolution, Freudian psychology and Keynesian economics, among other falsehoods" put forward by social scientists playacting as historians.[16]

The Boyers have been disturbed especially by the loss of "divine heroes" in the historical literature offered to children in public schools. They believe that most textbooks used in public institutions purposefully avoid narratives that highlight human agents acting out God's plan. The result has been a troubling diminution of biography as a genre in history curricula and a concomitant reduction in the perceived relevance of founding figures. "I once sat in a college classroom and heard the professor ask the class how many of us knew who Nathan Hale was," Rick Boyer wrote. "Since I grew up in a time when we still learned about 'heroes' instead of 'role models,' I was surprised to see that only about half the class raised their hands. That was thirty years ago and I'm sure that very few hands indeed would go up were that question asked in college now." We don't learn about a hero such as Hale, Boyer suggests, because the "moral judgments" and "virtue of character" implicit in the term "are considered out of bounds" in today's history classrooms. We "mustn't pass judgment on anybody's character by suggesting that someone else's is superior," Boyer adds derisively; rather, "we talk about 'role models,' which seems to simply mean somebody who is good at something he does. He may or may not give a rip about what's right and wrong; in fact he may be selfish, rude, promiscuous, boorish and abusive—but he sure can throw a ball through a hoop. He is a good model for the role because he's good in that role himself." The Learning Parent website moralizes further: "We worship people who pretend to be other people in movies, though their personal lives are moral cesspools. We admire people who invest years of discipline into playing games that only entertain, yet scarcely recognize others who have made the world better for the entire human race." The golfer Tiger Woods "bumps little balls into holes in the ground," yet "how many people know who Jonas Salk was?" the Boyers ask. "Think about it."[17]

Why are heroes so important? Heroes serve as moral exempla for students who need guidance in a rudderless world, the Learning Parent website asserts. "Kids who want their lives to amount to something have people, living and long gone, to look to for examples," Rick Boyer writes. "Their heroes both raise the bar and at the same time show the way to get over it. To have a hero—not just a role model—is to be inspired to rise above the ordinary. It is a constant reproof to laziness, low standards and unworthy attitudes." People who are recognized as great leaders render us humble and motivate us to do better as well, according to the Boyers. They "make us dissatisfied with ourselves, impatient rather than comfortable with our faults, and ashamed of complaining about our difficulties, most of which pale in comparison to those once shrugged off by our heroes," Boyer adds. "Many of our heroes—the real ones, I mean—came from humble circumstances but were raised by virtue to dizzying heights of honor and achievement." Young people who have access to the biographies of heroes "aspire to rise above their circumstances too," he concludes. "To dream of being worthy of honor is an honorable thing in itself. It is surely the most direct path to becoming a hero to some kid who will come along in a future day."[18]

For the Boyers there is a hagiographic quality to this hero-worshiping impulse that is crucial to the continuation of the Christian church in America. A literary genre devoted to the study of saints and ecclesiastical leaders whose lives were marked by miracles wondrous enough to warrant the designation sacred, hagiography was a rhetorical form that gave religious leaders a shorthand for disseminating accounts of the exemplary lives of saints. "Why does the Bible say so much about people who stood out? 'Honorable' people?" the couple asks. The Boyers believe it is "because heroes remind us that there really is such a thing as greatness." Nowadays, however, the worship of public figures has given way to endless self-contemplation by students, a narcissistic condition that has confused them about the appropriate standards for judging behavior. "We're not taught as youngsters to think in terms of right and wrong, but in terms of our own 'values,'" they write. "Hence we don't learn ethics but values clarification in school." That change has been disastrous in regard to the moral training of American youth. "Heaven forbid (if you still believe in heaven) that we should endorse one person's values over another's, let alone assert that there are absolutes of good and evil," Rick Boyer notes wryly. He longs for "earlier days when it was generally recognized that God was the judge of good and evil and that His opinions were immutable" and when the only values that mattered were those "that God places on things." Youngsters of prior generations understood almost instinctively and in ways they do not today, he summarizes, that "no man had the right to determine morality for himself but must bow to the Creator of all things and His valuation."[19]

Continued failure to appreciate the lives of heroes, the Boyers prophesize, will lead to the degradation and destruction of the culture. The solution to avoiding such a nightmarish end, they imply, is reviving old works of history for use as godly instruments in setting young readers on the path of moral righteousness. "The teaching of history is being systematically eased out of public schooling in America," the Boyers write, "because education is in the control of people whose political opinions are radically different from those of the men who made this country." Historians, especially on the Left, "don't want us to know that America was viewed by her national patriarchs as having been raised up specially by God to be a city on a hill to the whole world," the Boyers reason. "If we were aware of the portentous quality of our beginnings," they add, "we might hold our leaders accountable to the same Biblical values in government that our Founders held." In this day "of small men casting long shadows," the Boyers note, "it's worth the trouble for parents to find heroes, past and present who will challenge their sons to become the men our society needs to lead us back to the way of our fathers."[20] Where public school educators have failed, Rick Boyer asserts, homeschool instructors must succeed. "As homeschoolers, we have the ability to design a curriculum that honors true American history," he asserts. "We should fill our homes with the great old books that tell the truth, the ones that were written before Political Correctness robbed us of our godly national heritage. We at The Learning Parent are working on a number of new projects to bring the old books back to American homes," he concludes. "We're gearing up to do our part. I hope we can help you do yours. The children are counting on us."[21]

This "mission statement" begs certain questions regarding the efficacy of the Learning Parent's republication and literacy strategies. Toward which "great old books that tell the truth" should young readers gravitate? and at what kinds of students are these works directed? What are the consequences of centering a history curriculum on such recycled nineteenth-century works? and how exactly do they reveal a "godly national heritage"? What definitions of heroism emerge from these works? and can the heroes depicted in them accomplish all the rehabilitative tasks the Boyers expect of them?

Elbridge S. Brooks and "Small Men Casting Shadows"

Answers to these questions are linked to a generational perspective regarding tradition and the relevance of parental authority. In a public talk titled "Take Back the Land," Rick Boyer refers to the homeschooling parents of the 1980s and 1990s as "the Moses generation" since, like the ancient Israelites in search of Canaan, "they left Egypt [read government schooling] and headed for the Promised Land," getting as far as the Jordan River before giving way to the "Joshua generation," which completed the mission. The Moses generation of homeschoolers encountered all manner of resistance to their efforts to bring religion back to the study of history, suffering their metaphoric forty years in the wilderness during the first half of the twentieth century, when court case after court case went against them. Owing to the tireless work of a few devoted disciples to the cause, however, the tide began to turn in the mid-twentieth century. "Today, home schooling parents have broken free from the bondage of Godless philosophies and are raising up the Joshua generation that will carry the battle over the Jordan," Rick Boyer says, "taking the banner of Christ back into American government, law, medicine, business, education and the arts, where God and His Word were once universally honored." The field of history will benefit especially from this crusade, he predicts.[22] "Going to school is just enough to turn you against history altogether," he claims, but the home education victories of the last three decades have saved the discipline, revealing that a "better way to teach history is as the unfolding of God's story." Since "all of History is in fact His Story," Boyer notes, "God . . . wants us to know it and understand it."[23] The reward for doing so will be substantial for children as they experience the future that the past presages: "The enemies of God [and history] are trembling today at the thunderous approach of the Joshua generation!!"[24]

In order to prepare the Joshua generation for its redemptive mission, the Boyers have begun reviving nineteenth-century texts that they insist will provide homeschoolers with the proper foundations for understanding history and implementing its lessons. Rick Boyer, for instance, markets a series of CD recordings in which he reads from nineteenth-century popular biographies that he believes convey a proper spiritual outlook on history for children (fig. 17). "My experience with audio recording biographies of great Americans has become something of a fetish," Boyer admits. "Biographies written a hundred or more years ago reflect the values that used to be standard in America,"

FIGURE 17. CD cover: "Uncle Rick Reads *The True Story of George Washington.*"

he adds, "before political correctness robbed kids' literature of real heroes." Addicted to a class of books that "emphasizes character" and that "quotes Scripture repeatedly," Boyer proclaims, "It's exciting to know that in the years to come, thousands of kids around the country will hear old *Uncle Rick* read to them on CD about people worthy to be their heroes. They'll learn an awful lot of our nation's history at the same time."[25] The fact that these older volumes are being reissued and recycled is a positive thing, he adds, because repetition allows young readers to "see the principles of God illustrated as they work themselves out over and over and over and over." Quoting Ecclesiastes 1:9 ("There's nothing new under the sun"), Boyer reaffirms the power of the reiterative in history. "If we understand what's happened in the past when people did certain things, then we can understand what's likely to happen to us if we do those certain things," he declares, in keeping with his reading of Santayana. "That way we don't have to make the same mistakes people were making 300 years ago, if we learn from their mistakes."[26]

Respondents write glowingly of Boyer's CDs. "I am a homeschooling mom of 4 boys (ages 2 to 9) and I want to tell you what my oldest son, Joel, told me last night," wrote one pleased customer. "All 4 boys share a room and they take turns choosing a CD to listen to as they fall asleep. Joel wanted to know if he could put in an Uncle Rick CD after the Charlotte's Web CD (that his younger brother chose) ended. I told him yes, since the younger 3 were all asleep." He then declared, "Uncle Rick is my favorite person that reads audio CDs." Joel's mother added in a postscript to her endorsement that Uncle Rick was her favorite as well. "I especially love the American history CDs," she wrote to Boyer, since your materials have "given me a passion for our Godly heritage, and I want my boys to grow up loving and knowing their heritage. Thank you SO much!"[27] In response to the CD "Uncle Rick Reads True Stories of Great Americans for Young Americans," another satisfied purchaser enthused as follows: "This is probably meant for ages 7–14, but our 4 year old grandchildren LOVE and REMEMBER the true stories and ASK to hear them again and again, often while riding in the car." For these grandparents, at least, the repetition served to stabilize and justify historical meaning. "We firmly believe in letting them listen while young," wrote this contented customer. "Let them grow up hearing the hero stories again and again and be inspired by the heritage left to us in this country."[28]

What are these histories that Uncle Rick reads to young children and what do we know about their authors? Among the most popular in Boyer's repertoire are biographies of famous Americans written by one of the nineteenth century's most popular children's historians, Elbridge S. Brooks (fig. 18). Brooks was born in 1846 in Somerville, Massachusetts, into a family of ministers. His father, a clergyman and an important figure in the early development of the Universalist Church in New England, "moved the family around from parish to parish in Bath, Maine; Lynn, Massachusetts; and New York City." His mother was described as a "cultivated and homemaking Christian gentlewoman," descended from those "who fought so bravely at Lexington, and whose farm lands and grist mills were near the site of General Putnam's earthworks on Prospect Hill."[29] The *Somerville Journal* referred to Brooks's great-grandfather as "among the first to respond to the alarm from Lexington" as well as a soldier who was "probably at Bunker Hill, and certainly was present during the large part of the siege of Boston."[30] That Brooks's works "should be mainly historical and patriotic naturally follows from the nature of his ancestry and the quality of the Yankee blood which flowed through his veins," a biographical notation in a hometown journal, *Historic Leaves,* opined, since "of the seventy minutemen in line at the battle of Lexington, eleven were relatives on his mother's side" and "three of the names on the monument erected to the memory of the fallen heroes were those of blood relations."[31]

FIGURE 18. Portrait of Elbridge S. Brooks. Print Collection, Miriam and Ira D. Wallach Division of Art, Prints and Photographs, The New York Public Library, Astor, Lenox and Tilden Foundations.

Brooks studied at the Free Academy (later the College of the City of New York), "taking excellent rank in literature, history, and the classics," but left for financial reasons in the middle of his junior year to become a salesman for D. Appleton & Co. Publishers. He later worked for J. B. Ford & Co. and Sheldon & Co. before becoming an editor at the newly formed publishing corporation of D. Lothrop Company in Boston.[32] Here he honed his skills as a reviewer of and contributor to the juvenile book market. Brooks was prolific and specialized in children's history books with an emphasis on American heroes, publishing *Tales of Heroism, Historic Boys* (1885), *Historic Girls* (1887), and *Heroic Happenings Told in Verse and Story* (1893) in an eight-year span.[33] He also maintained an interest in religious history, writing a prize-winning work of fiction titled "A Son of Issachar" in an effort to "see if a religious novel would have a chance with a secular public." The positive reactions to the book, he reported, "easily proved that such was possible."[34]

An advertisement for CDs on the Learning Parent website points out that Brooks's works were recognized in their day as morally grounded and spiritually centered. An editor at *Youth's Companion,* F. L. Harbour, applauded Brooks for "writing safe books for the young in an age when so many unsafe books for our boys and girls are being written." The popular historian is "a steadfast and sympathetic friend" to children, the editor added, and "a potent power for good" in the world of literature.[35] Brooks's biography of Ben Franklin was a case in point, the Learning Parent website adds. "While modern biographies portray Franklin as a deist, Brooks' version makes plain the God-fearing philosophy that impelled Franklin to contribute his own funds to many various Christian ministries, including the famous evangelist George Whitefield." The Boyers make special note of the fact that, according to Brooks, Franklin, "died with his eyes on a painting of Jesus that hung on his bedroom wall."[36]

The Learning Parent website highlights the tradition-based, convention-affirming quality of Brooks's juvenile histories. Like many of the popular historians of the nineteenth century on whose works he drew, Brooks believed in the value and necessity of repetition, especially for training young readers to recognize the most salient features of the master narrative of American history. "The Story of the United States of America has already been told and re-told for young Americans by competent writers, and yet there is room for another re-telling," Brooks wrote in the introduction to one of his bestselling works. His justification for offering another version of the master narrative of the American past was that children benefited from constant repetition. The "future of the Republic depends on the upbringing of the boys and girls of to-day," he added, an incentive that justified shedding renewed light "on the doings of the boys and girls of America's past when they grew to manhood and womanhood," even at the risk of redundancy. Operating on the assumption that children "have been the same in all ages of the world," Brooks held that because "their essential natures are the same," the narratives that appeal to youth will have a certain consistency and should garner attention so long as the historian is willing "to put a living, everyday interest into the historical story."[37]

To the extent that Brooks offered anything new to his young readers, it was a commitment to writing about famous Americans before they achieved greatness. He recounted the stories of their childhoods when they were boys and girls. He noted that heroic episodes in the later lives of future heroes often derived from small, seemingly insignificant events in their infancies and youths. In this sense, private history was prologue to public history. "Heroism is always happening," Brooks informed America's young readers, although "much of it is unrecorded."[38] As the historian Scott Casper has acknowledged, readers of works by popular biographers like Brooks were invited to "study biography for examples of character and its formation, and for the inspiration provided by the lives of those who had risen from obscurity and poverty to fame and fortune." Additionally they were urged to appreciate the "direct relationship between public and private" existences and to recognize that the "character one cultivated in private life placed one on the permanent path to fortune or ruin."[39] Brooks reminded young readers of a turn-of-the-century Joshua generation that examples of heroism were scattered all around them for their consideration and emulation. "If [my works] may be found of interest or of help to the boys and girls of to-day, in the way of developing the heroic element that is common to all ages and all lands, the purpose of the collection will have well been served," he concluded.[40]

Brooks borrowed extensively from the techniques and methodologies of his predecessors in the field of popular history. Like Charles Carleton Coffin, he never "wrote down" to children, and he respected their limitations without restricting their ambitions. "They know more than their elders give them credit for, and the proper way is to write to lift them up," he insisted. The preeminent literary journal the *Dial* placed Brooks next to Thomas Wentworth Higginson as one of the very few historical writers for children who knew "their [readers'] needs and their tastes" and who understood "the art of blending simplicity and strength, without straining the one or weakening the other."[41] Like Josephine Pollard, Brooks embraced an age-appropriate approach to historical literacy in children, and he was not afraid to "start 'em" young. "I believe in leading children gradually, and that you cannot begin too early with healthful and instructive reading, especially that of a patriotic nature,"[42] Brooks wrote. This gradualist approach encouraged him to write books in the series format favored by the Abbott brothers. Throughout the 1880s and 1890s Brooks produced serial biographies of famous Americans for three levels of young readers: the Heroic Life series for children of primary school age, published by DeWolfe, Fiske and Co.; the Century Book series for the middle grades, produced by the Century Company; and the True Stories collection for teenagers and young adults, issued by Lothrop, Lee and Shepard.

The first of these series, the Heroic Life volumes, consisted of small, orange books of fewer than one hundred pages that highlighted the boyhoods of some of the nation's most notable figures, especially presidents and military figures such as John Paul Jones, George Washington, Abraham Lincoln, Ulysses S. Grant, and William McKinley (fig. 19). It is easy to see why Heroic Life texts have appealed to the Boyers and patrons of the Learning Parent website. For one thing, they emphasize consistently the role of God in the machinations of human history. Before racing ahead to study Washington's military and political career, Brooks advised, boys and girls should read the passages in *The Heroic Life of George Washington* that underscored "the position of affairs of that period, and what led up to the great war of

Independence, and how God in His Providence had prepared a man for the time."[43] In *The Heroic Life of Abraham Lincoln*, Brooks reminded young readers that although the sixteenth president struggled with many weighty decisions, he was equipped for the tasks he faced because "God had prepared the man for the hour."[44]

The Heroic Life volumes implied that the key to achieving greatness was for children to exhibit deference where appropriate and to be patient in waiting for their "inner virtues" to disclose themselves. Impetuous children were rarely successful adults, Brooks warned. Accordingly, he informed young readers of *The Heroic Life of George Washington* that the first president "may have wanted some of the meteor-like brilliance, some of the poetic or romantic side of life which might dazzle and delight the people," but his humble boyhood demeanor and his steadfast commitment to moral values revealed eventually that he "possessed a rarer union of virtues than perhaps ever fell to the lot of one man."[45] Even the swashbuckling John Paul Jones was admired by Brooks less for his romantic impulses than for his deliberate lifelong pursuit of freedom as a political objective. Despite his public reputation for rambunctiousness, Brooks noted, American boys and girls should care more about the private life of Captain Jones and his personal commitment to liberty, always remembering "with grateful feelings the brave deeds and noble heroism of him who fought so well to win it for them."[46] With respect to President William McKinley, recently martyred, Brooks insisted that although

FIGURE 19. Three books by Elbridge S. Brooks: *The Heroic Life of George Washington, The Heroic Life of Abraham Lincoln,* and *The Heroic Life of William McKinley.* All were published in Boston in 1902 by the D. Lothrop Publishing Company.

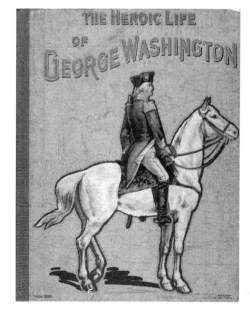

he was an inconspicuous, unassuming little boy, McKinley developed into an impressive man, serving as a brevet major in the Civil War and later as the twenty-fifth president of the United States. His life should serve as an example for all youth, Brooks noted, since it suggested that "truly in these United States it may be said of every boy, when he is a striving, industrious, studious and honest lad, that he may be a possible President."[47]

Extrapolating from seemingly insignificant private experiences to their larger civic consequences, Brooks worried (in ways reminiscent of Comer) that his young readers in the late nineteenth century might not appreciate fully the instructional value of the biographies of Washington or McKinley for achieving an understanding of the relative benefits they enjoyed over the youth of an earlier era. "Truly, the last half of the nineteenth century has been a great time in which to live," Brooks wrote, "even though the boys and girls of to-day—who are indeed the heirs of all the ages of thought and work that went before them—do not appreciate their advantages."[48] It was his job as a biographer to remind young readers of this important inheritance and to elucidate its attendant ethical responsibilities. In this sense, Brooks anticipated by almost a century the Boyers' appeal for a return to the "concept of moral excellence" as the standard for judging historical worth. He also provided the intellectual underpinnings for the Learning Parent's pronouncement that in evaluating heroes there must be "absolute and definable values of good and evil and that some actions and attitudes are better than others."[49]

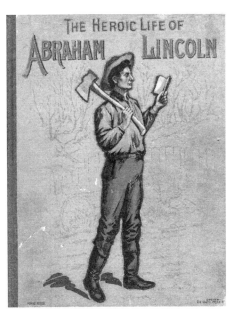
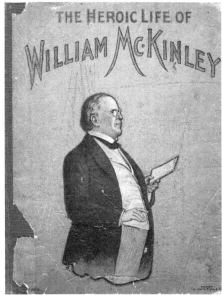

In *The Heroic Life of Ulysses S. Grant,* for instance, Brooks recounted how the future president learned valuable lessons while still a young boy, when he was swindled by a horse trader, signaling a lifelong vulnerability to "tricksters who traded on his singleness and honesty of purpose." This susceptibility was unfortunate for Grant personally, Brooks noted, but his heroic efforts to overcome such disappointments assured his place in the pantheon of national leadership and provided meaningful exemplary lessons for all students of American biography. "You, the young people of to-day, will do well to read and ponder over the story of the great General who did so much to preserve for us the liberties and the independence which that other great General, George Washington, who, as no doubt you have read, was justly styled the 'Father of his Country,' fought to win for us," Brooks moralized.[50] This associationalist strategy was consistent across all of the volumes of the Heroic Life series, and it buttressed Brooks's goal of continually reminding his audience that leaders like Grant and Washington embodied what Casper has called "practical models to help them surmount obstacles to success."[51]

The second of Brooks's series, the Century Book volumes, expanded these lessons in patriotic heroism to slightly older readers (fig. 20). Providing a masculine shadowing to Ella Stratton's strategy of teaching history to youngsters through the aegis of "Mamma Nelson" and the "Old White House Club," Brooks centered this four-volume series on a group of peripatetic cousins who convince their Uncle Tom to take them "on a tour of investigation" of the United States in hopes of learning the great history lessons of the nation's past.[52] They begin their travels by visiting the nation's capital, where the children discuss democratic principles while standing in front of an original copy of the Constitution. Focusing on the power of material culture to evoke a sense of the living past, Uncle Tom conducts tours of other historic sites around the country. His nephews and nieces come into close contact with artifacts redolent of historical meaning, including those found at birthplaces, document archives, battlefields, homes, monuments, and gravesites. While the volumes in the Century Book series focus tangentially on the power of individuals to affect the course of human history, they are more concerned with the physical residues of the past and with the ways in which children can be made to understand the commemorative power of history through material objects. "The riches of a nation are her dead," Uncle Tom intones, instructing the boys and girls accompanying him to recognize in the nation's "historic shrines" their protection against the transiency of history.[53]

Inventing dialogue and foreshortening travel distances in order to move his Century Book narratives along, Brooks employed some of the fictional devices reminiscent of Peter Parley to interest middle-school-aged children in

FIGURE 20. Elbridge S. Brooks, *The Century Book of Famous Americans* (New York: The Century Co., 1896).

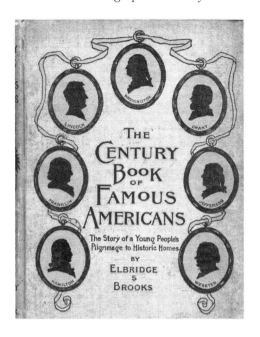

the tremendous range of history. In one remarkable instance, Uncle Tom and his consorts walk, ride, and "hike" over nearly 180 square miles of Chicago in a matter of hours, showing remarkable energy and little wear for having shot "up to the roofs of its 'sky-scrapers,'" "tunneled far beneath its divided river," "strolled along its lake front," "shopped in its great stores," and bicycled Chicago's "four thousand acres of park land and its hundred miles of boulevard." They found time even to visit the legendary spot on DeKoven Street where Mrs. O'Leary's fabled cow "kicked over the equally historic lamp, and laid a city in ashes."[54] Most reviewers accepted the contrived quality of this improbable travel itinerary because they understood how impatient young readers were with plodding narratives that insisted on exact temporal sequencing. Foreshortening in ways more fictional than factual was acceptable if the result was a marked improvement of their appreciation of history. A critic for the *Brooklyn Times* noted, for instance, that "Mr. Brooks has the rare facility of combining history and fiction so that each shall happily play into the hands of the other. The story makes the history interesting, and the history makes the story interesting. Mr. Brooks does this deliberately, because it is his aim to do this very thing; and we know no writer of stories for young people (or for old, either, for that matter) who understands better how to mix these two elements so that they shall not seek to instruct too much, or to entertain too little."[55]

Revealingly, the children in Uncle Tom's entourage are remarkably proper and decorous during this fast-paced journey, displaying none of the impertinence or insolence about which Comer complained in describing the "rising generation" of American youth at the outset of the twentieth century. They were precisely the kind of well-behaved children Rick and Marilyn Boyer have targeted in the Learning Parent publications—respectful, curious, and attentive. They value and respect tradition, especially "received tradition," as channeled through their elders. Many of Brooks's readers appreciated the wholesomeness of these characters and patronized the works of their creator, who recycled them over and over again in each of the subsequent volumes in the Century Book series. Remaining committed to a small stock of moral figures and historical themes that he reconditioned in sequential narratives, Brooks "secured the approbation of the reading world" and was rewarded for his consistency with high sales by a paying public. According to the *Somerville Journal*, *The Century Book for Young Americans* alone had "the unprecedented sale of 20,000 volumes in the first three months after its publication."[56]

Brooks's third biographical series, True Stories, was aimed at an older, secondary-school audience, but it too presented the story of the American past as told from the perspective of the childhood experiences of famous Americans, stressing what heroic figures were like before they became distinguished. In these biographical volumes Brooks tackled a version of the question that obsessed Jack Nicholson in *A Few Good Men,* namely, at what age is one old enough to "handle the truth" of history? Some felt as if young readers needed to be protected from the realities of the past and that juvenile histories should be packaged in purely sentimental forms. Eschewing the excesses of Grimm's fairy stories so despised by Goodrich and the contrivances of the popular "to be continued" series, however, Brooks reminded the slightly older readers of his True Stories books that a compelling biography such as Washington's "needs none of the over-wrought little stories that have so long been told to boys and girls, to strengthen his character or give point to his record. The true story of his life is fine enough and full enough to interest, to inspire and to help, without adding the things that would make a prig of the boy and a god of the man who was always a truth-teller, truth-liver, and truth-doer, both as boy and man" (fig. 21).[57] Brooks added that Lincoln's true story was far more marvelous than any fairy tale insofar as it was a narrative of a "brave, romantic, generous, noble-hearted and devoted man." The Marquis de Lafayette's personal history was as "crammed with adventure as 'Robinson Crusoe,'" "as crowded with fighting as 'Ivanhoe,' or as full of noble deeds as 'Westward Ho!'" Lincoln's was the story of a "brave, romantic, generous, noble-hearted and devoted man."[58]

FIGURE 21. Elbridge S. Brooks,
*The True Story of George
Washington* (Boston: D. Lothrop
Publishing Company, 1895).

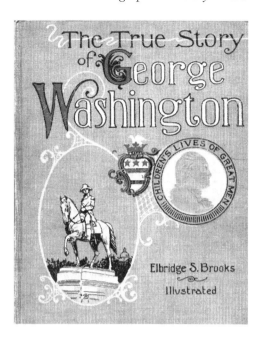

Among the things Brooks believed older children *could* handle was the idea that heroes were not necessarily born great and that they often developed slowly and inconsistently in their roles. Washington "was not a bright nor a brilliant boy," Brooks wrote, "but if he had anything to do he set about doing it at once. And as he grew older and mixed with men, he saw that what made men respected and obeyed by others was reliability—that is, keeping one's promises, and promising only what one felt he could do.[59] In most instances of future eminence, however, Brooks conceded that there were subtle indicators of potential from a young age. In *Greatness: Who Makes History and Why,* Dean Simonton explains the logic: "A person's childhood and adolescence provide vital clues about an individual's prospects in adulthood and old age," he writes. "If we only knew the significant signs, we could raise our own children to join the greats of history. So how can we detect the antecedents of achieved eminence?"[60] This was a question Brooks took upon himself to answer.

The examples of Lincoln and Washington were instructive. In the case of Lincoln, Brooks wrote in *The True Story of Abraham Lincoln,* the future president was "a funny-looking boy" with "sallow" skin who wore "a linsey-woolsey shirt, buckskin breeches, a coon-skin cap and heavy 'clumps' of shoes." Like the young Washington, he "was not a genius"; rather, he was a "slow, but sure" youngster who, "by regular stages of growth," taught himself "gradually to think clearly, to reason out things and to give himself, what we call, a 'logical mind.'" From these characteristics, Brooks reasoned that it "is not the brilliant boys and the prize scholars who make the best mark in the world; it is the patient and persistent ones, who stick to a thing until they understand and master it, and learn, by practice, how to do and how to say things with the best results." Not many youngsters "do have remarkable boyhoods or do great things at a time when their chief business should be growing and learning," Brooks moralized. "The world's historic boys are few and far between," he added, "but it is from the sturdy, active, healthy, hearty, wide-awake, honest, honorable and commonplace boys that the world's best men have been made."[61]

Early adversities and challenges helped make these figures the heroes they became. In making this case, Brooks again implied that any American child might grow up to become president if he or she demonstrated the necessary luck and pluck. The story of General Grant "seems to me one that all the boys and girls of America can take to heart," Brooks wrote in *The True Story of U. S. Grant,* since they will find in it "how, out of obscurity came honor, out of failure fame, out of hindrances perseverance, out of indifference patriotism, out of dullness genius, out of silence success, and, out of all these combined, a glorious renown." In reading of Grant's advance into greatness, Brooks believed, children would find reasons for doing "their best patiently, unhesitatingly, persistently." For it was thus that "Grant rose to honor and renown; it was thus that the tanner's son of Georgetown became the general of the armies of the Republic, that the horse-boy of the Ohio farm became the President of the United States."[62] And young Lincoln endured still more, including "a life of poverty, privation, hard work, little play and less money." The son of a father who "was rough and often harsh and hard to him," Abraham nonetheless persevered, "learning lessons of self-denial, independence, pluck, shrewdness, kindness and persistence" in his comfortless boyhood. "They were the very things that made him the ambitious, large-hearted, strong-souled, loving and kindly man he afterwards rounded into, and they fitted him to 'endure all things' as he rose to eminence and fame," Brooks wrote.[63]

Brooks's nascent heroes were effective as character types because they were realistic figures who made mistakes and learned corresponding lessons. From errors came remedies, and from remedies came solutions and triumphs. Despite evidence in his young life of many human inadequacies, for instance, heroes such as Lincoln "always kept going ahead" in Brooks's account. Lincoln "broadened his mind, enlarged his outlook, and led his companions rather than let them lead him," Brooks wrote in *The True Story of Abraham Lincoln*. "He was jolly company, good-natured, kind-hearted, fond of jokes and stories and a good time generally; but he was the champion of the weak, the friend of the friendless, as true a knight and as full of chivalry as any of the heroes in armor of whom you read in *Ivanhoe* or *The Talisman*." Brooks maintained that Lincoln "never cheated, never lied, never took an unfair advantage of anyone; but he was ambitious, strong-willed, a bold fighter and a tough adversary—a fellow who would 'never say die'; and who, therefore, succeeded." Lest his readers miss the point of this life lived in exemplary public service, Brooks added, "Take well to heart, boys and girls of America, the story of the plucky boy who . . . was all unconsciously training himself to be *the* American." "[Study] his trials and his troubles, his desires and his drawbacks, his determination, his pluck and his ambition," Brooks advised, while making sure not "to think of him as a man without faults; for he had them—but he rose above them," creating in the process a record of "statesmanship, leadership and greatness that made his work enduring and his name immortal."[64] Washington's life taught the same lessons. The future first president "hated a lie; he was never mean, nor low; he never did an underhand action; and he knew that the first lesson to learn is obedience to parents, respect toward older people, and kindness to all," Brooks wrote." From these attributes he developed into a preeminent world leader.[65]

Most of the remaining books in the True Stories series were devoted to cataloguing for young readers the emergent character traits that most revealed greatness among its subjects. The list included *persistence:* "[even as a boy Columbus] had an idea of what he wished to try and what he was bound to do. He kept right at that idea, no matter what might happen to annoy him or set him back";[66] *patience:* "Columbus never lost hope. He never stopped trying";[67] *resolution:* "through it all, Abraham Lincoln stood firm";[68] *honesty:* "That was Lafayette's chief characteristic,—unflinching integrity and absolute loyalty to his convictions";[69] *self-control:* "even when [Washington] was a small boy, he had learned to control his temper";[70] *preparedness:* "[Grant] did not just go at [a thing] thoughtlessly; he sat down and planned it out";[71] *morality:* "[Franklin was] an interested and earnest supporter of [abolitionism]";[72] and most of all, *humility:* "George Washington was simply a Virginia gentleman who did his duty and helped his fellowmen."[73] These values constituted a timeless glossary of behaviors that, if adhered to strictly, would allow children to engineer for the future. "As the years pass, the greatness of Washington grows on the world," Brooks summarized. "His story is not yet at an end; and it will never end, while men and women honor nobility of character, while boys and girls love to hear the story of how a farmer's boy grew into a hero, and a simple gentleman into a great man. His story will never end, for the world will never cease to love, to honor and to reverence the name of George Washington."[74]

The popular reactions to the volumes in all three of Brooks's historical series—Heroic Life, Century Book, and True Stories—were generally very positive at the time of their publication. An occasional reviewer fussed about redundancies, but by and large the volumes were praised for their historical value. A critic for the *Christian Advocate* commented that Brooks's works were "worthy of hearty commendation" not only from children but also from adults. "Every grown-up person who has read one of them will wish to buy the whole series for the young folks at home," the journal noted of the True Stories series.[75] The *Chicago Evening Post* judged that "the story of Lincoln was never more ably told," while the *Journal of the National Education Association* praised the same volume for "interest[ing] children and foster[ing] a feeling of veneration."[76] The *Pilgrim Teacher* agreed, assessing that Brooks's narrative of Grant was "carefully written in that style which makes Mr. Brooks so popular a writer with his young readers."[77] The *True Story of the United States of America* even received a commendation from home study readers, who observed that it is "largely used for home and supplementary reading, and is accepted as the most popular 'story' of the United States yet told for young people." Evaluating the book as "more like a charming fireside legend, told by a grandfather to eager children, than the dry and pompous chronicles commonly labelled history," the *Critic* applauded *The True Story of George Washington* for its emphasis on "heroic aspects and illustrating with many pictures of home and surroundings."[78]

These endorsements go a long way toward explaining why homeschooling parents such as the Boyers might be interested in republishing Brooks's biographies. His volumes were didactic and respectful and were characterized by clear expressions of what constituted bad and good behavior in history. Yet one still must ask, are these works really suitable for educating homeschooled children in the twenty-first century? do they meet all the standards established by the Boyers for effective history? and do they supply the proper information and tools necessary to allow youth to benefit from a study of the past? The answer, as the reviewer of Brooks's career in the *Dictionary of American Biography* claimed, is, "Not in this day and age."[79]

"Character Commentary" and Correcting History

At the beginning of the twentieth century Brooks was regarded as one of America's most significant and respected writers of children's historical literature. "Until a short time before his death at Somerville," one reviewer of his career wrote, "Brooks was to be seen regularly at his office, a man of intellectual appearance, with large head, aquiline nose, deep, keen, spectacled eyes, white hair, and full white beard."[80] When he died in 1902 he left a number of projects unfinished with the "apparent prospect of producing as many good books in the future as he had already produced in the past." The expectation was that his works would be read for years to come.[81] Members of the Somerville Historical Society honored him at his funeral for his "acknowledged ability as a writer of authentic history for the young, presenting, as he did, the study of history in its most attractive form to the impressible minds of youth." It was the historian's "modesty and gentlemanly bearing," his "honorable record . . . made among his contemporaries," and "his upright and manly life in our midst" that warranted celebration," the eulogist, John Ayer, proclaimed.[82]

The popular historian Hezekiah Butterworth, who was also at the funeral service, remarked that Brooks had once said to him, "My desire is to write historical books that will make the past live again."[83] Note, however, that Brooks did not say he expected his *books* to live again. Their resurrection has been the work of publishing enterprises like the Learning Parent, whose proprietors have argued for their continued relevance in the twenty-first century, more than a century after their publication. Yet only forty years after Butterworth's remarks, a contributor to the *Dictionary of American Biography* affirmed that while Brooks's legacy was intact, new outlooks on historical literacy in young readers in the twentieth century suggested his growing obsolescence. "The popularity of his books among young people," the reviewer remarked, "has continued almost unabated and, although experts in juvenile literature criticize them as 'machine-made,' they still find them so decidedly interesting that they grudgingly approve of them."[84] Such damning with faint praise was not severe enough to deter the Boyers from recycling Brooks's nineteenth-century works for twenty-first-century readers, and yet, as this critic implies, there is much that is problematic with all three of Brooks's biographical series.

Brooks's works suffer from at least four kinds of defects that jeopardize their usefulness in the twenty-first century. First, his juvenile histories contain more than a fair share of factual errors, even as measured by the low evidentiary standards of the genre of popular history. Some of these mistakes are clearly inadvertent and can be attributed to failings in the copyediting process. In *The Heroic Life of George Washington,* for instance, Brooks notes that at the opening session of the Second General Congress held at Philadelphia on May 10, 1775, "the difficult question as to who should be appointed Commander-in-Chief was settled . . . by John Quincy Adams, a very able man from Massachusetts advancing the name of Washington, who was unanimously elected by ballot June 15, 1775." Brooks meant to acknowledge John Adams, not his son, John Quincy Adams, who was born in 1767 and was therefore in no position to influence the Continental Congress.[85] Brooks was also guilty of perpetuating certain anachronisms, such as when he claimed, in imitation of Pollard, that John Smith's map of New England inspired Henry Hudson's discovery of the Hudson River in 1609. Smith, who was in Jamestown, Virginia, at the time of Hudson's voyage, did not produce his famous map of New England until 1614. By the time the map was published in London, Hudson had been dead for three years, the victim of a mutiny by disgruntled crewmen in the bay that now bears his name.[86]

More problematic in this line were the exaggerations and embellishments to which Brooks was prone, which compromised the integrity of some of his works. Despite his warning to young readers about overindulgence in hagiographic activities, for instance, *The True Story of Abraham Lincoln* included several legends "still accepted around Abraham Lincoln's boyhood home" that contributed to a distorted portrait of the future statesman. Brooks alleged, for instance, that Lincoln "could carry easily a load that three men would stagger under" and that he once "picked up and walked away with a chicken-coop that weighed six hundred pounds." That accomplishment alone would have earned him a place on the podium for weightlifting at the most recent Olympics. Brooks also depicted Lincoln as a more ardent abolitionist than the historical record indicates, claiming inaccurately that "Lincoln always declared that no man had a right by law or justice to own slaves." Confusing Lincoln the antislavery advocate with Lincoln the abolitionist, Brooks wrote that the statesman's "house divided speech" "sent a death-shot straight to the heart of slavery" and "made Abraham Lincoln President of the United States." As Lincoln said in his first inaugural address, however, his real goal was not to end slavery but to preserve the Union, and he was willing to accept the existence of the former in order to secure the future of the latter.[87]

Furthermore, Brooks was not above manipulating primary sources to suit his didactic purposes. Anxious to demonstrate that the founding fathers acted from Christian intentions in their personal lives, Brooks embellished certain passages in *The True Story of Ben Franklin* as derived from the *Autobiography*. For instance, Brooks recited the much-repeated story of Franklin's first day in Philadelphia, when his only meal consisted of loaves of bread he had purchased in excess because of his unfamiliarity with the currencies in use in Philadelphia. In retelling this narrative, Brooks had written of Franklin, "The boy wandered about the town, taking in everything as he walked, in his usual wide-awake way, and at last found himself again at the place where he had landed—on Market-street wharf. He still had his extra bread under his arm, for, although he was hungry, one of those big loaves was really a meal. So he took a drink of river water, gave his remaining loaves to a poor woman who had a little boy with her, and who looked quite as friendless and just as hungry as himself."[88] This noble act of charity, Brooks's young readers were led to believe, was characteristic of this benevolent man who always had his fellow citizens' best interests in mind. If one consults the original chapter in *The Autobiography of Benjamin Franklin* from which this passage comes, however, it is obvious that Brooks imputed charitable motives to Franklin that he did not intend. The original text reads, "Then I turned and went down Chestnut-street and part of Walnut-street, eating my roll all the way, and, coming round, found myself again at Market-street wharf, near the boat I came in, to which I went for a draught of the river water; and, being filled with one of my rolls, gave the other two to a woman and her child that came down the river in the boat with us, and were waiting to go farther."[89] In Franklin's version of the story, the woman and child are not destitute, and in fact they are not even strangers to this newest resident of Philadelphia; rather they have been his traveling companions. Brooks manages to turn Franklin's act of common courtesy (sharing food with friends) into a highly selfless and epic deed with vital but distorting implications vis-à-vis his later heroic stature.

Second, Brooks's histories are less useful to homeschoolers than those at the Learning Parent might think because they emphasize themes and devices that often contradict the message the Boyers are trying to deliver to young readers. For one thing, Brooks and the Boyers disagree about the relative importance of heroic figures as agents of historical change. Despite the fact that he wrote about the "heroic lives" of great Americans, Brooks felt that hero worship was a practice that should not be overindulged in by children. Young readers must come to understand that prominent historical figures were human beings and therefore subject to all manner of human failings. Aware that most young readers "love to linger over the names and deeds of those who have contributed to the success of great principles," Brooks warned that they must choose wisely when deciding which heroes to proclaim "great and grand and noble."[90] He cautioned, "Boys and girls, be careful how you pick out your hero." Despite John S. C. Abbott's assertions to the contrary, for instance, Brooks warned that one should avoid conquerors such as Napoleon Bonaparte, who, "though a mighty genius," was nevertheless a man "who loved power and war simply for his own ends." Such a man is "not . . . worthy to be selected by you as a real hero," Brooks instructed; nor should the man "who is powerful because he is rich, or because he is strong, or because he is smart, alone, . . . be chosen by you as your hero." Only a personage as august as Washington, "who, knowing what is right, dares to do it, and, doing it, is able to do it nobly and well," should command enough respect from young readers to justify the consistent use of the term *heroic* in reference to him.[91]

Brooks understood in ways that the Boyers have underestimated that the genre of biography is susceptible to distortions of the role of the individual in history. As Ray Raphael has noted, all written history consists of narrative and as such is subject to the literary tropes and conventions associated with storytelling. "Sentences written in the active voice require protagonists," Raphael points out of his works and those of his fellow historians, but in narratives charting historical causality, "we don't always know the exact identities of the subjects of our sentences." Therefore, our literary tendencies cause us to attribute historical change to the actions of "individual *people* rather than abstract *groups*," he adds, because "we like that, we revert to it unconsciously. It's a default mode in the writing of history." But the use of the term *heroic leader* has "a perilous side-effect," Raphael adds, since "if some are leaders, all the others become followers." He notes that popular historical literature is often peopled by "a few important individuals [who] make things happen," whereas "the rest only tag along." By "adopting and extending this default grammar, history writers cast about for 'leaders' to serve as subjects for their sentences and protagonists for their narratives," whereas in reality "so-called leaders emerge from the people—they gain influence by expressing views that others espouse."[92]

As Raphael articulates and Brooks understood, this "simplistic model—that a few individuals make history happen—works well with children," and since "what most Americans know about the Revolution they learned in the fifth grade," these distorted causal patterns become concretized.[93] "When you watch a baseball game what is it that interests you most through it all—the players or the result of their play?" Brooks asked. "Do you not soon forget this or that boy in whose good work you place so much confidence and think more of the score that is being made or wonder whether the great playing of your favorite nine is really going to give them the victory?" As was his habit, Brooks appended a moral: "It is so in life. Acts are more than actors; principles are more than men. What a city, a State or a nation is striving for is of more importance than the leaders in the struggle or the great men whose names we reverence and applaud."[94]

As a result of these insights, Brooks urged young readers to resist the temptation to think of heroes as imbued with providential self-awareness about their own future greatness. This should give the Boyers pause with respect to their republication ambitions, although it has not. Brooks claimed that Christopher Columbus's heroism, for instance, was a gradual achievement whose full import the explorer never comprehended fully at any point in his career.

During his lifetime Columbus was largely discontented and restless. "You say, why couldn't Columbus have lived happily, after he had gone through so much, and done so much, and discovered America, and given us who came after him so splendid a land to live in?" Brooks asked. The response was instructive for young readers who might be inclined to exaggerate the role of Providence in the Columbus story: "Now, just here comes the real point of the story. Wise men tell us that millions upon millions of busy little insects die to make the beautiful coral islands of the Southern seas. . . . Millions and millions of men and women have lived and labored, died and been forgotten by the world they helped to make the bright, and beautiful, and prosperous place to live in that it is to-day. Columbus was one of these millions; but he was a leader among them and has not been forgotten." Temporal distance has played tricks on our memories, Brooks recognized, and has caused us to concentrate our historical attention on Columbus in ways that are unavoidable but not wholly justified. "As the world has got farther away from the time in which he lived, the man Columbus, who did so much and yet died almost unnoticed, has grown more and more famous," Brooks acknowledged. His name "is immortal, and to-day he is the hero Columbus—one of the world's greatest men."[95]

In fact, Brooks was inclined to attribute the alleged discovery of the New World more to happenstance than to heroic destiny. He reminded young readers that Columbus had been induced on his first voyage to alter his course by Captain Alonso Pinzón, who had seen parrots flying southward and took them to be a sign that "the land they sought was off in that direction." If Columbus had not changed his course or had ignored the parrots, Brooks argued, "the Santa Maria, with the Pinta and the Niña, would have sailed on until they had entered the harbor of Savannah or Charleston, or perhaps the broad waters of Chesapeake Bay." The result would have been that "the United States of to-day would have been discovered and settled by Spaniards, and the whole history of the land would have been quite different from what it has been." Betraying some of the Anglo-Saxon bias evidenced in the works of the Abbotts, Brooks wrote, "Spanish blood has peopled, but not uplifted, the countries of South America and the Spanish Main." English blood, however, "peopled, saved and upbuilt the whole magnificent northern land that Spain missed and lost." And this is what a flying parrot did, he recorded: "It turned the tide of lawless adventure, of gold-hunting, of slave-driving, and of selfish strife for gain to the south; it left the north yet unvisited until it was ready for the strong, and sturdy, and determined men and women who, hunting for liberty, came across the seas and founded the colonies that became in time the free and independent republic of the United States of America." And the fate of the nation this parrot helped influence, Brooks noted, was equally random and storybook-inspired. "And thus has the story of Columbus really turned out," he concluded. "Happier than any fairy tale, more marvelous than any wonder book, the story of the United States of America is one that begins, 'Once upon a time,' and has come to the point where it depends upon the boys and girls who read it, to say whether or not they shall 'live happily ever after.' "[96]

A third factor that undermines the usefulness of Brooks's works as repurposed by the Boyers is that Uncle Rick's stylistic embellishments, especially the various verbal manipulations and emendations he introduces in the CDs, suggest that there are substantial differences between his republished texts and Brooks's originals. Hoping to appeal to young readers, for instance, Boyer cultivates a colloquial casualness in his recordings that is inconsistent with the more formal narrative voice of Brooks's literary presentation. For instance, Boyer adopts a folksy, Garrison Keillor-like persona in "Uncle Rick Reads *The True Story of George Washington*," an effort to appeal especially to young listeners who desire a personal connection to their storytellers. The recording begins as follows: "Hey little buddies, it's Uncle Rick coming to you from the Little House in the Pasture" (the Boyer home in Virginia), "where you can hear the birds sing, the cows moo, the horses neigh and Uncle Rick talk to his little buddies." He continues,

> Today is a beautiful sunshiney day; I don't see a cloud in the sky. It happens to be early March as we're recording this today and I'm looking out across the pasture of the farm of Mr. Titus, and I see lovely sights. I see my pond down there where I will soon be fishing with the grandkids. I see maple trees across the little spring, they're just turning red getting ready to bloom out in green as they always do at this time of year. The willow trees are starting to get good and green, and I mean Virginia's a lovely place right now and getting prettier by the day. I am here at the Little House in the Pasture with my faithful bloodhound Sadie May (Hmmm . . . I thought maybe she'd say hello, but she's just laying on the couch asleep; that's the way she usually does when we're not outside).

According to the packaging of this CD, Uncle Rick's "friendly, informal style brings to colorful life some of America's brightest luminaries to entertain and inspire boys and girls everywhere!"[97] Such insights are accompanied, however, by the sounds of farm animals emanating from the pasture behind the farmhouse where the CD is being recorded.

These Learning Parent soundtracks also include "Uncle Rick's Character Commentaries," in which he highlights the personality traits of his "sterling" biographical subjects while moralizing about their relevance to twenty-first-century listeners. The term *character commentaries* turns out to be a euphemism for an editorial prerogative employed indiscriminately by Boyer, often with distorting consequences for historical accuracy. In "Uncle Rick Reads *The True Story of George Washington*," for instance, Boyer disrupts the flow of the narrative to second-guess his pronunciation of Augustine Washington's first name, which he pronounces three times, with the accent on the first, second, and third syllable, respectively; he then stops reading in order to get his "tongue-[un]tied," as he puts it. Elsewhere he asks his readers out loud if "Bar-BA-dos" is the correct pronunciation of the Caribbean nation Washington visited for two months in 1751, and he consults a dictionary to confirm the intonation. Boyer employs a comically bad British accent to imitate the dialogue of British colonials—distracting listeners from the serious points Brooks was making in his text about the rising tensions in the 1770s—but he differentiates very little among the voices of the dozens of other historical actors whose stories he narrates. He loses his place several times in the reading of Brooks's text and hums until he finds it again, proclaiming, "Boy, it's tough to get old, isn't it?" At one point Uncle Rick appears confused by a bit of text that wraps around both sides of a picture in the original Brooks volume, and he reads vertically when he should be reading horizontally until he discovers his mistake, apologizing with a distracting "oops" but choosing not to re-record. Most distracting of all (because of its anachronistic implications) is the announcement Boyer makes part way through the reading that he has run out of space on the twenty-first-century compact disk he is using to record Brooks's nineteenth-century words.[98]

Some of Boyer's character commentaries reflect current politics and his ideological preferences, such as when he interrupts Brooks's discussion of the efforts to honor Washington's birthday as a national holiday to complain about the more generic, denatured Presidents' Day celebrations observed in the twenty-first century. Boyer disdains the current practice of commemorating collectively the administrations of all America's executive leaders, primarily because he does not think them all equally worthy of recognition. In an accompanying blog, he editorializes, "When I was a kid, we learned about such people as George Washington . . . not just because of their part in the writing of America's history, but because they were virtuous men."[99] Nowadays, Boyer reflects, no one studies Washington, a hero who has lost ground to less worthy figures in history textbooks, curricula, and National Standards. "Would you believe [it]," he asks, "if I told you that a lot of the young men who have worked for me in my business in the past did not even know who George Washington was?" In a congratulatory comment to the homeschooled children of parents who had the good sense to purchase and play his recordings, Boyer adds, "That is why you should be so thankful that your mom and dad are teaching you about great men like this." This self-serving statement was accompanied by his earnest plea to young listeners to embrace the Learning Parent's mission of reconstituting veneration for the father of our country and, by extension, all fathers. "Aren't we thankful to God that we have had people like him in our history?" Boyer asked, adding hopefully, "I am counting on you to grow up to be like him and let God use you greatly in making American history, too."[100]

Still more distracting is Uncle Rick's tendency to call attention to every instance in the biographies in which Brooks cited a line of scripture and to connect that propensity to the greater piety of nineteenth-century historians. "There's another Bible quote for you," Boyer noted in one case. "That's how they used to write biographies in the old days, guys." Elsewhere Uncle Rick editorialized, "Boys and girls, isn't it great to hear the Bible quoted. To hear the words of Jesus quoted in a history book about an American hero. That's the way people used to write books, and that's why you want to read these old books."[101] In an accompanying blog Boyer associates the loss of biblical and heroic language in current histories with the rise of multiculturalism in American schools. "New social studies standards are more concerned that American children empathize with Islam through the teaching of 'Islamic Studies' than that they understand the importance of George Washington to our present free society," he argues. "It's deemed so important to think 'multiculturally' that we don't delve deeply into the principles of our own society but study a smattering of facts from many different societies." That "is nonsense," Boyer concludes, because "America, built on biblical ideals, is still the one nation in the world that all other nations envy."[102]

Even when Boyer does stay close to Brooks's texts, his readings are marred by the distance of more than a century that has elapsed since the original writings were produced. Given this temporal gap, it is the things that Uncle Rick does not change that sometimes have the greatest impact on the quality of the CDs he markets. As Boyer reads the text of *The True Story of George Washington*, for instance, he fails to adjust language used by Brooks that is clearly germane only to the century in which the book first was written. Hence he does not attempt to update Brooks's terminology, even when, given new uses, it appears anachronistic, such as when he refers to James Russell Lowell as a "modern American." Elsewhere in his CD recordings he quotes Brooks to the effect that General Washington gathered his troops in 1775 under an elm tree on the Cambridge Commons in Massachusetts "which still stands—an old tree now, carefully preserved and made famous through all the land."[103] In fact, however, the tree died in 1923, several decades after Brooks had written his biography, and it was cut into a thousand pieces and distributed as relics.

In this case, Uncle Rick's literal reading gives young listeners of his CDs a false impression of the durability of that terrestrial symbol.

Additionally, Boyer misses opportunities to correct obvious errors in Brooks's narrative, even when he recognizes that Brooks may have gotten things wrong. Uncle Rick reads a passage from *The True Story of George Washington* on the creation of the Constitution in which Brooks declares erroneously that Alexander Hamilton was the "Father of the Constitution." Boyer is brought up short by this revelation. "Now that's interesting," he notes. Brooks "says that Alexander Hamilton was called the Father of the Constitution. I've always heard that James Madison was called the Father of the Constitution." His doubts about this assertion are well founded, but his impulse is to blame himself for the mislabeling rather than to second-guess Brooks. Better yet, Uncle Rick prefers to indict the public school system in which he was trained for his ignorance on the matter. "Now I wonder if there's a lot about this that I don't know because I went to public schools and didn't read about the important things very much and so I'm not as familiar with the Constitution as I should be," Boyer mutters aloud on the CD. "I wonder, I wonder, I wonder, I wonder here, if Hamilton may have had more to do with the Constitution than even Madison did. Hmmm. It just shows we need to keep reading and learning fellas and gals, we need to always keep reading and learning."[104] Ironically, Boyer's public school education actually served him quite well in this instance, but to acknowledge that fact would obviously contradict his central argument about the advantages of homeschooling, so he chooses not to challenge the point further. Evidently Boyer would rather take the blame for being wrong about the Constitutional Convention in order to confirm his thesis about the inadequacies of public schools than admit to being right about the events in Philadelphia in 1787 at the expense of exposing the weakness of his fundamental premises. Either way, the value of public school training is confirmed.

These sins of commission and omission further suggest the methodological distinctions between aural and written expression. Some have argued, for instance, that listening to tapes at bedtime is a poor substitute for reading books and that the practice slows literacy acquisition. The reading specialist Serge Tisseron writes that "the child who *listens* to stories when he is a baby, lives within the stories, like they were part of him," but that the child must also learn to "keep the stories at a distance, like something exterior to him" that "he can integrate on his terms." This can be accomplished only if the child has the skills "to understand what he has read, to integrate it in his own context and personal experiences by analysing it in a critical way so he is able to take a stand on what he has read. Only this kind of complete and deep reading education will take children toward a real, integrated literacy." Unless a child has access to "the letters, as graphic elements, that come together to form words, then sentences, then paragraphs and chapters of a book," Tisseron concludes, he or she cannot achieve reading competency. In terms of historical literacy, then, the orthographic perspective gained by reading rather than merely listening to narratives of memorable episodes of the past is obscured rather than facilitated by Uncle Rick's auditory strategies.[105] Insofar as Uncle Rick's recordings are marketed as texts suitable for use in homeschooling environments, these deficiencies are even more glaring. In short, listening to the Learning Parent versions of the historian's works is a very different experience from reading Brooks's first editions.

And fourth, Brooks employed a developmental scheme in his writings that drew extensively on those philosophies of the child study and child first movements so detested by the Boyers and others on the Christian Right. For instance, Brooks endorsed G. Stanley Hall's conception of a stepped, progressive approach to historical literacy, emphasizing the relevance of emergent heroism and character evolution in his biographies. Believing that children should be able to choose books that comported with their personal levels of reading comprehension, Brooks wrote multiple biographies of the same heroic figures, each intended for a different stage of a child's intellectual life. Additionally, Brooks embraced the philosophy of those early twentieth-century progressive educators who argued that history should be made useful to students by focusing on current events and featuring contemporary perspectives. Brooks sought to "bring the events of former ages out into the clearer light of our every-day trials and triumphs," urging young readers to recognize that "an eternal correlation does exist between dead actions and living endeavors."[106] This pragmatic approach to learning, reminiscent of Arnold's plea that education for the young must "begin with that which appeals to their child life" in the "present interest," is incompatible with the Boyers' belief in a ubiquitous, universal history that transcends time and that presumably protects children from the aforementioned "vain speculations" and "soft intellectualism" of secular, progressive educators who operated without religious commitment or character.

Brooks never endorsed the brand of submissiveness required of children toward their parents in the Learning Parent model. It is true that in his Heroic Life volumes Brooks urged patience and compliance on the part of his very youngest readers with respect to parental authority and tradition. In his True Story series for older readers, however, Brooks backed away from the most stringent requirements of obedience and advanced a model of childhood compliance more in keeping with the tenets of the child first movement.

Such figures as Franklin were heroic, he argued, not because they deferred always to their parents' authority but because they sometimes rejected it. Brooks pointed out that Franklin, who had grown up in a "strict but happy home," had to leave his parents in order to strike an independent course in life. Choosing to break an apprenticeship with his overbearing brother and against the wishes of his father, the "restless and unsettled" Franklin had, in Brooks's estimation, "provocation" to run away from his parents' house and to make a new home for himself in Philadelphia.[107]

These distinctions can be made clear by comparing the parenting strategies of Brooks and the Boyers. Brooks was committed to child-first philosophies in his personal life, both as a son and a father. Elbridge Gerry Brooks, his father, was not an "impossible good little boy" of the sort that "glared so reprovingly at every healthy, human child from the covers of Sunday-school books," Brooks noted proudly in a biography he wrote to honor him after his death. Reviewing his predecessor's boyhood records and talking to relatives in preparation for such work, Brooks was happy to report that he found "no namby-pamby ways, no unnatural saintlinesses, no mawkish sentimentalities to disfigure the wholesome childhood of [a] manly, clear-headed, sportive, and mischievous boy." In fact, he acknowledged his father's rebelliousness as a natural and necessary stage in the development of a child.[108] Brooks applied the same lessons to his own parenting, raising two daughters to be independent and even iconoclastic thinkers. One of his daughters, Geraldine Brooks, became a historian in her own right, writing books for young readers on the crucial role of women in the colonial and early national periods. Her sympathetic portrait of Dolley Madison in *Dames and Daughters of the Young Republic* told the story of a future first lady who, as a young Quaker girl, played the part of the "wayward little daughter" rebelling against the "forms and regulations that . . . hemmed her about so rigidly." Restricted in her actions by a "severely religious papa," Geraldine Brooks noted, Dolley proved "not nearly so demure as she appeared." For Dolley, as for Geraldine and many other women in every age, self-actualization required independence from parental authority rather than unquestioning acquiescence to it.[109]

The Boyers adopt a radically different perspective on raising nontraditional, potentially rebellious children. For this couple, strict obedience to parental authority is a must, especially among daughters. In a public lecture titled "Teaching Character Through History," Rick Boyer comments critically on the potential place of women in a culture "that's forgotten what manhood and womanhood are." Claiming that women in the military have less chance of being "good soldiers" than he has of being a "good La Leche League member," he announces that "men and women are different." A woman "is the flower of God's creation, and we're trying to make men out of them," Boyer argues. "For Pete's sake, it's like trying to make a jackass out of a Kentucky Derby winner. It's using the Hope diamond for a doorstop to use a woman for something a man can do."[110] In her lecture "If My People . . . How We Can and Must Make a Difference," one of Boyer's homeschooled daughters, Kate Boyer Brown, endorses these stereotypes, advising American women to concentrate not on the military front but on the home front, where they face enough problems as it is. Brown claims it takes a heroic effort each day for women to battle against the corrupting forces that serve as harbingers of "bad news about the moral state" of our country. "Homosexuals are 'getting married,'" she complains, "the Ten Commandments are thrown out of our courtrooms, the morale of the military is low and character is often lower, divorce consumes half of our marriages, and alarming numbers of teenagers and women are having children out of wedlock." She asks imploringly, "How did things get so bad? Will it ever get better?"[111]

For all these reasons—factual errors and embellishments, rejection of providential agency, ideologically driven emendations, and progressive pedagogies—Uncle Rick provides a very different educational experience for youngsters who listen to his CDs than they would have undergone had they read Brooks's original narratives instead. The CDs reveal the degree to which the Boyers have manipulated the past in an effort to make its realities conform to their expectations of it. The effect has been to beguile children with an imaginary vision of the world that is ahistorical (because contrary to the historical record) and thereby to stifle rather than encourage historical-mindedness among the young.

Barefoot Boys and the Desecration of History

If the Boyers are not content to import wholesale to the twenty-first century an unadulterated vision of the past as shaped in nineteenth-century works such as those by Brooks, then what kind of history do they endorse? The answer: one that is nostalgic and that may be unrepresentative of the experiences of the majority of Americans, both in the nineteenth century and the twenty-first. In "Breaking the Shackles," for instance, Rick Boyer longs for the day when Americans might return to the lifestyles of those who held ice cream socials on country farms, as he imagines they did in Brooks's time. "All the houses it seems had big front porches with swings and solid wood handrails for barefoot boys to sit on and dangle their feet," Boyer writes dreamily of eras gone by. In the old days, "if you lived in the country, it was brothers and cousins you wrestled with or pulled weeds with or bucked hay with or walked barefoot with down a path carrying poles on your shoulders and fishing worms in a tin can with a jagged edge lid and a shepherd dog nosing along in the bushes for rabbit scents." Boyer alleges that industrialists and social engineers spoiled this utopian vision. According to him, these minions of the monied interests influenced boards of education and public school officials to advance their nefarious ends. Devoted slavishly to the false preaching of Karl Marx and Friedrich Engels, whom Boyer accuses of "smoking dope together in Germany," American political leaders with leftist leanings funded public schools in which children were confined "in cell blocks with people of their own age, taught by strangers, [and] separated from their parents and siblings," all on behalf of "people claiming to want to help the unwashed masses to become enlightened." "But it was money that made it possible," he concluded cynically. Teachers' colleges emerged, in turn, to train "the priests of a new secular religion" who devoted their lives to the reconfiguring of public schools into "government concentration camps."[112]

As these descriptions suggest, the Boyers long for a history that is "an ideal construct," a temporal place "without conflicts . . . malice or stupidity." Their idealization of the past through embellishments of republished history books is consistent with what the historiographer Frances FitzGerald calls "the negative face of the demand that the books portray the world as a utopia of the eternal present."[113] Admittedly, some of the nostalgia of the Boyers derives from the language and tone of Brooks's original works, in which literary analogies are developed to appeal to a child's naïve perspective on the world. The Boyers, however, are among those purists whom David Lowenthal describes as seeking to "maintain rigid allegiance to the past, whose authority they vindicate by imbuing it with traditionalist symbols and institutions to be brought back in a redemptive future." By recycling Brooks's popular histories for children, the Boyers hope to recover a "primordial state that blends childhood memory with the religious ritual of rebirth; and this imagined golden age shapes the vision of [the] future." Such traditionalists also seek "refuge in mystical connection with his great and ennobling heritage." As Lowenthal observes, in some societies tradition is therefore "the pre-eminent guide for behavior, especially if the precedent is believed ancient and constant. The past is an infallible source of truth and merit" while "things are deemed correct simply because they have happened."[114]

It is perhaps not surprising that calls for a redemptive return to tradition from those on the Christian Right, like the Boyers, are especially loud in times of rapid change and perceived crisis such as many are experiencing in the twenty-first century. As the historian Michael Clark has pointed out, however, this is nothing new. The same traditionalist impulse pervaded the late nineteenth century, when the unsettling forces of widespread manufacturing and mass culture compelled Americans to be "more conscious of tradition as a social force" than ever before.[115] Lowenthal writes that "massive industrialization and mass immigration likewise led disillusioned Americans to seek refuge in the past. Noisome and odious industrial cities seemed more and more remote from the old agrarian ideal, and late nineteenth-century immigration accentuated urban evils. The millions of newcomers from southern and eastern Europe, manifestly alien in religion, language, family practices, and temperament, seemed unassimilable and dangerously un-American," causing many older Americans to retreat "defensively into history." These nativists envisioned the past as "a haven for traditional values that might, in time, restore their idealized America, and would, in the meantime, safeguard them from the sordid present." The rise of numerous genealogical organizations in the United States in the last third of the nineteenth century—for example, the Daughters of the American Revolution, whose membership boasted ancestral associations with vital historical events from the American past—bespoke "times of archaistic zeal which vilified the present in favour of a lost or revived past." The heritage-based elements of these associations reaffirmed the connections between temporal and parental authority; in such a climate, "to renounce the past meant especially to reject parental influence."[116]

The problem with such a filiopietistic approach to history is that it links challenges to authority by children with infidelity toward parents. It thereby preempts the prospects of young people participating meaningfully in contestations over a negotiated past by prohibiting them from developing the deliberative skills necessary to work through contentious matters. Such a strategy, psychologists warrant, flies in the face of history itself by ignoring the natural anti-authoritarian impulses evident in the developmental histories of most young people. While some children "cling forever to their self-image as dutiful followers" and "others give it up only at great psychic cost," Lowenthal writes, the majority "become ardent iconoclasts" who exercise their right to determine their own heroes and choose to fight for their generation's own place in history. All youth experience growing up as a "ceaseless struggle between ingrained assumptions that parents desire our homage and developing needs for autonomy that impel us to spurn their authority and example." These conditions, which informed the controversies over the child first movement in ways that commentators like Comer may not have understood, require that while parents "may acknowledge the virtues of yesteryear and the benefits of relics and roots," they must also know "that the old has to give way, that youth must be served, that new ideas need room to develop—that the past does indeed constrain the present." If the "most faithful followers of tradition" would but realize that neither parents nor children can avoid challenges, which are, after all, just the first steps toward innovation, Lowenthal concludes wisely, then they would learn to accept that "living in ever new configurations of nature and culture, we must think and act *de novo* even to survive." In this sense, "change is as inescapable as tradition."[117]

At the very least, the heroes whom young nineteenth-century readers learned to appreciate in Brooks's histories should not be expected to fulfill the needs of the twenty-first-century listeners exposed to Boyer's CDs. Brooks's goal as a biographer was not to paint an everlasting portrait of concretized subjects from which there could be no dissent or change but to represent dynamic figures whose lives were open to all manner of revisionist interpretation. The narrative forms Brooks applied to the lives of his heroes were as fluid and fungible as those figures themselves. Brooks understood that children could not be constrained by the interpretations of their parents; they must have the strength of their own convictions if they are to achieve a full sense of self-identity. Were children required to believe in the idealized pasts of their parents, even those designed to protect them, FitzGerald has noted, they would be unable to overcome psychologically or physically the harsh realities they face in their own lives that challenge such idealizations. The effects would also be highly confusing to developing minds. Slavish commitment to the historical forms and outlooks of others, FitzGerald notes, "give[s] young people no warning of the real dangers ahead, and later they may well make these young people feel that their own experience of conflict or suffering is unique in history and perhaps un-American. To the extent that children can see the contrast between these fictions and the world around them, this kind of instruction can only make them cynical."[118]

Cynicism is certainly not the disposition Elbridge Brooks wished to cultivate in the juvenile readers for whom he wrote; rather, he understood intuitively that each new Joshua generation must find its own path through the historical wilderness to the Promised Land. The Learning Parent website insists that children should obey their parents unquestioningly in order to understand God's intentions for them and their history, but Brooks's writings implied that real learning could not be achieved until parents recognized that their children must make their own way in the world by bending the lessons of the past to suit their personal needs. These acts of rebellion can be painful at first, especially for nonconforming children, but, as the historian Richard Hofstadter put it, they are part of the necessary and "perennial battle we wage with our elders." He added insightfully, "If we are to have any new thoughts, if we are to have an intellectual identity of our own, we must make the effort to distinguish ourselves from those who preceded us, and perhaps pre-eminently from those to whom we once had the greatest indebtedness."[119] For Brooks, at least, the long-term liberating effects of such intellectual insurgency far outweighed the short-term generational tensions it might engender. For him, *child first* was not merely a vague philosophical abstraction suitable only for some theoretical handbook on how to teach children about the past; rather, it was a practical, working strategy that parents should employ to improve the historical literacy and personal development of their children. In a very real sense, then, Brooks believed, in ways the Boyers seem not to have comprehended, that the term *learning parent* applies best to mothers and fathers who are capable of seeing the wisdom of setting free their learning children by allowing them to act on their revisionist impulses.

CHAPTER 6

Doctrinal History

Charles Morris and the Search for "Lost History"

> The originals are not original. There is imitation, model, and suggestion, to the very arch-angels, if we knew their history.
>
> Ralph Waldo Emerson, "Quotation and Originality"

God as Historian and the "Winds of Doctrine"

If tradition is the foundation of historical knowledge, as Rick and Marilyn Boyer, of the Learning Parent enterprise claim, then the consistency of the master narrative to which Elbridge S. Brooks and others in the nineteenth century contributed has given the couple hope that a return to such texts in the twenty-first century will reinvigorate the consensus championed therein. The replication of the texts of antiquated volumes, however, does not guarantee a transference of the cultural and intellectual milieu in which they were written originally. Studying the context of works by popular historians reveals the extent to which the master narrative emerged out of explicit historical settings in which tradition was being challenged at every turn. Brooks was an active contributor to the discussions among educators in the 1890s about how children might react to new pedagogical approaches to historical literacy. While his narratives did not seriously challenge tradition in terms of subject matter or structure, they were new and unconventional in their expectations for student learning. Republishing the texts of popular juvenile historians such as Brooks without appreciating these contexts not only distorts his words but also misrepresents the intellectual intentions that motivated him to express himself in distinct ways in the first place. In an age when the needs of children were foregrounded by educational specialists in the child first movement, the power and authority to control language mattered more than the subject or structure of language itself.

217

Even if one could transpose nineteenth-century texts to twenty-first-century contexts without affecting the conditions of reception, there is no proof that the utopian, nonpartisan consensus the Boyers believe existed in the mid-nineteenth century ever really did. The brutal reality of the bloody Civil War, among other things, would suggest otherwise. In fact, one could argue that the intensity of the Boyers' efforts to recover a pure lost childhood— a world unaffected by politics, ideologies, and doctrines—is an indicator of the unlikelihood of its existence, of obsessive longing betraying a desperation for the improbable. The practice of republishers of recycling original nineteenth-century works can be attributed to their fixation with creating a "desired past," one in which, according to David Lowenthal, "we convince ourselves that things really were that way" and that "what ought to have happened becomes what did happen."[1] The misdirected yearning for such a past was not original to the Boyers, of course; indeed, it was a widespread sentiment among the very nineteenth-century Americans of the late Victorian era whose popular histories they have republished. The Learning Parent is responsible not for creating the mythology of a lost golden age of youth but for failing to distinguish between the regressive fantasies in which these popular historians indulged and the realities they obscured in doing so.

This psychology of desire persists today among others on the Christian Right, as evidenced by the republication efforts of the Christian Liberty Press, headquartered in Arlington Heights, Illinois. A branch of the Christian Liberty Academy School System and affiliated with the Church of Christian Liberty, the Christian Liberty Press is dedicated to "finding, evaluating, and producing curriculum materials that are rooted in the Word of God and express a biblical worldview." The press advertises a "Christ-centered curriculum" that prepares students "for services within His Kingdom" and that includes recommended reading and exercises from preschool to high school and beyond.[2] Arguing that "it is only possible to honor God when we insist on high standards in our academic program," the promoters of the Christian Liberty Academy Satellite Schools (CLASS) curriculum consider scripture the foundation of all learning. "Because God created the world, it reflects His order," the curriculum designers write. "As a result, all aspects of the world in which God has placed us should be taught in an organized and systematic fashion," with God's unity "conveyed from subject to subject and from grade to grade." Fragmented curricula promote "a disjointed conception of reality" and teach the student that "there is no one philosophy that accounts for everything," they argue in support of a single truth theory.[3] As the Boyers reaffirm in their endorsements of the Christian Liberty Press, there *is* a single philosophy that does explain everything, and it is embodied in the "old style," "uncompromisingly Christian" vision of the CLASS curriculum.[4]

The study of history, especially Bible history, is a central element of the Christian Liberty curriculum. Therefore, the press's educational specialists encourage homeschooling parents to begin preparations for teaching their children about the past by reading a booklet produced by Bob Jones University titled "The Christian Teaching of History" and by linking its principles to the biblical exercises outlined in the CLASS curriculum kits for history.[5] These beliefs include an acknowledgment that "God is the Lord of history" and that "history has not only been planned by God but proceeds according to His purpose." Those who complete the Christian Liberty regimen of history courses, the promoters claim, will learn that "God created every part of the universe according to His own wisdom." Therefore, the Christian Liberty Press materials advance a teleological curriculum for the study of history reminiscent of Coffin's, one that seeks "to uncover the facts which [God] created and the laws which He ordained." Eschewing "secular models as the standard of what is best," the advertisers assure parents that the CLASS history curriculum is not, like those used in public schools, subject to "every wind of doctrine"; instead, it is forged from a stable "Christian approach through building on the achievements of sound Christian scholars."[6]

The Christian Liberty Press's emphasis on scriptural approaches to the past reflects its designers' fears that the lessons of the Bible are being lost on young readers because they are too distracted by social media to focus on the word of God. Overwhelmed by the "materialism, secularism, big statism, humanism, and denominational apostasy" of the twenty-first century, children have little permanence in their lives; indeed, the very idea of consistency either in practice or belief is foreign to them, the Bob Jones pamphlet avows. The solution to this unpredictability is to return to the stability of the Holy Word and a consensual past. "The biblical accounts raise history to its highest function," especially "the revelation and demonstration of the facts fundamental to Christian belief and godliness," write the authors of "The Christian Teaching of History." Central to these principles is the sanctity of parental authority as depicted in the Bible. Students are instructed to read the Old Testament for what it illustrates about the "divine precepts" as they relate to "the consequences of obedience and disobedience," while the New Testament establishes for young learners "the basis of Christian belief and hope." Through scripture reading, the curriculum asserts, students who study the past will recognize that "God Himself is a historian and holds man responsible for obeying the truths taught by the inspired record" of the divine being. It is God who "allows memory of the past for our learning and commands us not to forget our heritage," the Bob Jones publication asserts. A child's failure to understand history, in this scenario, is a form of blasphemy that must be addressed by parents in a swift, vigorous manner. Students must learn at a very young age that "the biblical account of man's creation and redemption" represents "God's will for man on earth" and constitutes the one true expression of how "God Himself looks at human history."[7]

This scriptural approach to education is connected to a larger conception of generational relations that harkens back to some of the child-rearing practices of the seventeenth century. In keeping with the thinking of the Boyers, Christian Liberty Press publications assert that educational materials should aid children in learning how to obey their elders and to respect their obligations to serve both God and family in traditional approaches to the past. This concept of a useful childhood (as opposed to sheltered or protected ones) derives from a belief that children should contribute to the financial and emotional well-being of the domestic circle and that they must not expect special concessions because of their young age. Implicit in biblical study is the recognition that the scriptures afford historical models for constructive behavior in children as exemplified by the "conformity to the image of God" evidenced by his disciples. "Family ties and other expressions of natural affection [found in the Bible] testify to the close attentiveness and protective love with which the Heavenly Father observes and provides for His children," the Bob Jones pamphlet instructs. In "unselfish acts of heroism" featured in the Old and New Testaments, it adds, children "may see reflections of the great self-sacrifice of the Redeemer" and apply these lessons to their own lives. The value of respecting tradition, one of the fundamental obligations of any true Christian, is not only revealed by "the privation and ultimate destruction" of biblical figures who ignored this tenet, but also evidenced in the "divine principles of personal discipline and submission to authority" that are prerequisites to studying the lessons of the Bible in the first place. Children must be obedient and useful to others if they expect to demonstrate their humility and value before God.[8]

Tradition-based principles had a noticeable effect on ideas about literacy at the beginning of the twentieth century, especially in terms of the pedagogical strategies used for language acquisition by children. Most public school teachers in the United States instructed students in English, a technique that parents of immigrants saw as both an avenue of success in the new culture and a threat to the traditions of the old. For the young, losing verbal and written facility in the language of the parents meant not being able to converse across generations. To ameliorate the effects of the potential estrangement resulting from this condition, some parents insisted that their children continue to train domestically in the old ways even as they studied their new history in the public schools. The sons and daughters of many Jewish immigrants, for instance, studied Hebrew at home, not only to be able to understand the Torah in synagogue but also so that they might converse with their parents and grand-parents who acquired knowledge of American history through Yiddish texts on the subject.[9] Similarly, Christian fundamentalists homeschooled their children in the practice of "biblical literalism" in reaction to the gradual removal of the Bible as an instructional tool in public schools.[10] If "the Word of God is the Truth," as they averred, then children must be made to understand what the words in the Bible say literally and what they mean in a Christian context. As public schools abandoned this task, homeschooling parents took it upon themselves to train their children to read not only by memorizing the words in the Bible but also by studying their syntax and lexical-grammatical properties as well. Tradition was bound up not only with literacy achieved through the reading of canonical passages in the scriptures but also with the study and usage of their specialized literary forms.

These traditional nineteenth-century strategies of biblical hermeneutics have found a new place in the Christian Liberty Press CLASS curriculum. In this system, children are encouraged at a very early age to familiarize themselves both with the words and the modes of presentation of the Bible. For instance, parents of homeschooled kindergarteners using the CLASS program are requested to purchase *Studying God's Word: A* by Michael J. McHugh, a workbook that uses a phonics approach to teaching reading comprehension in conjunction with Bible stories from both the Old and New Testaments.[11] "Great care must be given to understand the exact meaning of the words used," fundamentalist pedagogues like McHugh warn, "and how words are repeated, or combined, or presented in lexical and syntactic patterns."[12] These and other literalist techniques for acquiring reading competency focus on such things as how many times a word occurs in scripture and the original meaning of terms that recur in multiple usages throughout the Bible. Approaching literacy in this way gives children and their parents the confidence that they are reading passages that convey the explicit words of God without error or contradiction. In a piece endorsing these practices titled "Teaching Reading Using the Bible," the educators Dave and Debbie Klein note that "literacy is so important to God" because it is necessary "for the purpose of learning his Word." In this sense, the Bible is both the subject and the means by which children learn of God's intentions for them.[13]

With respect to the study of history, CLASS materials insist that parents avoid modern, newfangled pedagogies in favor of traditional, historically proven ones. Reflecting the attitudes of many people on the Christian Right, the progressive teaching strategies of the early decades of the twentieth century are special targets of contempt. The Christian Liberty Press embraces Bob Jones's assertion that "history teaching that is distinctly Christian rejects certain philosophical attitudes and approaches that stem from modern unbelief. In particular it opposes humanism, which denies the existence of a personal God, rejects all value systems external to man, and trusts in human self-sufficiency." The Christian teacher also shuns and condemns forms of modern cynicism, including "the practice of debunking genuine heroes and creating unwholesome ones, of debasing good men and exalting sinners."[14] To teach children, Christian educators seek instead to recover lost texts in which the distinctions between heroes and antiheroes are manifest and undeniable. Adopting a strategy characteristic of Renaissance scholars, who sought to revive the classical past by resurrecting volumes of the ancient Greek and Roman worlds, such teachers practice what Lowenthal calls bibliographic "acts of unearthing and resurrecting, metaphors brought to mind by the past's remoteness and resultant fragmentation and burial."[15] As it was for Rick and Marilyn Boyer, the quest to recover a "lost history" is at the heart of the efforts by the Christian Liberty Press to republish nineteenth-century texts they believe evoke original visions of a bygone, golden past buried for too long beneath the rubble of modernist and revisionist methodologies.

"It Is Surprising What Book Makers Can Do": Charles Morris's Histories

A good example of the Christian Liberty Press's commitment to the "unearthing and resurrecting" of lost history is its republication of *The Child's Story of America,* written originally as *The Child's History of the United States* in 1900 by the popular historian Charles Morris and reissued in 1989 and again in 1998 by Christian Liberty Press.[16] The press advertises the book as "a comprehensive overview of United States history from Columbus through the late twentieth century" and recommends it as an anchor text in the CLASS fourth grade homeschooling curriculum. The republished version of Morris's volume comes with a test packet and an answer key, and it is advertised as a "politically conservative resource that will hold your fourth-grader's attention while covering some of our nation's most pivotal figures and events." Written in "a casual, conversational style," the promoters note, the revised version of Morris's book includes approaches to early American history that are unlike anything found in history textbooks used in public schools today insofar as they emphasize traditional narratives for students who "read about the history of America from Columbus to the 1980s, with plenty of attention paid to Christian figures and the current need for revival in the United States." Covering "historical events that are important in a Christian context," a "Providential history" approach "is plainly evident here," one reviewer notes, while another applauds the fact that the Christian Liberty Press edition "does not remove God entirely from our history, and that's certainly more than I can say for the texts that most public school children encounter."[17]

In one sense, Morris's *The Child's History of the United States* is a likely choice for resurrection by a Christian press because its author was a schoolteacher in Philadelphia in the 1850s whose early works emphasized moral development in young people (fig. 22).[18] Born in 1833 in Chester, Pennsylvania, Morris was raised in a Christian home in which discussions of moral challenges like temperance encouraged him to publish diatribes such as *Broken Fetters: The Light of Ages on Intoxication.*[19] Morris also was affiliated with the nineteenth-century homeschooling movement. After leaving the teaching profession, he wrote *The Home Educator in Necessary Knowledge,* a general information resource that became a standard in many home study programs.[20] Additionally he published the *Home School of American History,* in which he focused on the needs of readers outside traditional public school settings for the comprehension of basic historical facts as packaged in a popular narrative.[21] Most of these juvenile histories were infused as well with the didacticism typical of mid-nineteenth-century works by Goodrich, the Abbott brothers, and others, including clear articulations of what constitutes good and bad behavior and an inventory of sound principles by which children could learn to live their lives. Hence, in *The Child's History of the United States,* Morris explained to young readers that Hernando de Soto "deserved a bad fate" since he "brought bloodhounds to hunt the poor Indians, and chains to fasten on their hands and feet"; Cavaliers in Virginia were proclaimed to be shameful people because they were "too proud to work, and expected others to work for them, while they hoped to live by gambling and cheating." These examples were contrasted with "good souls" such as Ben Franklin, who was "not ashamed of hard work," and George Washington, who led a truly "noble life."[22]

Morris was very attentive to tradition and to the moral principles he believed were preconditions required for establishing greatness as a nation. In *The Young People's History of the World,* for instance, he highlighted the crucial and consistent role of distinguished individuals who had advanced the causes of human liberty and freedom through time. Adopting a long view of history, he encouraged young readers to imagine themselves on a mountaintop watching the vast panorama of the past unfold before them as eminent figures acted out their historical dramas. "All history is interesting but that which deals with the great achievements of the race and the great leaders of men is fascinating and entrancing," he wrote. "Standing here at the dawn of the Twentieth Century, as at the summit of a lofty peak of time, we may gaze far backward over the road we have traversed, losing sight of its minor

FIGURE 22. Portrait of Charles Morris. Courtesy of Northern Illinois University Libraries.

incidents, but seeing its great events loom up in startling prominence before our eyes." These "striking events, the critical epochs, the mighty crises through which the world has passed," he wrote, served as the historical residue of humanity's most treasured traditions and experiences and helped push "the world forward in its career." Less interested in "the trifling occurrences which signify nothing" and "passing actions which have borne no fruit in human affairs," Morris urged young readers to study the moral "turning points" and "critical periods" in the history of the world that constituted its "deepest and best aspect" and that, from his metaphoric summit, appeared to impart most meaningfully the wisdom of the ages.[23]

In another sense, however, Morris's works constitute unusual selections for republication by the Christian Liberty Press in that they often emphasized progressive change over stable tradition and questioned the desirability or even feasibility of attempting to live in a golden past when the present looked so promising. In fact, Morris viewed it as his greatest challenge as a historian to convey adequately to inexperienced young readers how crude and even savage the world was a mere one hundred years before they lived and to explain why the past must be subservient to the present. "I am afraid none of you quite understand how great the change has been," he wrote in *The Child's Story of the Greatest Century*, a work that depicts the nineteenth century as a tradition-altering epoch in which the old gave way to the new in startlingly abrupt ways. "Why, there are hundreds of little things we possess today which it seems to us the world must always have had, for we do not see how people

could ever have got along without them," Morris wrote in a manner reminiscent of Brooks. When the nineteenth century began, he pointed out, most
people worked with their hands as opposed to the machines they used at the
end of the century. Oil lamps and candles substituted for electricity and gas;
houses were not well heated, and bedrooms were still "as cold as Greenland";
floors were not carpeted and "pictures and books were few and poor." By
the end of the century, however, the material and spiritual conditions of life
had altered dramatically. "See what a change," he told young readers; "never
was there so much done in so short a time in any other part of the earth."
It was now "a century of science," Morris observed, one in which inventors
harnessed the "great forces and forms of the universe" that had once been
obscured by vague cosmologies but now had become self-evident.[24]

As the editors at the Christian Liberty Press doubtless appreciated, *The
Child's History of the United States* also charted the enormous advancements
that had been made in the area of human rights by the late nineteenth century.
Such accomplishments separated the past from the present in highly dramatic
ways. For instance, Morris cited the fact that earlier in the century there had
been "millions of men" who "were held as slaves in America and Europe" and
who "could be bought and sold like so many cattle, could be whipped by their
masters, and had no more rights than so many brutes." By the 1890s, however,
there was not a slave in Europe or America, all of them having been set free.
"Do you not think I am right in saying that the world has grown better as
well as richer?" he asked his young readers. Commenting rather controver-
sially that fin de siècle Americans had "higher ideas of right and wrong than
our forefathers had," Morris took pride in emphasizing the rapid progress of
the American nation since its creation moment. He reminded young readers
that there is a fresh "new history before us in which we shall live and act and
of which our own doings will form part." Morris wrote confidently, "In the
time to come each of my youthful readers will help make the history of the
country, and you will see its events pass before your eyes like the pictures on
a panorama which slowly unrolls and reveals to you its hidden secrets. Let us
hope that the pictures to be seen will be those of peace and happiness, not
those of war and ruin."[25]

Morris also had a reputation for narrating the exciting details of the recent
past for the purposes of literary effect rather than belaboring the minutiae
of ancient times as a means of conveying the authority of tradition. He had
begun his writing career as the author of dozens of dime novels, quickly
penned works whose moral messages were often obscured by the sensationalized rhetoric used to convey them.[26] Appearing in periodicals like *Beadle's
Saturday Journal* and characterized by the use of melodramatic devices,

inflated language, and formulaic structure, such dime novel literature had been condemned by teachers and clergy as impertinent and irreverent insofar as it despiritualized the past. Many of Morris's first serialized pieces in popular magazines were adventure novels, especially troubling to Christian educators because they encouraged children, as Comstock noted of the genre, to "run away from respectable homes" and "to seek their fortune[s]" in places where they inevitably degenerated into "boy-bandits" and "little villains."[27] When Morris turned to writing history almost exclusively in the late 1880s and 1890s, he encountered similar criticisms from professionals, who deemed his work too subjective to qualify as real history.[28] His fifteen-volume series titled Historical Tales was disparaged in the New York Times as not altogether suitable for school-age children because it lacked precision and fidelity to the facts: "Where the romantic element is so frankly sought, scientific historical accuracy is not perhaps to be expected."[29]

While the original publishers of The Child's History of the United States, W. H. Ferguson in Cincinnati, made every effort to assure parents that its author was not a mere petty dime novelist but a reputable historian to whom they could entrust their children's historical education, they did not always succeed (fig. 23). Salesmen's samples of the original volume suggest that Ferguson hoped to convince readers that "the author of this book is a man well known as a writer and is an authority on the History of the United States." "Dummies," or guidelines issued to book agents who were selling The Child's History of the United States door to door and by subscription, advised salesmen to downplay Morris's reputation as a dime novelist. Scripted instructions urged canvassers to inform would-be buyers that while there was some animated prose in Morris's text, its most sensational elements derived naturally from the episodes he described rather than from some artificial impulse to embellish. "No story book is so fascinating to children as the thrilling and romantic passages of real history," Ferguson's agents reminded readers, the master narrative of the country needing little embroidery or revision.[30]

Much in The Child's History of the United States was derivative of the subject matter and themes of the popular juvenile histories of the day, especially those written by Brooks, but Morris's text was less sanctimonious in tone. He began with "A Talk with the Young Reader About the History of Our Country," in which he discussed what children would see if they were to take a train trip across the continent of North America. In only three hundred years of American development, a "rich and prosperous scene" had been created, he remarked, one that revealed the technological wonders of an advancing age. The emphasis throughout Morris's narrative was on men as agents of change (women are largely absent). Morris rarely attributed this growth to

FIGURE 23. Charles Morris, *The Child's History of the United States* (Cincinnati: W. H. Ferguson Company, 1900).

some guiding spiritual or providential force, as Coffin had; instead, the glory of its accomplishment belonged to noble Americans acting out their parts on numerous historical stages. "No doubt many of you have read in fairy tales of wonderful things done by the Genii of the East, of palaces built in a night, of cities moved miles away from their sites," Morris wrote in his introduction, "but here is a thing as wonderful and at the same time true, a marvel wrought by men instead of magical beings." The fact that human beings had engineered these triumphs was significant to Morris, since it reminded young readers that the genius necessary for success was all around them and ready for appropriation. Best of all, he added, the story of its gradual emergence was a true story. "Is not this as wonderful as the most marvelous fairy tale?" he asked in a tone reminiscent of Goodrich. "And is it not better to read the true tale of how this was done than stories of the work of fairies and magicians? Let us forget the Genii of the West; men are the Genii of the West, and the magic of their work is as great as that we read of in the fables of the 'Arabian Nights,'" he concluded.[31]

The Child's History of the United States did not treat the kinds of providential themes typical of many of nineteenth-century histories for children, such as those by Coffin, but it did highlight elements of patriotism and hero worship characteristic of its day. In the case of patriotism, the salesman's dummy for the book capitalized on the filiopiety that was still the mainstay of biographical studies in the early twentieth century. "The story of the Revolution always arouses the fire of Patriotism in the young," the prospectus noted, "and enough is told here to make you wish there were more of such heroes to-day." In making their pitches to would-be clients, agents were advised to turn to page 143 of the subscription sample and to point to the page, saying, "Here is a very important chapter called 'The Voyage of Our Ship of State.' It tells how this government of ours is conducted. It tells how the President is elected and what he does, also how the laws are made. It tells what every boy and girl should know to become good citizens." The inference was that all American youth had the potential to become heroic patriots, provided they understood, embraced, and modeled the political beliefs of the founders. "It is surprising how many of our voters to-day know so little about our Government," the publisher added. "We know it is a dry subject to many. But our author has made it interesting, and I am sure profitable as well."[32]

In cultivating hero worship, Morris was especially gifted at creating memorable biographical sketches of political and military heroes whose exemplary public lives revealed underlying private virtues. Again, agents soliciting subscriptions to Morris's work were instructed to turn the pages of the sample slowly so the vetted child could see that "great men are brought before him."[33] Like Brooks in his series Childhood Lives of Great Men, Morris recounted the public achievements of American heroes, focusing on their boyhood experiences and extrapolating from these to their adult accomplishments. He informed readers, for example, that Columbus began life as a "poor woolcarder" who grew up hearing magical tales of the West. No divine revelation started him down the path to greatness, as others alleged; instead, he earned his reputation gradually through dogged persistence and pragmatic adaptation. Morris repeated the Washington Irving legend employed by Goodrich, Pollard, and others to the effect that Columbus confounded scholars at the Spanish court with the knowledge that the earth was round. "At the time some of the most learned people had odd notions about the earth," Morris wrote, adding, "Most of them thought that the earth was as flat as a table, and that any one who sailed too far over the ocean would come to the edge of the earth and fall off." He noted, however, that such insights were not preordained or celestial in origin but were the results of Columbus's special insights into nature's ways based on practical experience with them. The same was true of the unconventional John Smith, an impious but spirited hero who made his own way in the world. This colonizer may have "bragged a little" too much about his accomplishments, Morris admitted, but Smith had much to celebrate in his heroic life, having shaped his own destiny by dint of his courageous and independent actions. He was not a minion of God, Morris noted but "a brave and bold man, and just the man to help settle a new country where there were savage red men to deal with."[34]

Readers of *The Child's History of the United States* responded well to these subtle shifts in the role that human agency was presumed to play in the telling of the American past. As Scott Casper has commented, such transitions were consistent with the gradual secularization of the genre of biography at the turn of the century, when readers increasingly preferred narratives of "public deeds to private foibles" and asserted that "it was public virtue rather than personal individuality which they most wished to cultivate."[35] Children also appreciated the efforts Morris made to write with their specific needs in mind. "This story you have before you in the book you now hold," the author instructed, "is written for the boys and girls of our land . . . who do not have time to read large histories, which try to tell all that has taken place. For those this little history will be of great service, in showing them how, from a few half-starved settlers on a wild coast, this great nation has grown up."[36] These promotional materials certainly made a convincing case for purchase. "It is surprising what the book makers can do," the salesman's sample indicates. "I am sure you want it—and you will sign your name here."[37] *The Child's History of the United States* sold thousands of copies, which is testimony to the fact that many parents and perhaps some young readers did just that. These arguments doubtless persuaded managing editors at the Christian Liberty Press to republish Morris's work in the late twentieth century as well, motivated as they were by the expectation that not just "boys and girls of our great land" but "many of their fathers and mothers may also find it pleasant and useful to read."[38]

Nevertheless, some in Morris's day identified substantial problems in his works and would not have recommended republication. Reviewers complained that the popular historian wrote too much like a journalist, issuing text too quickly and without enough reflection, even compromising accuracy for the sake of publishing deadlines. "The American genius for the prompt and proper appreciation of market values is illustrated in nothing better than by its facility for constructing books for the demand of the hour," wrote one reviewer of Morris's histories. "The work may not be well done," the critic noted in a backhanded manner, "but it is marvelous that it could have been done at all in so short a space of time."[39] *The Child's History of the United States* provoked a similar lackluster review from the Yale University historian Charles M. Andrews, who opined that the text was "neither better nor worse than many others of its kind. It is without special merits or serious defects;

repeats stock anecdotes and contains illustrations that are merely imaginative. . . . It displays neither originality nor a knowledge of modern methods of instruction."[40] Nor have Morris's works necessarily aged well. The historian Michael Kammen noted that Morris's discussion of the Constitutional Convention in *The Child's History of the United States* was so "unclear, superficial, inconsistent, and inaccurate" as to be unusable by young readers. "We find John Adams and Thomas Jefferson active at the Convention when, in fact, they were serving in 1787 as our ministers to Great Britain and France, respectively," Kammen wrote. "And strangest of all, we get a picture of Carpenter's Hall, where, we are told, the Convention met. Most people have at least heard of Independence Hall, but not Mr. Morris. His editor and publisher didn't blink an eye, apparently." Kammen added derisively, "One wonders whether they read the text? One hopes that few American schoolchildren did."[41]

Furthermore, Morris was accused of being a federalist partisan who favored strong executive leadership and disparaged those who advocated for states' rights over a powerful central government. Hence, the anti-Federalist Thomas Jefferson receives virtually no attention in *The Child's History of the United States* beyond the misattributed activities at the Constitutional Convention mentioned by Kammen, while the states' rights advocate Andrew Jackson is dismissed as an obstructionist who impeded government operations. "I cannot say that [Jackson] was a very good President," Morris wrote, allowing only that the Tennessean "was a very obstinate man, who always wanted to have his own way, and that is better in a soldier than in a president."[42] Morris's favorite president was Theodore Roosevelt, who receives no mention in *The Child's History of the United States* because the book was published prior to the assassination of McKinley. However, Roosevelt's virtues are in strong evidence in Morris's laudatory biography of him, *Battling for the Right: The Life-Story of Theodore Roosevelt* (1910). In this work, the popular historian highlighted the progressive reformer's heroic principles and policies in the struggle for human rights. Describing Roosevelt as a "man of inborn genius, of unsurpassed capacity for affairs, of extraordinary insight, and of wonderful power for 'doing things,'" Morris applauded Roosevelt's daring in using the authority of government to take "the bulls of corruption by the horns." He would have been "a man of prominence in political life and a worker for reform at almost any time in the history of our country," Morris noted, "but fortune willed that he should come into the office of President at a date excellently fitted for a man of his calibre to make his work effective." What was needed to deal effectively with corrupt corporate interests, Morris suggested at a time when others had not, was "an able and aggressive leader" such as Roosevelt who was not afraid to employ the power of the executive branch in order to "put the country in the way of finally bringing to an end the whole evil."[43]

Morris was a self-proclaimed advocate of many causes, including anti-imperialism, and he urged even his youngest readers to take a strong interest in the peace movement of the late nineteenth century. In *The Child's History of the United States* he was solicitous of the restraint that leaders in the United States had shown with respect to warfare in the years after the Civil War: "During your short lives there has been no war which came near to us in our homes." Morris cited the advantages enjoyed by the post–Civil War generation of children: "The angel of peace has spread her white wings over our land, and plenty and prosperity have been the rule." He was not unmindful of the Spanish-American War, which had concluded a few months before the publication of his popular history, but that war did not take place on American soil and was an aberration of sorts, he argued. For the most part, Morris concluded, "Uncle Sam wants to keep out of war."[44]

Additionally, Morris had very specific and principled beliefs on the most central and vitriolic topic of debate of his era, the origins of the human race. In 1900 Morris published a work titled *Man and His Ancestor: A Study in Evolution* in which he argued that the chapters of the Bible that charted the beginnings of life on earth were pure fiction. "It might have been better for civilized mankind if the opening pages of Genesis had never been written, since they have played a potent part in checking the development of thought," Morris argued in a manner more candid than some of his turn-of-the-century readers appreciated. "As the case now stands, the cosmological doctrines they contain can no longer claim even a shadow of divine authority, since they have been distinctly traced back to a human origin." Contending that the Pentateuch was "simply a restatement of the Babylonian cosmology, as given in a literary production ages older than the Bible," he insisted that those who accept the first five chapters of the Old Testament as conveying sacred truth "must do so on the basis of belief in their probability; it is no longer permissible to claim for them the warrant of divine origin."[45] Creationism was devoid of the kind of evidentiary proof that professional historians demanded of the past. Facts are "absolutely and necessarily wanting in support of the creation doctrine," Morris wrote, "and the only argument its advocates can advance is one that deals in negatives, and demands its acceptance on the ground that the opposite doctrine has not been proved." Such an approach is valueless, he averred, and could never "have any standing in science, since it is impossible to adduce any facts to sustain it. We shall therefore dismiss it from further consideration, and proceed to state certain general facts in favor of the evolutionary hypothesis of the origin of man."[46]

Finally, despite the fact that he wrote for the home study market, Morris was no different from most of the other popular historians I've discussed in this book on the subject of public education. As a former teacher himself, he was a spirited supporter of public schools, characterizing them as a major formative institution in the progress of humanity. "In talking of the wonder of the nineteenth century, it will not do to forget the school," Morris wrote, "for it is the mould in which the men and women of our time are formed." The grand progress of the human race, he added, was predicated on the fact that once the "great mass of population could not even read or write, while the higher branches of education were only to be had by children of the rich." Questioning the class bias inherent in private education, Morris reminded readers that "a good education is free for all" in the United States. This democratizing impulse extended to the vast improvements made in public school textbooks (such as *The Child's History of the United States*), which he claimed, somewhat immodestly, eclipsed those "poor, little school books our fathers studied" that "we would laugh at to-day." Morris's message to young readers in the early twentieth century was clear: things have changed, and for the better, and responsible citizens must abandon traditional texts and beliefs and those elements of the past that inhibit continued progress. It is not always easy to recall the minute details of what life was like a century ago, Morris reminded American youth, but "you can thank your lucky stars that you live to-day instead of living then."[47]

Child specialists at the beginning of the twentieth century believed that young people were capable of thinking and acting as political creatures and that their parents and teachers had a responsibility to help them in their efforts to formulate opinions and question authority. Critics of the child first movement rejected these assumptions, however, and clung to the idea that children could and should be nondoctrinal in their outlooks and unwaveringly conventional in their learning practices. Morris's political affinities did not endear him to this latter group, including a reviewer for the *Nation*, who criticized the historian for his careless politicizing, which "seriously affects [his] utility."[48] The themes emphasized by Morris in his popular history—especially his deemphasis of the role of Providence, his support for a strong federal government, his distrust of the military, and his rejection of creationism—are not compatible with the principles of the Christian Right today either. Why, then, one might ask, are his works being republished for homeschool use by publishers like the Christian Liberty Press? why excavate a "lost history" like Morris's *The Child's History of the United States* that might be better left buried?

Family Values and a "Desired Past"

Part of the answer to these questions lies with the misplaced nostalgia some on the Christian Right feel for a bygone era that they imagine was better in its values and moral living than the present age. Some operators of Christian presses believe that profound truths lie entombed in original historical texts, truths that, when brought to the light of day, will serve as unimpeachable guides to proper behavior for children. But is it possible to recover an original historical experience of any kind with complete fidelity? The zealous idealism with which many Christian educators approach the possibility of repossessing an unadulterated past by reviving its most representative and popular texts ignores the complex, subtle processes by which any past is made evident to those in the present. As Lowenthal points out, while the recovery impulse associated with the past takes many forms—copying, imitating, and emulating, all of which "stem from or arouse a desire to protect or enhance the originals"—these acts of retrieval inevitably alter the conditions of the primary texts themselves. Republishing a work of history, even without alterations, Lowenthal notes, "affects its form or our impressions" in the same way that "selective recall skews memory and subjectivity shapes historical insight." Privileging some older works and ignoring others also changes the context in which the originals were introduced and impacts their reception in our own day as well. When republished works are embellished or changed in ways to suit publishers such as the Christian Liberty Press, these distorting conditions are exacerbated. The result is that "preservation sets in train the extensive remodeling of the very past it aims to protect." Even if we "profess only to rectify our predecessors' prejudices and errors and to restore pre-existing conditions," Lowenthal argues, "we fail to see that today's past is as much a thing of today as it is of the past." When we "bolster faith that the past originally existed in the form we now devise, we minimize or forget our own alterations."[49] This, he avers, is a dangerous practice.

Certainly Morris was not one to insist on the sanctity and inviolability of his nineteenth-century texts. During his lifetime he rewrote many of his volumes, making changes to the text to suit the idiosyncratic needs of specific publishers and readers. The Library of Congress website records 188 volumes produced by Morris over a fifty-year writing career, for instance, but these include nine listings for separate revised editions of his *Elementary History of the United* States, which itself had been reworked six times in the modified *Primary History of the United States* and eight times for his *School History of the United States*. Few popular histories were safe "from editorial intervention," Frances FitzGerald has suggested, since successful volumes were "revised and reissued every three of four years, in time to be presented anew to the school systems." Such works as *The Child's History of the United States* changed "like a Brunswick stew," she noted wittily, as they moved from one iteration to the next.[50] Morris's popular histories were also mimicked and revised by presses that appropriated not only his texts but also his design strategies. W. B. Conkey Company, for instance, "borrowed" both the title and the cover art (without attribution) for *A Child's History of the United States* by John Wesley Hanson Jr., including a colorful chromolithograph depicting young children seated awkwardly around an equestrian, sword-wielding Washington taken directly from the pictorial cover art of Morris's volume (fig. 24).[51]

The Christian Liberty Press likewise has not been absolutely faithful to the original texts it has reproduced for young readers, as evidenced especially by the kinds of revisions introduced in its republished versions of Morris's *The Child's History of the United States* (fig. 25). The publishers at Christian Liberty Press have done more than merely recycle Morris's text, that is; they have also sought to improve upon it in ways that serve their present ideological needs. In a manner reminiscent of the subjective character commentaries of Uncle Rick Boyer, the publishers at Christian Liberty Press have introduced an expanded, embellished, altered text in place of Morris's original as a means of adapting it to their Christian purposes and in ways that would be unrecognizable to its author. These editorial adjustments have been made by collaborators hired by Christian Liberty Press to add and subtract material from the 1901 text, although the emendations they have made are not always obvious to the casual reader. In the edition of 1989 of *A Child's Story of America,* for instance, Michael J. McHugh is listed as a coauthor, although he wrote only four of the twenty-nine chapters in the book, the remainder coming from Morris's original work. The second reissue by Christian Liberty Press, in 1998, cites McHugh and Edward Edwin Shewan as Morris's collaborators, although McHugh's name alone appears at the end of the preface. This imprimatur is misleading in that the text of the republished introduction is virtually identical to the one written by Morris at the turn of the century. The few words that have been altered do so in ways that do not essentially affect the original, an act of editorial appropriation that is as confusing as it is unethical, since, without acknowledging the nineteenth-century historian who composed the original text, McHugh assumes Morris's first-person voice ("I only lay this introduction before you . . ."), implying that he is the author of its sentiments and insights.[52]

Among the changes made by McHugh and Shewan are small alterations to the wording of passages to emphasize how divine causal laws operate in the universe. The treatment of Columbus is a case in point. In *The Child's History*

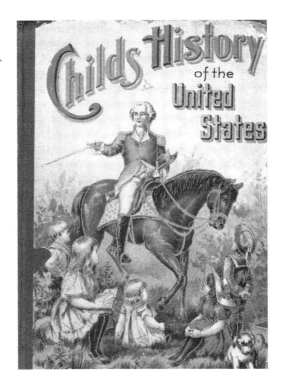

FIGURE 24. John Wesley Hanson Jr., *A Child's History of the United States* (Chicago: W. B. Conkey Company, [1896]).

FIGURE 25. Charles Morris, Michael J. McHugh, and Edward J. Shewan, *A Child's Story of America,* 2nd ed. (Arlington Heights, Ill.: Christian Liberty Press, 1998).

of the United States, Morris depicted the discoverer as a self-made man who relied on his wits and persistence to achieve greatness.[53] In McHugh's and Shewan's rewrite, however, the explorer is a beneficiary of God's grace and his accomplishments are preordained. In *A Child's Story of America,* Columbus evidences a sincere belief that "God had destined him to be the one to spread the Christian faith to people who were lost in pagan darkness." This goal trumped all other personal ambitions as far as the editors at Christian Liberty Press are concerned. "The desire that Columbus had for glory and worldly wealth was never as strong as his desire to promote the cause of Christ," the coauthors surmised.[54] Additionally, in the first edition of the history, Morris had written that Columbus was saved from almost certain disaster on his first voyage by the whims of "good fortune."[55] This passage was altered by McHugh and Shewan to read, "Only God's grace preserved the life of the great sea captain."[56] Not surprisingly, perhaps, the Christian Liberty Press republication of Morris's work took specific doctrinal positions relative to the decisions of the Spanish supporters of Columbus. While in the original Morris wrote that the Spaniards were "at war with a people called the Moors" in the fifteenth century, McHugh and Shewan revised the text to read that Spain was "at war . . . with a *heathen* people called the Moors."[57] Presumably this change was introduced to ensure that young Christian readers coming of age in an era of Islamic fundamentalism would not assume that all religious peoples were equally appointed to carry out God's work. Evidencing some of the anti-Catholicism of which Coffin was accused in *The Story of Liberty,* McHugh and Shewan also changed Morris's description of the "good monks" at La Rábida monastery who aided Columbus prior to his first voyage to just "monks," ostensibly, again, because they considered the term *good monks* to be an oxymoron.[58]

McHugh and Shewan also adjusted Morris's portraits of the founding fathers. Like most nineteenth-century popular historians, Morris paid tribute to the heroism of the original creators of the nation in *The Child's History of the United States,* and he included lengthy encomia to heroic figures such as Washington and Hamilton. Like Brooks, however, he concentrated less on the role of great individuals in the founding of the nation than on the energies and accomplishments of the democratic masses whose anonymous efforts on behalf of liberty secured freedom and established a representative form of government in the United States. Our country's "great feature," Morris wrote, "is that it is a republic—a government 'of the people, by the people, and for the people.'"[59] The rewrite by McHugh and Shewan, however, echoes the thoughts of conservatives in the National Standards debates of the 1990s, who bemoaned the fact that liberals had reduced the space devoted to the founders in order to make room for figures revealing of the new social history told from the bottom up. One satirist has referred to this lament as part of a vast left-wing conspiracy designed to obscure the true story of how "conservatives fought and died for our freedoms, while cowardly liberals subverted our government and our way of life, making us all slaves to the liberal socialist government that we have today."[60] In the Christian Liberty Press's *A Child's Story of America* there is a nearly audible cry of bereavement for a vanishing age in which erstwhile heroes were recognized as intrepid and God's status as the "first cause" of history was unassailable.

Feeling this loss of historical perspective especially in the case of Jefferson, the Christian Liberty Press rewriters added a supplementary chapter to Morris's text focused on the new nation during the third president's two terms in office. Interestingly, this chapter has virtually nothing to say about Jefferson's antifederalist politics; there is no mention of the cantankerous nature of the election of 1800 or of his well-publicized battles with John Adams and John Marshall. Rather, most of the attention in this chapter is focused on the "new spiritual revival" that occurred during Jefferson's administrations, a "Second Great Awakening," as McHugh and Shewan describe it, that proved that "God did not abandon America." The redactors' references in *A Child's Story of America* to Jefferson's Declaration of Independence as a Christian document helped solidify the connection between the founding fathers and the Christian roots of American government. The same pattern is evident in McHugh's and Shewan's reconceiving of Morris's passages on Andrew Jackson's presidency. No longer an obstinate man who always demanded his way, as Morris characterized him, Jackson was transformed into "a Christian man who honored the Bible." According to McHugh and Shewan, the validity of this characterization of Jackson is borne out by his utterance, "The Bible, Sir, is the foundation upon which our republic rests."[61] This quote (which actually reads, "That book, sir, is the rock on which our republic rests") is the only commentary offered on Jackson's administrations by the two rewriters, and it is allowed to stand in for any discussion of decidedly irreligious battles such as those over the Mother Bank, the Trail of Tears, and the Nullification Crisis.

McHugh and Shewan took other liberties with Morris's treatment of the American colonial period as well, especially with respect to the theme of the separation of church and state. Morris had not written much about the Puritans in *The Child's History of the United States* because he did not admire their theocratic approaches to government. He spent comparatively more time on Roger Williams, however, since that persecuted religious figure's desire to "worship as he pleased" was compatible with Morris's own sentiments about religious toleration. According to the popular historian, the Puritans "were as hard to live with as the people [in England], for they wanted to force everybody else into their way," while Williams suffered unnecessarily by comparison because he had "different beliefs from the Puritans." Like Brooks, Morris admired historical figures who were noteworthy not for their slavish adherence to established tradition but for their self-willed pursuit of personal truth. Williams "was not a captain" like other colonial heroes, such as John Smith and Myles Standish, Morris wrote, "but a preacher" and a "brave man" who "showed in his way as much courage as either of the captains." Williams "did not kill any one," Morris added. "He was not that kind of hero. But he did much to make men happy and good and to do justice to all men, and I think that is the best kind of hero." The historian also praised Williams for his ability to anticipate the kind of religious toleration that would characterize the future. "This was in the year 1634, just about the time Roger Williams went to Rhode Island," he wrote in *The Child's History of the United States,* adding that "he gave the people religious liberty" by proclaiming that "every Christian . . . had the right to worship God in his own way."[62]

Revealingly, McHugh and Shewan, who were disposed more favorably toward theocratic leadership than Morris, deleted Williams altogether from the text of their reissued volume and expanded proportionally the treatment of an alternative religious figure—the strong, authoritative Puritan leader John Winthrop, about whom Morris had written little. They noted that it was Winthrop who had "traveled to America to find freedom to worship God and to secure that same liberty for others," making the Massachusetts Bay Colony "a blessed haven for the God-fearing Puritans and for many persecuted refugees." Disturbingly, however, in making these revisions McHugh and Shewan did not generate new prose with which to celebrate Winthrop's accomplishments as a civic leader; rather, they merely rewrote deleted passages from Morris's description of Williams, substituting Winthrop's name for that of the deposed Rhode Island hero. Hence, Winthrop was described in the McHugh and Shewan revised text as "not a captain like the others, but a political leader. He was a brave man and showed, in his own way, just as much courage as either of the captains. . . . Do you not think John Winthrop was as brave a man as John Smith or Miles [*sic*] Standish, and as much a hero?" they asked. "He did not kill anyone. He was not that kind of hero. He did much, however, to make men happy and good and to do justice to all men, and I think that is the best kind of hero. It is because of the sacrifices of brave men like Governor Winthrop that all Americans have the great blessing of religious freedom." So sloppy were McHugh and Shewan in making these substitutions that they failed to correct dates and suppositions in transposed passages that were relevant to Williams but not to Winthrop. They noted incorrectly, "This was in the year 1634, just about the time John Winthrop went to Massachusetts," where "he gave the people religious liberty," proclaiming that "every Christian . . . had the right to worship God as he believed the Bible dictated." These revelations would have startled the Massachusetts Bay governor, to be sure, since he arrived in Massachusetts four years earlier, in 1630, at which time the colony was governed by a theocratic system in which religious toleration was not recognized or countenanced.[63]

Mischaracterizing Winthrop as an advocate of religious liberty required altering Morris's original historical language in ways that distorted his intentions. A similar strategy was evident in the reworking of Morris's descriptions of the sometimes oppressive church services that Puritan children were forced to endure. In *The Child's History of the United States,* Morris wrote condemningly of the psychological tyranny exercised by Puritan theocrats: "And, mercy on us, what sermons they preached in those cold old churches, prosing away sometimes for three or four hours at a time! . . . The boys and girls had to listen to them, as well as the men and women, and you know how hard it is now to listen for one hour." With a sympathetic tone characteristic of the child first movement, Morris added, "To-day we would call that sort of sermon cruelty to children, and I think it was cruelty to the old folks also."[64] Apparently not wanting vulnerable young Christian readers to believe that Puritan children were inattentive to their church lessons, however, McHugh and Shewan rewrote Morris's passage as follows: "Almost everybody liked to go to church. . . . What marvelous sermons they preached in those old churches, preaching away sometimes for three or four hours at a time! The boys and girls listened to them, as well as the men and women. It was only natural for these people to want to spend as much time as possible in fellowship with God."[65]

Other modifications to Morris's text were equally deliberate and ideologically motivated. Wishing to support the family values platforms popular with Republicans in the 1980s and 1990s, McHugh and Shewan altered Morris's history to accommodate political attitudes regarding the importance of home life in America. For instance, whereas Morris noted that the explorer John Smith "ran away from home when a boy," the Christian Liberty Press edition claims that Smith "*foolishly* ran away from home when a boy," a subtle adverbial addition that transformed Smith from a rugged individualist to a selfish apostate.[66] Addressing the concerns of mid-nineteenth-century readers of Morris's dime novels who disapproved of his protagonists' tendencies to flee their homes to make their way in the world, McHugh and Shewan passed swift moral judgment on such youthful abandon.

The republishers at Christian Liberty Press avoided scrupulously any mention of alcohol and drugs in their revised texts. So temperate were they in these matters, in fact, that they chose to eliminate from their revision of *The Child's History of the United States* a story Morris had included about Henry Hudson and the Dutch swindling the Native Americans on Long Island Sound by dispensing brandy and getting them drunk. "Captain Hudson and the Dutch no doubt thought that this was great fun. People often do much harm without stopping to think" when they are intoxicated, Morris preached, whereas McHugh and Shewan commented only that the Dutch "paid the Indians for the island with some cheap goods."[67] While the elimination of passages in the original that related to alcohol might offer a tactical advantage to those interested in shielding children from the evils of drink, their removal simultaneously prevented McHugh and Shewan from warning young readers about those evils in a way Morris thought was absolutely necessary to the temperance campaign he supported so ardently. No mention of alcohol, in other words, would have been more harmful to children in the estimation of the author of *Broken Fetters* than the Christian Liberty Press's muted reference to it.

Additional changes in language made by McHugh and Shewan reflect other biases of the Christian Liberty Press. The press wanted young readers to understand that nothing in the universe happens by chance, that every experience is scripted carefully by an omniscient being; they were meticulous, therefore, about removing from Morris's work any reference to mystical or supernatural motive forces operating in history. Morris's passage in *The Child's History of the United States* celebrating Americans as the "Genii of the West" was eliminated altogether in the McHugh and Shewan edition, while the term *fairy tale* was changed to "a marvelous tale of fiction" and the phrase "the work of fairies and magicians" was altered to "certain imaginary stories."[68] Some of this editorial strategy might reflect a lingering suspicion of fables as articulated by Goodrich more than 150 years earlier, but one suspects that the real reason for the substitutions has to do with the desire of the writers of the Christian Liberty Press edition of Morris's work to diminish the role of human agency in his narrative of the American past.

Hypersensitive to any language that might be imagined to have sexual connotations, the bowdlerizers at Christian Liberty Press were unwilling to let the word "naked" be used in *A Child's Story of America,* even though it appeared in a direct, well-known quote. In describing the excesses of Governor William Berkeley of Virginia in punishing those who participated in Bacon's Rebellion, Morris had cited accurately King Charles II, who said of Berkeley, "That old fool has hung more men in that naked land than I did for the murder of my father."[69] McHugh and Shewan altered the quotation to accommodate their priggishness: "That old fool has hung more men in the Virginia colony than I have in crowded England."[70] And the Christian Liberty Press editions of Morris's *The Child's History of the United States* tolerated no language that was suggestive in any way of homosexual behavior. Homophobia is evidenced in the subtle (and frankly sad) alterations made by McHugh and Shewan to several innocuous and nonsexual passages in Morris's original text. The authors felt compelled, for instance, to change Morris's line describing Francisco Pizzaro's crew as a "gay and hopeful band" to "a happy and hopeful band."[71] Elsewhere, Morris's portrayal of Hudson's "queer-looking Dutch vessel" was expurgated to read, "a strange-looking Dutch vessel."[72]

The most noticeable and disturbing of all of the editorial revisions to Morris's text by McHugh and Shewan, however, are those that are politically motivated. Morris had not avoided partisanship in *The Child's History of the United States,* but he embraced the doctrinal propensities of the child first movement with its allowances for expressions of ideological perspective by and for children. Operating in an environment they claim to be free of the "wind of doctrine," however, McHugh and Shewan wrote new chapters on the twentieth-century American experience as a way of updating Morris's text. Yet they did so hypocritically from an unabashedly conservative point of view and with explicit evangelical intentions. There is a distinctly antigovernment bias throughout the later chapters of McHugh's and Shewan's *A Child's Story of America.* Young readers are told that the "federal government was never supposed to be spending great sums of money to provide for the social needs of the American people." Noting that the Communist threat in the 1950s was very real—"our nation's fortieth president, Ronald Reagan, was right when he called Communism an 'evil empire,'" the authors claim—McHugh and Shewan blamed creeping socialism for the fact that the "richest country in the world" is now "bankrupt and forced to borrow money from others." The federal government "must get out of the business of social welfare," the authors preach, "before America is destroyed financially." McHugh and Shewan also blamed the central government for initiating a movement "to remove God from our society and destroy our nation's Christian heritage." Irresponsibly, they noted, "Our country's Supreme Court ruled in 1962 that it was illegal for children to pray in the public schools." Such rulings, they claimed in their rewritten version of Morris's work, "permitted God and the Bible to be removed from our society" and "opened the way for many evil forces to gain power in our land." The result, they concluded, is that America today "is staggering under a heavy load of sin."[73]

Liberal Democrats of the twentieth century, not surprisingly, fare badly in McHugh's and Shewan's *A Child's Story of America*. Presidents Lyndon Johnson and John Kennedy are blamed for the war in Vietnam, in which the "federal government was so afraid of starting another world war that it often would not let its soldiers wage full scale war against the North Vietnamese." Additionally, President Jimmy Carter is castigated for ceding claims to the Panama Canal, for mishandling the Iran hostage crisis, and for negotiating trade agreements with Communist China. (Revealingly, Nixon's role in these negotiations was ignored.) "In short, our country had sunk to new lows during the Carter years," McHugh and Shewan reported. President Bill Clinton was an even more conspicuous target, identified as he was with the rise of huge government debt, "meddling in Bosnia and other war-torn nations, promoting homosexuality, and [the] Monica Lewinsky" scandal. The 1990s were "a sad time in American history," the authors of the rewritten text concluded with respect to Democratic leadership, since during Clinton's two administrations the "enemies of freedom had managed to damage the noble spirit of America."[74]

Republican presidents and administrations, by contrast, had done little wrong in the estimation of the authors of *A Child's Story of America*. "Thankfully, our nation decided to elect a president who could motivate the American people to return to the values that made our country great," McHugh and Shewan editorialized, choosing Reagan as a leader who convinced voters that "they should not look to big government to save them; they were told to look to God for help and strength." In just "a few short years," they added, President Reagan "helped to remind people that it was love of God, hard work, and a compassion toward our fellow citizens that made America great." The result was a "stronger economy and a stronger military," both of which allowed the United States to "regain respect around the world." That legacy was carried on as well in the presidencies of the two Bushes, readers are told. "One of the most encouraging aspects of the 2004 election," the back cover of the most recent edition of *A Child's Story of America* states, "was that a significant number of voters chose their candidate largely upon moral and religious considerations."[75]

Hardly producers of the kind of history from which the "winds of doctrine" have been purged, then, McHugh and Shewan are far more doctrinal and ideological in their revised history than Morris ever was in his original text. There is a significant irony in this. Publishers like Christian Liberty Press condemn the supposed revisionism of twentieth-century progressive educators as despoiling the purity of original nineteenth-century texts, yet they do not hesitate to revise works deliberately when doing so serves their ideological purposes. Their republication efforts remind one that revision is endemic to all historical pursuits. As Lowenthal has pointed out, when historians impose a narrative structure on the past, they appropriate it for their own literary uses and, in the process, alter it irrecoverably. "Copying or celebrating relics makes the originals better known and alters our view of them," he writes, admitting that "impressions of the past reflect all subsequent acts of appreciation and derogation, our own included." Recycled versions of the past "thus take on careers of their own, often submerging their prototypes in the service of subsequent demands," causing work "later inspired by past exemplars [to] loom larger in the present landscape than do its original relics."[76]

Some republishers accept these conditions, likening them to the unavoidable changes that occur when preservationists relocate old buildings or transplant monuments. Dislocations and embellishments are concessions that must be made in order to safeguard antiquities against the ravages of time, they recognize. There are obvious dangers, however, in the radical repositioning of artifacts, especially those that require the transposition of objects from original to new contexts. "The removal of relics whose lineaments are indissolubly of their place annuls their testamentary worth and forfeits their myriad ties with place," Lowenthal writes. "The whole value of many antiquities inheres in their locale; the landmark must stay put if it is to mark the land." As the architectural historian William Morris (no relation to Charles) advised, the "proper way to treat a relic [is] to leave it alone. Resist all tampering with either the fabric or ornament of the building as it stands; if it has become inconvenient for its present use . . . raise another building rather than alter or enlarge the old one." Even though books are made to travel, the same restrictions may be said to apply to their relationship to the temporal landscapes in which they emerged. Transposing a work of history such as Morris's from the early twentieth-century context in which it was written to twenty-first-century usages can distort the intentions of the author in major ways, sometimes "altering them beyond recognition."[77]

Many purchasers of Christian Liberty Press's *A Child's Story of America* approve of these alterations without considering that they render the original texts "inconvenient for [their] present use." Some justify modifications to Morris's volume on the grounds that McHugh and Shewan have spiritual truth on their side, implying that adjustments of the right kind are permissible. The homeschooling curriculum reviewer Cathy Duffy, for instance, refers to *A Child's Story of America* as "one of the most delightful history books I have ever come across" because its authors have "taken pains to update the language and correct inaccurate and incomplete information while still reflecting some of the original attitude" of its author.[78] There is something insidious about the use of the word *inaccurate* in this context, since it implies that McHugh and Shewan understood better than Morris himself what he intended for his narrative. "Unlike fakes designed to deceive," Lowenthal notes, "good intentions extenuate the crimes of those who distort or destroy original relics under the illusion of restoring them." Others accept the distortions because they do not find them significant or permanent. "Faith that the actual past is too closely interwoven to be permanently subverted also mitigates the offence of tampering with history, for few expect the alterations to endure," Lowenthal adds.[79] Recognizing that all authors exhibit a bias, a mother of four homeschooled boys sees nothing wrong with parents altering Morris's text in accordance with their personal Christian beliefs. "I felt i[t] was far easier to modify it than use something from a completely secular and/ or liberal bias that left God entirely out of our history or had a pro-liberal agenda," she asserted.[80] That may be the path of least resistance, but it is also the most hypocritical with respect to the professed goal of Christian fundamentalists to promote an original, supposedly pure version of history. Such advice, if followed to its illogical extreme, adds yet another layer of revisionist interpretation to a history already subject to considerable alterations during its production history.

A Child's Story of America has come under attack by people who do not share the political outlooks of McHugh, Shewan, and Christian Liberty Press. "The book is nothing more than a 'sanitized' version of American history," wrote one unhappy customer, who added, "Michael McHugh has rewritten [and] revised American History to fit the theology of the Reformed Church and Christian Liberty School, thus making the text politically correct. In the end I returned my copy to Amazon.com."[81] Another disgruntled reader complained, "This book is written in an engaging fashion for younger readers, so that's why I gave it 2 [out of a possible 5] stars. But I found the attitudes conveyed towards slavery, Native Americans, and Democrats unsettling." Recognizing that there are "political motives behind this book," the reviewer warned potential purchasers that "the author is trying to indoctrinate youngsters into ultra-conservative Southern Republican political ideas, and a brand of Christianity that makes people outside the church (you know, the OTHER people God loves) think Christ-followers are hateful and crazy." Noting that only two pages of the book deal with slavery—whereas Morris had devoted an entire chapter to the institution in The Child's History of the United States— this reader was taken aback especially by McHugh's and Shewan's assertion that "the slave trade was profitable for the traders, but 'hard on the slaves' who were shipped to the colonies 'under difficult conditions.'" That's a "bit of an understatement," the reviewer correctly pointed out. Additionally, there is "no mention of how compassionate Christians (and others) were vehemently opposed to the way slave owners viewed, kept and treated their slaves, or what they did to abolish slavery." The reader conceded that his complaints might be more appropriately directed at Morris than at McHugh and Shewan "who are, after all, merely repeating Morris's sentiments," but he asked, again reasonably, why these new authors have not "changed the text" in these instances in light of the fact that they have altered it in so many other ways. For these reasons, he concluded of the Christian Liberty Press rewrite that "no one should b[u]y it."[82]

America's Forgotten History and Heroes

The frustrations expressed in reviews such as these reflect an ongoing concern about the persistent efforts of those on the Christian Right to revise history as a means of justifying a distinctive ideological position. Fundamentalists are not the only ones who manipulate history in this way, as advocates of causes on the Right and the Left use the past to establish precedents for their claims. As the Bob Jones University pamphlet "The Christian Teaching of History" points out, people on the Left often employ partisan historical strategies to buttress their political positions as well. "Modern instances of such propaganda include pseudo-documentaries on television and 'new leftist' interpretations narrowly based on the authors' revolutionary presuppositions without regard to historical accuracy," the booklet notes. "Political parties and candidates evidence pragmatism when they cite Thomas Jefferson, Washington's Farewell Address, or even passages of scripture out of context in order to win votes."[83]

While those on the Christian Right understand the dangerous ideological implications of reassessments when they are associated with leftist interpretations, however, they rarely recognize such tendencies in themselves. In the case of advocates for the "Christian heritage" movement, this blindness is particularly concerning because it encourages revisionist uses of the past in the name of those who denounce revisionism. The "apparently solid, authoritative tomes" that republishers advertise as the unimpeachable relics of an earlier era are, in fact, the most "nervous of objects, constantly changing in style as well as in political content," FitzGerald notes.[84] When the marketers at Christian Liberty Press seek to recover a lost past by republishing nineteenth-century histories while failing to admit that they are engaged essentially in a revisionist act, they participate in a ritualistic denial that has treacherous consequences for historical practice. Consider, for instance, what might happen if an original historical source is lost or cannot be recovered except in its revised form. "Not only are emulations more numerous than surviving originals, but many a past now survives only or mainly in subsequent refractions of it," Lowenthal reminds readers. Just as "our image of 'classical', depends far less on actual Greek and Roman survivals than on Hellinistic and later evocations," so books like *The Child's History of the United States* might have their authority usurped by more prominent revised texts such as McHugh's and Shewan's *A Child's Story of America*.[85]

There have been mixed reactions to these falsifying tendencies on the part of supporters of the Christian Right. Some have pardoned them as an evil made necessary by the honorable end goal of reaffirming the sanctity of a Christian historical tradition. This can hardly be a satisfactory rationale for most Christians, however. Apart from the obvious contradictions associated with using evil to promote good, such a position relies on the willingness of readers to suspend their belief in the very truths that have motivated them to study the past in the first place. Toleration of any embellishment and distortion in the name of fundamentalism appears especially hypocritical given the strong emphasis many Christians place on a literal interpretation of the Word of God as found in the Bible. If respect for literalism is the foundation of reading literacy in homeschooling curricula like that of the CLASS program, for instance, then any alterations to the nineteenth-century texts used to teach reading skills to the young should be thought of as corrupting of the originals and counterproductive to learning in the Christian manner.

Scholars and casual readers of history alike have begun as well to attack the ways in which those on the Christian Right revise the past in the name of reaffirming rather than reinventing righteous traditions. This can be seen most clearly in the reaction to a work such as Jody D. Kimbrell's *Lost History of America: Information Not Found in Modern History Books* (2008), marketed by Tate Publishing and Enterprises, a Christian vanity press. A self-described "real estate broker, rental manager, wife, mother, daughter, and servant to God" from Illinois, not far from Arlington Heights, where the Christian Liberty Press operates, Kimbrell came to the field of historiography through her hobby of book collecting. She believes that modern history books used in public schools betray children by ignoring, challenging, and eviscerating the "true history" recorded by popular historians from the early and mid-nineteenth century. Volumes with a decidedly moral message, she notes, in keeping with the Christian Liberty Press philosophy, have been repressed or hidden from students as part of a conspiracy among progressive educators to ensure that "God has been banished from our government, our schools, and even the public square." The insidious goal of these self-proclaimed experts, she alleges, is "to make this a secular, Godless country." Insisting that "America's history has been revised with half-truths, lies, and the ideology of those who would rejoice in the complete removal of God from our society," Kimbrell rejects the revisionist impulses of nearly all professional educators and historians. "Let me tell you," she declares succinctly, "a lot of their interpretation is bunk."[86]

Kimbrell offers *Lost History of America* as a "de-bunking" reclamation project of sorts, featuring paraphrased passages from original nineteenth-century works with commentary interspersed for moral emphasis. She rewords selections from histories such as Goodrich's *A Pictorial History of America* as well as from other volumes she has collected through the years that she thinks remain relevant for children. Kimbrell vows in her preface that readers will discover in her translations of excerpts from these works a sense of what life at the beginning of the American experiment was really like. Suggesting that *Lost History of America* provides the kind of participatory experiences achieved among young readers of popular histories, such as Coffin, she writes, "You, the reader, will be joining George Washington as he grows to manhood and starts his journey to the birth of our beloved country. You will stand next to him on the battlefield, feeling his anxious concerns and reveling in his triumphs. You will meet the everyday people who rose up and fought for liberty and freedom you enjoy today." Kimbrell asserts further that the powerful sentiments of the historians whose volumes she paraphrases "will embrace you as you read the events that led to a free America, and your heart will swell with love for the greatest country ever created by the Hand of God." Such "lost history," she adds, is a treasure trove of spiritual material that can protect young readers from the sacrilegious offerings of profane revisionists. Unlike the blasphemous writings of professional historians, whose motives she distrusts, Kimbrell's book, she confidently declares, "gives the true and uncorrupted history of America."[87]

A close reading of *Lost History of America* reveals how much Kimbrell has in common with McHugh and Shewan, all three of whom claim to have recovered lost relics of American historiography. "Little do [revisionist historians] know the power of the Heavenly Father, who chose not the scholar or the rich and famous, but a Midwestern mother of three to inform America and her people of the true benefits of its Founders," the promoters at Tate Publishing and Enterprises note of Kimbrell. "I soon learned that Providence was at work," Kimbrell added in her text of the various book-finding missions she conducted, and not a minute too early. God's "plan to give back America's history had me gathering books, and what I found would make you cry," she claimed. "Books written and read by our Founders, ancestors, and people who walked this earth when America was born were abused, burned, ripped, and filthy," their covers and spines "torn off and in total, unwanted condition."

Such works, she wrote, like God's forgotten people, "held the *Lost History of America* I was searching for." In pursuit of this holy grail, Kimbrell devoted herself to the messianic challenge of resurrecting that which had been presumed dead for the sake of the living. "Armed with deerskin, glue, and leather cleaner/conditioner, I learned how to save books, thus saving America's history," she wrote. She felt compelled to revive these old histories by a "Holy Providence" that had "overseen the gathering of the original books written, published, and held by our Founders and everyday people who faced down a tyrannical empire for love of God, country, family, and freedom." In this endeavor Kimbrell suffered and sacrificed for the sins of unfeeling revisionists, whom she holds accountable for obscuring and abandoning these sacred texts.[88]

Despite considerable evidence of the viability of multiple interpretations of events and personages in the American past, republishers such as the Christian Liberty Press and Tate Publishing and Enterprises insist that their brand of providential history is the only acceptable one, and they congratulate themselves for discovering it on behalf of American children. "Much is expected from the American youth, and a deep responsibility rests on our shoulders to make sure they are instructed in the truth," Kimbrell notes. Here, truth is what it was for McHugh and Shewan: a presumably nonpolitical realm in which the "winds of doctrine" introduced by revisionists have been eliminated. But these doctrinal conceits have not been banished. To think they have constitutes "an essentially medieval state of mind," FitzGerald notes, showing obvious disdain for the "multiple perspectives" evident in the "modernist aesthetic and theory of knowledge."[89] Because republishers do not recognize the ideological underpinnings of historical writing at the time of the founding, they fail to see how distinctly political and misguided their republished works are in claiming a nonideological perspective for themselves. They do not comprehend that in resurrecting the so-called lost histories of an earlier period they are really substituting one set of ideological priorities for another, declaring their preferred histories more truthful than those they reject by virtue of their closer temporal association with the events they described. This argument would be dubious under any circumstances given that, as historians have long remarked, eyewitness accounts of historical events, though enlivened by the passions of the moment, lack the advantages of perspective.

The assumption is presumably that historians such as Samuel and Charles Goodrich and Charles Morris, like the founders themselves, could clairvoyantly anticipate what children in the late twentieth and early twenty-first century would need in terms of historical guidance and that they wrote about and prophesied these requirements in nonideological ways. This concept of an absolute Truth in history is hard to support. As we have seen throughout this book, historical narratives are always influenced by the conditions of the cultural moments in which they were produced and circulated and by the idiosyncrasies of the historians who write them. To imagine that historians working within a few decades of the founding of the nation were closer to the truth by virtue of their temporal proximity to the creation of the nation than those who came after is similar to believing that the founders were nearer to understanding the elusive origin of the universe because they were born closer to its moment of inception. The failure to see that all historians (whether of the eighteenth century or the twenty-first) have particular, personalized points of view represents a fundamental misconception of what history is and what historians do. As the historian Jill Lepore has noted, such "originalism" is ahistorical because it denies the vital role of change in the historical process, the study of which, after all, is the primary function of history.[90] Christian Liberty Press's philosophy of history denies that the founders were human, that they made mistakes, and that they could not predict the future; and it presumes that those historians who followed shortly in their wake shared these traits. It also posits a prelapsarian golden age of historical writing in the nineteenth century during which children's historians like the Goodriches and the Abbott brothers stepped out of time and thereby avoided the constraints of context that limit the works of so many well-meaning students of the past.

Originalism contains another inherent flaw as well. Even if we were to accept that the founders were less susceptible to human failings than most other human beings, we still cannot assume the same of the historians who wrote the biographies and histories chronicling the lives of the founders, at least not from what we've seen in terms of the various factual and interpretive mistakes made in most of the children's histories analyzed here. Popular texts like Morris's *The Child's History of the United States* served their purpose in a day of nation building and hero worshipping, but they have outgrown their usefulness in our own era, when national exceptionalism has come under scrutiny, when filiopiety seems as inappropriate as it is ineffectual, and when unity of condition appears so much less attainable and less desirable than diversity. Today, Americans need a more serviceable history, one that acknowledges the failings as well as the successes of those who lived in the past and who wrote about it. If history is to meet our broad, cultural needs— if it is to be more usable than abuse-able—then it must be appropriate to the concerns and prejudices of our day. Ideological perspective is a natural and unavoidable part of that process, as most of the historians studied in this book understood. They even reveled in its power to bring about change. As Lowenthal has noted, the recognition of our own cultural relativism can be liberating: "Once aware that relics, history, and memory are continually refashioned, we are less inhibited by the past, less frustrated by a fruitless quest for sacrosanct originals." Realizing that "the past and present are not exclusive but inseparable realms, we cast off preservation's self-defeating insistence on a fixed and stable past."[91]

The collective failure of the quixotic searches for a "lost history" on the part of McHugh, Shewan, and Kimbrell is a reminder that the past is not static and recoverable in any meaningful ontological and objective sense; rather, it is always a subjective reconstruction of events as filtered through the experience of the present and subject to constant change and reinterpretation. This was true for Morris when he wrote the original text of *The Child's History of the United States* and for McHugh and Shewan when they composed their revision. The belief that one can retrieve from the vast records of human history a past that is pure and unadulterated with respect to lived experience is a fantasy whose rhetoric betrays its own chimerical aspirations. And the charge that the truths of history are knowable but are deliberately obscured by iconoclastic revisionists is an example of tilting at windmills that would have made Miguel de Cervantes blush. Traditions have meaning for historians insofar as they allow centuries of historical experience to be condensed into a collection of compelling cultural narratives, but traditions do not inhere in the past. They are imposed on it post hoc and represent artificial constructions that reveal as much about those who narrate the past in the present as it does about those who experienced it. As Lowenthal notes, both "stability and change are essential" to historical understanding. "Survival requires an inheritable culture, but it must be malleable as well as stable."[92]

When history appears to repeat itself in accordance with tradition, then, it does so not because it must but because we prefer that it would. Lacking recognition of this fundamental epistemological circumstance, historians on the Christian Right are deluded into thinking that they can know the past as it actually happened by recovering its artifacts or by resurrecting the narratives of those erstwhile chroniclers who first constructed, described, and catalogued them. In making such assumptions, these historians eventually find themselves wandering aimlessly in a temporal wilderness in search of a path that does not exist. With respect to history, it can be said, they are truly lost.

CONCLUSION
The Recycled Past

I don't often read books twice. There are too many I haven't read once.

Chuck Klosterman, *Newsweek*, 23 February 2009

I had three goals in mind when I started this book. The first was *historical* and related to the charting of shifting educational and ideological contexts in the production of children's historical literature in the nineteenth century. I have considered how changing conceptions of childhood influenced the impact of popular historians on young readers. In the early nineteenth century, when children were viewed as vulnerable little adults, juvenile histories such as Samuel Goodrich's *Peter Parley's Tales* guided young readers quickly forward into adulthood under the watchful eye of an elderly, wise fictional narrator. When childhood was reenvisioned as a "time set apart" during which the pace of maturation slowed, volumes such as those in Jacob and John S. C. Abbott's series Makers of History allowed young readers to linger over biographical portraits of historical heroes whose lives they were urged to emulate. Concessions were made to young children whose literacy was deemed emergent in works like Josephine Pollard's *The History of the United States Told in Words of One Syllable*. As the science of child study emerged in the late nineteenth century, with its use of the new developmental psychology of child rearing, students of history found value in Charles Carleton Coffin's *The Story of Liberty*. By the beginning of the twentieth century, history books like Elbridge Brooks's *The True Story of the United States* and Charles Morris's *The Child's History of the United States* complemented the growing spirit of independence among American youth affiliated with the child first movement, as children now demanded a literature of their own, stripped of the most blatant moral aphorisms and devoid of any guiding narrative voice. In this sense, "history repeating itself" refers to the alternating contexts in which these juvenile histories were published, including their fluid production processes, their fluctuating narrative choices, and their variable challenges, successes, and failures as judged historically. With respect to these matters, change was emphasized over consensus, although, as we have noted, all these popular histories had more in common in terms of subject matter and thematic content than they had differences in terms of pedagogy and approaches to readership.

The second goal of this book was *scholarly* and involved tracing the rise and expansion of a genre of juvenile historical literature from the early to the late nineteenth century, focusing on how the authors of popular nineteenth-century texts originated and then vigorously defended a master narrative of the American past for school-age children. These works of juvenile popular history provided young readers with suggestions for conceptualizing the American past according to the religious and patriotic conventions of their day. I have noted especially their consistencies across decades as like-minded authors and publishers borrowed (and sometimes stole) from each other to produce texts that were remarkably similar in subject matter, historical tone, and pictorial effect. In this sense "history repeating itself" refers to the redundancies that emerged in the nineteenth century with respect to this consensus about what to include in the story of the American past and what to exclude. What Leslie Howsam has identified as the "narrative duplication" of popular British historians applies to American authors as well: that is, repetitions and piracies meant that "writers of history often found themselves charged with retelling an account of events already well known—to themselves, to their imagined readers, as well as to their publisher." This implied that most readers of history, even young ones, "already knew the story, or expected to know it, when they picked up the book."[1] My thesis is that such consistency of approach reveals a psychological aversion on the part of popular authors and readers to change and a resistance by some to the idea of a contested and revised past. A truly multiperspectival approach to American history, at least, had to wait until the revisionist movements of the twentieth century.[2]

My third goal has been *philosophical*, treating the epistemological aspects of the revisionist impulse. In the case of the twenty-first-century uses of these works, I have considered the current attraction of much of this literature of consensus, especially its stability. Its emphasis on established tradition has convinced some, especially homeschooling parents, to educate their children via recycled, nineteenth-century history texts. Over the past two decades, dozens of new presses (some with throwback names like Nothing New Press and Dodo Press) and burgeoning publishing and marketing enterprises, including Hearthstone Publishing, Mantle Ministries, Heritage History, Maranatha Publications, The Learning Parent, and Christian Liberty Press, have reprinted these nineteenth-century juvenile histories, advertising them as pure volumes uncorrupted by the revisionist, professional scholarship of the twentieth century. I have dissected the arguments of Christian home-schoolers who have asserted that these centuries-old histories should be used in the home as "anchor texts" for learning about the past. Common patterns of justification for this practice have emerged among these presses and institutions. Their works are promoted as alternatives to the progressive-minded, left-leaning, politically correct ideologues who have betrayed American children by foisting upon them social scientific volumes that distort the truth. Implicit in this criticism is the assumption that pre-twentieth-century history was synonymous with true history, written by authors who were immune to the kinds of politics and doctrines in which twentieth- and twenty-first-century professional historians traffic. I trust I have made clear that the phrase "history repeating itself" in this context references my considerable concerns about a critical misunderstanding on the part of republishers of the ideological underpinnings of these original texts. I have established that it is fallacious to assume that nineteenth-century popular historians were above the politics of history or insulated from its doctrines. I likewise do not believe it is appropriate to argue that historians in the nineteenth century were somehow pre-ideological and that they were not revisionists in their own right.

Anyone who imagines that these issues are irrelevant today should consider how the debates over the value of such republished works are mirrored in current deliberations over textbook selection for public schools in various states, especially Texas. In 2010 the *New York Times Magazine,* in an article on how textbook selections are made in the state, observed that every ten years professional educators in Texas report on current texts and make recommendations for changes to a fifteen-member, publicly elected board. As the author of the article, Russell Shorto, reports, the Texas State Board of Education at that time had seven conservative members "who are quite open about the fact that they vote in concert to advance a Christian agenda." A meeting of the board in January 2010 was dominated by a conservative named Don McLeroy, who, according to the *Times,* "proposed amendment after amendment on social issues to the document that teams of professional educators had drawn up over 12 months, in what would have to be described as a single-handed display of archconservative political strong-arming." McLeroy recommended, for instance, that "language be inserted about Ronald Reagan's 'leadership in restoring national confidence' following Jimmy Carter's presidency and that students be instructed to 'describe the causes and key organizations and individuals of the conservative resurgence of the 1980s and 1990s, including Phyllis Schlafly, the Contract With America, the Heritage Foundation, the Moral Majority and the National Rifle Association.'" This obvious campaigning on behalf of partisan politics "went so far," *the Times* reported, "that at one point another Republican board member burst out in seemingly embarrassed exasperation" saying, "Guys, you're rewriting history now!" Nevertheless, most of McLeroy's proposed amendments "passed by a show of hands," Shorto remarked, adding discouragingly, "This is how history is made, or rather, how the hue and cry of the present and near past gets lodged into the long-term cultural memory or else is allowed to quietly fade into an inaudible whisper."[3]

The Texas board operates from a distinct ideological position, to be sure, although some of its members believe they have the advantage of backing the right ideology (understood both in terms of political leaning and propriety of outlook). McLeroy is a "young-earth creationist," for instance, who insists that the planet "was created in six days, as the book of Genesis has it, less than 10,000 years ago," and he believes this knowledge should be the starting point for all studies of the human race, as it had been for *Peter Parley's History of the World*. Such predispositions, however, can lead to some very poor decision making when it comes to textbook selection, Shorto asserts. "Few of these elected overseers are trained in the fields they are reviewing," he writes. "'In general, the board members don't know anything at all about content,' Tom Barber, the textbook executive says. Kathy Miller, the watchdog, who has been monitoring the board for 15 years, notes with reference to Don McLeroy and another board member: 'it is the most crazy-making thing to sit there and watch a dentist and an insurance salesman rewrite curriculum standards in science and history.'"[4]

Still more disturbing are the methods McLeroy employs to pressure textbook companies into catering to his ideological preferences. "In the language-arts re-evaluation, the members of the Christian bloc wanted books to include classic myths and fables rather than newly written stories whose messages they didn't agree with," the *Times* records. "They didn't get what they wanted from the writing teams, so they did an end run around them once the public battles were over. 'I met with all the publishers,' McLeroy said. 'We went out for Mexican food. I told them this is what we want. We want stories with morals, not P.C. stories.' He then showed me an e-mail message from an executive at Pearson, a major educational publisher, indicating the results of his effort. 'Hi Don. Thanks for the impact that you have had on the development of Pearson's Scott Foresman Reading Street series. Attached is a list of some of the Fairy tales and fables that we included in the series."[5] The board did not quite accomplish everything on its agenda, the article notes, but it made deep inroads into the programs of professional educators and historians who are increasingly at the mercy of people like McLeroy, described in a recent documentary as "Revisionaries."[6] As the satirist Steven Colbert pointed out in an interview with McLeroy about the documentary, we are now in the untenable position with respect to historical knowledge where school boards (whose members are not trained historians) vote "as to what is true."[7] This was an insight Charles Coffin had more than one hundred years ago in dealing with the Boston City School Board.

What's revealing about this exchange is how much it mimics the debates among educators of the early 1900s about how extensively and quickly children can achieve historical literacy. As we have seen, as early as the 1840s educators were asking pertinent questions about the degree to which young readers could process causality, ambiguity, and multiple perspectives in regard to the study of the past. And the solutions advanced in that earlier era anticipated many of the discussions being held today in Texas and elsewhere about the pace and direction of historical learning. At the beginning of the twentieth century, some rejected the emerging child study initiatives and their attendant scientific pedagogies in favor of traditional home study approaches that centered on time-tested principles of recitation and memory building. In more recent iterations of the debate, parents, worried that public schools were eroding their religious and educational beliefs, have pulled their children out of public schools. In all such cases they have exercised a protected right, but those who have chosen to instruct their children in the field of history via the exclusive use of books written more than a century and a half ago as a way of protecting them from public school infidelities, have limited severely the range and value of the educations they make available to their children as alternatives. In my estimation, the factual inaccuracies, skewed perspectives, blatant proselytizing, and inadequate coverage of these older works disqualifies them as suitable texts around which to build a history curriculum in the twenty-first century.

I did not write this book to demean the nineteenth-century books written by the popular historians analyzed here. As I've noted in my *Popular History and the Literary Marketplace,* I believe these works have value as artifacts of a bygone age and as reminders of what popular history was in the early period of American development.[8] I also have no objection to their republication if undertaken for preservationist or antiquarian purposes. The works of Goodrich, the Abbotts, Pollard, Coffin, Brooks, and Morris are valuable as pieces of the historiographic record, and I'm glad that more people are getting a chance to read them through the efforts of staffs at the various presses and publishing companies that are reproducing them.

Where I draw the line is in the use of these nineteenth-century books to educate students in the twenty-first century about the meaning of the past for the present. I hope the detailed analysis of these popular works has convinced at least some readers that popular nineteenth-century juvenile histories were products distinctive to the eras in which they were produced and that they reflect the virtues but also the shortcomings of those time periods. The revisionist efforts of the twentieth century, initiated by professional historians committed to regularizing practices in the discipline of history, though not flawless themselves, represented a serious and even noble attempt to bring new thinking to bear on old events. We should not simply dismiss these labors out of hand, therefore, on the assumption that everything useful to be said about the American past has been recorded by those who told the story first, as Jody Kimbrell implies. It is an act of denial of the most dangerous sort to ignore revisionist scholarship, I believe, even if one disagrees with the directions it is taking. We cannot repeal the twentieth century, despite the fact that many on the Christian Right would like to do so, nor should we seek to reverse the recognition attained by progressive educators (with considerable struggle, I might add) that history has many perspectives and that it has always been and will always be contested. The twentieth century has taught us much about historical methodology, including the insight that Santayana's notion of "history repeating itself" is not an inescapable axiom but a philosophical choice with consequences. The philosopher reminds us that we should acknowledge the powerful didactic, even moral, value of nineteenth-century texts in their own day, but that we should not feel compelled correspondingly to accept their authority or to embrace them as agents of salvation in our own.

One might say that there should be room in modern historiography for any histories that adopt specialized perspectives, such as Uncle Rick Reads The True Story of George Washington. These works take liberties with the past, to be sure, but is that not the case to some degree with all histories? Many historians, including the inimitable Charles Beard, have argued that the concept of an "objective past" cherished by scholars has been at best a "noble dream" and at worst a distracting delusion.[9] Some historians still cling tenaciously to the idea that we can know the past definitively and with precise reference to what actually happened, but over the past three decades of postmodern reflection the very concept of objectivity as a heuristic device for structuring and evaluating past experience has been questioned. If all history is but a "choice of fictions," as James Wilkinson has argued, are the fictions created by historians on the Christian Right any more objectionable than any others?[10]

The answer, in my opinion, is yes. In the postmodern world, in which the rise of relativism has been achieved sometimes at the expense of objectivity, we may be forced to admit, as Beard did almost a century ago, that history is always an act of faith.[11] Those on the Christian Right would agree in principle with such a faith-based conviction, but they would insist on the existence of a single truth in regard to the past that would invalidate all competing historical interpretations and systems. Theirs is an omniscient vision that will admit of no grounds for revision. For most people whose profession is history (and it is a profession in the religious sense of that term for some), however, historical faith is not doctrinal or centered on teleological tenets independent of or prior to lived experience; rather, it is grounded in sufficient and convincing data collected from actual observation and subjected to agreed-upon evidentiary standards that can change over time. In history, one cannot simply make things up, no matter how desperate one is to prove the truthfulness of an ideological proposition about the past or a forewarning of the future. Faith in this sense is not a priori, then, but a posteriori, derived from practical circumstances and requiring persuasive proof for its validation. Failure to meet this benchmark is what invalidates most of the efforts of Christian presses today whose editors republish so-called original histories not as a way of determining what happened in the past, but as a means for controlling the present and anticipating the future. In extrapolating directly from nineteenth-century histories to apocalyptic visions of the coming Armageddon, such republishers have attempted "to reduce history to eschatology," notes the philosopher of history Kerwin Lee Klein, and that is an impulse professional historians can neither embrace nor condone.[12]

Perhaps Santayana deserves the final word, as his thoughts on historical repetition have informed this book so profoundly. With respect to the misuse of the philosopher's most famous phrase about history repeating itself, one is reminded of the quip of a recent blogger that "those who misquote George Santayana are condemned to paraphrase him."[13] George W. Bush got himself into trouble with some members of the press when, in a speech of August 2007 to the Veterans of Foreign Wars, he tried to rephrase Santayana by noting the similarities between the war in Iraq and the Vietnam conflict. "I recognize that history cannot predict the future with absolute certainty," he said. "I understand that. But history does remind us that there are lessons applicable to our time. And we can learn something from history." Members of the press corps rightly asked which lessons and what is there to learn?[14] Trudy Rubin of the *Baltimore Sun* complained that people like Bush "who raise false historical analogies may harm their cause as much as the memory-challenged."[15] Mark Twain was even less convinced that history could teach any of us much at all, especially politicians who pursued imperialistic wars. "History doesn't repeat itself," Twain was credited with saying; "at best it sometimes rhymes."[16]

Twain's comic quip may hold true with respect to historical events, but *historical writing* does repeat itself and with more frequency because of the proliferation of the recycled texts I've analyzed here. If, as I suspect, Santayana was saying we should study history not as a record of absolute truth on which to base practice but as an "imaginative reconstruction" for use as a coping mechanism against chaos, then we must embrace revisionism or become victims of its relativism. The efforts of the Christian Right to recycle volumes of allegedly lost and sacred history as protection against a more frightening (because more uncertain and contested) past suggest that these presses are motivated less by a desire to escape the implications of the past than by a wish to avoid the complexities of the present and the challenges of the future. That would be an abnegation of the responsibilities of the historian as defined in Santayana's writings, which were characterized less by "a moral exhortation to pay attention to history" than by the philosopher's "subtle, paradoxical, and occasionally humorous" ambition to make history serviceable to those who understand best its relativistic challenges and benefits.[17] More important, it would do a great disservice to children, who are highly vulnerable to a historiography based on the decisions of school boards whose members are untrained in the field of history and who operate on the principle that Colbert derides as "reality by majority vote."[18]

Such an arbitrary standard for judging the value of history hints that perhaps we really are condemned, and in ways Santayana anticipated we would be. Having acknowledged the propensity of humans to seek "consecutiveness and persistence" in their historical accounts, Santayana recognized that our need for self-renewal and our related aversion to change make us vulnerable to the kinds of recycling practices in which republishers are engaged today. In order to avoid repeating history in the slavish ways warned against by Santayana, we must resist the inclination merely to duplicate older texts— the path of least resistance in most cases—and somehow find the creative energy and finances to write new histories that speak more directly to our own age. We should not underestimate the challenges or the stakes involved in this enterprise either. For such a mission will require acts of faith on the part of twenty-first-century revisionist historians every bit as powerful and spiritual as the impulses that motivate publishers on the Christian Right to reprint nineteenth-century popular histories for children in the name of family, country, and God. For the sake of the young, revisionists must challenge polemicists such as those on the Texas State Board of Education by pursuing a standard of objectivity that not only rejects "orthodoxy for orthodoxy's sake" but also allows children to study the discipline of history on their terms and according to narrative forms appropriate to their present circumstances.[19] In this final sense, the phrase *history repeating itself* evokes the concept of consistency that many associate with Santayana's famous dictum, but it does so in a paradoxical manner, by calling attention to the "consistency of inconsistency" at the heart of all historical investigation. It acknowledges the central role revisionism must play in the pursuit of a meaningful and usable past, a past we are not "condemned to repeat" unless we choose consciously to do so by promoting republishing practices that encourage our children to "remember" history in repetitive, unimaginative, and anachronistic ways.

NOTES

Introduction

1. Josephine Pollard, *The History of the United States Told in One Syllable Words* (New York: McLoughlin Brothers, 1884); and Josephine Pollard, *A Child's History of America Told in One-Syllable Words* (Bulverde, Tex.: Mantle Ministries, 1998).

2. "Resources for Homeschoolers," *Valerie's Living Books,* www.valerieslivingbooks.com.

3. "Kessinger Publishing's Rare Reprints," www.kessinger.net.

4. Bruce VanSledright, *In Search of America's Past: Learning to Read History in Elementary School* (New York: Teachers College Press, 2002), 142.

5. Gilbert T. Sewall, *World History Textbooks: A Review* (New York: American Textbook Council, 2004).

6. Dylan Lovan, "Top Home School Texts Dismiss Darwin, Evolution," 6 March 2010, www.hostednews/ap/article.

7. For statistics on the number of Americans homeschooling, see "Homeschooling in the United States: 2003, Statistical Analysis Report," *U.S. Department of Education Report NCES 2003-42,* http://nces.ed.gov.

8. Diane Ravitch and Chester E. Finn, *What Do Our 17-Year-Olds Know? A Report on the First National Assessment of History and Literature* (New York: Harper and Row, 1987), 49, 62, 54. See also Ravitch, "The Precarious State of History," *American Educator* (Spring 1985): 12–15; and Ravitch, "From History to Social Studies: Dilemmas and Problems," in Diane Ravitch, *The Schools We Deserve* (New York: Basic Books, 1985).

9. Bradley Commission on History Schools, *Building a History Curriculum: Guidelines for Teaching History in the Schools* (Washington, D.C.: Education Excellent Network, 1988). See also "Preface," in *Historical Literacy: The Case for History in American Education,* ed. Paul A. Gagnon (New York: Macmillan, 1989), xii.

10. Robert Rothman, "1.5 Million Awarded for Center on History," *Education Week,* 30 March 1988.

11. National Center for History in the Schools, *National Standards for United States History: Exploring the American Experience* (Los Angeles: Regents, University of California, Los Angeles, 1994). Archival records for the NCHS's work on the standards can be found at Administrative Files, Record Series #667, UCLA Archives, National Center for History in the Schools, Los Angeles, California.

12. Gary B. Nash, Charlotte Crabtree, and Ross E. Dunn, *History on Trial: Culture Wars and the Teaching of the Past* (New York: Alfred A. Knopf, 1997), 83–84. See also, Sheldon M. Stern, "Why the Battle over History Standards?," in *What's at Stake in the Standards Wars? A Primer for Educational Policy Makers,* ed. Sandra Stotsky (New York: Peter Lang, 2000), 149–68.

13. Lynne V. Cheney, "The End of History," *Wall Street Journal*, 20 October 1994. See also Charles Krauthammer, "History Hijacked," *Washington Post*, 4 November 1994, and John Leo, "The Hijacking of American History," *U.S. News and World Report*, 14 November 1994. For a good general discussion of these exchanges, see Linda Symcox, *Whose History? The Struggle for National Standards in American Classrooms* (New York: Teachers College Press, 2002), 129–30.

14. Woody West, "Schools Are Crucial Battlefield in the War of American Ideals," *Washington Times*, 28 November 1994. See also Diane Ravitch, "Standards in U.S. History: Solid Material Interwoven with Political Bias," *Education Week*, 7 December 1994.

15. Patricia Avery and Theresa Johnson, "How Newspapers Framed the U.S. History Standards Debate," *Social Education* 63, no. 4 (May–June 1999): 220–24. See also Carol Innerst, "P. C. Pressures May Shape Teaching of U.S. History," *Washington Times*, 21 November 1994.

16. For the defense by Nash and others, see Nash et al., *History on Trial*, 193–200; and Ross E. Dunn, "A History of the History Standards: The Making of a Controversy of Historic Proportions," *UCLA Magazine* (Winter 1995): 32–35. On the reactions of conservatives, see Sabrina W. M. Lutz, "Whose Standards?: Conservative Citizen Groups and Standards-based Reform," *Educational Horizons* 75 (1997): 133–42.

17. VanSledright, *In Search of America's Past*, 22.

18. Bruce VanSledright, "And Santayana Lives On: Students' Views on the Purposes for Studying History," *Journal of Curriculum Studies* 29, no. 5 (1997): 529.

19. VanSledright, *In Search of America's Past*, 142.

20. VanSledright, "And Santayana Lives On," 550. See also Lynne V. Cheney, *Telling the Truth: Why Our Culture and Our Country Have Stopped Making Sense—and What We Can Do About It* (New York: Touchstone, 1995).

21. Nash et al., *History on Trial*, xxi.

22. VanSledright, *In Search of America's Past*, 139.

23. For a discussion of the moral implications of the New History, see Gertrude Himmelfarb, *The New History and the Old: Critical Essays and Reappraisals* (Cambridge: Harvard University Press, 1987), esp. 155–70. See also VanSledright, "And Santayana Lives On," 550.

24. For more on the relationship between reading capacity and historical learning, see Kieran Egan, "Teaching History to Young Children," *Phi Beta Kappan* (March 1982): 439–41.

25. Bruno Bettelheim, *The Uses of Enchantment: The Meaning and Importance of Fairy Tales* (New York: Vintage Books, 1975), as summarized in Symcox, *Whose History?* 72.

26. "H. A. Guerber's Histories," *Nothing New Press*, www.nothingnewpress.com.

27. Charlotte Crabtree, "Returning History to the Elementary School," in *Historical Literacy*, 177.

28. VanSledright, *In Search of America's Past*, 15.

29. Ibid., 141, 92.

30. VanSledright, "And Santayana Lives On," 553. See also Diane Ravitch, "Tot Sociology: Or What Happened to History in the Grade Schools?," *American Scholar* 56 (Summer 1987): 343–54; and Kieran Egan, *Teaching as Story Telling: An Alternative Approach to Teaching and Curriculum in the Elementary School* (Ontario: Althousde Press, 1986).

31. Nash et al., *History on Trial*, 218. See also Christian Coalition, *Contact with the American Family, A Bold Plan by the Christian Coalition to Strengthen the Family and Restore Common-Sense Values* (Nashville: Moorings, 1995).

32. Parents choose to homeschool their children for many reasons; some may keep their children at home because they feel the schools are not doing enough to promote the new agenda of the standards. For negative reactions of homeschoolers to the National Standards,

see "Follies and Failures of the National Education Association," in *Phyllis Schlafly Reports,* www.eagleform.org; and "We are Being Misled by Claims that Adopting and Enforcing Standards in Education Will Improve Our Educational System," *Home Education Magazine,* www.homeedmag.com.

33. "The History Thieves," Letters to the Editor, *Wall Street Journal,* 8 November 1994, as cited in Nash et al., *History on Trial,* 189.

34. Melissa Worcester, Review of "Guerber's Historical Readers," *Practical Homeschooling Magazine* 64 (1 May 2005): 54.

35. Diane Ravitch, "Standards in U.S. History: Solid Material Interwoven with Political Bias," *Education Week,* 7 December 1994, as cited in Symcox, *Whose History?,* 134.

36. Lynne V. Cheney, "Kill My Old Agency, Please," *Wall Street Journal,* 24 January, 1995. See also Lynne V. Cheney, "The National History (Sub)Standards," *Wall Street Journal,* 23 October 1995.

37. *Congressional* Record (18 January 1995), S1080, as cited in Symcox, *Whose History?,* 1.

38. Joanna [from] California, "Guerber History Customer Comments," *Nothing New Press,* www.nothingnewpress.com.

39. Doug Morris, *Knoxville Journal,* 19 April 1986, as cited in Michael A. Lofaro and Joe Cummings, eds., *Crockett at Two Hundred: New Perspectives on the Man and the Myth* (Knoxville: University of Tennessee Press, 1989), 25.

40. "Parents' Reasons for Homeschooling," in "Homeschooling in the United States: 2003, Statistical Analysis Report."

41. Symcox, *Whose History?,* 151, 160.

42. See, for instance, Louise Adler and Kip Tellez, "Curriculum from the Religious Right: The 'Impressions' Reading Series," *Urban Education* 27, no. 2 (July 1992): 152–73; David C. Berliner, "Educational Psychology Meets the Christian Right: Differing Views of Children, Schooling, Teaching, and Learning," *Teacher's College Record* 98, no. 3 (Spring 1997): 381–416; and Lesley H. Browder Jr., "The Religious Right, the Secular Left, and Their Shared Dilemma: The Public School," *International Journal of Educational Reform* 7, no. 4 (October 1998): 309–18.

43. Richard Wheeler, "Biography, Richard 'Little Bear' Wheeler," *Mantle Ministries,* www.mantleministries.com.

44. Cathy Duffy, "Guerber History Customer Comments," *Nothing New Press,* www.nothingnewpress.com.

45. Frances FitzGerald, *America Revised: What History Textbooks Have Taught Our Children about Their Country, and How and Why Those Textbooks Have Changed in Different Decades* (New York: Vintage Books, 1979), 10, 59.

46. George Santayana, *The Life of Reason; or, The Phases of Human Progress,* 5 vols. (New York: Charles Scribner's Sons, 1905–22), 1:284.

47. Ibid., 5:39.

48. Henry Adams, "The Rule of Phase Applied to History," in *The Degradation of the Democratic Dogma, by Henry Adams; with an introduction by Brooks Adams* (New York: Macmillan, 1919), 267–311; see also Henry Adams, *The Education of Henry Adams: An Autobiography* (Boston: Houghton, Mifflin, 1918), 497–98.

49. Santayana, *Life of Reason,* 5:39, 45, 284.

50. I have adapted the notion of inversion from Peter Collier and David Horowitz, *Destructive Generation: Second Thoughts About the Sixties* (New York: Free Press, 1996), 371.

51. For more on the concept of self-renewal, see Leonard S. Marcus, *Minders of Make-Believe: Idealists, Entrepreneurs, and the Shaping of American Children's Literature* (Boston: Houghton Mifflin, 2008), xi.

52. See John Bryant, *The Fluid Text* (Ann Arbor: University of Michigan Press, 2002); Jerome McCann, *Radiant Textuality: Literature after the World Wide Web* (New York: Palgrave Macmillan, 2001); and Meredith McGill, *American Literature and the Culture of Reprinting* (Philadelphia: University of Pennsylvania Press, 2007).

53. Ralph Waldo Emerson, "Self-Reliance" (1841), in *The Complete Essays and Other Writings of Ralph Waldo Emerson*, ed. Brooks Atkinson (New York: Modern Library, 1940), 152.

54. E. D. Hirsch Jr., Joseph F. Kent, and James Trefil, *The New Dictionary of Cultural Literacy*, 3rd ed. (Boston: Houghton Mifflin, 2002), 202.

1. Narrative History

1. N[oah]. W. Hutchings, "Foreword," in Samuel G. Goodrich, *Parley's History of the World* (Oklahoma City: Hearthstone Publishing, [2002]), 16.

2. "History Books: Parley's History of the World," www.virtueunknowledge.com.

3. Goodrich, *Parley's History of the World*, 5, back cover.

4. Noah W. Hutchings and Larry Spargimino, *Y2K=666* (Oklahoma City: Hearthstone Publishing, 1998), n.p.; Hutchings, who used to refer to himself as "Doctor of Theology," had his academic credentials challenged by critics, and he later admitted that the only degree he possesses is a bachelor's in accounting. For more on this incident, see Bill Alnor's comments in the *Christian Sentinel*, August 2004, as summarized in "Suspect Credentials and Phony Degrees in the Church," www.degreeinfo.com.

5. See, for instance, "The F.I.R.E." (Freedom is Real Education) website, www.ignitethefire.com, which advises homeschooling parents about "incorporating tried-and-true antique readers and children's books [from the nineteenth century] into their 21st century homeschooling programs." Peter Parley's work is one of the books inventoried.

6. "Parley's History of the World," Item Description and Condition, http://egi.ebay.com.

7. Goodrich, *Parley's History of the World*, 15.

8. "Authorcraft," *Littell's Living Age*, 6 June 1846, 488.

9. Samuel G. Goodrich, *Recollections of a Lifetime*, 2 vols. (New York: Miller, Orton and Mulligan, 1856), 2:333–34.

10. Hearthstone was not the only publisher, or even the first, to reprint Goodrich's juvenile histories. In 1974 Dover Press reissued Goodrich's volume *Peter Parley Tales of America* (1828) as a "lost classic." For the details of this republication effort, see Barrow Mussey to Harmon S. Boyd, 17 July 1972, folder 65, box I: Correspondence, Samuel G. Goodrich Collection, Amherst College Archives and Special Collections, Amherst College, Amherst, Mass.

11. Steven Mintz, *Huck's Raft: A History of American Childhood* (Cambridge: Harvard University Press, 2004), viii; see also Peter Hunt, *Children's Literature: An Illustrated History* (New York: Oxford University Press, 1995), ix.

12. Gillian Avery, *Behold the Child: American Children and Their Books, 1621–1922* (Baltimore: Johns Hopkins University Press, 1994), 16–21.

13. For more on children as little adults, see John Demos, *A Little Commonwealth: Family Life in Plymouth Colony* (New York: Oxford University Press, 1970), 182.

14. Gillian Avery, "Beginnings of Children's Reading to c. 1700," in Hunt, *Children's Literature*, 7.

15. Mintz, *Huck's Raft*, 16–17.

16. Samuel Osgood, "Books for Our Children," *Atlantic Monthly*, December 1865, as cited in Avery, *Behold the Child*, 121; also Leonard S. Marcus, *Minders of Make-Believe: Idealists, Entrepreneurs, and the Shaping of American Children's Literature* (Boston: Houghton Mifflin, 2008), 32–33.

17. Therese Yelverton, *Teresina in America* (London: R. Bentley, 1875), 263, as cited in Avery, *Behold the Child,* 6–8.

18. Marcus, *Minders of Make-Believe,* 2.

19. Avery, *Behold the Child,* 58; Amy Weinstein, *Once Upon a Time: Illustrations from Fairytales, Fables, Primers, Pop-ups and Other Children's Books* (New York: Princeton Architectural Press, 2005), 69.

20. Daniel Roselle, *Samuel Goodrich: Creator of Peter Parley* (Albany: State University of New York Press, 1968), 56. The most thorough bibliographic source on Goodrich is Pat Pflieger, "Nineteenth Century American Children and What They Read," www.merrycoz.org. See also Jacob Blanck, *Peter Parley to Penrod: A Bibliographical Description of the Best-Loved American Juvenile Books* (New York: R. R. Bowker, 1956).

21. Mason L. Weems, *The Life of Washington,* ed. Marcus Cunliffe (Cambridge: Harvard University Press, 1962), xiii–xxiii.

22. The phrase "picturesque and lurid" comes from comments by James Harvey Robinson, "The New History," in *The New History: Essays Illustrating the Modern Historical Outlook* (New York: Macmillan, 1912), 10.

23. William Oliver Stevens, " 'Uncle' Peter Parley," *St. Nicholas Magazine,* November 1925, 78.

24. N. A. Calkins, "Report of the Committee of Ten on Secondary Schools Studies, with the Reports of the Conference Arranged by Committee" (New York: American Book Company for the National Educational Association, 1893), 3, 6–7. See also American Historical Association, *The Study of History in Schools: Report of the American Historical Association by the Committee of Seven* (New York: Macmillan, 1900).

25. Anne Scott MacLeod, "Children's Literature in America from the Puritan Beginnings to 1870," in Hunt, ed., *Children's Literature,* 114.

26. Avery, *Behold the Child,* 36–62.

27. Mintz, *Huck's Raft,* viii, 17.

28. MacLeod, "Children's Literature in America," 128.

29. Julia Briggs, "Transitions, 1890–1914," in Hunt, *Children's Literature,* 167.

30. *Painted Picture Play Book,* 1855, as quoted in Weinstein, *Once Upon a Time,* 1.

31. Avery, "Beginnings of Children's Reading to c. 1700," 13. The book referred to here is Charles Dudley Warner's *Being a Boy* (1877).

32. Samuel G. Goodrich, *Fireside Education* (Boston: Geo. A. and J. Curtis S Type and Stereotype Foundry, 1838), vi–vii, 72–73.

33. George Callcott, *History in the United States 1800–1860: Its Practice and Purpose* (Baltimore: Johns Hopkins University Press, 1970), 56–57.

34. Mintz, *Huck's Raft,* 82. See also Gail Schmunk Murray, "Good Girls, Bad Boys, 1850–1890," in *American Children's Literature and the Construction of Childhood* (New York: Twayne Publishers, 1998), 51–81.

35. Avery, *Behold the Child,* 186.

36. Callcott, *History in the United States,* 66.

37. Goodrich, *First Book of History* (Boston: Richardson, Lord and Holbrook, 1831), 5.

38. Emily Goodrich Smith, " 'Peter Parley'—As Known to His Daughter," *Connecticut Quarterly* 4, no. 3 (July, August, September 1898): 304.

39. Roselle, *Samuel Goodrich,* 20–21; see also Bruce A. Harvey, *American Geographies: U.S. National Narratives and the Representation of the Non-European World, 1830–1865* (Palo Alto: Stanford University Press, 2001), 45.

40. Goodrich, *Recollections,* 1:89, 22–23.

41. For a discussion of Freud's concept of family romance with reference to Goodrich's midcentury "post-heroic" generation, see George Forgie, *Patricide in the House Divided: A Psychological Interpretation of Lincoln and His Age* (New York: Norton, 1979), 31–32.

42. Goodrich, *Recollections*, 1:489, 240–41.

43. Ibid., 1:173, 23, 284.

44. Ibid., 1:275.

45. Ibid., 1:170, 167–68, 168–69.

46. Ibid., 2:311–12.

47. Wordsworth as cited in Roselle, *Samuel Goodrich*, 48.

48. Weinstein, *Once Upon a Time*, 70.

49. Goodrich, *Recollections*, 2:312.

50. Sir Henry Cole in *The Home Treasury* (1842), as cited in Dennis Butts, "The Beginnings of Victorianism, 1820–1850," Hunt, ed., *Children's Literature*, 88.

51. Michael Angelo Titmarsh [William Makepeace Thackeray], "On Some Illustrated Children's Books," *Fraser's Magazine for Town and Country* 33 (April 1846), 495, as cited in Roselle, *Samuel Goodrich*, 2; F. J. Harvey Darton, "Two New Englands: 'Peter Parley' and 'Felix Summerly,'" *Children's Books in England*, 3rd ed. (London: Cambridge University Press, 1982); "Review of Puck's Reports to Oberon, by Felix Summerly," *Littell's Living Age*, 21 September 1844, 427.

52. Goodrich, *Recollections*, 2:317–18.

53. Julia Briggs and Dennis Butts, "The Emergence of Form, 1850–1890," in Hunt, *Children's Literature*, 137.

54. Annie Cole Cady, *The American Continent and Its Inhabitants before Its Discovery by Columbus: A Unique History Communicated by Robin Goodfellow, Fairy Historian and Written by Annie Cole Cady (illustrated by Henry Cady and Others)* (Philadelphia, Gebbie, 1893).

55. For more on the etymologies of the names Robin Goodfellow and Puck, see Katherin Mary Briggs, *Anatomy of Puck* (New York: Arno Press, 1977).

56. Goodrich, *Recollections*, 2:320n–321n.

57. Charles Dickens, *A Child's History of England*, 3 vols. (New York: Harper and Brothers, 1869), 2:201, 1:106.

58. "A Child's History of England," review, www.amazon.com/Child's-History-England-Penny.

59. Samuel Griswold Goodrich, *A Pictorial History of England* (1845; reprint Philadelphia: J. H. Butler, 1879), 11.

60. "Samuel Griswold Goodrich," in *American Authors 1600–1900*, ed. Stanley J. Kunitz and Howard Hycraft (New York: H. H. Wilson, 1938), 308–9.

61. Goodrich, *Recollections*, 2:167–68; 1:172.

62. Ibid., 2:112, 321, 308.

63. Ruth K. MacDonald, "Samuel Griswold Goodrich (Peter Parley)," in *American Writers for Children Before 1900*, ed. Glenn E. Estes, vol. 42 of the *Dictionary of Literary Biography* (Detroit: Gale Research, 1985), 193.

64. Goodrich, *Recollections*, 2:308–9, 311.

65. *Goodrich's Second Reader*, 61, as cited in Roselle, *Samuel Goodrich*, 64, 68np, 66.

66. On Gallaudet and the "sight-word method," see Mitford M. Mathews, *Teaching to Read: Historically Considered* (Chicago: University of Chicago Press, 1966), 55–57.

67. For more on nineteenth-century concepts of memory and memory exercises, see Douwe Draaisma, *Metaphors of Memory: A History of Ideas About the Mind* (Cambridge: Cambridge University Press, 2000), 68–102.

68. On Horace Mann and his teaching methods, see Mathews, *Teaching to Read, Historically Considered*, 77–85.

69. Goodrich, *Recollections*, 2:311–12.

70. Goodrich, *Third Book of History, Containing Ancient History in Connection with Ancient Geography* (Boston: Jenks, Palmer, 1850), 9.

71. Goodrich "Chronological Index," *First Book of History*, 227.

72. "Appreciations and Criticisms by G. K. Chesterton," review of Charles Dickens, *A Child's History of England*, www.dickens-literature.com, [1–3].

73. Captain, H. A. Chambers of Chattanooga, Tennessee, "An Iredell Neighborhood Fifty Years Ago, 1845–1853," as cited in "North Carolina in the Civil War," www.ncgenweb.us, letter marked 30 March 1900.

74. "Appreciations and Criticisms by G. K. Chesterton," [3].

75. "Samuel Griswold Goodrich," *Southern Literary Messenger*, 7 October 1841, 736–37.

76. [S. G. Goodrich], *Peter Parley's Method of Telling about Geography to Children*, preface, as cited in Roselle, *Samuel Goodrich*, 70.

77. Pflieger, "Nineteenth-Century American Children and What They Read," www.merry-coz.org. See also Gladys Scott, "Peter Parley: His Magazine and His Books," *Peabody Journal of Education* 19, no. 5 (March 1942): 290–92; Helen S. Canfield, "Peter Parley," *Horn Book Magazine* (April 1970): 135–41; (June 1970): 274–82; (August 1970): 412–18; F. J. Harvey Darton, "Peter Parley and the Battle of the Children's Books," *Cornhill Magazine*, November 1932, 542–58.

78. Goodrich, *Recollections of a Lifetime*, 2:326.

79. "Politics," *The Youth's Casket*, 1 (October 1852): 164.

80. Fillmore to Goodrich, 31 August 1850, Boyd Collection, as cited in Roselle, *Samuel Goodrich*, 61.

81. Smith, " 'Peter Parley'—As Known to His Daughter," 307.

82. Goodrich, *Recollections*, 1:144.

83. Goodrich, *The Third Reader for the Use of Schools* (Louisville: Morton and Griswold, 1839), iii, 11–13.

84. Ibid., 11–13.

85. Goodrich, *Recollections*, 1:86.

86. Samuel G. Goodrich, *Tales of Peter Parley About America* (Boston: S. G. Goodrich, 1827), 3–4.

87. Goodrich, *First Book of History*, 5.

88. Ibid.

89. Samuel Goodrich, *The American Child's Pictorial History of the United States* (Philadelphia: E. H. Butler, 1860).

90. Roselle, *Samuel Goodrich*, 79. See Goodrich, *A Pictorial History of England*.

91. Roselle, *Samuel Goodrich*, 80.

92. *London and Westminster Review* 33, no. 1, p. 149, as cited in Roselle, *Samuel Goodrich*, 43.

93. *American Annals of Education and Instruction for the Year 1832*, 2:579, as cited in Roselle, *Samuel Goodrich*, 62.

94. Peter Parley, *Universal History on the Basis of Geography* (London: William Tegg, 1869).

95. Rose H. Lathrop, *Memoirs of Hawthorne* (Boston: Houghton, Mifflin, 1897), 336. From a letter to Elizabeth Peabody, as cited in Roselle, *Samuel Goodrich*, 76–77.

96. *The American Monthly Review* (November 1832), 354, as cited in Roselle, *Samuel Goodrich*, 62.

97. Goodrich, *Tales of Peter Parley About America*, 9.

98. Francis Parsons, "Who Was Peter Parley?" *The Friendly Club and Other Portraits* (Hartford: Edwin Valentine Mitchell, 1922), 109–19.

99. Allan Luke, *Literacy, Textbooks and Ideology: Postwar Literacy Instruction and the Mythology of Dick and Jane* (New York: Falmer Press, 1988), 37.

100. Goodrich, *First Book of History,* 29, 32.

101. Goodrich, *Tales of Peter Parley About America,* 100, 72, 75.

102. Goodrich, *Parley's Universal History,* 14–15.

103. Goodrich, *Parley's Method of Telling About the History,* 11–12, 124–26.

104. David Lowenthal, "The Timeless Past: Some Anglo-American Historical Preconceptions," in *Memory and American History,* ed. David Thelan (Bloomington: Indiana University Press, 1989), 134, 138.

105. Goodrich, *Recollections,* 2:311.

106. Goodrich, *Parley's Universal History,* 239.

107. Goodrich, *Recollections,* 2:320n–21n.

108. Goodrich, *First Book of History,* 29.

109. Stevens, "'Uncle' Peter Parley," 81.

110. I have borrowed the phrase "the sober narration . . ." from Peter Novick, *That Noble Dream: The 'Objectivity Question' and the American Historical Profession* (New York: Cambridge University Press, 1988), 45.

111. Hayden White, "Fictions of Factual Representation," *Tropics of Discourse* (Baltimore: Johns Hopkins University Press, 1985), 85, 123.

112. Goodrich, *Recollections,* 2:279–80.

113. *Boston Daily Courier,* 8 December 1855, as cited in Roselle, *Samuel Goodrich,* 97.

114. Roselle, *Samuel Goodrich,* 89.

115. Goodrich, *Recollections,* 2:279–80.

116. "Samuel Griswold Goodrich," *Southern Literary Messenger,* October 1841, 738.

117. Goodrich, *Recollections,* 2:323–24.

118. Ibid., 2:322.

119. Roselle, *Samuel Goodrich,* 40.

120. Donald G. Mitchell, *"Peter Parley" in American Lands and Letters* (New York: Charles Scribner's Sons, 1897), 1:330–35.

121. Augustus Gaylord to J. C. Derby, 18 October 1883, as cited in Roselle, *Samuel Goodrich,* 40. See also J. C. Derby, "S. G. Goodrich," in *Fifty Years Among Authors, Books and Publishers* (Hartford: M. A. Winter and Hatch, 1884), 110–23.

122. "Samuel Griswold Goodrich," *Southern Literary Messenger,* 738.

123. For an indication of this self-consciousness, see [Poem signed by S. G. Goodrich], folder 41, box 1, Correspondence, The Samuel Goodrich Collection, Amherst College Archives and Special Collections. Amherst, Mass.

124. Hutchings, *Parley's History of the World,* 15–16.

125. Ibid. On illegitimate births in the pre–Civil War period, see Laurel Ulrich, *A Midwife's Tale: The Life of Martha Ballard Based on Her Diary, 1785–1812* (New York: Vintage Books, 1991).

126. Hutchings, *Parley's History of the World,* 15–16.

127. "Editorial Note," *Parley's History of the World,* 3.

128. Samuel Goodrich, *Parley's Common School History Revised: A Pictorial History of the World, Ancient and Modern (1858)* (Kessinger Legacy Reprints, n.d.).

129. Efforts to pass an international copyright law failed during Goodrich's lifetime, in part, according to Charles Dickens, because of the recalcitrance of American authors such as Goodrich, whom Dickens pronounced "a scoundrel and a Liar" and a man who, "if he would present himself at my door, he would, as he very well knows, be summarily pitched in to the street." See Goodrich, *Recollections,* 2:355–72.

130. Leslie Howsam, "Sustained Literary Ventures: The Series in Victorian Book Publishing," *Publishing History* 32 (1992): 11, 18; see also William St. Clair, *The Reading Nation in the Romantic Period* (New York: Cambridge University Press, 2004).

131. "Peter Parley's Farewell," as cited in Roselle, *Samuel Goodrich,* 93, 97–98; see also Michael V. Belock, "Spurious Peter Parley Books," *American Book Collector* 18 (Summer 1968): 23–24.

132. Goodrich, *Tales of Peter Parley About America,* 77–78, 81.

133. Ibid., 107–9.

134. Goodrich, *Peter Parley's Tales About America and Australia,* ed. T. Wilson (London: Darton and Clark, Holborn Hill, c. 1845), 52.

135. Roselle, *Samuel Goodrich,* 89, 94.

136. Goodrich, *Recollections,* 2:304. Darton said in his defense that Goodrich was guilty of the same sort of piracy with respect to publishing works without acknowledging the author by royalties. See F. J. Darton, *Children's Books in England: Five Centuries of Social Life* (Cambridge: Cambridge University Press, 1932), 228.

137. Smith, "'Peter Parley'—As Known to His Daughter," 405.

138. Page iii, as cited in Pat Pflieger, "Literary Activities of Samuel G. Goodrich: An Evolving Bibliography," in "Nineteenth Century American Children and What They Read."

139. Pflieger, "Not Quite Goodrich: Works *Not* by Samuel G, Goodrich," in "Nineteenth Century American Children and What They Read."

140. Goodrich, *Recollections,* 2:552, appendix 1.

141. Roselle, *Samuel Goodrich,* 98.

142. ["To the Black-ey'd and Blue-ey'd Friends of Robert Merry"] 2 (December 1841): 184, as cited in "Nineteenth Century American Children and What They Read."

143. Goodrich, *Recollections,* 2:550, appendix 1, 2:338.

144. *Peter Parley's Own Story: From the Personal Narrative of the Late Samuel G. Goodrich ("Peter Parley").* (New York: Sheldon, 1863).

145. "Death of S. G. Goodrich," *Littell's Living Age,* 9 June 1860, 619–20.

146. Smith, "'Peter Parley'—As Known to His Daughter," 407.

147. Roselle, *Samuel Goodrich,* 53–54. For more on this revival, see L. H. Martin, "Peter Parley," *Congregationalist,* 14 October 1897, 553.

148. Smith, "'Peter Parley'—As Known to His Daughter," 304.

149. "More Blog Things: Parley's History of the World," https://sites.google.com.

150. Jill Lepore, *The Whites of Their Eyes: The Tea Party's Revolution and the Battle over American History* (Princeton: Princeton University Press, 2010), 16.

151. Hutchings, *Parley's History of the World,* 15–16.

152. Ibid.

2. Pedagogical History

1. Samuel G. Goodrich, *Recollections of a Lifetime,* 2 vols. (New York: Miller, Orton, and Mulligan, 1856), 1:174.

2. "Nothing New Press: Curriculum Honoring the Ancient Paths," www.nothingnewpress.com.

3. Christine Miller, All Through the Ages, as described in "Classical Christian Home Schooling," www.classical-homeschooling.org.

4. http://m.vi-vn.connect.facebook.com/nothingnewpress.

5. "Old-fashioned history straight from your great-grandparents' bookshelf," Heritage History, www.heritage-history.com.

6. "Heritage Classic Curriculum User Guide: Introduction," Heritage History.

7. "Modern History vs. Traditional History," Heritage History.

8. Ibid.

9. "Why Should I Study History?," Heritage History.

10. "History from Grandfather's Bookshelf: Why the Latest Is Not the Greatest," Heritage History.

11. Ibid.

12. "Why Should I Study History?," Heritage History website.

13. See advertisement for "Illustrated Histories," p. 4 of brochure marked "Abbott's Juvenile Series," added to the final pages of Jacob Abbott, *Margaret of Anjou; Queen of Henry VI of England* (New York: Harper and Brothers, 1861).

14. "Rev. John S. C. Abbott," *New York Tribune,* 18 June 1887, as collected in M1.2 Folio, vol. 16, John S. C. Abbott Scrapbook, Abbott Memorial Collection, George J. Mitchell Department of Special Collections and Archives, Bowdoin College Library, Brunswick, Maine.

15. R. H. Fleming, "Rev. Jacob Abbott," in M1.6, volume 13, Scrapbook, Abbott Memorial Collection, Bowdoin.

16. William Randel, *Edward Eggleston* (New York: Twayne, 1963), 35.

17. "What Abraham Lincoln Said about the 'Makers of History,'" *McClure's Magazine* 21 October 1903, advertising insert, p. 24.

18. "Vintage Children's Living History Books: Understanding the Old-Fashioned Story Book Approach," Happy Hearts at Home Homeschooling and Frugal Living on One Income, http://happyheartsathome.blogspot.com.

19. "All Through the Ages Introduction: Using Literature to Teach History," Nothing New Press.

20. "History from Grandfather's Bookshelf: Why the Latest Is Not the Greatest," Heritage History.

21. Steven Mintz, *Huck's Raft: A History of American Childhood* (Cambridge: Harvard University Press, 2004), 78, 77.

22. The original family name was Abbot (with one *t*). Jacob added the second *t*, as did some of his brothers. Hence, Gorham is Gorham Abbot while John is John S. C. Abbott. See Christopher L. Nesmith, "Jacob Abbott," in *The American Renaissance in New England, Fourth Series,* ed. Wesley T. Mott, vol. 243 of the *Dictionary of Literary Biography* (Detroit: Gale Group, 2001), 8.

23. Mary Titcomb, "A Delightful Grand Father," *Intermediate Monthly: An Illustrated Magazine of Entertaining and Instructive Stories for Boys and Girls* 12 (1 October 1887): 23–52.

24. For more on this period, see Jacob Abbott, "A Lecture on Moral Education: Delivered in Boston Before the American Institute of Instruction, August 26, 1831," Pams. A132 Lect. 1831, Record ID# 222887, American Antiquarian Society, Worcester, Mass.

25. For details on this and other pedagogical theories considered by the Abbotts, see "Jacob Abbott's Writings—Mount Vernon School and Abbott's Institution—Contract," in M1.6, box 24, folder 5, Abbott Memorial Collection, Bowdoin. See also in the same collection the *Christian Union,* 7 August 1884, in M1.6, box 24, folder 6, "Jacob Abbott, Clippings," Abbott Memorial Collection, Bowdoin.

26. Jacob Abbott, "The Teacher; or Moral Influences Employed in the Instruction and Government of the Young; intended chiefly to assist young teachers in organizing and conducting their schools" (Boston: William Pierce, No. 9 Cornhill, 1834), as collected at G351 A132 T834, Record ID# 22905, American Antiquarian Society; See also John S. C. Abbott, "The School-Boy; or, A Guide for Youth to Truth and Duty" (Boston: Crocker and Brewster, 1849), CL A135 S372 1849, Record ID# 213573, American Antiquarian Society.

27. See Jacob Abbott, "A Description of the Mount Vernon School in 1832, Being a Brief Account of the Internal Arrangements and Plans of the Institution" (Boston: Peirce and Parker [1832]), iii–iv.

28. Mintz, *Huck's Raft,* 174.

29. Johann Heinrich Pestalozzi, *How Gertrude Teaches Her Children: an attempt to help mothers to teach their own children and an account of the method, by Johann Heinrich Pestalozzi,* trans. Lucy E. Holland and Francis C. Turner, edited with introduction and notes by Ebenezer Cooke (London: G. Allen and Unwin; Syracuse: C. W. Bardeen [1915]).

30. John Manning, "Charles Dickens and the Oswego System," *Journal of the History of Ideas* 18, no. 4 (October 1957): 580. See also "Vocational Normal School for Training Primary School Teachers, being 'Lessons on Education,' from the Syllabus of Students in Training at the Home and Colonial School Society,'" *American Journal of Education* 23 (December 1860): 449–66, as cited by Manning, "Charles Dickens and the Oswego System," 581.

31. "College Journal," Amherst College, [1825], M1.6, box 24, folder 11, Abbott Memorial Collection, Bowdoin.

32. See Jacob Abbott, "Harlie's Letter; or, How to Learn with Little Teaching" (New York: Sheldon, 1863), CL A132 H2855h 1863, Record ID# 213298, American Antiquarian Society.

33. Lyman Abbott, "Jacob Abbott, Friend of Children," in *Silhouettes of My Contemporaries* (Garden City: Doubleday, Page, 1921), 333.

34. Robert McCole Wilson, "Teaching Reading—a History," www.zona-pellucida.com.

35. Abbott, "A Description of Mount Vernon School," iv–vi, 27.

36. Ibid., 27.

37. "The Cabinet of Nature for the Year: Containing Curious Particulars Characteristic of Each Month: Intended to Direct Young People to the Innocent and Agreeable Employment of Observing Nature" (New York: Printed and Sold by Samuel Wood and Sons, 1817), CL-Pam C115 N2851 1817, Record ID# 293655, American Antiquarian Society.

38. "Memorial Tablet to Jacob Abbott Dedicated," *Lewiston Evening Journal,* 14 August 1907, in "Jacob Abbott Clippings," M1.6, folder 6, Abbott Memorial Collection, Bowdoin College.

39. Lydia Maria Francis Child, *On the Management and Education of Children* (London: John W. Parker, West Strand, 1835), 87. For an application of these ideas to the works of the Abbotts, see Jacob Abbott, "The Little Learner. Learning about Common Things; or, Familiar instructions for children in respect to the objects around them, that attract their attention, and awaken their curiosity, in the earliest years of life" (New York: Harper and Brothers, 1857), CL A132 L779d 1857, Record ID# 213372, American Antiquarian Society.

40. Joseph M. Rice, *The Public School System of the United States* (1893), in *Turning Points in American Educational History,* ed. David B. Tyack (Waltham, Mass.: Blaisdell, 1967), 330, as cited in Mintz, *Huck's Raft,* 92.

41. Manning, "Charles Dickens and the Oswego System," 580.

42. For more on the Rollo and Lucy series, see Carl J. Weber, *A Bibliography of Jacob Abbott* (Waterville, Maine: Colby College Press, 1948), 33.

43. Abbott, *Rollo Learning to Read,* vi.

44. Daniel Hager, "Competition in Education: The Case of Reading; Only the Marketplace Can Determine the Best Pedagogy" 47, no. 4 (April 1997), as cited in www.thefreemanonline. org; Linnea C. Ehri, Simone R. Nunes, Steven A. Stahl, and Dale M. Willows, "Systematic Phonics Instruction Helps Students Learn to Read: Evidence from the National Reading Panel's Meta-Analysis," http://rer.sagepub.com.

45. Allan Luke, *Literacy, Textbooks, and Ideology: Postwar Literacy Instruction and the Mythology of Dick and Jane* (New York: Falmer Press, 1988), 2, 37. On literacy in the nineteenth century,

see Harvey J. Graff, *The Literacy Myth: Literacy and Social Structure in the Nineteenth-Century City* (New York: Academic Press, 1979).

46. Hager, "Competition in Education," www.thefreemanonline.org. Attacks on the sight/word method of teaching reading persisted into the twentieth century, especially in the research of Rudolph Flesch, who, in the 1950s, complained in *Why Johnny Can't Read* about the inability of students to "learn rules for decoding unknown words." Rudolph Flesch, *Why Johnny Still Can't Read* (New York: Harper Colophon Books, 1981), 4, 5, 65.

47. William Elliott Griffis, "Memorial: Charles Carleton Coffin" (Boston: Geo. H. Wright, 1896), 20.3.1 COF, Charles Carleton Coffin Collection, Congregational Library, Boston, 20.

48. Hager, "Competition in Education," [4], www.thefreemanonline.org.

49. Diane McGuinness, *Why Our Children Can't Read, and What We Can Do About It: A Scientific Revolution in Reading* (New York: Free Press, 1997), 50.

50. See, for instance, the instructional guidelines in *The Mount Vernon Reader: a course of reading lessons, selected with reference to their moral influence on the hearts and lives of the young; by Messrs. Abbott* (New York: Collins, Keese, 1837), CL M928 V539 1837, Record ID# 237064, American Antiquarian Society.

51. Bruce VanSledright, *In Search of America's Past: Learning to Read History in Elementary School* (New York: Teachers College Press, 2002), 8, 14; see esp., Larry Cuban, "Foreword," vii–viii, 7.

52. For a description of the Abbotts' School for Young Ladies in its infancy from the perspective of one of its faculty members, see *The Story of a Musical Life: An Autobiography by Geo. F. Root* (Cincinnati: John Church, 1891), 37. Root remarks, "Abbott's school for young ladies at that time was in one of the fine houses in the white marble row in Lafayette Place, New York, spacious and convenient beyond anything I had seen before. I found the work delightful."

53. *Abbot Memorial Book* (Poughkeepsie: Privately Printed, A. V. Haight, n.d.), 4–5.

54. "Address by Rev. Lyman Abbott," in Edward Abbott, "A Brief Memorial: of Gorham D. Abbot, Rebecca S., his wife, and Elizabeth R., their Daughter," (Cambridge, Mass.: Thomas Todd, printer, Congregational House, Boston, 1876), R A126 Abbo B876, Record ID# 415762, American Antiquarian Society. See also John S. C. Abbott and Jacob Abbott, *Abbotts' Institution for the Education of Young Ladies* (New York: Printed by S. W. Benedict, 1849), 3.

55. Also called Abbot Collegiate Institute for Young Ladies. See "Abbot Collegiate Institute for Young Ladies, New York, NY" (New York: Printed by S. W. Benedict, 1849); Schools Abbo, Record ID# 414937, American Antiquarian Society; "Collegiate Institution for the Education of Young Ladies; the Spingler Institute, Union Square," Schools Abbo, Record ID# 30342 (New York: Printed by John F. Trow, 1859–60), American Antiquarian Society; and "Institution of the Messrs. Abbott, for the Education of Young Ladies,: at 412 Houston Street, and the Mount Vernon School for Boys, at 54 Bleecker Street" (New York: Printed by Edward O. Jenkins, 1846), Schools Abbo, Record ID# 414936, American Antiquarian Society.

56. "Jacob Abbott," *Christian Union*, 7 August 1884, as collected in M1.6, box 24, folder 6, "Jacob Abbott, Clippings," Abbott Memorial Collection, Bowdoin. See also the notes on the diaries of two sisters, Matilda and Catherine Schermerhorn, who attended Spingler in 1850, in Jane Hanna Pease, "Boarding School, 1850 Style," *University of Rochester Library Bulletin* 10, no. 2 (Winter 1955): n.p. The notes indicate that Spingler cost five hundred dollars a year and that the price included "Board, Washing and Seat at Church."

57. "Letter book to JA—History Class—Abbott's School, New York, 1845," M1.6, box 24, vol. 11, Abbott Memorial Collection, Bowdoin.

58. Child, *On the Management and Education of Children*, 88.

59. "Letter book to JA—History Class—Abbott's School, New York, 1845, M1.6, box 24, vol. 11, Abbott Memorial Collection, Bowdoin.

60. *Abbot Memorial Book,* 43–44, 58.

61. Adaline T. Allen, "Diary, 1858–59, and class notes, 1856–57," MG 896, Allen, Adaline T. Papers, 1856–69, New Jersey Historical Society, Newark.

62. *Abbot Memorial Book,* 95–96.

63. VanSledright, *In Search of America's Past,* back cover.

64. Abigail Ann Hamblen, "The Abbott Series: Maine's Gift to Young Scholars," 61, as collected in M1.2, box B – Biographical Records, folder 61, Abbott Memorial Collection, Bowdoin College.

65. Mary Stovell Stimpson, "Farmington, Maine," *New England Magazine* 30, no. 4 (June 1904): 402, 397; and "Lyman Abbott Notebook," folder 9, M1.7, box 30, Abbott Memorial Collection, Bowdoin.

66. Jacob Abbott, *History of Alexander the Great* (New York: Harper and Brothers, 1854), vii–viii.

67. Jacob Abbott, *History of William the Conqueror* (New York: Harper, 1854), 93, 239.

68. Ibid., 122.

69. Stanley P. Chase and Robert Edmond Ham, "John S. C. Abbott," in *Dictionary of American Biography,* 20 vols. (New York: Charles Scribner's Sons, 1928): 1:23.

70. Jacob Abbott, *The Young Christian; or, A Familiar Illustration of the Principles of Christian Duty* (Edinburgh, Scotland: Waugh and Innes, 1835), 5.

71. Gillian Avery, *Behold the Child: American Children and Their Books, 1621–1922* (Baltimore: Johns Hopkins University Press, 1994), 98.

72. R. H. Fleming, "Rev. Jacob Abbott," in M1.6, vol. 13, Scrapbook, Abbott Memorial Collection, Bowdoin.

73. *Lutheran Observer,* 21 November 1879, M1.6, vol. 13, Scrapbook, Abbott Memorial Collection, Bowdoin.

74. Abbott, *William the Conqueror,* preface n.p.

75. John S. C. Abbott, *History of Louis Philippe, King of the French* (New York: Harper and Brothers, 1871), viii.

76. Jacob Abbott, *History of King Richard the First of England* (New York: Harper and Brothers, 1857), vii–viii.

77. Jacob Abbott, *History of Pyrrhus* (New York: Harper and Brothers, 1854), v–vi.

78. Gorham Abbot helped found the American Society for the Diffusion of Useful Knowledge to combat these problems; see "The American Society for the Diffusion of Useful Knowledge: Incorporated May 16, 1837. Prospectus of the American Library for Schools and Families" (New York: Published by the Committee, 1837), NatIn S678 Amer 1837a, Record ID# 223634, American Antiquarian Society.

79. Jacob Abbott, *History of Cyrus the Great* (New York: Harper and Brothers [1850]), vi.

80. Jacob Abbott, *History of Nero* (New York: Harper, 1854), [iii].

81. John S. C. Abbott, *History of King Philip* (New York, Harper and Brothers, 1857), back pages, 4.

82. Leslie Howsam, "Sustained Literary Ventures: The Series in Victorian Book Publishing," *Publishing History* 32 (1992): 5.

83. Leslie Howsam, *Past into Print: The Publishing of History in Britain, 1850–1950* (Toronto: University of Toronto Press, 2000), 61.

84. Rowland Lorimer, "The Business of Literacy: The Making of the Educational Textbook," in *Literacy, Society and Schooling,* ed. S. de Castell, A. Luke, and K. Egan (Cambridge: Cambridge University Press, 1986), 36, as cited in Luke, *Literacy, Textbooks, and Ideology,* 70–71.

85. *Publisher's Circular,* September 1884, as cited in Howsam, "Sustained Literary Ventures," 5.

86. Luke, *Literacy, Textbooks, and Ideology,* 67, 116, 77.

87. For more on these advertising strategies, see Richard D. Altick, "From Aldire to Everyman: Cheap Reprint Series of the English Classics from 1830–1906," *Studies in Bibliography* (1958): 3–24.

88. Abbott, *William the Conqueror,* 16.

89. Jacob Abbott, *History of Genghis Khan* (New York: Harper and Brothers, 1860), 308, 335.

90. Hamblen, "The Abbott Series: Maine's Gift to Young Scholars," 63.

91. Abbott, *History of Genghis Khan,* 24.

92. Hamblen, "The Abbott Series: Maine's Gift to Young Scholars," 62.

93. John S. C. Abbott, *History of Madame Roland* (New York: Harper and Brothers, 1850), 291.

94. "Women in History—History Curriculum Homeschool," Heritage History.

95. *New York Tribune,* 18 June 1877, in M1.2 Folio, vol. 16, John S. C. Abbott Scrapbook, Abbott Memorial Collection, Bowdoin.

96. *Christian Leader,* 23 June [1877], in M1.2 Folio, vol. 16, John S. C. Abbott Scrapbook, Abbott Memorial Collection, Bowdoin.

97. Gorham D. Gilman to Julius A. Ward, 27 May 1896, Mss. Misc. boxes A, Record ID# 271112, American Antiquarian Society.

98. Here Abbott references the six-volume edition of his *Napoleon Bonaparte [His Complete Life] and the Story of the French Revolution* (New York: Harper and Brothers, n.d.), which includes two volumes on the French Revolution. See "Review of John S. C. Abbott's Works, #15," in M1.2 Folio, vol. 16, John S. C. Abbott Scrapbook, Abbott Memorial Collection, Bowdoin.

99. John S. C. Abbott, *The History of Napoleon Bonaparte,* 4 vols. (New York: Harper and Brothers, 1883), 1:iv.

100. John S. C. Abbott, *History of Josephine* (New York: Harper and Brothers, 1870), 298–99.

101. Abbott, *The History of Napoleon Bonaparte,* 1:19, 2:306, 310, 1:v.

102. John S. C. Abbott, *The History of Queen Hortense* (New York: Harper and Brothers, 1870), 877.

103. Rev. Horatio O. Ladd, *A Memorial of John S. C. Abbott, D. D.* (Boston: A. Williams, 1878), 28.

104. *Christian Leader,* 27 June [1877], in M1.2 Folio, vol. 16, John S. C. Abbott Scrapbook, Abbott Memorial Collection, Bowdoin.

105. Lyman Abbott, "John S. C. Abbott," *Christian Union,* 27 June [1877], in M1.2 Folio, vol. 16. John S. C. Abbott Scrapbook, Abbott Memorial Collection, Bowdoin.

106. Edward Abbott, "The Writings of John S. C. Abbott," *Christian Science Mirror,* 15 September 1877, in M1.2 folio vol. 16, John S. C. Abbott Scrapbook, Abbott Memorial Collection, Bowdoin.

107. Gorham D. Gilman to Julius A. Ward, 27 May 1896, in the John S. C. Abbott Letters, 1833–67, Mss. Misc, box A, folder 1, American Antiquarian Society.

108. E[dwin]. S. G[odkin]. "Literary Topics: Abbott's Napoleon: The Man of War as Viewed by the Man of Peace," *New York Evening Post,* as found in M1.2 Folio vol. 16, John S. C. Abbott Scrapbook, Abbott Memorial Collection, Bowdoin.

109. *Universalist,* 30 June 1877, in M1.2 Folio, vol. 16, John S. C. Abbott Scrapbook, Abbott Memorial Collection, Bowdoin.

110. Elbert Hubbard, *Little Journeys to the Homes of Eminent Artists* (New York: G. P. Putnam's Sons, 1907), 171.

111. *The Jewell* (Liberty, Missouri) 3, no. 1 in M1.2 Folio, vol. 16, John S. C. Abbott Scrapbook, Abbott Memorial Collection, Bowdoin.

112. William Henry Fry, ["Review of John S. C. Abbott's History of Napoleon Bonaparte"], 15 February 1856, *New-York Daily Tribune*, 5–10.

113. Ibid.

114. "Literary Gossip," *Criterion; Art, Science and Literature*, 23 February 1856, 266.

115. Edward Abbott, "The Writings of John S. C. Abbott," *Christian Science Mirror*, 15 September 1877, in M1.2 Folio, vol. 16, John S. C. Abbott Scrapbook, Abbott Memorial Collection, Bowdoin.

116. "The Editor's Waste Basket," *Literary World* 26, no. 19 (7 September 1895).

117. "John S. C. Abbott: A Visit to the Bedside of the Most Prolific of American Authors," *New York World*, 26 February 1877, as collected in M1.6, vol. 13, Scrapbook, Abbott Memorial Collection, Bowdoin.

118. Nathaniel Hawthorne to Samuel Colman, 27 September 1843, Berg Collection, New York Public Library, as cited in Daniel Roselle, *Samuel Goodrich: Creator of Peter Parley* (Albany: State University of New York Press, 1968), 125.

119. Algernon Tassin, "Mrs. Child; *Youth's Companion*; Goodrich; Jacob Abbott," in *The Cambridge History of English and American Literature: An Encyclopedia in Eighteen Volumes*, ed. A. W. Ward, A. R. Waller, W. P. Trent, J. Erskine, S. P. Sherman, and C. Van Doren (New York: G. P. Putnam's Sons, 1907–21), 3:173.

120. Abbott, "Jacob Abbott, Friend of Children," *Silhouettes of My Contemporaries*, 359.

121. See Stimpson, "Farmington, Maine," 402; for fundraising materials, see also M1.7, box 30, Lyman Abbott Notebook, folder 9, Abbott Memorial Collection, Bowdoin.

122. See Janice Durrell, "National Register of Historic Places Includes Noted Author's Former Home," manuscript, Colby College Archives, Waterville, Maine.

123. Fletcher Osgood, "Jacob Abbott, A Neglected New England Author," in *New England Magazine* 30 (March 1904–August 1904): 472.

124. For a depiction of John S. C. Abbott's final days, see "Description of John S. C. Abbott's House at Fair Haven, Conn.," 27 March, [1877], in M1.2 Folio, vol. 16, John S. C. Abbott Scrapbook, Abbott Memorial Collection, Bowdoin. See also John S. C. Abbott, "Letter from John S. C. Abbott: A Parting Message to a Chance Traveling Acquaintance—His Severe Illness," 11 March 1877, *New York Times*.

125. *New York Tribune*, 18 June 1877, in M1.2 Folio, vol. 16, John S. C. Abbott Scrapbook, Abbott Memorial Collection, Bowdoin.

126. *Methodist*, 30 June 1877, in M1.2 Folio, vol. 16, John S. C. Abbott Scrapbook, Abbott Memorial Collection, Bowdoin.

127. Edward Abbott, "The Writings of John S. C. Abbott," *Christian Science Mirror*, 15 September 1877, in M1.2 Folio, vol. 16, John S. C. Abbott Scrapbook, Abbott Memorial Collection, Bowdoin.

128. "History from Grandfather's Bookshelf: Why the Latest Is Not the Greatest," Heritage History.

129. Christine Miller is an exception to this rule, as she advocates teaching history through literature. See All Through the Ages as described in "Classical Christian Home Schooling," www.classical-homeschooling.org.

130. See John S. C. Abbott, *Napoleon Bonaparte* (Dodo Press, e-Book, 2006), 42–46. See also Henry Mills Alden, "The Church of the Cup of Cold Water," *Harper's New Monthly Magazine* 5, no. 25 (June 1852): 35–37; and Jacob Abbott, "Memoirs of the Holy Land," *Harper's New Monthly Magazine*, 5, no. 27 (August 1852): 304–5.

131. "Heritage Electronic Books," Heritage History.

132. Shakeel Rai, "Dodo Press or why you might give E-Readers a second chance," Open Source Living, http://opensource-living.blogspot.com.

133. "e-Book Conversions," ReadHowYouWant, www.readhowyouwant.com.

134. Carl Becker, "Everyman His Own Historian," in *Everyman His Own Historian* (New York, 1935), 233–55.

135. Osgood, "Jacob Abbott," 473.

3. Gendered History

1. Ann Curthoys and John Docker, *Is History Fiction?* (Ann Arbor: University of Michigan Press, 2005), 6.

2. "Biography: Richard 'Little Bear' Wheeler," Mantle Ministries Website, www.mantleministries.com. The "About the Author" segment of Richard Wheeler's *Warning! Public Schools Aren't for Christians!* (Bulverde, Tex.: Mantle Ministries Press, n.d.) notes that Little Bear (a nickname derived from a frontier moniker given to Wheeler by the Royal Rangers, a "worldwide Christian ministry") received "music and theater arts training at the Los Angeles Metropolitan Civic Light Opera."

3. Josephine Pollard, *A Child's History of America Told in One-Syllable Words* (Bulverde, Tex.: Mantle Ministries Press, 1998); *A Child's History of the Life of Christopher Columbus Told in One-Syllable Words* (Bulverde, Tex.: Mantle Ministries Press, 2000); *A Child's History of the Life of George Washington Told in One-Syllable Words* (Bulverde, Tex.: Mantle Ministries Press, 1998); *A Child's History of Our Naval Heros* [sic] *Told in One-Syllable Words* (Bulverde, Tex.: Mantle Ministries Press, no date). For more on Wheeler's "Living-History" reenactment camps, see Richard "Little Bear" Wheeler, *Confessions of a Former Retarded Gopher Skinner, The Old Schoolhouse: The Magazine for Homeschool Families* (Summer 2004).

4. Book synopsis on back cover of Wheeler's version of *A Child's History of the Life of Christopher Columbus.*

5. Wheeler, "About the Author," *Warning! Public Schools Aren't for Christians!,* [p. 54].

6. "Homeschooling Mommies," www.homeschoolauctions.com.

7. See "Warning! Public Schools Aren't for Christians! A Biblical Perspective on the Dangers of Public Schools," and audio CD that "exposes the dangers of current government education in America from a biblical perspective." Mantle Ministries Website, www.mantleministries.com.

8. Wheeler, *Warning! Public Schools Aren't for Christians!,* [6–7].

9. Christopher Klicka, *Home School Heroes: The Struggle and Triumph of Home Schooling in America* (Nashville: Broadman and Holman, 2006).

10. Book synopsis on back cover of Pollard, *A Child's History of America Told in One-Syllable Words.*

11. Advertising "Summary," CARE Books, www.carebooksandmore.com.

12. Helen W[all]. Pierson, *History of Germany in Words of One Syllable* (New York: George Routledge and Sons, 1884), 139.

13. Caryl Rivers and Rosalind C. Barnett, "The Difference Myth: We Shouldn't Believe the Increasingly Popular Claims That Boys and Girls Think Differently, Learn Differently, and Need to Be Treated Differently," *Boston Globe online,* www.boston.com.

14. Josephine Pollard, *The History of Battles of America in Words of One Syllable* (New York: George Routledge and Sons, 1889), 2–3.

15. Josephine Pollard, "Prefatory," *Our Hero: General U. S. Grant: When, Where, and How He Fought* (New York: McLoughlin Brothers, 1885), [1].

16. Lydia Child, *The History and Condition of Women, in Various Ages and Nations,* 2 vols. (Bos-

ton: John Allen, 1835), 2:210–11, as cited in Nina Baym, *American Women Writers and the Work of History, 1790–1860* (New Brunswick, N.J.: Rutgers University Press, 1995), 227.

17. Steven Mintz, *Huck's Raft: A History of American Childhood* (Cambridge: Harvard University Press, 2004), 82. See also Annette Atkins, *We Grew Up Together: Brothers and Sisters in Nineteenth-Century America* (Urbana: University of Illinois Press, 1995), 11.

18. Leonard Sax, *Why Gender Matters: What Parents and Teachers Need to Know about the Emerging Science of Sex Differences* (New York: Three Rivers Press, 2006).

19. Rivers and Barnett, "The Difference Myth."

20. Richard "Little Bear" Wheeler, "Confessions of a Former Retarded Gopher Skinner," *The Old Schoolhouse* (Summer 2004), as cited on the Mantle Ministries website, http://mantleministries.com.

21. Wheeler, *Warning! Public Schools Aren't for Christians!*, 42–43.

22. For more on how children absorb and retain historical material, see James W. Loewen, *Teaching What Really Happened: How to Avoid the Tyranny of Textbooks and Get Students Excited About Doing History* (New York: Teachers College, Columbia University, 2010), 10–18.

23. Bruce VanSledright, *In Search of America's Past: Learning to Read History in Elementary School* (New York: Teachers College Press, 2002), vii–viii.

24. "Boys' Brains vs. Girls' Brains: What Sex Segregation Teaches Students," ACLU Women's Rights Project, 19 May 2008 as cited in www.aclu.org.

25. Mintz, *Huck's Raft,* 152–54.

26. See Jacob A. Riis, *How the Other Half Lives* (New York: Charles Scribner's Sons, 1890); also George C. Needham, *The Child-Mother: Street Arabs and Gutter Snipes; The Pathetic and Humorous Side of Young Vagabond Life in the Great Cities, with Records of Work for Their Reclamation* (Boston: D. L. Guernsey, 1884).

27. Mintz, *Huck's Raft,* 161.

28. Ibid., 164.

29. Catherine Beecher, "The American People Starved and Posisoned," *Harper's New Monthly Magazine* 32 (December 1865–May 1866): 772.

30. Gail Schmunk Murray, *American Children's Literature and the Construction of Childhood* (New York: Twayne, 1998), 96.

31. "Introduction," Baldwin Library Collection of Historical Children's Literature, 1850–1869, Special and Area Studies Collections, Smathers Libraries, University of Florida, [viii], http://microformguides.gale.com.

32. Anthony Comstock, *Traps for the Young* (1883; reprint, Cambridge: Harvard University Press, 1967), 20, 32–33.

33. For more on Comstock's crusade as it applies to popular historians, see Gregory M. Pfitzer, *Popular History and the Literary Marketplace, 1840–1920* (Amherst: University of Massachusetts Press, 2008), 230–39.

34. Lydia Sigourney, *Evening Readings in History: The History of Assyria, Egypt, Tyre, Syria, Persia, and the Sacred Scriptures; With Questions Arranged for the Use of the Young, and of Family Circles* (Springfield, Mass.: G. and C. Merriam, 1833), as cited in Baym, *American Women Writers and the Work of History,* 34.

35. Mantle Ministries website, www.mantleministries.com. The full title of the work is *Young Folks' Stories of American History and Home Life,* ed. "Pansy" (San Antonio: Mantle Ministries, 1990; reprint of original 1886 publication).

36. See *Memoirs, Miscellanies and Letters of Lucy Aikin* (London: Longman, Green, Longman, Roberts, and Green, 1864); also Linda J. Turzynski, "Lucy Aikin," *Dictionary of Literary Biography: British Children's Writers, 1800–1880* (Detroit: Gale Research, 1996), 163:3.

37. Mary Godolphin, *The Pilgrim's Progress, In Words of One Syllable* (New York: McLoughlin Brothers, 1884).

38. Amy Weinstein, *Once Upon a Time: Illustrations from Fairytales, Fables, Primers, Pop-Ups, and Other Children's Books* (New York: Princeton Architectural Press, 2005), 115.

39. Godolphin, *Pilgrim's Progress*, iii–iv.

40. Gillian Furlong, comp. *The Archives of Routledge & Kegan Paul Ltd., 1853–1973* (London: University College Library, 1978).

41. James J. Barnes and Patience P. Barnes, "George Routledge and Sons," in *British Literary Publishing Houses, 1820–1880*, in *Dictionary of Literary Biography*, ed. Patricia J. Anderson and Jonathan Rose (Detroit: A Bruccoli Clark Layman Book, 1991), 106:262.

42. "Notes" from the archivist of the Routledge papers, Furlong, *The Archives of Routledge & Kegan Paul Ltd.*, n. p.; see also Norman Franklin, *150 Years of British Publishing: Routledge & Kegan Paul* (London: Routledge and Kegan Paul, 1985).

43. Aileen Fyfe, "Copyrights and Competition: Producing and Protecting Children's Books in the Nineteenth Century," *Publishing History* 45, *The Critic* (1999), 50.

44. For more on the details of copyright laws and how they affected publishers such as Routledge, see Barnes and Barnes, "George Routledge and Sons," 262.

45. Fyfe, "Copyrights and Competition," 41.

46. Ibid., 35.

47. Advertisement on the end pages of Helen Ainslie Smith, *History of Japan in Words of One Syllable* (New York: George Routledge and Sons, 1887), [211–12].

48. See "Publication Books," Furlong, comp., *The Archives of Routledge & Kegan Paul*, 340, 377.

49. Helen A. Smith to F. A. Adams, 29 February 1888, box 1, folder 1, Helen Ainslie Smith Papers, 1875–95, Roger and Julie Baskes, Department of Special Collections, Newberry Library, Chicago.

50. H. A. Smith to F. A. Adams, 20 December 1886, box 1, folder 1, Helen Ainslie Smith Papers, 1875–95, Newberry Library. For more on Smith's background, see "Family History," box 2 in the same collection. In writing *History of Russia in Words of One Syllable* (New York: George Routledge and Sons, 1887), Smith drew heavily on Alfred Nicolas Rambaud, *The History of Russia from the Earliest Times to 1877*, trans. Leonora B. Lang (New York: John B. Alden, 1886). For a discussion of Smith's reliance on this work, see H. A. Smith to F. A. Adams, 12 January 1887, box 1, folder 1, Helen Ainslie Smith Papers, 1875–95, Newberry Library.

51. See, for instance, Virginia Conser Shaffer, *How to Remember History. A method of memorizing dates, with a summary of the most important events of the sixteenth, seventeenth, eighteenth and nineteenth centuries* (Philadelphia, J. B. Lippincott, 1890).

52. Helen W[all]. Pierson, *History of the United States in Words of One Syllable* (New York: George Routledge and Sons, 1884), 17.

53. Smith, *History of Japan*, 10, 38.

54. "Historians in One Word," *The Critic* 3, no. 207 (17 December 1887): 14.

55. For more on these various publishers, see Cary Sternick, *A Bibliography of 19th Century Children's Series Books, with Price Guide* (2003), [note 957].

56. George E. Tylutki, "A. L. Burt Company," in *American Literary Publishing Houses, 1638–1899, Part 1: A–M, Dictionary of Literary Biography*, ed. Peter Dzwonkoski (Detroit: A Bruccoli Clark Book, 1986), 49:68.

57. "Introduction," Baldwin Library Collection of Historical Children's Literature, 1850–69, [x].

58. Pollard, "Prefatory," *Our Hero Grant*, [1]. For more on the McLoughlin Brothers Publish-

ers, see "John McLoughlin," [obituary], *Publishers Weekly* 67 (6 May 1905): 1286–87; "McLoughlin's 125 Years," *Publishers Weekly* 163 (14 March 1953): 1290–92.

59. Theodore Mills, "McLoughlin Brothers," in *Dictionary of Literary Biography*, ed. Peter Dzwonkoski (Detroit: Bruccoli Clark Book, 1986), 49:301. For more on these illustrated works, see "Drawings, Proofs, and Print Samples Identified by Illustrator, Title, or Subject, 1858–(1880–1900)–1920," 19 oversize boxes, 7 manuscript boxes, 2 double oversize boxes in "McLoughlin Brothers Archival Drawings and Prints," American Antiquarian Society. See also Laura Wasowicz, "Brief History of McLoughlin Bros.," in Wasowicz, "Box List of McLoughlin Bros. Archival Drawings and Proofs Held at the American Antiquarian Society" (unpublished checklist, 1999) and the McLoughlin Brothers Papers in the De Grummond Collection of the University of Southern Mississippi Library.

60. See for instance, "75 Cent Books; One Syllable series, No. 744.—History of the United States—Half Bound," Catalogue of McLoughlin Brothers, 19.

61. Ira R. Snyder, curator, "World of the Child: Two Hundred Years of Children's Books," Special Collections Department, Hugh M. Morris Library, University of Delaware, Newark, Delaware, www.lib.udel.edu.

62. Ruth McGurk, "Early Children's Books: The Fox Collection at San Francisco Public Library," http://sfpl.lib.ca.us, [3].

63. Pierson, *History of the United States,* 10.

64. Pollard, *The History of the United States,* 13.

65. Godolphin, *Pilgrim's Progress,* iii–iv.

66. Jacob Abbott, *Rollo Learning to Read* (Boston: Thomas H. Webb, 1835), v–vi.

67. Annie Cole Cady, *The American Continent and Its Inhabitants before its Discovery by Columbus: A Unique History Communicated by Robin Goodfellow, Fairy Historian and Written by Annie Cole Cady (illustrated by Henry Cady and Others)* (Philadelphia: Gebbie, 1893).

68. Harry Thurston, *Bookman* (December 1896), as cited in Peter Hunt, "Retreatism and Advance, 1914–1945," in *Children's Literature: An Illustrated History,* ed. Peter Hunt (New York: Oxford University Press, 1995), 229.

69. Gillian Avery, *Behold the Child: American Children and Their Books, 1621–1922* (Baltimore: Johns Hopkins University Press, 1994), 125.

70. *New York School Journal,* advertisement at the end of Pierson, *History of the United States,* [190].

71. *The New York Journal of Education,* advertisement at the end of Pierson, *History of the United States,* [190].

72. M. Louise Comstock, endorsements at the end of Helen W[all]. Pierson, *History of England in Words of One Syllable* (New York: George Routledge and Sons, 1884), [225].

73. H. A. Smith to F. A. Adams, 20 December 1886, box 1, folder 1, Helen Ainslie Smith Papers, 1875–95, Newberry Library, Chicago.

74. "Catalogue of the McLoughlin Brothers, 1886," 19.

75. *Putnam's Magazine* 2 (December 1868): 760, as cited in Leonard S. Marcus, *Minders of Make-Believe: Idealists, Entrepreneurs, and the Shaping of American Children's Literature* (Boston: Houghton Mifflin, 2008), 34.

76. For more on women historians in the nineteenth century, see Natalie Zemon Davis, "Gender and Genre, Women as Historical Writers, 1400–1820," in *Beyond Their Sex: Learned Women of the European Past,* ed. P. Latialme (New York: New York University Press, 1980): 153–82; see also B. G. Smith, *The Gender of History: Men, Women, and Historical Practice* (Cambridge: Harvard University Press, 1986).

77. Mintz, *Huck's Raft*, 54.

78. "Books for Children," *American Annals of Education* (1828): 100.

79. Lydia Sigourney, *History of Marcus Aurelius* (Hartford: Oliver D. Cooke and Sons, 1834), as cited in Baym, *American Women Writers and the Work of History*, 34; see also 35, 38–39.

80. Ella Hine Stratton, *Child's History of Our Great Country* (Philadelphia: National Publishing, 1902), 132. Stratton also wrote more adventuresome works, including *Our Jolly Trip Around the World with the Captain Parker, or, The Lucky Thirteen and Their Long Voyage of Discovery in Search of Knowledge* (Philadelphia: National Publishing, 1902).

81. Baym, *American Women Writers and the Work of History*, 35, 43.

82. Leslie Howsam, *Past into Print: The Publishing of History in Britain, 1850–1950* (London: British Library, 2009), 3.

83. Charlotte M. Yonge, *Aunt Charlotte's Stories of Bible History for Young Disciples* (W. E. Scull, 1909), 11.

84. Lucy Lombardi Barber, *A Nursery History of the United States* (New York: Frederick A. Stokes, 1916).

85. "Girl History vs. Boy History," Heritage History, www.heritage-history.com.

86. Kate Dickinson Sweetser, *Ten Boys from History* (New York: Duffield, 1910); *Ten Girls from History* (New York: Duffield, 1912).

87. Charles Dickens, *The Boys of Dickens Retold* (New York: McLoughlin Brothers, [n.d.]).

88. Howsam, *Past into Print*, 10–11.

89. Ibid., 20.

90. Julie Des Jardins, *Women and the Historical Enterprise in America: Gender, Race, and the Politics of Memory, 1880–1945* (Chapel Hill: University of North Carolina Press, 2003), 9.

91. Annie Cole Cady, *The History of Pennsylvania in Words of One Syllable* (New York: Belford, Clarke, 1889), 229–30.

92. Josephine Pollard, *Our Naval Heroes Told in One Syllable Words* (New York: McLoughlin Brothers, 1896), 6–7, [1], 7–8; 41.

93. Pollard, *Life of Washington*, 7.

94. Pfitzer, *Popular History and the Literary Marketplace*, 204.

95. On Pollard and her literary range, see "Josephine Pollard," in *Appleton's Cyclopaedia of American Biography*, ed. James Grant Wilson, John Fiske, and Stanley L. Klos, 6 vols. (New York: D. Appleton, 1887–1889), 5:59.

96. Frances E. Willard and Mary A. Livermore, eds., *A Woman of the Century: Fourteen Hundred-Seventy Biographical Sketches Accompanied by Portraits of Leading American Women in All Walks of Life* (Buffalo: Charles Wells Moulton, 1893), 578. On the architect Calvin Pollard, Josephine's father, see "Guide to the Calvin Pollard Architectural Drawing Collection, 1834–1852, undated)," PR 051, New York Historical Society, New York.

97. For more on Don Alonzo Pollard and the 7th Regiment, see "7th Regiment New York State Militia New York National Guard," New York State Military Museum and Veterans Research Center, Saratoga Springs, New York, http://72.14.104.

98. Josephine Pollard to My Dearest Brother, 3 August 1862, Sec. A, box 106, Josephine Pollard Papers, 1862–97, David M. Rubenstein Rare Book and Manuscript Library, Duke University. Pollard made the acquaintance of a neighbor, Horatio Oliver Ladd, who became the son-in-law of John S. C. Abbott, who had also moved to Connecticut during the war, and she claimed to have heard the Abbotts speak frequently of the family. See Josephine Pollard to My Dearest Brother, 14 June 1862, Josephine Pollard Papers, Duke University.

99. Josephine Pollard to Marcus Benjamin, 8 February 1888, SIA RU007085, Marcus Ben-

jamin Papers, 1886–1929, Smithsonian Institution Archives, Washington; see also Josephine Pollard to My Darling Brother, 21 June 1862, Josephine Pollard Papers, Duke University.

100. See "Chautauqua Beginnings: Early Images from the Chautauqua Institution," at http://xroadsvirgina.edu.

101. "Literature," in *The National Sunday School Teacher; Chicago Sunday School Union* 10 (1875): 42.

102. William Bok, "Historic Memories: Men and Women of National Renown Who Once Lived in Patchogue and Its Environs," *Patchogue Advance* 45 (10 August 1900): 1.

103. Josephine Pollard to Dear Sir, 14 October 1890, McClure Mss IV, 1884–1922, MC 1690, Lilly Library Manuscript Collections, Indiana University, Bloomington. On McClure's correspondence with other female writers, see the McClure Publishing Company Archives, Special Collections Department, University of Delaware Library, Newark, Delaware.

104. H. A. Smith to F. A. Adams, 20 June 1887, box 1, folder 1, Helen Ainslie Smith Papers, 1875–95, Newberry Library.

105. Des Jardins, *Women and the Historical Enterprise in America,* 7–9.

106. Howsam, *Past into Print,* 123.

107. Rosemary Mitchell, "'The Busy Daughters of Clio': Women Writers of History from 1820 to 1880," *Women's History Review* 711 (1998): 123, 115, 119.

108. In 1847 Adams took charge of the Young Ladies Seminary and Boarding School in Orange, New Jersey, where Smith was a student. For more on Adams, see "Obituary," 14 April 1888, *Orange Journal.* See also F. A. Adams to Rev. Dr. [William A.] Ward, 28 March 1883, box 1, folder 1, Helen Ainslie Smith Papers, 1875–95, Newberry Library.

109. H. A. Smith to F. A. Adams, 23 November 1886, box 1, folder 1, Helen Ainslie Smith Papers, 1875–95, Newberry Library.

110. H. A. Smith to F. A. Adams, 14 February 1888, box 1, folder 1, Helen Ainslie Smith Papers, 1875–95, Newberry Library.

111. F. A. Adams to H. A. Smith, 15 January 1887, box 1, folder 1, Helen Ainslie Smith Papers, 1875–95, Newberry Library.

112. F. A. Adams to H. A. Smith, 12 November [1886], box 1, folder 1, Helen Ainslie Smith Papers, 1875–95, Newberry Library.

113. H. A. Smith to F. A. Adams, 25 August 1887, box 1, folder 1, Helen Ainslie Smith Papers, 1875–95, Newberry Library.

114. F. A. Adams to H. A. Smith, 20 June 1887, box 1, folder 1, Helen Ainslie Smith Papers, 1875–95, Newberry Library.

115. Pierson, *History of the United States,* 118. Henry Clay died on 29 June 1852 and Daniel Webster on 24 October 1852. See also Helen Wall Pierson, *Lives of the Presidents* (New York: G. Routledge and Sons [c1885]), 102.

116. Annie Cole Cady, *The History of Ohio in Words of One Syllable* (New York: Belford, Clarke, 1888), 24.

117. Pollard, *The History of the United States,* 55.

118. Pierson, *History of England,* 148, 16.

119. Cady, *History of Pennsylvania,* 13.

120. Pierson, *Lives of the Presidents,* 17.

121. "Colonel George Washington—General Braddock—Fort Necessity," http://webcache.googleusercontent.com.

122. Pierson, *Lives of the Presidents,* 58, 70, 121.

123. John Greenleaf Whittier, "Brown of Osawatomie," as cited in James C. Malin, "The

John Brown Legend in Pictures, Kissing the Negro Baby," *Kansas Historical Quarterly* 9, no. 4 (November 1940): 339–41.

124. Benson Lossing, *The Pictorial Field-book of the Revolution; or, illustrations, by pen and pencil, of the history, biography, scenery, relics, and traditions of the war for independence,* 2 vols. (New York: Harper and Brothers, 1851–52). For a discussion of Lossing's project, see Gregory M. Pfitzer, *Picturing the Past: Illustrated Histories and the American Historical Imagination* (Washington: Smithsonian Institution Press, 2002), 45–61.

125. "America's Wars Fact Sheet," United States Department of Veterans' Affairs, www.va.gov.

126. Pierson, *History of the United States,* 46.

127. Stratton, *Child's History of Our Great Country,* 5, 18, 53.

128. Josephine Pollard, *History of the New Testament in Words of One Syllable* (New York: George Routledge and Sons, 1882), [5]. See also Josephine Pollard, *History of the Old Testament in Words of One Syllable* (New York: George Routledge and Sons, 1882).

129. Helen W[all]. Pierson, *The Gospel Story in Easy Words for Children* (New York: McLoughlin Brothers, n.d.).

130. Pierson, *History of the United States,* 86.

131. Helen W[all]. Pierson, *Life and Battles of Napoleon Bonaparte in Words of One Syllable* (New York: McLoughlin Brothers, 1887), 48, 108.

132. Pierson, *Lives of the Presidents,* [5].

133. Pierson, "Prefatory," *Life and Battles of Napoleon Bonaparte,* [1].

134. "Collecting Children's Books: Monosyllabic Monographs of Antediluvian Yesteryears," http://collectingchildrensbook.blogspot.com.

135. Cady, *History of Pennsylvania,* 97.

136. Pierson, *History of the United States,* 80, 39.

137. Pierson, *History of the United States,* 101.

138. Cady, *History of Pennsylvania,* 181.

139. Pollard, *The Life of Christopher Columbus,* 62.

140. Pollard, *Life of Washington,* 47.

141. Sadlier, *History of Ireland,* 144.

142. Bruce VanSledright, "And Santayana Lives On: Students' Views on the Purposes for Studying History," *Journal of Curriculum Studies* 29, no. 5 (1997): 529.

143. Salesman's dummy, Stratton, *Lives of Our Presidents,* ii.

144. Pollard to Dear Sir, 14 October 1890, McClure MSS IV LMC 1690, Lilly Library.

145. Susan Higginbotham, "Short Post Re: Short Words in a Long Book," *Reading, Raving and Ranting by a Historical Fiction Writer: April 2006* in http://72.14.205.104/ at susanhigginbotham.blogspot.com/2.

146. "An Interview with Audrey Geisel," www.readingrockets.org. See also Ruth K. MacDonald, "The Beginnings of the Empire: *The Cat in the Hat* and Its Legacy," in *Dr. Seuss* (New York: Twayne Publishers, 1988), 105–46.

147. "Basal Reader," www.answers.com.

148. See Dave Blum, "In Praise of Small Words," in *Floating off the Page: The Best Stories from the Wall Street Journal Middle Column,* ed. Ken Wells (New York: A Wall Street Journal Book, 2002), 254–56.

149. Wheeler, *Warning! Public Schools Aren't for Christians!,* 18.

150. Back cover synopsis, Pollard, *A Child's History of America.*

151. Wheeler, *Warning! Public Schools Aren't for Christians!,* 42–43.

152. Josephine Pollard to My Dear Brother, 24 August 1871, Josephine Pollard Papers, Duke University.

153. Wheeler, *Warning! Public Schools Aren't for Christians!*, 42–43.

154. Josephine Pollard, "Co-education," (New York: E. F. Birmingham, 1883), 57, 61.

155. Pollard, *A Child's History of America*, 157–58.

156. Wheeler, *Warning! Public Schools Aren't for Christians!*, viii, 1, 10, 27, 14, 12–13.

157. "How Dickens Unwittingly Started the First Woman's Club Here," *New York Times*, 4 February 1912. Owing to her continued ill health, Pollard felt constrained to withdraw. She remained "in warm sympathy with the club and was always interested in its welfare." Willard and Livermore, eds., *A Woman of the Century*, 578.

158. Box 17, folder 7: Constitution, By-Laws and Roll of Members, Sorosis Records, 1856–1972, Sophia Smith Collection, Smith College Archives, Northampton, Mass.

159. Box 14, folder 2 "Yearbooks" – 1869 – Sorosis: Constitution and By-Laws. See Marguerite Dawson Winant, *A Century of Sorosis, 1868–1968* (Uniondale, N.Y.: Salisbury, 1968). See also "The Sorosis Dinner, The Seventh Anniversary Celebrated with Feasting," *New York Times*, 16 May 1875; and "The General Federation of Women's Clubs," La Retama Club: Corpus Christi Public Libraries, www.library.ci.

160. "How Dickens Unwittingly Started the First Woman's Club Here," *New York Times*, 4 February 1912.

161. Charles G. Bush, "Sorosis, 1869," HarpWeek "Cartoon of the Day" (originally published 15 May 1869), www.harpweek.com.

162. J. C. Croly, *The History of the Women's Club Movement in America* (New York: Henry G. Allen, 1898), 21–22.

163. Pollard, *The History of the United States*, 12.

164. Ibid., 61.

165. Breckinridge, who claimed Pollard had elicited the matrimonial pledge at gunpoint, assembled a team of defense attorneys who worked actively to impugn her character. "The trial was further enlivened on the third day by a fist fight between the teams of opposing lawyers," a reporter noted. "The next day Breckinridge's lawyers had to deny formally to the judge that they were carrying concealed weapons." *The Celebrated Case of W. C. P. Breckinridge and Madeline Pollard*, Fin de Siècle Series 50, no. 1 (Chicago: Current Events, 1894), 238. A publishing firm that specialized in "popular novels" brought out a fifty-cent edition of the story of the Breckinridge spy titled *A Diary of Ten Weeks' Intimate Association with the Real Madeline Pollard*. See also Agnes Parker, *The Real Madeline Pollard: A Diary of Ten Weeks' Association with the Plaintiff in the Famous Breckinridge–Pollard Suit* (New York: G. W. Dillingham, 1894); and Stephen Hess, *America's Political Dynasties* (New Brunswick, N.J.: Transaction, 1997), 260.

166. "Miss Pollard on the Stand," *New York Times*, 20 March 1894.

167. An unnamed woman testified, for instance, that she had met Breckinridge's accuser in July 1892 at a summer writers' institute—Breadloaf, in Vermont—where Madeline Pollard recited lines from Josephine Pollard's poem "Love's Power," which she claimed to have written. The Brooklyn woman concluded her testimony by calling Madeline Pollard "the most polished and consummate liar I have ever met." These quotes come from *Standard Union*, Brooklyn, 17 March 1894; the story of the Pollard trial can also be followed in articles from the same paper from March 12, 15, 16, 19–22, 1894.

168. "Little Bear Live," audio CD, Mantle Ministries website, http://mantleministries.com.

4. Providential History

1. Bob and Rose Weiner, "One Million Youth, One Billion Souls," Weiner Ministries, http://youthnow.org/.

2. "Reaching Youth with Evangelism Teams," Editorial Staff, *The Forerunner*, 1 December 1987, http://forerunner.com.

3. "Weiner Ministries International," www.manta.com.

4. Bob and Rose Weiner, "History of Revival and Young People," Weiner Ministries, www.youthnow.org.

5. "The Story of Liberty," WeinerMedia: Biblestudybooks.com, www.biblestudybooks.com.

6. Nina Baym, *American Women Writers and the Work of History, 1790–1860* (New Brunswick, N.J.: Rutgers University Press, 1995), 46.

7. Bob and Rose Weiner, "What's Wrong With Education," *The Forerunner*, 2 April 1991, www.forerunner.com.

8. Bob and Rose Weiner, "Seven Reasons to Reach College Students," Weiner Ministries, www.youthnow.org.

9. "Maranatha Books and More," www.maranathabooksandmore.com.

10. These texts were originally published by Coffin as *The Story of Liberty* (New York: Harper and Brothers, 1879) and *Old Times in the Colonies* (New York: Harper and Brothers, 1881).

11. Charles Carleton Coffin, *The Story of Liberty* (Gainesville, Fla.: Maranatha Publications; reprinted from the original 1879 manuscript, 1987), 5–6.

12. "Wisdom's 7 Pillars: HisStory," *L.E.D. Resources and Recommendations*, http://frommeandmyhouse.com.

13. Gregg Harris, "The Christian Home School," as cited in *L. E. D. HisStory Resources and Recommendations*, http://frommeandmyhouse.com.

14. "Charles Carleton Coffin: In-depth History Readings," Mantle Ministries, http://mantleministries.com.

15. "Books for Education: Homeschool Curriculum and Educational Resources," Exodus Books, www.exodusbooks.com.

16. Jane Hier, "Product Reviews," 10 July 2011, WeinerMedia: BibleStudyBooks.com, www.biblestudybooks.com.

17. Charles H. Sylvester, *Journeys Through Bookland: A New and Original Plan for Reading Applied to the World's Best Literature for Children*, Vol. 10: *The Guide* (Chicago: Edwin Bellows, 1922), 1–6.

18. As cited in Milton Gaither, *Homeschool: An American History* (New York: Palgrave Macmillan, 2008), 43–44.

19. Rev. William H. Lyon, "The Responsibility of the Parent in the Education of the Child," *Year Book of the Brookline Education Society, Third Year, 1897–8*, 17.

20. Sylvester, *Journeys Through Bookland*, 10:1–6.

21. "William Rainey Harper: Young Man in a Hurry," Harper College Archives, http://dept.harpercollege.edu.

22. *Harvard Daily Echo* 3, no. 7 (2 January 1881): [3].

23. For more on the home study program in Wisconsin, see *Wisconsin Journal of Education* 30, no. 2 (February 1900): 31.

24. See Samuel Eliot, Mrs. Louis Aggasiz, et al., *Society to Encourage Studies at Home* (Cambridge, Mass.: Riverside Press, 1897). See also Harriet F. Bergmann, "'The Silent University': The Society to Encourage Studies at Home, 1873–1897," *New England Quarterly* 74, no. 3 (September 2001): 447–77; and Anne L. Bruder, "'Dear Alma Mater': Women's Epistolary Education in the Society to Encourage Studies at Home, 1873–1897," *New England Quarterly* 84, no. 4 (December 2011): 588–620.

25. "Annual Report: Society to Encourage Studies at Home: Fifth Annual Report, 1878" (Boston: Rockwell and Churchill, 1878), 15–16.

26. *The Automatic Instructor: A Practical System for Home Study* (St. Paul, Minn.: G. W. Read, 1898).

27. Sylvester, *Journeys Through Bookland,* 10:1–6.

28. Circular for Edward S. Ellis, *The History of Our Country for the "History as Home Study" Series* (Cincinnati: Jones Brothers), [n. p.]. In possession of the author.

29. Benson Lossing, *Young People's Story of American Achievements, a Graphic History of the Republic and its Builders with over 300 Portraits and Biographical Outlines of Illustrious Americans* (New Haven: American Manufacturing Company for the Home Education League of America, 1901).

30. Seymour Eaton, ed., *Home Study Circle Library,* 15 vols. (New York: Doubleday and McClure, 1900).

31. Frederick Sanders, "In Praise of Books: The Autumn Outlook: Reports as to the Conditions in the Chief Literary Centres of the United States," *New York Times,* 7 October 1899.

32. William Swinton, *First Lessons in Our Country's History* (New York: American Book Company, 1872), 3–4. For more on Swinton, see Thomas Marshall Spaulding, "William Swinton" in *Dictionary of American Biography* under the auspices of American Council of Learned Societies, 22 vols. (New York: Charles Scribner's Sons, 1943), 18:252–53.

33. L. P. M. [Levi Parsons Morton?], "Edward S. Ellis, A. M.," in Edward S. Ellis, *Popular History of the World: From Dawn of Information to Present Time: Including Complete Triumphs of the 19th Century* (George Spiel, 1900), vii–viii.

34. Albert Johannsen, *The House of Beadle and Adams and Its Dime and Nickel Novels: The Story of a Vanished Literature,* 2 vols. (Norman: University of Oklahoma Press, 1950), 1:31–37, 2:93–100.

35. Jordan, "[The] *Boys of '76.* Charles Carleton Coffin. Harper, illus. 398 p. $2," in "Our Own Country," Congress of Mothers Literature Reading List, 14.

36. William Elliot Griffis, *Charles Carleton Coffin: War Correspondent, Traveller, Author, and Statesman* (Charleston, S.C.: BiblioBazaar, 2007), 122, 142.

37. Ibid., 328. See also Charles Carleton Coffin, *Daughters of the Revolution and Their Times, 1769–1776: A Historical Romance* (Boston: Houghton, Mifflin, [1895]).

38. Penelope Niven, "Living in the Library: Writers Reading, Writers Writing," 22 April 2006, www.kzoo.edu.

39. Griffis, *Charles Carleton Coffin,* [9], 130, 174.

40. Ibid., 131, 122, 60–61.

41. Ibid., 20, 31. Griffis's biography of Coffin has been republished recently by a press called Boomerang Books.

42. "Obituary Record: Charles Carleton Coffin," *New York Times,* 3 March 1896.

43. Griffis, *Charles Carleton Coffin,* 52, 55.

44. Dispatches as cited in Charles Carleton Coffin, *The Boys of '61' or, Four Years of Fighting: Personal Observation with the Army and Navy* (1881; reprint, Boston: Estes and Lauriat, 1884), 243–47.

45. Diane Loms Weber, "Coffin, Charles Carleton," in *American National Biography,* 24 vols. (New York: Oxford University Press, 1999), 5:140. On Coffin's style, see C. C. Coffin to Mr. Buell, 16 January 1886; 1 March 1886; 8 March 1866; n. d., MSS and Archives Division, New York Public Library, New York.

46. For a sample of the kind of lectures Coffin delivered, see "Lecture on the War: C. C. Coffin, Esq. known as 'Carleton' of the Boston journal, will deliver a lecture at the Temple, on Wednesday evening, May 27, at 1-4 before 8 o'clock, in which he will give his own experience as an eye-witness in the principal battles of the present war!" "Archive of Americana," American Broadsides and Ephemera, Series 1, no. 11495. See also Charles Carleton Coffin to Prof.

Mowry, 29 June 1881, ALS [Autographed Letter Signed], in "A Guide to the Charles Carleton Coffin Collection," no. 8592, University of Virginia Library, Special Collections Dept. Alderman Library, University of Virginia, Charlottesville.

47. Griffis, *Charles Carleton Coffin,* 59.

48. "Review of *Young Folks' Book of American Explorers,*" *The Nation* 51 (26 April 1877): 465.

49. "Review of *Four Years of Fighting,*" *The Nation* 2 (12 June 1866): 741; Edwin E. Sparks, *The Literature of American History: A Bibliographical Guide,* ed. J. N. Larned (Boston: Published for the American Library Association by Houghton, Mifflin, 1902), 224; "Review of *My Days and Nights on the Battle-Field,*" *Atlantic Monthly* 13, no. 75 (January 1864): 516.

50. Griffis, *Charles Carleton Coffin,* 37.

51. Published by Ticknor and Fields, *Four Years of Fighting* was reissued in 1882 by Estes and Lauriat under the title *Boys of '61.*

52. "Good Books for Boys . . . by Chas. Carleton Coffin," *Spokane Daily Chronicle,* 13 August 1891.

53. Griffis, *Charles Carleton Coffin,* 133–34.

54. "Review of *Drum-Beat of the Nation,*" *The Nation.* 45, no. 1170 (1 December 1887): 442; "Review of *Redeeming the Republic,*" *The Nation* 49, no. 1273 (2 November 1889): 415.

55. Alice Fahs, *The Imagined Civil War: Popular Literature of the North and South, 1861–1865* (Chapel Hill: University of North Carolina Press, 2001), 257–58.

56. Coffin, *The Story of Liberty* (New York: Harper and Brothers, 1879), 9.

57. Coffin, *Old Times in the Colonies,* 7–8.

58. Coffin, *The Story of Liberty,* 9.

59. Coffin, *Old Times in the Colonies,* 7–8.

60. Ibid., 288.

61. Karen, "Andreola Reviews," Christianbook.com, www.christianbook.com.

62. "Review of *My Days and Nights on the Battle-Field,*" *Atlantic Monthly,* 516.

63. Susannah Rowntree, "In Which I Read Vintage Novels: A Guide to Bestsellers of Yesterday," http://inwhichireadvintagenovels.blogspot.com.

64. Susan Rushing, former homeschooler and current teacher at Cornerstone Academy, as cited in Jacketflap Reviews, www.jacketflap.com.

65. Steven Mintz, *Huck's Raft: A History of American Childhood* (Cambridge: Harvard University Press, 2004), 189–90.

66. For background on G. Stanley Hall, see "Preface," in L. T. Benjamin Jr., ed., *G. Stanley Hall Lecture Series,* 9 vols. (Washington: American Psychological Association, 1981), 1:1–6; L. A. Diehl, "The Paradox of G. Stanley Hall: Foe of Coeducation and Educator of Women," *American Psychologist* 41, no. 8 (August 1986): 868–78; and L. F. Goodchild, "G. Stanley Hall and the Study of Higher Education," *Review of Higher Education* 20 (1996): 69–99.

67. Mintz, *Huck's Raft,* 188–89.

68. Emily S. Davidson and Ludy T. Benjamin Jr., "A History of the Child Study Movement in America," in *Historical Foundations of Educational Psychology,* ed. John A. Glover and Royce R. Ronning (New York: Plenum Press, 1987), 41, 48–49.

69. Mintz, *Huck's Raft,* 188–89, 190.

70. Davidson and Benjamin, "A History of the Child Study Movement in America," 53.

71. E. M. Hartwell, "Year Book of the Brookline Education Society, First Year, 1895–6," (Brookline, Mass.: Riverdale Press: C. A. W. Spencer, 1896), 9. See also Walter Channing, "Parental Responsibility in Education," ibid., 34.

72. "Emergent Writing Stages and History of Emergent Writing," www.brighthub.com.

73. G. Stanley Hall, ed., *Methods of Teaching History* (Boston: Ginn, Heath, 1883), ix–x.

74. Andrew White, "Historical Instruction in Course of History and Political Science at Cornell University," in Hall, ed., *Methods of Teaching History,* 74–75, 76.

75. C. C. Soule, "Third Regular Meeting," *Year Book of the Brookline Education Society, First Year, 1895–6* (Brookline, Mass.: Riverdale Press: C. A. W. Spencer, 1896), 16.

76. Thomas Wentworth Higginson, "Why Do Children Dislike History?," in Hall, *Methods of Teaching History,* 227–30.

77. Thomas Wentworth Higginson, *A Larger History of the United States of America, to the Close of President Jackson's Administration* (New York: Harper and Brothers, 1886), vi.

78. For more on the production and reception of this history, see Thomas Wentworth Higginson, additional scrapbooks and other papers 1823–1911, MS AM 2545, *Young Folks' History of the United States:* scrapbook of clippings, 1874–79, Series I: B (20), Houghton Library, Harvard.

79. Thomas Wentworth Higginson, *Young Folks' History of the United States* (Boston: Lee and Shepard, 1875), iv.

80. J. H. Vincent, President of the Chautauqua Literary and Scientific Circle, "Advertisement," back leaf pages of Higginson, *Young Folks' History of the United States.*

81. "Boston: Literary Notes," [n.p.], in Thomas Wentworth Higginson, additional scrapbooks and other papers 1823–1911, MS AM 2545, *Young Folks' History of the United States:* scrapbooks of clippings, 1882–85, vol. 1, scrapbook 1 (20), Scrapbooks, Houghton Library, Harvard.

82. "Specimen Sheets for *Young Folks' History of the United States,*" in Thomas Wentworth Higginson, additional scrapbooks and other papers 1823–1911, MS AM 2545, *Young Folks' History of the United States:* scrapbooks of clippings, 1882–85, vol. 1, scrapbook 1 (20), Scrapbooks, Houghton Library, Harvard.

83. "History for Young Folks," *Chicago Tribune,* 30 January [1875], in Thomas Wentworth Higginson, additional scrapbooks and other papers 1823–1911, MS AM 2545, *Young Folks' History of the United States:* scrapbooks of clippings, 1882–85, vol. 1, scrapbook 1 (20), Scrapbooks, Houghton Library, Harvard.

84. Higginson, *Young Folks' History of the United States,* 145.

85. Herbert B. Adams, "Special Methods of Historical Study," in Hall, ed., *Methods of Teaching History,* 138.

86. Thomas Wentworth Higginson, "History in Easy Lessons," *Atlantic Monthly* 96 (July 1905): 389.

87. Thomas Wentworth Higginson, *Part of a Man's Life* (Boston: Houghton Mifflin, 1905), 281–82.

88. Higginson, *Young Folks History of the United States,* 68, 136–37.

89. Coffin, *The Story of Liberty,* 8, 34, 37, 39.

90. James K. Hosmer, "Review of *The Story of Liberty,*" in *The Literature of American History: A Bibliographical Guide,* ed. J. N. Larned, 296.

91. Thomas K. Hanna, "Boys' Books Criticized: At Least One of Coffin's Held to Implant Prejudice," Letters to the Editor, *New York Times,* 2 May 1943. The letter to which Hanna was responding was "Others Wrote Boys' Books," *New York Times,* 25 April 1943.

92. "The Catholics Object: A Religious War Waged in the Indiana Legislature," *New York Times,* 22 February 1897.

93. "Course of Study for the Common Schools of Illinois," Third General Revision, with Agriculture and Household Arts, August 1903. Revised by the Standing Committee of the County Superintendents' Section of the State Teachers' Association (Taylorville, Ill.: O. M. Parker, 1904), 84–85.

94. [Review of Higginson's *Young Folks' History of the United States*], *Wisconsin Journal of Education* 5, no. 2 (February 1875), in Thomas Wentworth Higginson, additional scrapbooks and other papers 1823–1911, MS AM 2545, *Young Folks' History of the United States:* scrapbooks of clippings, 1882–85, vol. 1, scrapbook 1 (20), Scrapbooks, Houghton Library, Harvard.

95. Frederick Sheldon, *The Nation*, 11 February 1875, in Thomas Wentworth Higginson, additional scrapbooks and other papers 1823–1911, MS AM 2545, *Young Folks' History of the United States:* scrapbooks of clippings, 1882–85, vol. 1, scrapbook 1 (20), Scrapbooks, Houghton Library, Harvard.

96. Mary Potter Thacher Higginson, *Thomas Wentworth Higginson: The Story of His Life* (Boston: Houghton Mifflin, 1914), 364–65.

97. "Thoughts and Experiences In and Out of School by John B. Peaslee, LLB., Ph.D., Ex-Superintendent of the Public Schools of Cincinnati, Ohio," (Cincinnati: Printed for the Author by Curtis & Jennings, 1900), 38–39, 359–61.

98. "Higginson's U. S. History," *Springfield Republican*, 29 January 1875, in Thomas Wentworth Higginson, additional scrapbooks and other papers 1823–1911, MS AM 2545, *Young Folks' History of the United States:* scrapbooks of clippings, 1882–85, vol. 1, scrapbook 1 (20), Scrapbooks, Houghton Library, Harvard.

99. Higginson, *Thomas Wentworth Higginson*, 286–87, 285–86.

100. Griffis, *Charles Carleton Coffin*, 57, 13, 134–35.

101. The seven volumes included *The Complaint of Labor* (Washington: Government Printing Office, 1879); *The Story of Liberty* (New York: Harper and Brothers, 1879); *The Life of James A. Garfield* (Boston: J. H. Earle, 1880); *Our New Way Round the World* (Boston: Estes and Lauriat, 1881); *The Boys of '61: or, Four Years of Fighting* (Boston, Estes and Lauriat, 1881); *The Future of New Hampshire* (Boston: Printed by the Boston Stereotype Foundry, 1881); *Old Times in the Colonies* (New York: Harper and Brothers, 1881).

102. Coffin, *The Story of Liberty*, 360–61.

103. Coffin, *My Days and Nights on the Battle-Field*, 3–4.

104. Griffis, *Charles Carleton Coffin*, 18, 132.

105. Ibid., 13, 150, 148–49.

106. Rose Weiner, "A Note from the Publisher," *Sweet Land of Liberty*, [3–4].

107. Griffis, *Charles Carleton Coffin*, 152–56, 108.

108. "Ad Hoc Committee: *A Statement of Evaluation Regarding Maranatha Campus Ministries / Maranatha Christian Ministries / Maranatha Christian Church*," www.rickross.com.

109. John Fialka, "Maranatha Christians, Backing Rightist Ideas, Draw Fire Over Tactics," *Wall Street Journal*, 16 August 1985.

110. Randy Frame, "A Team of Cult Watchers Challenges a Growing Campus Ministry," *Christianity Today*, 10 August 1984.

111. Charles Carleton Coffin, "Our Schools: Speech given before the Congregational Club," 26 November 1888, 5, 10, 18, 25–26, in MSS 40, box 1, folder 9, Charles Carleton Coffin Papers, New England Historic and Genealogical Society, Boston.

112. William Swinton, *Outlines of the world's history: ancient, mediæval, and modern, with special relation to the history of civilization and the progress of mankind, with special relation to the history of civilization and the progress of mankind* (New York and Chicago: Ivison, Blakeman, Taylor, 1874); John J. Anderson, *A complete course in history: New manual of general history: with particular attention to ancient and modern civilizations: with numerous engravings and maps: for the use of colleges, high schools, academies, etc* (New York: Clark and Maynard, 1881–82).

113. Coffin, "Our Schools," 10, 29–30.

114. Ibid., 34.

115. Ibid., 2.

116. For indications of the importance Coffin attached to public education in American history, see Coffin, *Old Times in the Colonies*, 12–13, 140.

117. Griffis, *Charles Carleton Coffin*, 158.

118. Higginson, "Appendix I: Books for Consultation," *Young Folks' History of the United States*, 336.

119. [Review of Charles Carleton Coffin, *Boys of '76*], *Pennsylvania Monthly* (December 1876), in Thomas Wentworth Higginson, additional scrapbooks and other papers 1823–1911, MS AM 2545, *Young Folks' History of the United States*: scrapbooks of clippings, 1882–85, vol. 1, scrapbook 1 (20), Scrapbooks, Houghton Library, Harvard.

120. See, for instance, Samuel Blumenfeld, "Dumbing Down America," in "Home School News, Ministers for Christ Assembly of Churches," www.ordination.org.

121. [D. S. Sanford], *Year Book of the Brookline Education Society, First Year, 1895–6*, 17.

122. G. Stanley Hall, "Child Study: Some of Its Methods and Results," referenced in "First Meeting of the Brookline Education Society," *Year Book of the Brookline Education Society, First Year, 1895–6*, 18, 24.

123. "Report of the Committee on History," *Year Book of the Brookline Education Society, First Year, 1895–6*, 35.

124. *Year Book of the Brookline Education Society, First Year, 1895–6*, 13, 14.

125. Howard A. Bridgman in William Elliott Griffis, "Memorial: Charles Carleton Coffin" (Boston: Geo. H. Wright, 1896), 20.3.1 COF, Charles Carleton Coffin Collection, The Congregational Library, Boston, Massachusetts, 20. "Memorial: Charles Carleton Coffin," 34, 44.

126. Sarah Louise Arnold, *Reading: How to Teach It* (Boston: Silver, Burdett, 1899), 267, 269.

127. "Christian History Books," WeinerMedia: BibleStudyBooks.com, www.biblestudybooks .com.

128. Baym, *American Women Writers and the Work of History*, 46.

129. Griffis, "Memorial: Charles Carleton Coffin," 15–16.

5. Biographical History

1. Rick and Marilyn Boyer, *Home Educating with Confidence: How Ordinary Parents CAN Produce Extraordinary Children* (Elkton, Md.: Homeschool Press, 1996), 18–48. See also Rick Boyer, "Some Things We've Learned: Lessons from Over Two Decades of Home Education," www .thelearningparent.com.

2. "About: The Learning Parent blog," www.thelearningparentblog.com.

3. Rick Boyer, "Breaking the Shackles: Why Parents Should Trust Themselves, Not Schools," CD available at www.thelearningparent.com.

4. Rick and Marilyn Boyer, *Home Educating with Confidence*, 6, 7, 8, 27, 19.

5. Ibid., 151.

6. Louise Collier Willcox, "Our Supervised Morals," in *North American Review* 198, no. 696 (November 1913): 708, as cited in Steven Mintz, *Huck's Raft: A History of American Childhood* (Cambridge: Harvard University Press, 2004), 214–15.

7. Mintz, *Huck's Raft*, 219, 214, 226–27, 214–16.

8. Cornelia A. P. Comer, "A Letter to the Rising Generation," *Atlantic Monthly* (4 February 1911), 145, as cited in ibid., 231.

9. Mintz, *Huck's Raft*, 231–32.

10. Sarah Louise Arnold, *Reading: How to Teach It* (Boston: Silver, Burdett, 1899), 29, 33.

11. Rick and Marilyn Boyer, *Home Educating with Confidence*, 83, 112.

12. A Beka Books," www.abeka.com.

13. Rick and Marilyn Boyer, *Home Educating with Confidence*, 113.

14. Rick Boyer, "Why History Matters," The Learning Parent, www.thelearningparentblog.com.

15. Rick Boyer, "Breaking the Shackles."

16. Rick and Marilyn Boyer, *Home Educating with Confidence*, 41–42.

17. Rick Boyer, "What Do You Do With BOYS?," n.d.

18. Ibid.

19. Ibid.

20. Ibid.

21. Boyer, "Why History Matters."

22. Rick Boyer, "Take Back the Land," www.christianbook.com.

23. Rick Boyer, "Teaching Character Through History," www.characterconcepts.com.

24. Boyer, "Take Back the Land.

25. Boyer, "What Do You Do With BOYS?"

26. Boyer, "Teaching Character Through History."

27. Jamie, "Hear What our Customers Say! Uncle Rick Reads Biographies of Heroes from the American Revolution Collection," www.thelearningparent.com.

28. "Review of 'Uncle Rick Reads *True Stories of Great Americans for Young Americans*,'" www.thelearningparent.com.

29. "Elbridge Streeter Brooks: Biographical Sketch and Memorial Exercises," *Historic Leaves* 1 (April 1902–January 1903): 7, Somerville Local History Room, Somerville Historical Society, Somerville, Mass.

30. Rev. Anson Titus, "Elbridge Streeter Brooks," obituary, *Somerville Journal* (21 February 1902); see also "Elbridge S. Brooks: Death of Somerville's Famous Historian and Storywriter After a Remarkably Active and Useful Career—More Than 40 Volumes From His Pen," *Somerville Journal* (10 January 1902): 1, 8.

31. "Elbridge Streeter Brooks: Biographical Sketch and Memorial Exercises," *Historic Leaves*, 9.

32. With respect to Brooks's work at Lothrop, see Lothrop to Whitney, 12 January 1889, vol. 58, Whitney Papers, Library of Congress, as cited in Peter Karsten, "The Nature of 'Influence': Roosevelt, Mahan and the Concept of Sea Power," *American Quarterly* 23, no. 4 (October 1971): 599.

33. *Tales of Heroism, Historic Boys* (New York: G. P. Putnam's Sons, 1885); *Historic Girls* (New York: G. P. Putnam's Sons, 1887); and *Historic Happenings Told in Verse and Story* (New York: G. P. Putnam's Sons 1892). *Heroic Happenings: Told in Verse and Story* (New York: G. P. Putnam's Sons, 1893), iii–iv.

34. "Elbridge Streeter Brooks: Biographical Sketch and Memorial Exercises," *Historic Leaves*, 10–11.

35. F. L. Harbour, "Address by F. L. Harbour of the *Youth's Companion*," *Historic Leaves*, 16–17.

36. Boyer, "What Do You Do With BOYS?"

37. Elbridge S. Brooks, *The True Story of the United States of America: Told for Young People* (1891; reprint, Boston: Lothrop, Lee, and Shepard, 1922), 1.

38. Brooks, *Heroic Happenings: Told in Verse and Story*.

39. Scott E. Casper, *Constructing American Lives: Biography and Culture in Nineteenth-Century America* (Chapel Hill: University of North Carolina Press, 1999), 88.

40. Brooks, *Heroic Happenings*, iii–iv.

41. *The Dial*, as cited in "Brooks, Elbridge Streeter," *The National Cyclopaedia of American Biography*, 7 vols. (New York: James T. White, 1897): 7:157.

42. Brooks, *The True Story of the United States of America*, 1.

43. Elbridge S. Brooks, *The Heroic Life of General George Washington: First President of the United States* (Boston: DeWolfe, Fiske, 1902), 4.

44. Elbridge S. Brooks, *The Heroic Life of Abraham Lincoln*, 31.

45. Brooks, *The Heroic Life of General George Washington*, 48.

46. Elbridge S. Brooks, *The Heroic Life of Captain Paul Jones: The First Captain of the United States Navy* (Boston: DeWolfe, Fiske, 1902), 16, 47.

47. Elbridge S. Brooks, *The Heroic Life of William McKinley: Our Third Martyr President* (Boston: DeWolfe, Fiske, 1902), 4.

48. Brooks, *The True Story of the United States*, 239–40.

49. Boyer, "What Do You Do With BOYS?"

50. Elbridge S. Brooks, *The Heroic Life of Ulysses S. Grant: General of the Armies of the United States* (Boston: DeWolfe, Fiske, 1902), 6–7, 1.

51. Casper, *Constructing American Lives*, 89.

52. Elbridge S. Brooks, *The Century Book for Young Americans: Showing How a Party of Boys and Girls Who Knew to Use Their Eyes and Ears Found Out All About the Government of the United States* (New York: Century, 1894), 3–4.

53. Elbridge S. Brooks, *The Century Book of Famous Americans: The Story of a Young People's Pilgrimage to Historic Homes* (New York: Century, 1896), 247.

54. Ibid., 211.

55. *Brooklyn Times*, as cited in "Brooks, Elbridge Streeter," *National Cyclopaedia of American Biography*, 7:156–57.

56. Titus, "Elbridge Streeter Brooks," *Somerville Journal*, 10 January 1902.

57. Elbridge S. Brooks, *The True Story of George Washington: Called the Father of His Country* (Boston: Lothrop, Lee, and Shepard, 1895), iv.

58. Elbridge S. Brooks, *The True Story of Abraham Lincoln: The American* (Boston: Lothrop, Lee, and Shepard, 1896) [4]; Elbridge S. Brooks, *The True Story of Lafayette: Called the Friend of America* (Boston: Lothrop, Lee, and Shepard, 1899), 11–12.

59. Brooks, *The True Story of George Washington*, 196.

60. Dean Keith Simonton, *Greatness: Who Makes History and Why* (New York: Guilford Press, 1994), 142.

61. Brooks, *The True Story of Abraham Lincoln*, 42–43, 55; Elbridge S. Brooks, *The True Story of U. S. Grant: The American Soldier* (Boston: Lothrop, Lee, and Shepard, 1897), 31.

62. Brooks, *The True Story of U. S. Grant*, 12.

63. Brooks, *The True Story of Abraham Lincoln*, 48.

64. Ibid., 83, 223.

65. Brooks, *The True Story of George Washington*, 22–23.

66. Elbridge S. Brooks, *The True Story of Christopher Columbus: Called the Great Admiral* (Boston: Lothrop, Lee, and Shepard, 1892), 47.

67. Ibid., 35.

68. Brooks, *The True Story of Abraham Lincoln*, 92.

69. Brooks, *The True Story of Lafayette*, 225.

70. Brooks, *The True Story of George Washington*, 24.

71. Brooks, *The True Story of U. S. Grant*, 28.

72. Brooks, *The True Story of Ben Franklin: The American Statesman* (1898; reprint, Boston: Lothrop, Lee, and Shepard, 1926), 242.

73. Brooks, *The True Story of George Washington*, 192.

74. Ibid., 202.

75. [Endorsement], *Christian Advocate*, in "Books for Young Americans, by Elbridge S. Brooks: The Popular 'True Story' Series," Brooks, *The True Story of George Washington*, n. p. (back matter).

76. [*Chicago Evening Post*, review of *The True Story of Abraham Lincoln*], as cited in *Journal of the National Education Association* 11 (February 1922): 52.

77. [Endorsement], *Pilgrim Teacher* in "Books for Young Americans, by Elbridge S. Brooks: The Popular 'True Story' Series," Brooks, *The True Story of George Washington*, n. p. (back matter).

78. [Endorsement], *The Critic* in "Books for Young Americans, by Elbridge S. Brooks: The Popular 'True Story' Series," Brooks, *The True Story of George Washington*, n. p. (back matter).

79. S.G.B., "Brooks, Elbridge Streeter," *Dictionary of American Biography*, 22 vols., ed. Allen Johnson and Dumas Malone (New York: Charles Scribner's Sons, 1943), 3:76.

80. S.G.B., "Brooks, Elbridge Streeter," *Dictionary of American Biography*, 3:76.

81. Death Notice, "Elbridge Streeter Brooks," *Publishers Weekly* 61, no. 1563 (11 January 1902): 37–38.

82. John Ayer, "Address by John Ayer," *Historic Leaves*, 14–15.

83. Hezekiah Butterworth, "Address by Mr. Butterworth," *Historic Leaves*, 18.

84. S.G.B., "Brooks, Elbridge Streeter," *Dictionary of American Biography*, 3:76.

85. Brooks, *The Heroic Life of George Washington*, 24, 26.

86. Brooks, *The True Story of the United States*, 44.

87. Brooks, *The True Story of Abraham Lincoln*, 53, 141, 156, 159, 203.

88. Brooks, *The True Story of Ben Franklin*, 49.

89. Benjamin Franklin, *The Autobiography of Benjamin Franklin* (Rockville, Md.: Arc Manor, 2008), 25.

90. Brooks, *The True Story of the United States*, 109.

91. Brooks, *The True Story of George Washington*, 196–98, 237.

92. Ray Raphael, *Founding Myths: Stories That Hide Our Patriotic Past* (New York: Norton, 2004), 267–68, 269–70.

93. Ibid., 273.

94. Brooks, *The True Story of George Washington*, 196–98.

95. Brooks, *The True Story of Christopher Columbus*, 173–74.

96. Ibid., 185–87.

97. Rick Boyer, "Uncle Rick Reads *The True Story of George Washington*, by Elbridge S. Brooks. The Inspiring Life Story of America's Greatest Hero with Character Commentary by Uncle Rick," CD available at www.thelearningparent.com.

98. Ibid.

99. Rick Boyer, "Beware of Social Studies," The Learning Parent, 13 June 2012, www.thelearningparentblog.com.

100. Boyer, "Uncle Rick Reads *The True Story of George Washington*."

101. Ibid.

102. Boyer, "Beware of Social Studies."

103. Brooks, *The True Story of George Washington*, iv, 81.

104. Boyer, "Uncle Rick Reads *The True Story of George Washington*."

105. Denise von Stockar, The Importance of Books and Literacy in Children's Development: Intellectual, Affective and Social Dimensions, IBby, International Board on Books for Young People, www.ibby.org.

106. Elbridge Streeter Brooks, *The Life Work of Elbridge Gerry Brooks: Minister in the Universalist Church* (Boston: Universalist Publishing House, 1881), [vi].

107. Brooks, *The True Story of Ben Franklin,* 14–15, 42.

108. Brooks, *The Life Work of Elbridge Gerry Brooks,* 19, 60.

109. Geraldine Brooks, *Dames and Daughters of the Young Republic* (New York: Thomas Y. Crowell, 1901), 7–8, 11.

110. Boyer, "Teaching Character Through History."

111. Kate (Boyer) Brown, "If My People . . . How We Can and Must Make a Difference," www.thelearningparent.com.

112. Boyer, "Breaking the Shackles."

113. Frances FitzGerald, *America Revised: What history textbooks have taught our children about their country, and how and why those textbooks have changed in different decades* (New York: Vintage Books, 1979), 218.

114. David Lowenthal, *The Past Is a Foreign Country* (Cambridge: Cambridge University Press, 1985), 71, 369, 8, 9.

115. Michael D. Clark, *The American Discovery of Tradition, 1865–1942* (Baton Rouge: Louisiana State University Press, 2005), front flap.

116. Lowenthal, *The Past Is a Foreign Country,* 121–22, 123, 110.

117. Ibid., 72, 69, 70.

118. FitzGerald, *America Revised,* 218.

119. Richard Hofstadter, *The Progressive Historians: Turner, Beard, Parrington* (New York: Alfred A. Knopf, 1969), xiv.

6. Doctrinal History

1. David Lowenthal, *The Past Is a Foreign Country* (Cambridge: Cambridge University Press, 1985), 278.

2. "Christian Liberty Press," www.shopchristianliberty.com.

3. "What is CLASS," www.homeschools.org.

4. "Curriculum Choice: Curriculum Decisions Made Simple," http://thecurriculumchoice.com.

5. "The Christian Teaching of History" (Greenville, S.C.: Journey Forth, a Division of Bob Jones University Press, 1981).

6. "Christian Liberty Press," www.shopchristianliberty.com.

7. "The Christian Teaching of History," 11, 4, 6.

8. Ibid., 2–3.

9. See, for instance, Allen C. Thomas, *A History of the United States* (New York City: Jewish Press, 1916), with text printed in English and Yiddish on facing pages.

10. Collin Hansen, "Why Johnny Can't Read the Bible," *Christianity Today,* www.christianitytoday.com.

11. Michael J. McHugh, *Studying God's Word A: Bible Stories* (Arlington Heights, Ill.: Christian Liberty Press, 1996).

12. G. Devi, "English 225: Notes on Biblical Interpretation," 29 August 2012, www.wordpress.com.

13. Dave and Debbie Klein, "Teaching Reading Using the Bible," www.inkleinations.com.

14. "The Christian Teaching of History," 11, 12.

15. Lowenthal, *The Past Is a Foreign Country,* 77.

16. Charles Morris, *The Child's History of the United States* (Cincinnati: W. H. Ferguson, 1900); Michael J. McHugh and Charles Morris, *A Child's Story of America* (Arlington Heights, Ill.: Christian Liberty Press, 1989); Charles Morris, Michael J. McHugh, and Edward J. Shewan, *A Child's Story of America*, 2d ed. (Arlington Heights, Ill.: Christian Liberty Press, 1998).

17. "Our Honest Opinion," review of Charles Morris et al., *A Child's Story of America,* Exodus Books website, www.exodusbooks.com; and Mamaof4boys, "Product Description," Christianbook.com, www.christianbook.com.

18. There is very little biographical information about Charles Morris and even less archival material. There are nine letters collected at Boston College, mainly correspondence between Morris and various publishers regarding requests for permission to use passages from books. See Charles Morris Correspondence, 1885–86, MS 86–25, box 1, Thomas P. O'Neill Library, Boston College, Chestnut Hill, Massachusetts.

19. Charles Morris, *Broken Fetters: The Light of Ages on Intoxication* (Richmond, Va.: H. E. Grosh, c. 1884.

20. Charles Morris, ed., *The Home Educator in Necessary Knowledge* (Philadelphia: Charles Foster, 1905).

21. Charles Morris, *Home School of American History; embracing the growth and achievements of our country from the earliest days of discovery and settlement to the present eventful year* (Chicago: C. F. Beezley, [1899]).

22. Morris, *The Child's History of the United States,* 35–36, 57, 111, 150.

23. Charles Morris, *Young People's History of the World for the Past One Hundred* Years (Philadelphia: John C. Winston, 1902), 27, 33–34.

24. Charles Morris, *The Child's Story of the Greatest Century* (Philadelphia: J. C. Winston, 1901), 181, 20, 25, 29–30, vii.

25. Morris, *The Child's History of the United States,* 179–80, 181, 212, 237, 254.

26. "Morris, Charles," University Library, Northern Illinois University, Charles Morris, www.ulib.niu.edu/badndp/morris_charles.html.

27. Anthony Comstock, *Traps for the Young* (Cambridge: Belknap Press of Harvard University, 1967 [1883]), 32–33.

28. For reviews of Morris's work, see *Banner Weekly,* 9 January 1892 and 16 January 1892; and *Philadelphia Public Ledger,* September 7, 1922.

29. "The Poetry of History," *New York Times,* 23 July 1904.

30. "Explanation," [Salesman's dummy], *The Child's History of the United States,* n. p.

31. Morris, *The Child's History of the United States,* vii–viii.

32. "Description of the Child's History of the United States" [salesman's dummy], *The Child's History of the United States.*

33. Ibid., separate brochure folded in.

34. Morris, *The Child's History of the United States,* 19–20, 37–38.

35. "Review of Scott Casper's *Constructing Lives: Biography and Culture in Nineteenth-Century America,*" H. L. Watson, "Lies and Times: The Changing Genre of Biography," *Reviews in American History* 28, no. 1 (March 2000): 47.

36. Morris, *The Child's History of the United States,* x.

37. "Description of the Child's History of the United States," [salesman's dummy], *The Child's History of the United States.*

38. Morris, McHugh, and Shewan, *A Child's Story of America,* iv.

39. "Another Book on the Navy," *New York Times,* 17 September 1898.

40. Charles M. Andrews, *The Literature of American History: A Bibliographical Guide,* J. N. Larned, ed. (Boston: Published for the American Library Association by Houghton, Mifflin, 1902), 287.

41. Michael Kammen, *A Machine That Would Go of Itself: The Constitution in American Culture* (New York: St. Martin's Press, 1994), 24.

42. Morris, *The Child's History of the United States*, 170.

43. Charles Morris, *Battling for the right; the life-story of Theodore Roosevelt, including his early life struggles and victorious public career; his principles and policies; the story of his African trip; his memorable journey through Europe; and his leadership in the battle for human rights* (Philadelphia? c.1910]), 20, 150.

44. Morris, *The Child's History of the United States*, 179–80, 181, 212, 237.

45. Charles Morris, *Man and His Ancestor: A Study in Evolution* (London: Macmillan, 1900), 2–4.

46. Ibid., 3–4.

47. Morris, *The Child's History of the United States*, 223, 20.

48. Andrews, "The Nation's Navy," *The Nation* 67, no. 1735 (July–December 1898): 246, as cited in *The Literature of American History: A Bibliographical Guide*, 287.

49. Lowenthal, *The Past Is a Foreign Country*, 264, 278, 326.

50. Frances FitzGerald, *America Revised: What History Textbooks Have Taught Our Children about Their Country, and How and Why Those Textbooks Have Changed in Different Decades* (New York: Vintage Books, 1979), 26–27.

51. John Wesley Hanson Jr., *A Child's History of the United States* (Chicago: W. B. Conkey, [1896]).

52. Morris, McHugh, and Shewan, *A Child's Story of America*, iv.

53. Morris, *The Child's History of the United States*, 20.

54. Morris, McHugh and Shewan, *A Child's Story of America*, 4.

55. Morris, *The Child's History of the United States*, 26.

56. Morris, McHugh, and Shewan, *A Child's Story of America*, 6.

57. Morris, *The Child's History of the United States*, 23; Morris, McHugh, and Shewan, *A Child's Story of America*, 4.

58. Morris, *The Child's History of the United States*, 24; Morris, McHugh, and Shewan, *A Child's Story of America*, 5.

59. Morris, *The Child's History of the United States*, 149.

60. Karl Will Jr., "The Declaration of Constitution: An American Historical Story," The Smirking Chimp, www.smirkingchimp.com.

61. Morris, McHugh, and Shewan, *A Child's Story of America*, 108–9, 197, 122.

62. Morris, *The Child's History of the United States*, 46–47, 59.

63. Morris, McHugh, and Shewan, *A Child's Story of America*, 20–21, 31.

64. Morris, *The Child's History of the United States*, 88.

65. Morris, McHugh, and Shewan, *A Child's Story of America*, 52.

66. Morris, *The Child's History of the United States*, 37; Morris, McHugh, and Shewan, *A Child's Story of America*, 15.

67. Morris, *The Child's History of the United States*, 50; Morris, McHugh, and Shewan, *A Child's Story of America*, 25.

68. Morris, McHugh, and Shewan, *A Child's Story of America*, iv.

69. Morris, *The Child's History of the United States*, 83.

70. Morris, McHugh, and Shewan, *A Child's Story of America*, 48.

71. Morris, *The Child's History of the United States*, 33; Morris, McHugh, and Shewan, *A Child's Story of America*, 13.

72. Morris, *The Child's History of the United States*, 48; Morris, McHugh, and Shewan, *A Child's Story of America*, 23.

73. Morris, McHugh, and Shewan, *A Child's Story of America,* 263; 266–67.

74. Ibid., 265–66.

75. Ibid.; back cover of fourth printing, 2005.

76. Lowenthal, *The Past Is a Foreign Country,* 290.

77. Ibid., 287, 280.

78. "*A Story of America,*" Cathy Duffy Reviews, http://cathyduffyreviews.com.

79. Lowenthal, *The Past Is a Foreign* Country, 331.

80. "A Story of America," reviewed by Mamaof4boys@, Christianbook.com, http://ugc.christianbook.com.

81. K. Alphs, "Sanitized Version of American History," 19 September 2008, www.amazon.ca.

82. Kimm Hunt, "A Strange Version of 'Christian' History," www.amazon.com.

83. "The Christian Teaching of History," 13.

84. FitzGerald, *America Revised,* 47.

85. Lowenthal, *The Past Is a Foreign Country,* 309.

86. Jody D. Kimbrell, *Lost History of America: Information Not Found in Modern History Books* (Mustang, Okla.: Tate Publishing and Enterprises,, 2008), back cover, 13.

87. Ibid., 10, 12.

88. Ibid., back cover, 9, 10.

89. FitzGerald, *America Revised,* 164.

90. Jill Lepore, *The Whites of Their Eyes: The Tea Party's Revolution and the Battle over American History* (Princeton: Princeton University Press, 2010) 118–25.

91. Lowenthal, *The Past Is a Foreign Country,* 411–12.

92. Ibid., 69.

Conclusion

1. Leslie Howsam, *Past into Print: The Publishing of History in Britain, 1850–1950* (London: British Library, 2009), 3–4.

2. For a thorough history of the professionalization of the discipline, see Peter Novick, *That Noble Dream: The 'Objectivity Question' and the American Historical Profession* (New York: Cambridge University Press, 1988).

3. Russell Shorto, "How Christian Were the Founders?," *New York Times Magazine,* 11 February 2010.

4. Ibid., 35, 37.

5. Ibid., 46, 47.

6. "'Revisionaries' Tells Story of Texas Textbook Battle," 20 June 2012, NPR, www.npr.org.

7. Stephen Colbert, "*Don McLeroy* – The *Colbert Report* – 2012-23-04 – Video Clip," www.colbertnation.com.

8. Gregory M. Pfitzer, *Popular History and the Literary Marketplace, 1840–1920* (Amherst: University of Massachusetts Press, 2008).

9. Charles A. Beard, "That Noble Dream," *American Historical Review* 41, no. 1 (October 1935): 74–87.

10. James Wilkinson, "A Choice of Fictions: Historians, Memory, and Evidence," in "The States of Evidence," special issue, *PMLA* 111, no. 1 (January 1996): 80–92.

11. Charles A. Beard, "Written History as an Act of Faith," *American Historical Review* 39 (January 1934): 219–31.

12. Kerwin Lee Klein, *From History to Theory* (Berkeley: University of California Press, 2011), 16.

13. "Those who misquote George Santayana are condemned to paraphrase him" (1 September 2007), NewPublic News Coverage, www.nowpublic.com.

14. "Transcript of President Bush's Speech at the Veterans of Foreign Wars Convention," 22 August 2007, as cited at www.nytimes.com.

15. Trudy Rubin, "Bogus Parallels Won't Rally Americans to 'Stay the Course,'" *Baltimore Sun*, 28 August 2007, as cited in http://articles.baltimoresun.com.

16. I say "was credited" here because there is some doubt as to whether Twain used this phrase or not. For a more thorough discussion of its veracity, see Eugene Volokh, "History Doesn't Repeat Itself, But It Rhymes," The Volokh Conspiracy, 18 February 2005, at www.volokh.com.

17. "Those who misquote George Santayana are condemned to paraphrase him."

18. Colbert, *"Don McLeroy* – The *Colbert Report* – 2012-23-04 – Video Clip."

19. Thomas L. Haskell, *Objectivity Is Not Neutrality: Explanatory Schemes in History* (Baltimore: Johns Hopkins University Press, 1998), 150.

INDEX

Abbot, Gorham, 66, 72–73, 273n78

Abbott, Charles, 66, 72

Abbott, Edward, 86, 89, 91

Abbott, Jacob, 1, 3, 12, 62–83, 90–91, 99–103, 111, 144, 182

Abbott, John Stevens Cabot, 1, 3, 12, 62–95, 99–103, 127, 144, 147, 182, 203

Abbott, Lyman, 68, 86, 90–91

Abbott, Samuel, 66

Abbott's Juvenile Histories (series), 79. *See also* specific books

Abbotts' School for Young Ladies, 72. *See also* Spingler Institute

A Beka Book company, 182

Academy on the Plain, 150

Adam and Alice (Heritage History), 58–64, 75–76, 79, 82–83, 90, 92, 115, 178

Adams, Frederic A., 121–22

Adams, Henry, 11

Adams, Herbert B., 164

Adams, John, 123, 154, 201–2, 230, 237

Adams, John Quincy, 201–2

African Americans, 5, 128, 151, 161, 169, 244–45

Aikin, Lucy, 105. *See also* Godolphin, Mary

A. L. Burt Publishers, 108, 111, 113

Alcott, Louisa May, 103

Alfred the Great (Abbotts), 81

Allen, Adaline T., 73

All Through the Ages (series), 58

American Annals of Education and Instruction, 38, 113

American Civil Liberties Union (ACLU), 101

The American Continent and Its Inhabitants Before Its Discovery (Cady), 29

American Revolution, 49, 124, 227–28. *See also* founding fathers; United States

American Society for the Diffusion of Useful Knowledge, 273n78

Anabaptists, 171

Anderson, John J., 172–73

Andover Academy, 66

Andrews, Charles M., 229

antimodernism, 60–64. *See also* history; ideology; metahistorical issues

Arnold, Sarah Louise, 175, 182, 210

Atlantic Monthly, 156, 181

Autobiography of Benjamin Franklin (Franklin), 202–3

The Automatic Instructor (Sylvester), 145

Avery, Gillian, 19–20, 22, 77, 111

Bacon's Rebellion, 240

Baldwin Library Children's Collection, 103, 109

Baltimore Sun, 257

Barber, Lucy Lombardi, 115

Barber, Tom, 254

Barnes, James and Patience, 106

Battling for the Right (Morris), 230

Baym, Nina, 113–14, 140

Beadle's Saturday Journal, 225

Beard, Charles, 256

Becker, Carl, 94, 176

Beecher, Catherine, 103

Berkeley, William, 240

Bettelheim, Bruno, 7, 21

Bible, the: historical pedagogy and, 16–25, 138–42, 167, 207–8, 217–22; literacy training and, 19–25, 34–35, 125–26; moral lessons and, 36–37, 46–47, 138–47, 206–7, 223; Morris's work and, 231–32

biographies: child psychology and, 7, 182–86; heroes and, 183–86, 189–90; moral didacticism and, 21, 84–90, 186–200, 225–32; national heritage and, 200–216; usable past idea and, 75–83, 258–59. *See also* heroism; history; morality

Birrell, Augustine, 48

Blanchard Academy, 150

Blue-Backed Spellers (Webster), 70

Bob Jones University, 219, 221–22, 245
Bonaparte, Josephine, 83, 85
Bonaparte, Louis-Napoleon (Napoleon III), 85
Bonaparte, Napoleon, 84–93, 127, 203, 274n98
Bookman, 111
Boston Daily Courier, 43
Boston Journal, 151
Bowdoin College, 65, 73
Boyer, Kate, 212
Boyer, Rick and Marilyn, 177–80, 182–88, 196,
    200–201, 203–18, 222
Boys of '61 (Coffin), 152
The Boys of '76 (Coffin), 148, 154, 173
The Boys of Dickens Retold (Sweetser), 115
Brace, Charles Loring, 102
Braddock, Edward, 124
Bradley Commission, 4
"Breaking the Shackles" (Boyer), 178, 212
Breckenridge, William Campbell Preston,
    135–36, 283n165, 283n167
Bridgman, Howard A., 174
Briggs, Julia, 22
Broken Fetters (Morris), 223, 240
Brookline Massachusetts Education Society, 158,
    160, 174
Brooklyn Standard-Union, 135
Brooklyn Times, 195
Brooks, Elbridge Gerry, 211
Brooks, Elbridge Streeter, 3, 12, 187, 188–89,
    200–212, 215–17, 224–26, 251
Brooks, Geraldine, 211
Brothers Grimm, 21, 36, 196
Brown, J. G., 102
Brown, John, 124, 161
"Brown of Osawatomie" (Whittier), 124
Bryant, John, 13
Building a History Curriculum (Bradley Commission), 4
Building the Nation (Coffin), 154
Burnham, Charles G. M., 150
Burr, Aaron, 26
Bush, Charles G., 135
Bush, George W., 257
Butterworth, Hezekiah, 201

Cady, Annie Cole, 29–30, 111, 116, 123, 127–28
Callcott, George, 23–24
Callcott, Maria, 116
Canon Press, 64
Carter, Jimmy, 242, 253
Casper, Scott, 190, 194, 229
Catholicism, 165–67, 171–73, 236

The Century Book for Young Americans (Brooks), 196
The Century Book of Famous Americans (Brooks), 195
Century Book series, 191, 194, 196, 200
Cervantes, Miguel de, 250
Chambers, H. A., 34
Chautauqua movement, 119–20
Cheap Repository Tracts (More), 30
Cheney, Lynne, 5, 9, 59
Chesterton, G. K., 15, 33–34
Chicago Evening Post, 200
Chicago Tribune, 163
Child, Lydia, 69, 73, 99
child first movement, 180–86, 210–11, 216–17, 239,
    241, 251
childhood: child-centered education and, 9,
    64–75, 101–13, 157–67; children's literature and,
    75–86, 103–23, 137, 200–212, 252–53; Christian
    ministry and, 137–42; conceptions of, 19–25,
    28, 36–46, 64–66, 71, 73, 96–101, 103–23, 157,
    177, 180, 209–10, 232, 251–52; gendered learning differences and, 99–101, 113–23, 126–27;
    literacy and, 7, 19–35, 53–54, 96–113, 255;
    narrative strategies and, 15–19, 75–95, 155–56,
    162–63, 167
Children's Lives of Great Men series, 3, 228
child-savers, 102, 113, 120, 136
A Child's History of America (Mantle reproduction), 131
*A Child's History of America Told in One-Syllable
    Words* (Pollard): images of, 2
A Child's History of England (Dickens), 29–30, 31,
    33, 42, 106, 163
Child's History of Our Great Country from the Earliest Discoveries to the Present Time (Stratton),
    114, 125
A Child's History of the United States (Hanson),
    234, 235
The Child's History of the United States (Morris),
    222–23, 225–32, 227, 228, 234, 237, 239, 241,
    246, 250–51
A Child's Story of America (Morris, McHugh, and
    Shewan), 234–46
The Child's Story of America (Morris reissue),
    222–32
The Child's Story of the Greatest Century (Morris),
    224
"Child Study" (Hall), 174
child study movement, 157–68, 170, 178, 232, 251
Christ Church (Moscow, ID), 63
Christian Advocate, 200
Christian Coalition, 10

"The Christian Home-School" (Harris), 141
Christianity: Coffin and, 149–50, 164–67, 170–72; epistemology of, 6, 34–35, 60–64, 217–22, 233–50, 252–53; filiopiety and, 186–200, 219–22, 232–45; founding fathers and, 26, 46–47, 54–56, 97–101, 179, 202–3, 236–37; gender and, 99–101, 130–38, 211–12; hagiography and, 184–200, 202, 237–39, 245–50; pedagogical techniques and, 16–25, 99–101, 104–13, 138–42, 167, 217–22; providential history and, 3, 8–9, 15–19, 28–35, 97–101, 130–42, 154–56, 161, 165, 168–70, 175, 179, 191–92, 205, 222–45, 247–50; youth ministries and, 137–42. See also history; homeschooling; morality; specific denominations, people, publishers, and organizations
Christian Leader, 84, 86
Christian Liberty Press, 218–50, 252
"The Christian Teaching of History" (BJU), 219, 245
Church of Christian Liberty, 218
Cicero, 96
citizenship, 4, 6, 17, 24, 71, 104, 113, 144–47, 178, 228–32
Civil War, 47, 119, 129, 142, 147–48, 150, 152, 154, 161, 167, 169, 218
Clark, Michael, 213
CLASS (Christian Liberty Academy School System), 218–32, 246
class (socioeconomic term), 5, 128–29, 144, 232
Clay, Henry, 123
Clinton, Bill, 242
Coffin, Charles Carleton, 71, 140–42, 147–57, 161–77, 191, 219, 227, 236, 255
Coffin's Historical Reading for the Young, 147–48
Cohen, M. M., 35
Colbert, Steven, 254
Cole, Henry, 28
Columbus, Christopher, 13, 128, 131, 199, 204–6, 228, 234–36
Comer, Cornelia A. P., 181, 196, 214
Committee on Child Study, 158, 160
Communism, 241–42
A Complete Course in History (Anderson), 172
Comstock, Anthony, 103–4, 181
Comstock, M. Louise, 112
Congregational Club of Boston, 171
Congress of Mothers Literature, 147
consensus model (of history), 5–6, 10–12, 18, 55, 83–90, 137–38, 175–77, 251–52
constructivism, 66–75, 181–82. See also epistemology; progressives; social studies
Contract With America, 253

Cooper, James Fenimore, 48, 103
copyright, 48–54, 106, 108, 268n129, 269n136
Copyright Act of 1842 (England), 48
correspondence courses, 144–48
Crabtree, Charlotte, 4, 7–8
Critic, 200
Croly, Jane Cunningham, 133–34
Cruikshank, George, 29
cult of the child, 102–4, 136
Curthoys, Ann, 96

Dames and Daughters of the Young Republic (G. Brooks), 211
D. Appleton Publishers, 118, 189
Darton, John, 49–51, 269n136
Daughters of the American Revolution, 214
Davis, James, 123
Des Jardins, Julie, 120–21
de Soto, Hernando, 223
Dewey, John, 60, 63, 179, 182
DeWolfe, Fiske, and Co., 191
Dial, 191
Dickens, Charles, 28–30, 34, 42, 69, 102–3, 106, 115, 133, 268n129
Dictionary of American Biography, 200–201
dime novels, 103, 146, 225–26, 239
Disciples of Maranatha, 138–42
D. Lothrop Company, 189, 191
Docker, John, 96
Dodo Press, 3, 63, 92–93, 252
Donatien de Vimeur, Jean Baptiste, 127–28
Doubleday and McClure Company, 146
Dover Press, 264n10
Duffy, Cathy, 10, 243
Dustin, Hannah, 155, 163

Eco, Umberto, 80
Edison, Thomas, 5
education: Biblical pedagogy and, 16–25, 138–42, 167, 217–22; child study movement, 157–68, 170, 173, 178, 181; citizenship and, 4, 6, 17, 24, 71, 104, 113, 144–47, 178, 228–32; gender and, 72–73, 99–101, 113–23, 132–33, 144–45, 147–48, 152; home study movement and, 142–48; parents and, 160–67, 172–86, 219–22, 232–45, 255; pedagogical theory and, 3–4, 9–10, 19–37, 251–52; progressive movement and, 60–83, 95, 139, 150. See also childhood; Christianity; history; homeschooling; literacy; public schools
Eggleston, Edward, 62–63, 118
Elementary History of the United States (Morris), 233

Eliot, John, 165
Eliot, Samuel, 145
Ellis, Edward S., 146–47
Ely, John, 25–26, 36
Emerson, Ralph Waldo, 14
Encyclopedia Americana, 84
"The End of History" (Cheney), 5
Engels, Friedrich, 213
England, 20, 28–38, 48–50, 54, 80, 84–85, 107–10, 147
epistemology, 5–6, 10–12, 217–22, 248, 252, 256–57. *See also* childhood; Christianity; ideology; objectivity; pedagogical theories; progressives; revisionists (of history)
Estes and Lauriat publishers, 147–48
Evening-Post, 92
Exodus Books, 141

Fahs, Alice, 152
fairy tales, 7, 19–25, 27–29, 36–37, 39, 196, 227, 254
families. *See* childhood; Christianity; filiopiety; homeschooling; parents
Ferguson, W. H., 226
fiction, 7, 24, 27–31, 35–46, 78, 92, 103–4, 226, 251. *See also* history; narrative history; pedagogical theories
Field-Book of the Revolution (Lossing), 124
filiopiety, 186–200, 219–22, 227–28, 245–50
Fillmore, Millard, 35
Finn, Chester E., Jr., 4
F.I.R.E. (Freedom is Real Education), 264n5
Fireside Education (Goodrich), 23
The First Book of History (Goodrich), 33, 42
First Lessons in Our Country's History (Swinton), 146
First Reader (Goodrich), 32
First World War, 131
FitzGerald, Frances, 10, 213, 215, 233–34, 245
Fleming, R. H., 62, 77
fluid text concept, 46–56, 92–95, 107–10, 130–35, 168–69, 232–45
Following the Flag (Coffin), 152, *153*
founding fathers: heroism and, 5, 183–86, 206–12, 236–37; religious views of, 26, 46–47, 54–56, 97–101, 179, 202–3, 236–37. *See also* Christianity; history; republications and reissues; United States; *specific figures*
Four Years of Fighting (Coffin), 152
Franklin, Benjamin, 23, 190, 199, 211, 223
French and Indian War, 124
Froude, J. A., 121

Fry, William Henry, 88–89
Fyfe, Aileen, 106

Gallaudet, Thomas H., 32–33, 69, 107
gender, 5, 72–82, 99–101, 113–23, 130–38, 144–52, 211–12, 214. *See also* Christianity; filiopiety; history; homeschooling
Genghis Khan, 80–81
George Routledge and Company, 105–13, 118, 124–25, 129, 136
Gesell, Arnold, 181
Gingrich, Newt, 9
The Girls of Dickens Retold (Sweetser), 115
Godkin, Edwin, 87
Godolphin, Mary, 105, 110. *See also* Aikin, Lucy
Goodrich, Charles Augustus, 38
Goodrich, Emily, 51, 53
Goodrich, Samuel, 12–59, 69–71, 104–8, 157, 169, 196, 247–51
G. P. Putnam (publisher), 122
Grant, Ulysses S., 99, 191, 198, 200
Greatness (Simonton), 197
Greeley, Horace, 88–89
Griffis, William, 147, 150, 169, 176
Guerber's Historical Series, 9
Gurian, Michael, 100
Gypsy Books (series), 120

hagiography, 184–200, 202
Hale, Nathan, 183
Hale, Sarah J., 43
Hall, G. Stanley, 157–67, 173–75, 179, 181, 210
Hallowell Academy, 65
Hamblen, Abigail, 74, 81
Hamilton, Alexander, 26, 209
Hanna, Thomas K., 166
Hansel and Gretel (fairy tale), 21
Hanson, John Wesley, Jr., 234
Harbour, F. L., 189
Hard Times (Dickens), 69
Harper, William Rainey, 144
Harper and Brothers, 3, 62, 78–79, 81, 84, 147–48, 152
Harper's Magazine, 83, 88–89, 92–93, 129
Harper's Weekly, 134
Harris, Gregg, 141
Hartwell, E. M., 158–59
Harvard Daily Echo, 144
Hawthorne, Nathaniel, 38, 90
Heatherstone Publishing, 15–19, 27, 34–36, 39, 46, 53, 58–59, 178, 252, 264n10
Henry VIII, 85

Heritage Classical Curriculum, 58–59

Heritage Foundation, 253

Heritage History, 58–64, 75–76, 79, 82–83, 90, 92–93, 115, 178, 252

Heroic Happenings Told in Verse and Story (Brooks), 189

The Heroic Life of Abraham Lincoln (Brooks), 192, *193*

The Heroic Life of George Washington (Brooks), 191–92, *192*, 201–2

The Heroic Life of Ulysses S. Grant (Brooks), 194

The Heroic Life of William McKinley (Brooks), *193*

Heroic Life series, 191, 200, 210

heroism: biographical studies and, 176, 183–86; Christian doctrine and, 220–22; founding fathers and, 5, 183–84, 206–12, 236–38; moral education and, 5–6, 117, 154–55, 183–86, 202–5, 220–23

Higginson, Thomas Wentworth, 151, 161–67, 173, 175, 177, 191

Historical Reading for the Young series, 152–54

Historical Tales series, 226

Historic Boys (Brooks), 189

Historic Girls (Brooks), 189

Historic Leaves, 188

history: childhood's conception and, 19–25, 53–54, 103–23, 157–67, 178, 222–32, 251–52, 255; Christian homeschooling and, 1, 3, 8–10, 15–19, 57–64, 97–101, 130–42, 156, 165, 169–70, 212–16, 222–32; consensus model of, 5–6, 10, 12, 18, 55, 83–90, 137–38, 175, 177, 251–52; epistemology and, 11–12, 15–19, 83–95; factual accuracy and, 13, 42–46, 53–56, 78, 83–90, 123–25, 128–29, 168–76, 200–212, 215, 226, 228, 230, 232–45; the future and, 11, 13, 245–50, 252–53, 255–56; gender and, 113–23, 128–29, 133–34, 211, 214; genre and, 7, 15–46, 60, 75–83, 114, 155–56, 162–63, 183–87, 191, 194–95, 204, 226, 251; ideology and, 5–6, 83–92, 179, 185, 203–8, 222–45; moral didacticism and, 21–35, 58, 77–85, 103, 106–7, 116–18, 141–43, 145–47, 149–50, 154–56, 202–5, 222–24; national standards for, 4–5; National Standards for, 4–9, 55, 59, 206–7, 236–37, 273n32; objective truth and, 6, 34–35, 46–47, 75–90, 96, 217–22, 233–50, 256–58; racism and, 80–81, 110, 128–29, 205; scholarly methods and, 13, 41–46, 60–64, 78, 84, 90–95, 125–30, 137, 157–67, 209, 252–53, 255–56; social studies and, 60–64, 139, 141, 179, 208, 252–53. *See also* biographies; Christianity; homeschooling; multiculturalism; pedagogical theories

History as Home Study series, 146

History of Cyrus the Great (J. Abbott), 79

History of England (Hume), 116

History of England (Penrose), 116

History of England in Words of One Syllable (Pierson), 129

History of Henry IV (J. S. C. Abbott), 77

History of Ireland (Sadlier), 128

History of Japan in Words of One Syllable (H. Smith), 107

History of King Philip (Abbotts), 79

The History of Napoleon Bonaparte (J. S. C. Abbott), 83–95, 127, 203, 274n98

The History of Our Country (Ellis), 146

History of Pennsylvania (Cady), 127

History of the Battles of America in Words of One Syllable (Pollard), 120

History of the United States (Northrup), 125

History of the United States in Words of One Syllable (Pierson), *109*, 110–12, 123, 125

The History of the United States Told in One Syllable Words (Pollard), 1, *2*, *3*, 8, 13, 97–101, 106, *111*, 134, 251

History Through Literature (curriculum), 58–64

Hofstadter, Richard, 215

Holden, Mark, 100

Home Educating with Confidence (Boyer and Boyer), 179, 183

Home Education League of America, 146

The Home Educator in Necessary Knowledge (Morris), 223

Home Lessons (Routledge), 106

Home School Heroes (Klicka), 98

homeschooling: curricular materials for, 1, 3, 54–64, 74–83, 106–7, 140–42, 144–45, 169–70, 201–12, 223–24, 243–44, 264n5; filiopiety and, 180–200, 210–11, 214, 227–28, 232–45; gender and, 99–101, 211–12; national heritage and, 57–64, 239–44; pedagogical theories of, 3–4, 60–64, 210–16; public schools and, 8–9, 98–101, 130–38; religious motivations and, 10–19, 46–47, 97–101, 138–42, 177–78, 184–86, 223, 243–44, 263n32. *See also* Christianity; pedagogical theories; *specific figures, foundations, and publishers*

HomeschoolingMommies.com, 98

Home School of American History (Morris), 223

Home Study Circle Library, 146

home study movement, 142–48, 157, 173

homosexuality, 133, 212, 241–42

Hosmer, James K., 165–66

Household Words (magazine), 29

How Gertrude Teaches Her Children (Pestalozzi), 66
Howitt, Mary, 116
Howsam, Leslie, 79, 115–16, 121, 252
How the Other Half Lives (Riis), 102
"How to Read Right" (lesson), 70
Hubbard, Elbert, 87
Hudson, Henry, 123, 202, 240–41
Hume, David, 116
Hutchings, Noah W., 15–18, 36, 46–47, 55, 178, 264n4

ideology, 83–90, 92, 179, 185, 206–8, 222–45, 252–54
"If My People. . . How We Can and Must Make a Difference" (K. Boyer), 212
The Imagined Civil War (Fahs), 152
Indiana Reading Circle, 166
inquiry-based learning, 60–74, 95, 125
Inter-State School of Correspondence, 144
Iran hostage crisis, 242
Irving, Washington, 13, 48, 228
Islam, 208, 236

Jackson, Andrew, 230, 237
J. B. Ford & Co., 189
Jefferson, Thomas, 26, 123, 154, 230, 237
Jewell (magazine), 87
Johannsen, Albert, 147
Johnson, Lyndon, 242
Jones, John Paul, 191–92
Jones Brothers Publishers, 146
Journal of the National Education Association, 200
Journeys Through Bookland (Sylvester), 145, *145*

Kammen, Michael, 6, 230
Keillor, Garrison, 206
Kennedy, John, 242
Kessinger Publishing, 3
Kettell, Samuel, 38, 43
Kilborn, Eliphalet, 149
"Kill My Old Agency, Please" (Cheney), 9
Kimbrell, Jody D., 246–50, 256
Klein, Dave and Debbie, 221–22
Klein, Kerwin Lee, 257
Klicka, Christopher, 98
Klosterman, Chuck, 251

Ladd, Horatio Oliver, 280n98
Ladies' Magazine, 43
Lafayette, Jean, 199
Leadership Education through Discipleship (L.E.D.), 141

Learning Parent, 177–78, 184–85, 189, 196, 201, 206–18, 252
Lee and Shepard, 162–63, 191
Lepore, Jill, 55, 249
Letters to Mothers (Sigourney), 143
"A Letter to the Rising Generation" (Comer), 181–82
"Letting Go" (Holden), 100
Lewinsky, Monica, 242
liberty (as object of study), 140–41, 147–48, 152, 154–56, 159, 165–67, 192, 205
Life and Battles of Napoleon Bonaparte (Pierson), 127
Life and Times of George Villiers, Duke of Buckingham (Thomson), 121
Life of Washington (Weems), 21
The Life of Washington (Pollard), 128
Lincoln, Abraham, 4, 63, 150, 191, 196–98, 202
literacy: childhood's conception and, 53–54, 103–4, 151, 157–67, 191, 196–97, 209–10, 255; monosyllabic readers and, 96–113, 125–26, 130, 137; morality and, 17–18, 32–35, 58, 182; narrative genres and, 15–35, 37–46, 60, 75–83, 114, 155–56, 162–63, 167, 183–87, 191–95, 204, 226, 251; parent-child relations and, 181–86; pedagogical theories and, 32–37, 78, 95, 107, 149, 160, 192–200; phonetics and, 69–72, 127, 182, 221–22; sight/word technique and, 32–35, 69–70, 99, 107, 127, 182; whole language and, 130, 182
Literary World, 86
Little Arthur's History of England (Callcott), 116
Little Bear Adventure Camp, 100
Little Goody Two Shoes (story), 21
Little Journeys to the Homes of Eminent Artists (Hubbard), 87
Little Red Riding Hood (story), 28
Lives of the Presidents (Pierson), 124, 126
London and Westminster Review, 38
Lossing, Benson, 124–25, 146
Lost History of America (Kimbrell), 246–50
"Love's Power" (J. Pollard), 283n167
Lowell, James Russell, 135, 208
Lowenthal, David, 41, 213–15, 218, 233, 243–44, 246, 250
Luke, Allan, 39, 70, 80
Lyon, William H., 143

Macaulay, T. B., 121
MacLeod, Anne, 22
Madison, Dolley, 211
Madison, James, 209

Makers of History series (Abbott brothers), 1, 3, 10, 62–63, 65, 76, 79, 83–90

Malin, James C., 124

Man and His Ancestor (Morris), 231

Mann, Horace, 32–33, 69–70, 107

Manning, John, 68

Mantle Ministries, 1, 3, 10, 97–101, 130–38, 141–42, 178, 252

Maranatha Publications, 137–43, 156, 169, 171, 175–78, 252

Marshall, John, 237

Marx, Karl, 213

Master Stebbins's Seminary, 25

maturationists, 157–67. *See also* childhood; Hall, G. Stanley

McHugh, Michael J, 221–22, 234–50

McIntosh, Ebenezer, 5

McKinley, William, 191–92, 230

McLeroy, Don, 253–54

McLoughlin Brothers, 1, 109–13, 118, 125–26, 129, 136

MCM (Maranatha Christian Ministries), 138–42

"Memoirs of the Holy Land" (J. Abbott), 92

memorization (pedagogical technique), 6, 17, 32–35, 78, 95, 107, 149, 160

metahistorical issues, 60–64, 79–83, 92, 168–76. *See also* history; ideology; revisionists (of history)

Methodist, 91

Methods of Teaching History (Hall), 159–61, 164, 173

Miller, Christine, 58, 61, 275n129

Miller, Kathy, 254

Mintz, Steven, 65, 100, 103, 113, 157–58, 180–81

Mitchell, Rosemary, 121

Mogridge, George, 51

Mongols, 80–81

monosyllabic literacy theories, 96–113, 125–26, 130, 137

Montessori, Maria, 159

morality: biographies and, 77–85, 190–200, 228, 230–32; child psychology and, 102–4, 157–67; dime novels and, 225–26; fairy tales and, 21–25, 27; gender and, 99–101, 116–18, 130–38; heroic examples and, 5–6, 154–55, 183–86, 202–5, 220–22; homeschoolers' views of, 46–47, 138–43, 145–47, 206–7, 223; narrative history and, 25–46; public schools and, 239–44, 254–55

Moral Majority, 253

More, Hannah, 30

Morris, Charles, 12, 222–45, 248, 250–51, 294n18

Morris, William, 243

Mother Goose Tales (Newberry), 21, 27

Motley, John Lothrop, 91

Mount Vernon School, 66, 71–72, 144

multiculturalism, 5–6, 208, 236. *See also* history

Murray, Gail, 103

My Days and Nights on the Battle-Field (Coffin), 152, 169

Napoleon Bonaparte and the Story of the French Revolution (Abbott), 274n98

narrative history, 25–46, 60, 75–83, 90–95, 162–63, 204, 215, 225–26. *See also* history; literacy

Nash, Gary, 4–6, 8

Nation, 152, 167

National Center for History in the Schools (NCHS), 4–5, 9

National Education Association (NEA), 178–79

National Rifle Association, 253

National Standards (in history), 4–9, 55, 59, 206–7, 236–37, 263n32

Native Americans, 5, 42, 110, 128, 134, 155, 163, 223, 240, 244

Needham, George C., 102

Newberry, John, 21

New England Journal of Education, 112

New-York Daily Tribune, 88–89

New York Herald, 92

New York School Journal, 112

New York Times, 166

New York Times Magazine, 253

New York Tribune, 62, 91–92, 124

Nixon, Richard, 4, 242

Norcross, Grenville, 152

North American Review, 181

Northrup, Henry Davenport, 125

Norton, Charles Eliot, 177

nostalgia, 22, 212–13, 233–45

Nothing New Press, 3, 9, 57–64, 93, 252

A Nursery History of the United States (Barber), 115

objectivity, 6, 42–43, 45–47, 83–90, 217–22, 233–50, 252–58

object lessons, 68–69, 150

Old Times in the Colonies (Coffin), 154–55, 163, 170, 173, 175

One Hundred Famous Americans (Smith), 112

One-Syllable Histories (Routledge), 110

Open Source Living, 93

Osgood, Fletcher, 91

Osgood, Samuel, 20

Our Naval Heroes (Pollard), 117

"Our Schools" (Coffin), 171–72

Outlines of World History (Swinton), 172

Panama Canal, 242
parents, 160–67, 172–78, 180–86, 219–22, 232–45,
   255. *See also* childhood; education; filiopiety;
   history; homeschooling
Parley, Peter (character), 39–46, 194, 251
Parley's Common School History Revised
   (Goodrich), 48
Parley's History of the World (Goodrich), 15–19, *16*,
   24–35, 48–56, 254
Parley's Methods of Telling About History
   (Goodrich), 41
Parley's Peeps at Paris (anonymous), 52
Parley's Universal History (Goodrich and
   Hawthorne), 38, 40–41
Parton, James, 177
Patchogue Advance, 120
Pearson (publisher), 254
pedagogical theories: associationism and,
   192–200; child psychology and, 8, 19–25, 32–37,
   101–13, 126–27, 130, 148–67, 176–86, 191, 251–52;
   child study movement and, 157–68, 170, 178,
   232, 251; Christianity and, 16–17, 19–25, 138–42,
   167, 217–22; citizenship and, 4, 6, 17, 71, 104,
   113, 144–47, 178, 228–32; genres and, 15–19,
   25–35, 37–46, 60, 75–83, 114, 155–56, 162–63,
   183–87, 191–95, 204, 226, 251, 275n129; memorization and, 6, 17, 78, 107, 149, 160; progressive
   movement and, 60–83, 95, 139, 150; values-
   based teaching and, 180–200, 232–45. *See also*
   education; history; homeschooling; literacy
Pennsylvania Monthly, 173
Penrose, Elizabeth, 116
Pestalozzi, Johann Heinrich, 66, 68, 74, 102, 104,
   150, 157
Peter Parley's Annual (anonymous), 49–50
Peter Parley's Christmas Tales for 1839 (Goodrich),
   51
Peter Parley's Common School History (Goodrich),
   34, 38–46
Peter Parley's Farewell (Goodrich), 52
Peter Parley's Own Story (Goodrich), 52
Peter Parley's Tales of America (Goodrich), 264n10
*Peter Parley's Visit to London during the Coronation
   of Queen Victoria* (Till), 50
Pflieger, Pat, 51
phonetic learning, 21–23, 69–72, 127, 182, 221–22
A Pictorial History of America (Goodrich), 247
Pictorial History of England (Goodrich), 30, 38
Pierson, Helen Walls, 99, 105, *109*, 110, 112, 121,
   123–30, 132, 137, 168
Pilgrim Teacher, 200
Pinzón, Alonso, 205

Pizzaro, Francisco, 241
Plymouth Plantation, 97
political correctness, 6, 9, 59, 64, 92, 244. *See
   also* ideology; revisionists (of history); social
   studies
Pollard, Josephine, 1, 3, 8–13, 97–101, 112, 119–37,
   157, 251, 283n165
Pollard, Madeline, 135–36, 283n167
Pontiac's Rebellion, 123
Popham, George, 123
popular history, 23–35, 46–56, 201, 222–32. *See
   also* childhood; history; pedagogical theories
Popular History and the Literary Marketplace
   (Pfitzer), 255
pragmatism, 60–64
presentism, 61, 64, 96, 150, 156, 224, 233
PrestonSpeed Publications, 1–2
Primary History of the United States (Morris), 233
progressives, 60–75, 95, 125, 157–67, 173–75,
   178–79, 232, 256
psychology. *See* childhood; child study movement; literacy; pedagogical theories
public schools: child study movement and,
   157–68, 170, 173; church/state separation
   and, 46–47, 98–101, 171, 178–79, 237, 241,
   253–55; curriculum and, 4–6, 208, 236, 253–54;
   homeschooling's critiques of, 4, 8–9, 142–44,
   206–9, 212–16; home study movement and,
   142–48; parents' role and, 160–67, 172, 175,
   177–78, 180–86, 219–22, 255; progressive movement and, 64–75, 231–32. *See also* citizenship;
   literacy; National Standards (in history)
publishing industry: fluid texts and, 3, 9, 15–19,
   46–56, 92–95, 107–10, 130–35, 168–69, 217–22,
   232–45; gender and, 113–23; home study
   movement and, 143–48; international copyright issues and, 48–52, 54, 106, 108, 268n129,
   269n136; series publication and, 3, 79–80, 105,
   146, 191; textbook market and, 253–54. *See also*
   Christianity; education; history; homeschooling; pedagogical theories; republications and
   reissues
Puck's magazine, 28
Putnam's Magazine, 112

race, 5, 80–81, 110, 128, 151, 205
Raleigh, Walter, 123–24, 168–69
Raphael, Ray, 204
Ravitch, Diane, 4, 9
ReadHowYouWant, 93
Reading (Arnold), 175, 182
Reading Club for Young Ladies, 147–48

Reagan, Ronald, 241–42, 253

Recollections of a Lifetime (Goodrich), 52

republications and reissues: copyright and, 48–54, 106, 108, 268n129, 269n136; homeschooling market for, 1, 3, 54–64, 74–83, 106–7, 140–45, 169–70, 201–12, 223–24, 243–44, 264n5; ideological editing and, 46–47, 138–47, 206–9, 212, 232–45, 256; textual fluidity and, 46–56, 92–95, 107–10, 130–35, 168–69, 232–45. *See also* Christianity; history; homeschooling; morality; publishing industry

"The Responsibility of the Parent in the Education of the Child" (Lyon), 143

Resurrection Press, 3

revisionists (of history): Christian republications and, 222–45; homeschoolers' views of, 46–47, 54–56, 212–16; ideology charges and, 83–90, 130–38, 141–42, 178–79, 185, 206–8, 242–45, 247–50, 252–53; National Standards and, 4–9, 55, 206–7, 236–37, 273n32; postmodernism and, 17–18, 139, 141. *See also* history; social studies

Richard I, 78

Riis, Jacob, 102

Rittenhouse, David, 127

Robert Merry's Museum (magazine), 52

Rogers, Robert, 123

Rollins, Alice Wellington, 164

Rollins, Charles, 24

Rollo and Lucy stories, 69–70, 90–91

Rollo Learning to Read (Abbott), 70

Roosevelt, Theodore, 230

Roselle, Daniel, 21, 25, 35, 38, 53

rote learning. *See* memorization (pedagogical technique)

Routledge, George, 105, 107–13, 118, 124, 129, 136

Rubin, Trudy, 257

Rush, Benjamin, 24

Sadlier, Agnes, 105, 121, 123, 128, 134, 137

Salk, Jonas, 184

Sandburg, Carl, 148

Santayana, George, 1, 10–12, 187, 257–59

Saturday Review, 121

Sax, Leonard, 100

Schlafly, Phyllis, 253

School History of the United States (Morris), 233

Scott, Walter, 28, 84, 163

Scott Foresman Reading Street series, 254

Second Great Awakening, 237

Second Reader (Goodrich), 32

Second Republic, 85–86

Secret Six, 161

"Self-Reliance" (Emerson), 14

serialization, 29, 88, 226

sexism, 81–83. *See also* gender

Sheldon, Frederick, 167

Sheldon & Co., 189

Shewan, Edward Edwin, 234–50

Shorto, Russell, 253–54

sight / word technique, 32–35, 69–70, 99, 107, 127, 182

Sigourney, Lydia, 104, 113, 143

Simonton, Dean, 197

single truth theory, 218. *See also* objectivity

slavery, 5, 124, 128, 169, 202, 244–45

Smith, Ebenezer, 26–27, 36, 38

Smith, Helen Ainslie, 105, 107–8, 112, 120–23, 130, 134, 137

Smith, Henry Boynton, 73

Smith, John, 123, 202, 228–29, 238

Smith, Samuel Harrison, 24

Snow White (fairy tale), 21

social Darwinism, 102

social studies, 60–64, 75, 92, 139, 141, 208, 252–53

Society to Encourage Studies at Home, 144–45

Somerville Historical Society, 201

Somerville Journal, 188, 196

"A Son of Issachar" (Brooks), 189

"Sorosis, 1869" (Bush), *135*

Sorosis Club, 133–34

Soule, C. C., 160

Southern Literary Messenger, 34, 39, 44–45

Spanish-American War, 231

"Special Methods of Historical Study" (Adams), 164

Spingler Institute, 72–73, 119, 144

S. S. McClure (publisher), 120

Standish, Myles, 238

Stevens, Wallace, 21

Stimpson, Mary, 74

Stories of Bible History for Little Ones (Yonge), 115

The Story of Liberty (Coffin), 140, 142, 154–55, 159, 165–66, 168, 177, 236

Stratton, Ella, 114, 125, 129, 194

Street Arabs and Gutter Snipes (Needham), 102

Studying God's Word (McHugh), 221–22

Summerly, Felix, 28

Sumner, Charles, 35

Sweet Land of Liberty (Coffin), 140, 156

Sweetser, Kate Dickinson, 115

Swinton, William, 146–47, 172–73

Sylvester, C. H., 143–45

Symcox, Linda, 9–10

Tales of Heroism (Brooks), 189
Tales of Peter Parley About America (Goodrich), 39–40, 49
Tales of the Sea (Goodrich), 35
"A Talk with the Young Reader About the History of Our Country" (Morris), 226
Tate Publishing and Enterprises, 246–50
"Teaching Character through History" (Boyer), 211–12
"Teaching Reading Using the Bible" (Klein and Klein), 221–22
Tegg (publisher), 51–52
Ten Boys from History (Sweetser), 115
Ten Girls from History (Sweetser), 115
Texas (state), 253–54, 258
textual fluidity (term), 13, 46–56, 92–95, 107–10, 130–35, 168–69, 232–45
Thackeray, William Makepeace, 28
Third Reader (Goodrich), 36–37
Thomson, Katherine, 121
Thorne, Haley, 35
Thurston, Harry, 111
Ticknor, Anna Eliot, 144
Ticknor, George, 144
Ticknor and Fields (publisher and store), 30
Till, Charles, 50
Tisseron, Serge, 209–10
Traps for the Young (Comstock), 103
True Stories collection, 191, 196, 200, 210
The True Story of Abraham Lincoln (Brooks), 197, 199, 202
The True Story of Ben Franklin (Brooks), 202–3
The True Story of George Washington (Brooks), 187, 197, 200, 206–9
The True Story of the United States of America (Brooks), 200, 251
The True Story of U. S. Grant (Brooks), 198
Tubman, Harriet, 5
Twain, Mark, 257–58, 297n16

Ulrich, Laurel, 47
"Uncle Rick Reads *The True Story of George Washington*" (Boyer), 206–7, 209, 256
"Uncle Rick Reads True Stories of Great Americans for Young Americans" (Boyer), 187–88
Uncle Tom (character), 194–95
Union Theological Seminary, 73
United States: American Revolution and, 49, 124, 227–28; citizenship and, 4, 6, 17, 71, 104, 113, 144–47, 178, 228–32; Civil War and, 47, 119, 129, 147–48, 150, 152, 154, 161, 167, 169, 218; exceptionalism of, 137–42, 205–6; founding fathers and, 5, 46–47, 97–101, 183–86, 206–9, 236–38; immigration and, 142–43, 220–21; morality and, 47, 183–86, 202–5, 220–22, 241–44; nationalism and, 7–8, 46, 57–64, 128–29, 190–200, 212–16; public education and, 3–5, 132–33; religion and, 19–26, 138–42, 168–76, 179, 207–8, 223–45
The United States Catalogue of Books in Print, 53
Universal History (Rollins), 24
Universalist, 87
Upper Spingler, 72
usable past notion, 75–83, 258–59

values-based teaching, 180–200, 232–45
VanSledright, Bruce, 6–8, 71–72, 129
verisimilitude, 27, 30, 39
Veterans of Foreign Wars, 257
Victorian era, 22, 24, 28, 81, 91, 103–15, 157, 218
Vietnam War, 242

Wall Street Journal, 5, 171
Warning! Public Schools Aren't for Christians! (Wheeler), 98
Washington, George: heroism of, 5, 124, 128, 148, 169, 191–97, 203–4, 223; moral didacticism and, 21, 117, 154, 199–200
Washington Times, 5
Watergate, 4
W. B. Conkey Company, 234
Webster, Daniel, 123
Webster, Noah, 70
Weems, Mason, 21
Weiner, Bob and Rose, 138, 143, 150, 169–70, 172, 175, 178, 182
Weiner Ministries International, 138
Weinstein, Amy, 105
West, Woody, 5
West Lane School, 25
The Westminster Review, 50
What Do Our 17-Year-Olds Know? (Ravitch and Finn), 4
Wheeler, Richard, 10, 97–101, 104, 130–38, 141, 178
White, Andrew, 160
White, Hayden, 42–43
Whitefield, George, 190
Whittier, John Greenleaf, 124
whole language literacy, 130, 182
Wilbour, Charlotte, 134
Wilkinson, James, 256
Williams, Roger, 164, 237–39
William the Conqueror, 76, 80
Winning His Way (Coffin), 152

Winthrop, John, 238–39
Wisconsin Journal of Education, 167
Woods, Tiger, 184

Yale Child Study Center, 181
Yes Lord Ministries, 54
Yonge, Charlotte, 115
Young Folks' History of the United States (Higginson), 162–64, 166–67, 173, 175, 177

Young Ladies Seminary and Boarding School, 121
The Young People's History of the World (Morris), 223
Young People's Story of American Achievements (Lossing), 146
Youth's Companion, 189
The Youth's History of the United States (Ellis), 147

Born in Pittsburgh, GREGORY PFITZER grew up in various midwestern towns, primarily on the outskirts of Cincinnati. He earned a BA in American studies and history at Colby College, and an MA in history and a PhD in the History of American Civilization from Harvard University. Pfitzer is professor of American studies at Skidmore, where he has taught since 1989. In 2003–2004, he was honored with Skidmore's Ralph A. Ciancio Award for Excellence in Teaching. His previous books include *Samuel Eliot Morison's Historical World; Picturing the Past: Illustrated Histories and the American Historical Imagination, 1840–1920;* and *Popular History and the Literary Marketplace, 1840–1920.* In addition to his work on popular historical writing, he has published articles on the literary figures Thoreau, Melville, Hawthorne, Henry James, Charles Francis Adams Jr., and Mark Twain as well as on the painter Winslow Homer. More recently, he collaborated on an online exhibit for the CLIO Visualizing History: Picturing the Past project, "Illustrated Histories and the American Imagination, 1840–1900."